Freedom

Freedom

AN UNRULY HISTORY

Annelien de Dijn

Harvard University Press

Cambridge, Massachusetts · London, England

2020

First printing

Library of Congress Cataloging-in-Publication Data

Names: Dijn, Annelien de, 1977– author.
Title: Freedom : an unruly history / Annelien de Dijn.
Description: Cambridge, Massachusetts : Harvard University Press, 2020. |
Includes index.
Identifiers: LCCN 2019054434 | ISBN 9780674988330 (cloth)
Subjects: LCSH: Liberty. | Power (Social sciences) | Government, Resistance to.
Classification: LCC JC585 .D4865 2020 | DDC 323.44—dc23
LC record available at https://lccn.loc.gov/2019054434

Contents

Introduction

An Elusive Concept

TODAY MOST PEOPLE TEND TO equate freedom with the possession of inalienable individual rights, rights that demarcate a private sphere no government may infringe on. But has this always been the case? Does this definition, whereby freedom depends on the limitation of state power, really offer the only—or even the most—natural way of thinking about what it means to be free in a society or as a society? And if not, how and why did our understanding of freedom change?

These are the questions this book sets out to answer. It does so by surveying over 2,000 years of thinking and talking about political freedom in what is conventionally known as the West. The story starts with the invention of freedom in ancient Greece and continues to the present. Along the way, I explore the ideas of boldface names such as Plato, Cicero, John Locke, and Jean-Jacques Rousseau. But the story also includes individuals less celebrated for their contributions to political thought, such as the nineteenth-century lexicographer Noah Webster, who was the first to provide a definition of liberty in American English.

The results of this investigation are startling. Our current conception of freedom must be understood as a deliberate and dramatic rupture with long-established ways of thinking about liberty. For centuries Western thinkers and political actors identified freedom not with being left alone by the state but with exercising control over the way one is governed. Theirs was a *democratic* conception of freedom: a free state was one in which the people ruled itself, even if it lacked a bill of rights, an independent judiciary, and other mechanisms to patrol the boundaries of legitimate state power. This democratic conception of freedom was developed by ancient Greeks and Romans and was revived in modern times by Renaissance humanists and their pupils, such as Niccolò Machiavelli, Etienne de la Boétie, and Algernon Sidney. As Sidney, the seventeenth-century English author of *Discourses Concerning Government,* put it, a people could only be free if it was ruled "by laws of its own making."[1]

These humanist ideas in turn inspired the American, Dutch, Polish, and French revolutionaries of the late eighteenth century. When these revolutionaries rebelled, they did so in the name of freedom. But the freedom they fought for was not the freedom to quietly enjoy their lives and possessions: it was the freedom to govern themselves in the way of the ancient Greeks and Romans. The foundation of "all free government," the First Continental Congress stated in 1774, is "a right in the people to participate in their legislative council."[2] The same was heard on the other side of the Atlantic. "You cannot be said to be free if you do not govern yourself, your property, and your happiness," Pieter Vreede, a prominent Dutch Patriot, wrote in 1783.[3]

Visual representations illustrate the remarkable longevity of the ancient, democratic conception of liberty. The history of the so-called cap of liberty is a case in point. In ancient Rome freed slaves were given a conical cap during their emancipation ceremony. In time the cap came to represent freedom in a political sense, appearing, for instance, on coins issued to celebrate the introduction of the secret ballot in Rome. Centuries later, in the 1760s and 1770s, New York rebels announced their defiance of British rule by erecting freedom poles decorated with these liberty caps. In the 1790s the symbol became a part of the daily attire of French revolutionaries, who wore red woolen caps to signal their attachment to liberty.[4]

For over 2,000 years, then, freedom was equated with popular self-government. The coming chapters will show as much, in detail. It was only in the nineteenth and twentieth centuries that political thinkers in Europe and the United States began to propagate a different way of thinking about liberty. Freedom, many came to argue, was not a matter of *who* governed. Instead, what determined freedom was *the extent* to which one was governed. The German philosopher Johann August Eberhard was one of the earliest to make such claims. It was an "unfounded prejudice," he wrote in 1784, to think that liberty was only to be found in democratic republics. The subjects of enlightened kings enjoyed just as much—nay, more—civil liberty than the citizens of self-governing states. As Eberhard noted, under King Frederick the Great, Prussians had greater religious freedom and paid lower taxes than the self-governing Swiss people.[5]

What provoked this shift in thinking about freedom? Why was the democratic conception displaced by the idea that freedom depended on the limitation of government power? To the extent that historians ponder this question, they tend to find answers in long-standing trends in European history. Thus it is often claimed that the growth of religious tolerance in the West—an unintended consequence of the Reformation— sparked the emergence of a new way of thinking about freedom, as identical with private independence. Another popular narrative attributes the shift in thinking about liberty to the emergence of a market economy in the seventeenth and eighteenth centuries. This supposedly led to a more enlightened conception of freedom, centered on the notion of natural rights.[6] But contrary to widespread assumptions, neither the Reformation nor the transition to a market economy had much impact on the debate about freedom.

Instead, as this book shows, the shift to a new understanding of liberty was the outcome of a prolonged political struggle triggered by the Atlantic Revolutions of the late eighteenth century. These revolutions played a crucial role in establishing our modern, democratic political systems. But they also inspired a formidable reaction against democracy. Notably the French Revolution's descent into political violence—the Terror—turned many intellectuals and civic actors on both sides of the Atlantic Ocean against the effort to introduce bottom-up politics. The resulting counterrevolutionary movement propagated a new understanding of liberty, one that directly contested the democratic view by prioritizing the enjoyment of private independence. Eberhard's remarks about freedom, for instance, were directed against the "young republicans" who wanted to democratize Prussia by introducing institutions modeled on the Swiss and American examples.[7]

The counterrevolutionary redefinition of freedom, in turn, influenced new political movements that emerged in early nineteenth-century Europe, notably liberalism. Nineteenth-century liberals such as Benjamin Constant agreed wholeheartedly with conservatives like Eberhard and Edmund Burke that democracy was not only very different from freedom but also potentially harmful to it. Even as European liberals eventually came to accept democracy as a fait accompli, they continued to argue that democracy and freedom were different things. The best way to preserve freedom was not, they argued, to expand popular control over government but to create roadblocks against government interference in people's lives. In a democratic context, then, individual liberty could best be protected by institutions and norms that curtailed popular power. This idea, it is safe to say, would have stunned earlier freedom fighters.

When arguing that democracy needed to be limited in order to safeguard freedom, thinkers like Constant were, to an extent, motivated by concerns about the position of vulnerable minorities, such as religious dissenters. But more often the fight against democracy in the name of freedom was provoked by fears that the newly enfranchised masses would use state power for economic redistribution. In Europe these worries grew throughout the nineteenth century and reached fever pitch in the 1880s and 1890s. The French economist Paul Leroy-Beaulieu, to give but one example, lamented that "Western civilization" would soon be under the yoke of a "new serfdom." Modern democratic states were necessarily ruled in the interests of the working classes, he warned. The advent of "collectivism," and hence the destruction of all liberty, were virtually inevitable.[8]

In the United States, the counterrevolutionary conception of liberty took longer to catch on. While counterrevolutionary ideas about liberty were echoed by some disgruntled Federalists and conservative Whigs, most Americans in the first half of the nineteenth century embraced the democratic conception of freedom that had been central to the revolution. But this changed in the wake of the Civil War. Elite discontent with democracy increased as a result of the extension of voting rights to freedmen and of mass migration to the North: suddenly there were large numbers of blacks and recent immigrants demanding political rights that elites were loath to recognize. During the Gilded Age, the idea that freedom was best served by maximally curtailing the power of the masses gained wide currency in the United States. The leading lights of the period, such as the influential Yale professor William Graham Sumner, vehemently rejected the idea that freedom was to be equated with democratic self-government. Instead, Sumner argued, "laissez faire," or, in blunt English, "mind your own business," was "the doctrine of liberty."[9]

The new vision of freedom articulated by democracy's detractors did not go uncontested. In the wake of the Long Depression of 1873–1896, a growing number of radicals, socialists, populists, and progressives on both sides of the Atlantic rejected the equation of freedom with minimal government. That sort of freedom, they argued, was a false freedom, a thinly veiled defense of class interests. In order for a people to be truly free, both political and economic domination needed to end. Thus the revolutionary call for democratic freedom was revitalized and extended to the economic sphere by thinkers and politicians such as Jean Jaurès and Franklin Delano Roosevelt. After 1945, however, the Cold War drowned out these voices, and the identification of freedom with minimal government came to be accepted even by many left-leaning intellectuals, politicians, and voters. This remains true today.

As this thumbnail sketch suggests, understanding the long history of freedom shows, first and foremost, just how recently the concept became identified with the limitation of government power. But this history also reveals something crucial about the genealogy of current ways of thinking about freedom. Ideas about freedom commonplace today—such as the notion that freedom is best preserved by shrinking the sphere of government—were invented not by the revolutionaries of the eighteenth and nineteenth centuries but rather by their critics. Today's most ardent freedom fighters like to portray themselves as heirs of the revolutionaries who created our modern democracies. But with their call for minimal government, contemporary enthusiasts of freedom far more resemble democracy's opponents than its architects. They are the heirs of Johann August Eberhard and William Graham Sumner, not of Thomas Jefferson and Pieter Vreede.

Some Nuts and Bolts

Freedom is a lofty ideal, celebrated by poets, artists, and philosophers alike. But it is also a formidable ideological weapon. Those who have followed public debate in the United States and other countries over the past several decades will have no trouble recalling countless examples of liberty being invoked to achieve political ends of one sort or another. Pundits identify institutions and policies they disagree with as threats to liberty. Politicians accuse their rivals of being insufficiently freedom-loving. Foreign nations and actors are labeled a danger to national liberty in order to increase support for military action against them.

This book tells the story of how this ideological weapon was forged in antiquity, revived in the Renaissance, and transformed in the nineteenth and twentieth centuries. The history of freedom, it will become clear, is not one of polite debate between gray-haired philosophers tucked away in ivory towers. It is instead a story of fierce political battles, in which some people, quite literally, lost their heads. (The head of the Roman politician and self-professed freedom fighter Marcus Tullius Cicero, to give but one example, was cut off and nailed to the speakers' platform at the Forum.[10]) During these battles, different conceptions of freedom were invented and pitted against one another.

In short, the focus of this book is on the development of freedom as a political concept. I trace changing answers to fundamental questions: What kinds of political institutions will allow us to lead a free life? What does a free state look like? This means that a number of other aspects of the history of freedom will receive less attention. In particular, debates about what one might call legal freedom—how jurists distinguished between free persons and slaves and how philosophers legitimated or criticized these differences—are mostly out of scope. So are debates about moral freedom, which consider the extent to which individuals really are free to do what they want.

That is not to say that these questions are unimportant. To begin with, historians agree that the idea of freedom came into being in the first place to denote the opposite of slavery and legal bondage. Etymological evidence suggests as much. *Eleutheros,* Greek for "free," derives from the Indo-European ǂleudh-, meaning "belonging to the people." The Latin *liber* probably has the same root. This indicates that the ancient conception of freedom emerged as an antonym of slavery, for it was understood that most slaves were foreigners or outsiders and hence did not belong to the people. The written record further confirms this view. In Homer's *Iliad* and *Odyssey*, the oldest surviving Greek texts, words like "free" and "freedom" were consistently defined as the opposite of "slave" and "slavery."[11]

Freedom, then, came into being as a legal category: to be free was the opposite of being a slave. Attempts to define and legitimate these different categories loom large in the history of freedom. The existence of legal bondage created a host of ethical and practical problems that sparked intense debate. Legal scholars and philosophers battled over the question of who counted as free and who did not, and what it meant to be a slave. Perhaps the most pressing question was how the distinction between free and slave could be legitimated, if at all. Already in the fourth century BC, for instance, Aristotle wondered whether slavery was ethically justified. He believed it was, under specific circumstances, but this question continued to provoke debate throughout the ages.[12]

Similarly the issue of moral freedom was (and remains) one of the most hotly discussed topics in ethics, engaging philosophers and theologians from a wide variety of intellectual traditions and historical contexts. Their investigations revolved around a timeless question: Do human beings have free will? Or are we always ruled by forces we cannot control, such as our passions, our biology, or divine providence? This was a central problem in the philosophy of Zeno of Citium, the founding father of Stoicism, who wrote his main works in the third century BC. Nearly two millennia later, the British thinker Thomas Hobbes was grappling with the same issue.[13]

But these debates and their histories, while fascinating in their own right, have been dealt with extensively by other historians. Their work need not be rehashed here. This book will not attempt to explain why, for instance, most people in the West stopped thinking that chattel slavery was morally acceptable. Nor will it examine the origin of the notion of free will in any detail.[14] Instead, I will trace the centuries-long debate about how to be free in a society or as a society. My primary focus will be on the way in which political thinkers grappled with the question of how to institutionalize freedom within city-states or sovereign nations, rather than in the international arena. In the later parts of the story, as we shall see, these questions also sparked reflection on how to extend freedom to the economic order.

That brings me to a second point. As mentioned earlier, this book focuses on the history of freedom in what is conventionally known as the West. This is not because only Western philosophers have thought about what it means to be free in a society or as a society. Throughout history, people across the globe have reflected on this issue. The Wajo', for instance, an Indonesian sea-faring people, attached considerable value to political liberty. Their eighteenth-century chronicles contain several references to the importance of freedom or *merdeka*, a term of Sanskrit origin that was used in Malay, and in similar languages such as Buginese, in the sense of "free" as opposed to "slave." According to the chronicles, one of the founding fathers of the Wajo' had announced that "the people of Wajo' are free; free from birth." The Wajo' were also quite clear on what they meant by this. To secure freedom, their chronicles note, three things are crucial: "firstly not to interfere with people's wishes; secondly not to forbid the expression of opinions; thirdly not to prevent [people going] to the south, the north, the west, the east, upstream or downstream."[15]

The fact that this book nevertheless concentrates on Western thinkers and debates has much to do with the limitations of my own expertise. But there are more substantial reasons as well. Notably, the Western political tradition has had far more impact than other, comparable traditions when it comes to the ways in which people around the world think and talk about freedom. In the Arabic-speaking world, for instance, the concept of freedom (*hurriyya*) became increasingly politicized in the course of the nineteenth century as contact with the West and in particular with France increased. Similarly, in Japan, translations of European thinkers such as John Stuart Mill, whose *On Liberty* was published in Japanese in 1871, sparked new debate about the nature and meaning of liberty. A historical understanding of the development of the Western freedom tradition is therefore immediately relevant to contemporary debates about freedom more broadly speaking.[16]

At this point, it might be useful to clarify what I mean when I speak about the "West" or the "Western tradition." In recent years, scholars such as Kostas Vlassopoulos have drawn attention to the existence of an Occidentalist ideology, which wrongly assumes that "clearly bounded entities in world history," such as the West and the Orient, have existed since time immemorial, much like continents and other natural phenomena.[17] In this book, I try to avoid the pitfalls of Occidentalism by emphasizing that the emergence of a Western tradition of thinking about freedom was by no means natural or inevitable. I show instead how this tradition came into being through the largely contingent actions of historical agents while at the same time highlighting how its geographical and temporal boundaries remained contested throughout the ages.

It was by no means obvious, for instance, that early modern Europeans would come to think of themselves as the heirs of a freedom-centric outlook conceived by the ancient Greeks and Romans. After the fall of the Roman Empire, Greek and Roman texts celebrating freedom as the most important political value went unread for centuries. And many of the early modern Europeans who turned to these texts inhabited areas that had never been part of the Roman Republic, let alone the Greek world. Moreover, the social and political conditions under which they lived differed markedly from those of the ancients. That the words of these ancients came to seem relevant again to Europeans of a later age is not a function of some unbroken and inborn sense of unity within a Western tradition. Rather, the revival of interest in antique liberty in the early modern period depended on a series of contingent events.

To begin with, the revival of ancient liberty cannot be understood without taking into account the crucial role of a relatively small group of learned men and women: the Renaissance humanists. Following in the footsteps of the fourteenth-century Italian poet Petrarch, humanists had come to believe, for their own reasons, that ancient Greek and Roman texts represented the pinnacle of human civilization. Humanists therefore invested heavily in the dissemination of these texts, creating in the process an educational system based on the study of ancient authors like Cicero and Livy. These were deliberate choices but by no means predetermined. Just as importantly, the dissemination of humanist ideas coincided with the large-scale political upheaval of the sixteenth and seventeenth centuries, creating demand for new ways of thinking about politics. Without this coincidence, the revival of ancient ways of thinking about liberty might have left little mark on European political thought.

The notion of a Western tradition also is not the product of some un-broken fealty to Greco-Roman ideals. In the aftermath of the French Rev-olution, many came to believe that attempts to implement ancient ideas about how to live a free life were misguided and even dangerous. In re-sponse, Constant and others came up with a new genealogy of freedom. In their view, the modern, Western conception of freedom should not be understood as a legacy of Greco-Roman civilization. "Modern" ways of thinking about liberty were quite different from—indeed, opposite to—the ancient conception of freedom. Thus, Constant reconceptualized the Western tradition of freedom, now depicting it as having emerged *against* the ancient legacy, rather than being rooted in that legacy.[18]

The geographic contours of the West have, equally, been subject to debate. For instance, while most current invocations of the West as-sume France's inclusion, in his bestselling *On Civil Liberty and Self-Government,* German-American thinker Francis Lieber disagreed. He argued that Constant's distinction between ancient and modern liberty overlapped with another dichotomy: that between "Anglican" and "Gal-lican" ideas about freedom. Whereas the Gallicans were stuck on ancient ways of thinking, largely because of the pernicious influence of Rousseau, the Anglicans—the English and their American offspring—developed a truly modern understanding of liberty, thanks to their Protestant and Teu-tonic heritage. In other words, Lieber deliberately restricted the limits of the modern West to the Anglophone world.[19]

In short, to the extent that we can speak of a Western tradition in the history of political thought, we need to bear in mind that this tradition was both constructed and contested. This does not make this tradition other than "real," however, and it does not invalidate the usefulness of the concept of the West. Many people today understand their ideas about liberty to be Western in nature—products of a lineage running from the Greeks and Romans through the eighteenth-century revolutions unto the present. An intellectual history of freedom must show how we got to this point, while at the same time revealing the contingent nature of this tra-dition as well as the polemical claims underpinning it.[20]

One final editorial remark: Some readers might believe that the goal of this book—to outline the history of freedom, from antiquity to the present—is overly ambitious and perhaps even impossible to undertake. By tracing the history of a concept over such a long period of time, it might be argued, one runs the risk of producing a disembodied history in which concepts and ideas, rather than the men and women who produced them, become historical actors of their own. Unless one is willing to accept Hegel's view of ideas as the motor of world history, this necessarily leads to *bad* history; or, as Quentin Skinner has put it, it results in stories that might be more readily classified as mythologies rather than histories. In such mythological accounts of the history of ideas, motives and intentions are imputed to historical actors who could not possibly have had them—for instance, that they were engaged in the "elaboration" or "working out" of specific ideas they were never familiar with in the first place.[21]

These dangers, while real, are not insurmountable, as has been recently argued by David Armitage, Peter Gordon, and Darrin McMahon. The resurgence of "big" intellectual history illustrates this in practice.[22] As long as the historian of ideas keeps in mind that the history she recounts is a history produced by men and women for their own particular, context-bound reasons, it should be possible to avoid the pitfalls of mythologizing. Concretely, I would argue that the danger of mythologizing can be dodged by paying close attention to the transmission and reception of ideas; by demonstrating rather than imputing intention to historical agents; and finally by attributing changes in meaning to the documented intentions of historical actors rather than to some sort of inner logic of the ideas in question. When I claim, for instance, that eighteenth-century revolutionaries invoked the ancient conception of freedom, I am able to demonstrate that they had access to ancient texts in which the concept of freedom played a key role. I am also able to demonstrate that they themselves believed they were engaged in the practice of reviving a conception of freedom associated with antiquity.

Apart from these methodological considerations, there are other risks involved in a project of this scope. It is certainly true that in writing this book, I have had to reach far beyond my original area of expertise, which is eighteenth- and nineteenth-century French political thought. Such an endeavor involves hazards; however, I believe they are worth undertaking.

PART I

The Long History of Freedom

CHAPTER 1

Slaves to No Man

Freedom in Ancient Greece

IN 480 BC, two young Spartans named Sperthias and Bulis set out from their hometown to the Persian capital Susa. Their mission was a dangerous one. Several years earlier, the Persian king Darius had sent envoys to all Greek cities, demanding offerings of "earth and water"—a symbolic acknowledgment that they submitted to his power. Outraged by Darius's demand, the Spartans threw the unlucky messengers into a deep well, telling them to get their earth and water there. By doing so, they mortally offended not just Darius but also the gods, as envoys were thought to be under their protection. After much dithering, the Spartans decided to send two envoys of their own to Susa to make amends. Sperthias and Bulis had volunteered, fully understanding that the Persian king might give them a taste of their own medicine.

The young men showed themselves remarkably fearless—reckless even—as they carried out their perilous assignment. On their way to Susa, they made a stopover at the court of the Persian general Hydarnes, the governor of Ionia. Hydarnes received them with great hospitality, treating them as honored guests and welcoming them with an elaborate banquet. While Sperthias and Bulis dug into their food, conversation turned to the relations between Sparta and Persia, which were as bad as they had ever been. Shortly after his demand for earth and water, Darius had been defeated at Marathon by the combined forces of the Athenians and the Plataeans. But the Persians had continued to dream of conquest, and now, ten years later, Darius's son, Xerxes, was amassing a huge army to subjugate Sparta and other recalcitrant Greek cities.

Hydarnes tried to convince his guests that the Spartans would be better off voluntarily submitting to Xerxes instead of awaiting their defeat. If they put themselves in the king's hands, Hydarnes said, they would be well treated. Indeed, if they served Xerxes faithfully, they and their compatriots might even become rulers of the whole of Greece by the king's commission. If they continued to resist him, however, they should expect no mercy once the war was won. And Xerxes would surely win the war: the Persian army was far superior to any force the divided Greeks would be able to amass, with respect to both arms and manpower.

The advice was probably well meant, but Sperthias and Bulis would have none of it. Hydarnes knew what it was like to be a slave, they answered brusquely. But clearly he had no idea how sweet freedom tasted, or he would not have suggested they give it up to serve the Persian king. A free man would never consent to be ruled by another human being. He would defend his liberty—by force, if necessary. Hydarnes's reply to this remarkable outburst is undocumented, but it is tempting to think that the dining hall became chillier.

Unrepentant, Sperthias and Bulis continued to Susa, where they sought an audience with Xerxes. They must have felt more than a bit intimidated when they were escorted to the throne room. Their hometown Sparta was a small, provincial place, without buildings of any note. The Great King's palace, by contrast, was designed to inspire as much awe as possible. Visitors entered through the gate, a palace in and of itself, its fifteen-meter walls dwarfing all entrants. Next they crossed a huge open space that gave access to the royal palace, continuing on until they reached the enormous throne room. Here, Sperthias and Bulis found Xerxes seated on a large stone seat, surrounded by armed guards and retainers.

But the young Spartans were not cowed. When Xerxes's guards ordered them to prostrate themselves before the king—a traditional part of court ritual—Sperthias and Bulis refused. Even if the guards were to hurl them headlong onto the ground, they exclaimed, they would not prostrate themselves before another human being, because "that was not the Greek way." They were skating on thin ice: Xerxes would have been within his rights to have them executed for their insolence. Remarkably, they lived to tell the tale. Xerxes was amused rather than insulted by the Greeks' daring words, and he accepted their apologies for the Spartans' maltreatment of his envoys. After their return to Sparta, the two men became minor celebrities. Tales of their derring-do circulated among the Greek world, eventually reaching Herodotus, who gave them a central place in the *Histories*.[1]

The message of these anecdotes, as relayed by Herodotus, was clear: freedom was of paramount importance to the Greeks. Indeed, as Sperthias and Bulis demonstrated, the Greeks valued freedom more than social niceties—more, even, than their very lives. This distinguished them from the Persians, who were not only in thrall to absolute rulers like Xerxes but also seemed to accept their submission placidly. Herodotus was by no means the only Greek writer to make this point. The idea that Greece was the land of the free was a commonplace, much-repeated cliché. Aristotle, for instance, writing about a century after Herodotus, remarked that the main difference between the Greeks (the "Hellenes," as he called them) and Persians was that the Greeks were "free," whereas the Persians were "ruled and enslaved."[2]

By proudly describing themselves as "free," in contrast to the "slavish" Persians, the ancient Greeks made a key contribution to the history of freedom.[3] They were, of course, by no means the first to talk about freedom as the opposite of slavery. Quite the contrary, this distinction was familiar to all Near Eastern societies. Mesopotamian languages like Akkadian and Sumerian had words for "freedom" (respectively *andurarum* and *amargi*), which, as in ancient Greek, denoted the opposite of personal bondage. Indeed, we already find references to "freedom" as the opposite of legal slavery or bondage in Mesopotamian documents of the third millennium BC. Our sources also make clear that such freedom from bondage was a valued condition. In 2350 BC, for instance, the Sumerian king Urukagina boasted in an official history of his reign that he had "freed" his subjects from debt-slavery.[4]

Freedom in this sense of the word—as "liberation from bondage"—held an even more central place in Hebrew culture. The story of Exodus, which probably dates back to the sixth century BC (although the events it describes were supposed to have taken place many centuries earlier), tells how the Jews "groaned" under the "slavery" imposed on them by the Egyptian pharaoh. The Jews had settled in Egypt in search of a better life, and they had prospered. But their growing numbers frightened the Egyptian authorities, who worried the Jews might side with their enemies in case of war. Trying to break the Jews' spirit, the pharaoh set them to hard labor. When their bondage became unbearable, they called out to God for help, who delivered them with Moses's assistance. Ever after, their liberation from "the house of bondage" (as they called their time serving the pharaoh) was celebrated at Passover, an annual ceremony that included the consumption of bitter herbs meant to symbolize the harshness of slavery.[5]

But the freedom celebrated in Sumerian and Jewish texts was freedom from personal bondage, not political. The deliverance of the Jews was described not as a liberation from foreign domination but as a shift from slavery to the pharaoh to service to God. Leviticus 25:55 states this explicitly: "For onto me the children of Israel are servants; they are my servants whom I brought forth out of the land of Egypt: I am the Lord your God." That the Egyptian bondage must be understood as legal slavery rather than as political oppression by a foreign tyrant is also confirmed in Deuteronomy, where God commands the Jews to celebrate their deliverance from Egypt by freeing their household slaves every seven years. Only in the book of the Maccabees, written after contact with Greco-Roman civilization, is the term "freedom" used in a political sense, to describe the liberation of Judea from the Hellenistic Seleucid Empire.[6]

Before the Greeks, in short, no one seems to have used terms like "free" and "slave" to describe and evaluate types of government. Greek thinkers, however, clearly did. When Sperthias and Bulis called themselves "free" and accused their host Hydarnes of being a "slave," they did not mean that Hydarnes was in personal bondage. After all, their host was a respected and powerful nobleman, the commander of legions. But in the view of his Greek guests, Hydarnes was a "slave" nonetheless because he was the subject of an almighty king, whereas they, as members of a Greek polis, governed themselves. In this sense, the Greeks can be said to have invented the concept of political freedom. They were the first to think of freedom as a *political* value—as a condition that could be enjoyed in some

types of government but not in others. But they would not be the last.
Today, we still believe that the preservation of freedom requires specific
political institutions and that it is possible to distinguish between free and
unfree states. As such, Greek poets and philosophers stand at the beginning of a long story that leads us to the present.

It is crucial to realize, however, that the ancient Greeks did not invent
our conception of freedom. When they talked about themselves as free,
they did not mean they lived under a limited government or had such
things as a bill of rights, a written constitution, or a separation of powers.
Instead, they meant that, unlike the subjects of the Persian Great King,
they were not ruled by another but governed themselves. They had, in
other words, a *democratic* conception of freedom: in their view, a free state
was a state in which the people controlled the way it was governed; it was
not a state in which government interference was limited as much as
possible.[7]

In what follows, we will trace the history of this democratic conception of freedom through classical Greece. We will examine when and
under what conditions Greeks started thinking of themselves as free and
how they came to value freedom as a key political good. Greek thinkers
like Herodotus did not just invent a particular definition of freedom; they
were the first to come up with a coherent account of why a free life was
worth fighting for. But the cult of freedom also came to be fiercely contested in Greece. By the late fifth and fourth centuries, a powerful undercurrent took shape in Greek thought, which ultimately led some of the
most influential Greek thinkers to reject the value of freedom.

The Invention of Political Freedom in Ancient Greece

Freedom did not always hold a central place in Greek political culture.[8]
In his *Works and Days,* one of the earliest Greek literary sources, the poet
Hesiod never used the words "freedom" or "free." For him, justice was
the most important attribute of a well-functioning community. "They who
give straight judgments to strangers and to the men of the land, and go
not aside from what is just," Hesiod admonished his audience, "their city
flourishes, and the people prosper in it." At the same time, Hesiod was
enough of a realist to know that justice was rarely achieved in this world.

He therefore also counseled a quietist acceptance of the right of the strongest to do what they wanted, telling his audience that "he is a fool who tries to withstand the stronger, for he does not get the mastery and suffers pain besides his shame."[9]

Homer, one of our other major sources for the earliest period of Greek history, occasionally spoke of "free" individuals. But he always used the term to describe an individual's legal status, to distinguish free persons from slaves. Like Hesiod, he never talked about "freedom" as a political condition, something that could be enjoyed under one political system but not another. Thus, in the *Iliad,* the Trojan warrior Hector explained that he was fighting, first and foremost, to preserve the "freedom" of his wife Andromache. But what he feared was that his wife and other Trojan women would be carried off as booty by his enemies and turned into household slaves—not that they would be subjected to a tyrannical leader or oppressive political system.[10]

To the extent that Homer expressed a preference for one form of government over another, it was for one-man rule, not popular self-government. At the outset of the *Iliad,* Greek troops, weary of the ten-year battle against Troy, mutiny against Agamemnon's command. Longing to go home, they rush toward their ships and are all but ready to concede their defeat at the hands of the Trojans. But Odysseus, spurred on by the goddess Athena, forcefully restores order. Beating the soldiers with his staff, he commands them to obey their superiors. "The rule of many is not good," Homer has Odysseus remark while browbeating the soldiers, and "let there be one ruler, one king."[11]

These attitudes probably reflected existing power structures.[12] In the early Archaic period, Greek communities were in all likelihood dominated by the heads of powerful families who achieved and maintained their authority on the strength of their martial prowess and noble birth. Our evidence suggests that in the course of the seventh century BC, the power of these *basileis,* or "kings" as they are described in Homer's oeuvre, was eroded in favor of a broader aristocracy that shared power. As cities on the Greek mainland grew bigger and more prosperous, distinctions between the elite and the commoners became more pronounced. A telling indication is the appearance of terminology used to distinguish the elite—such as *kaloi* ("beautiful"), *agathoi* ("good"), and *esthloi* ("good" or "brave")—and that used to refer to commoners, such as *kakoi* ("ugly" or "bad") and *deiloi* ("cowardly" or "wretched"). The elites monopolized the growing number of public offices required to govern the increasingly complex communities of the late Archaic period.

There are some indications that freedom became a more important ideal in Greek political culture with the democratization of many city-states around 500 BC. It was then that ordinary male citizens came to exercise considerable power in several Greek cities. Important political decisions were now often addressed in assemblies in which all male citizens, in principle at least, had an equal say. These assemblies typically met in the marketplace or some specially designated space. This was the case in Athens, where reforms introduced by the politician Cleisthenes in 508 BC gave the *demos*, or "the people" (in this case, all adult male citizens), final say over all important decisions, including the election of public officials responsible for the state's day-to-day administration. Democracy was adopted in a number of other Greek cities too, although it was by no means universal: even after 500 BC many Greeks continued to be ruled by strongmen or elites.[13]

Why this shift to democracy happened remains disputed. Aristotle—one of the first thinkers to inquire into the origins of Greek democracy—believed that the democratization of Greek political regimes was a by-product of changes in warfare; more specifically, the rise of the hoplite army. Hoplites were heavily armed infantrymen who, Aristotle claimed, replaced the previously relied-upon cavalry. Since it cost much more to own a horse than to buy the weaponry needed by a hoplite, these military innovations would have increased the power of ordinary citizens and diminished that of aristocratic, horse-borne elites. As a result, non-elite men began to demand a greater say in communal decision-making—thus ushering in Greek democracy.[14]

Modern historians, however, tend to be skeptical about this explanation. There is little evidence, they point out, that before the hoplite, phalanx cavalries were the most important element in Greek armies. Moreover, even after the introduction of the hoplite army, distinctions continued to be made between the elite hoplites, who were regular soldiers and better (thus more expensively) armed. These facts cast doubt on the theory that the hoplite army was necessarily an equalizing force. However, so far, no consensus has emerged on an alternative explanation for the emergence of Greek democracy. Some historians point to long-term ideological developments that contributed to the creation of a culture of equality in Ancient Greece. Other explanations focus on the equalizing effects of the rise of tyranny in many Greek cities in the late Archaic period. In the late seventh and sixth centuries, aristocratic rule was replaced in a number of Greek poleis by more autocratic regimes, in which strongmen (called "tyrants" by the Greeks) relied on the support of commoners to assert their dominance over the local aristocrats, thus paving the way for genuinely popular governments.[15]

The exact causes of the transition to popular government in ancient Greece will probably remain contested. Less disputed is the idea that the emergence of more democratic political regimes gave greater prominence to freedom as a political ideal. One of the earliest references to the value of freedom in an explicitly political context can be found in the poems by the Athenian lawgiver Solon. During Solon's lifetime, in the early sixth century BC, Athens was mired in civil strife between rich and poor. These conflicts eventually facilitated the rise to power of Peisistratus, who promised to restore order and harmony between the classes but instead monopolized power for himself and his family. In poems that were probably sung at dinner parties, Solon cautioned his compatriots against the lure of tyranny, warning that one-man rule would reduce all Athenians to "slavery." ("The strength of snow and of hail is from a cloud, and thunder cometh of the bright lightning; a city is destroyed of great men, and the common folk fall into bondage unto a despot because of ignorance.")[16]

There are other indications of the growing importance of the cult of freedom in this period. Thus, in Athens, a tyrannicide cult emerged in the late sixth century to celebrate Harmodius and Aristogeiton, two citizens who had played a role in overthrowing the tyranny of the Peisistratids. According to tradition, they had killed Hipparchus, son and successor of Peisistratus, during a religious festival, thus "freeing" the city, as Herodotus put it, from tyranny.[17] Why they did so was much debated by the ancient Greeks: an influential tradition held that they had acted not out of hatred for tyranny as such, but because of a personal slight. Hipparchus (so the story went) had tried to seduce the handsome Harmodius, but his amorous overtures had been rejected. This made Hipparchus so angry that he insulted Harmodius's sister, prompting Harmodius to enlist his lover, Aristogeiton, to kill Hipparchus.[18]

Despite controversy about their motivations, the memory of Harmodius and Aristogeiton was widely venerated in Athens. The existence of this cult suggests veneration not just for Harmodius and Aristogeiton but for the value for which these two gave their lives: freedom from tyranny. Their statues were given a prominent position in the marketplace in 510 BC, immediately after the overthrow of the Peisistratid regime. When these statues were carried away by Xerxes's troops during the Persian wars, the Athenians replaced them with new figures, which are still known to us through Roman copies. The tyrannicide was also celebrated in songs, and Harmodius's and Aristogeiton's direct descendants were given special honors: they received meals at public expense, were exempt from taxes, and had special seats at public events.[19]

Evidence from the Greek island of Samos also hints at the existence of a freedom cult around this period. Initially, Samos was ruled by a strongman named Polycrates. But when Polycrates died in 522 BC, his right-hand man Meandrius came to power and abolished the tyranny, proclaiming *isonomia*, or "political equality," and access to power for all. According to Herodotus, Meandrius explicitly told the Samians that he had done this to "give [them] freedom." He also erected an altar dedicated to Zeus Eleutherios, or "Zeus the Liberator." Even though our report of these events comes from a much later date, that account may have been based on an older oral tradition, indicating that "freedom" was used in a political context as early as the 520s.[20]

There is no doubt, however, that it was mainly the experience of the Greco-Persian wars that encouraged the cult of freedom in Ancient Greece.[21] This conflict—or, rather, this series of conflicts—began when the Greek-speaking cities of Ionia, on the Asian coast, rebelled against their Persian rulers in 499 BC. A number of Greek cities on the mainland, notably the Athenians and their neighbors, the Eretrians, decided to help the Ionians with a small expeditionary force. They failed miserably, and the Persians easily put down the rebellion. However, in Sardis, one of the regional capitals of the Persian Empire, Athenians accidentally set fire to a temple. When the Persian king Darius learned who was responsible for

Sculpture of the Athenian tyrant-killers Harmodius and Aristogeiton.

the sacrilege, he vowed revenge and instructed a slave to remind him three times a day, "Master, do not forget the Athenians!"

It took Darius another eight years to follow through on his vow. But in 490, he invaded the Greek mainland with a massive army. The Persians' first stop after crossing the Aegean Sea was Eretria, where they burned temples, sacked the city, and enslaved the inhabitants. Then they landed at Marathon in northeast Attica and attacked Athens. Initially, things looked bad for the outnumbered Athenians, but they ended up achieving a massive victory, all the more spectacular because it was so unexpected. About 6,400 Persians reportedly died, against 192 (out of 10,000) Athenians. While these numbers are probably exaggerated, there is no doubt that the Greeks obtained an important victory and forced the Persians to retreat.

Ten years later, however, in 480, the Persians returned in full force. Now led by Darius's son, Xerxes, they crossed the Hellespont and marched to Athens, with the fleet sailing alongside. From the size of the expedition, which might have comprised as many as 200,000 men, it was clear that Xerxes intended nothing less than the conquest of Greece; it was not just the Athenians who had reason to be worried. In response, the Hellenic League was created: Sparta, the preeminent military power in Greece, was put in command, and control of the navy was given to Athens. Things looked bad for the Greeks at first: the Persian army wreaked havoc, razing Athens to the ground. (Most Athenians, however, had escaped by sea before the Persians arrived.)

But after two years of war, the Greeks' luck changed. A major turning point came with the battle of Salamis, when the Athenian navy inflicted a decisive defeat on the much larger Persian fleet. This setback so discouraged Xerxes that he went home to Susa, leaving his commander, Mardonius, to continue the fight on land. As Mardonius marched to Athens and occupied the city a second time, the Spartans seemed reluctant to defend their allies. But eventually, they sent a large army to meet the Persians at Plataea, where Mardonius was roundly defeated. The battle at Plataea marked the end of Persian attempts to conquer Greece.

The long, bloody confrontation with the Persians had a huge impact on the Greek political imagination. They began to think of Greekness as a collective identity, one largely defined in terms of what distinguished them from their foreign invaders. And the main way that the Greeks (at least in their own view) differed from the Persians was with regard to their political organization. The Persians and their allies, as Greek observers pointed out again and again, were under the thumb of an all-powerful autocrat. But that was not how things were done in Greece. Greek citizens were free, because they ruled themselves.

The earliest indication that the Greco-Persian war was seen as a conflict between freedom and slavery can be found in Aeschlylus's play *The Persians*. Produced in 472 BC, a mere eight years after the battle of Salamis (in which Aeschylus participated), *The Persians* described the battle's immediate aftermath. Remarkably, Aeschylus adopted the perspective of the defeated Persians. The play was set in the Persian capital Susa, and much of the action focused on Xerxes's mother Atossa as she anxiously awaited news of her son. Aeschylus thus seemed to humanize the enemy by focusing on the grief and despair of the Persians upon learning of Xerxes's defeat. But *The Persians* also did much to sharpen the contrast between Greeks and Persians, as Aeschylus depicted the Persians as a servile people, in thrall to their lord and master Xerxes. The Athenians, by contrast, were, as Aeschylus put it, "no man's slaves or subjects."[22]

Aeschylus brought this message home vividly in one of the most famous passages in the play: the account of Atossa's dream. Sick with worry about her son Xerxes, Atossa had a terrifying nightmare. Her son was trying to subdue two quarreling women and bridle them to his chariot. The first woman—representing Asia—stood tall and proud in the traces and "kept her mouth submissive to the reins." But Xerxes had less success with the second woman, Greece. She struggled and tore the chariot's harness apart with her hands, wrenching away the bridle and smashing the yoke. Finally, Xerxes was thrown to the ground and lay motionless. Aeschylus's message was clear: while the Persians were submissive agents of their king, the Greeks were proud and free, an "unbridled" people.[23]

Herodotus played an even more important role than Aeschylus in cementing the identification of Greeks as "free" and Persians as "slaves."[24] Born in Halicarnassus, a Greek town on the Asian seaboard, Herodotus was a small boy during the final stages of the wars between the Greeks and Persians. Although he was probably too young to remember much, he would have grown up hearing stories of the war. As an adult, Herodotus tried to learn more about the origins and development of this conflict, eventually recounting the results of his investigation in the *Histories* (*historiai* in Greek; literally translated, "inquiries"). Full of amusing anecdotes and digressions, the *Histories* was an instant success and was considered a classic throughout antiquity and beyond. Indeed, Herodotus was held in such high esteem as a writer and raconteur that he was called the "prose Homer."[25]

Today, Herodotus is remembered as the father of history, but his *Histories* also played a crucial role in the story of freedom. He was one of the earliest writers to identify freedom as a key political ideal, and—even more importantly—to expand at any length on its value. That is not to say that he reflected on these concepts in a systematic way. Far from being an analytic thinker, Herodotus had a highly conversational writing style. At first sight, the *Histories* resembles nothing more than the storytelling of a favorite uncle with an endless stream of tales—all equally entertaining but without any apparent logic connecting them.

A more careful reading, however, reveals that Herodotus developed a number of abstract ideas.[26] First and foremost, he left his readers no doubt that the battle between the Greeks and Persians was not just a military conflict: it was a clash of civilizations. In his rendering, the Greco-Persian wars pitted freedom-loving Greeks against an enemy with a completely different and far more hierarchical outlook. A Persian victory would not have just imposed a fiscal burden on the Greek cities; it would have ended the Greek way of life. Not only would the Greeks have been subjected to foreign domination; Persian rule, as Herodotus hinted repeatedly, would have meant the end of popular self-government in Greek cities. ("Despots support one another," a Spartan remarks in the *Histories*.)[27]

Herodotus brought this contrast home in different ways. As we have seen, he recounted anecdotes about the Spartan envoys Sperthias and Bulis to illustrate Greek devotion to freedom. But he also made this point more explicitly in the *Histories*, including speeches purportedly made by Greek military commanders (although more likely scripted by Herodotus) in which the war against the Persians was described as a war for freedom and against slavery. Thus, at the outset of the struggle, the Ionian general Dionysius warned his men that the war would decide whether they would be "free men or slaves, and runaway slaves at that."[28] Likewise, an Athenian general eager to engage the Persians tries to persuade his compatriots to vote with him by telling them that they must choose whether "to enslave Athens or make her free, and thereby leave behind for all posterity a memorial such as not even Harmodius and Aristogeiton left."[29]

In short, Herodotus portrayed the Greeks as a proud and freedom-loving race. That is not to say that he always depicted them in a positive light—he was by no means just a propagandist for the Greek cause. He made clear that the Athenians' involvement in the first phase of the war was motivated by a lust for lucre rather than the desire to liberate their Ionian cousins from the Persian yoke. But whatever their other qualities (or lack thereof), Herodotus's Greeks were genuinely devoted to freedom, and this stood in sharp contrast to the Persians. In the *Histories*, even wellborn and powerful noblemen addressed the Persian kings as "master." These kings made all decisions, and while they solicited advice from their inner circle, they ignored it if it did not suit their plans.[30]

The *Histories* thus played a key role in cementing the idea that the self-ruling Greeks were free, whereas the Persians, as subjects of an all-powerful king, were slaves. But this is not the only reason we should turn to Herodotus. Another reason is that he provided one of the earliest reflections on why freedom was valuable. Political freedom—that is, popular self-government—was important, he made clear, because only under this form of government could individuals order their lives as they wanted and enjoy personal security and independence. Only under a free government could people control their own destinies (as long as they were free adult males). Life under kingly rule was simply too precarious to be called free. Even a good king might suddenly turn bad and start to abuse his subjects.

Herodotus spelled out this idea quite explicitly in one of the most famous passages of the *Histories,* his account of the so-called Great Debate. After the death of Cambyses, one of the earliest Persian kings, Herodotus explained, a succession crisis occurred. Several of the most powerful Persian noblemen gathered to discuss their country's future government. A high-minded debate ensued about the pros and cons of democracy, aristocracy, and monarchy, with each man supporting one form of government. The debate was won by Darius, who argued that, given Persia's military success under a monarchy, they should stick with their ancestral form of government. Darius's advice was followed and Persia continued as an absolute monarchy.

But according to Herodotus, the moral victory went to Otanes, who made a long, rousing speech in favor of democracy. Otanes particularly stressed the fact that the continued existence of absolute monarchy in Persia would spell an end to personal security. "Monarchy is neither an attractive nor a noble institution," Otanes argued. He reminded his audience of how much ordinary Persians had suffered under Cambyses, a violent and cruel ruler. But, Otanes emphasized, their suffering was not just the result of Cambyses's personality; rather, oppression was an inevitable feature of autocracy. Herodotus quotes Otanes as saying, "Make a man a monarch, and even if he is the most moral person in the world, he will leave his customary ways of thinking. All the advantages of his position breed arrogant abusiveness in him, and envy is ingrained in human nature anyway."[31]

In short, giving one man all the power was bound to corrupt him and inflate his desires, leading him to follow his every whim and to tyrannize his subjects. This problem, Otanes continued, could only be avoided by introducing democracy to Persia. Democracy was "entirely free of the vices of monarchy," because "it is accountable government, and it refers all decisions to the common people."[32]

Herodotus repeated this message often in the *Histories*. After recounting, for instance, how Athens became a "free" city by expelling the tyrannical Peisistratid dynasty, Herodotus remarked, in a rare editorial aside, how this political change caused the city to flourish. "The advantages of everyone having a voice in the political procedure," he remarked, "are not restricted just to single instances, but are plain to see wherever one looks." Athenian military prowess offered a concrete example. While the Athenians were ruled by tyrants, they were no better at warfare than their neighbors. Once rid of the tyrants, however, they became a vastly superior fighting force. This went to show, Herodotus said, that under an oppressive regime, they did not do their best, because they served a master; whereas as free men they excelled in battle, because each wanted to "achieve something for himself."[33]

Herodotus brought this point home indirectly, as well, in his portrayal of the Persian regime. A large part of the *Histories* is devoted to an account of the reigns of the Persian kings, ranging from the founder of the empire, Cyrus the Great, up to Xerxes, the leader of the final, failed invasion of Greece. In this collective portrait of Persian rulers, Herodotus made it clear that the main downside to autocratic rule was that subjects lacked personal security. Throughout the *Histories,* subjects were always in danger of falling victim to the arbitrary whims of the Persian kings.[34]

This is not to say that Herodotus's Persian kings were cardboard despots. Rather, they were presented as distinct personalities and credited for their ability as strategists and administrators. But they were also capable of considerable cruelty. Cambyses, the successor to Cyrus the Great, Herodotus tells us, was an alcoholic sociopath whose reign was characterized by violence and random bloodshed. He murdered his own brother out of fear of usurpation, then, in defiance of all laws and customs, married two of his sisters, eventually killing one while she was pregnant with his child. Cambyses's bloodlust was not limited to his own family: he buried twelve Persian noblemen alive for no clear reason. When one of his most trusted advisers attempted to talk sense into him, Cambyses ordered him killed as well.[35]

Even when his wrath was justified, Cambyses characteristically expressed his anger by inflicting excessive cruelty, and his behavior toward Sisamnes, a royal judge, was no exception. Sisamnes, Herodotus recounted, had accepted a bribe to deliver an unfair verdict. To punish him, Cambyses ordered one of his servants to slit Sisamnes's throat and flay him. But Cambyses did not stop there. He had thongs made out of the flayed skin and used them to string the chair on which Sisamnes had sat to deliver his verdicts. Then Cambyses appointed Sisamnes's son to his father's previous role, forcing the terrified man to speak judgment from a chair made out of his own father's skin.[36]

Even a seemingly benign ruler, Herodotus made clear, could suddenly turn against his most faithful subjects. Darius, Cambyses's successor, restored peace and order and is generally depicted as a reasonable man. But he killed one of his military commanders along with his entire family, simply because he suspected that the man was plotting to overthrow him. In an even more chilling anecdote, one of Darius's subjects, who had three sons in the Persian army, asked if one son could remain home in Susa, out of harm's way. Darius replied, in a friendly manner, that all three could stay behind. He then ordered them to be killed. Herodotus dryly commented that "he did leave them there in Susa—with their throats cut."[37]

But it was especially Darius's son, Xerxes, who illustrated the idea that absolute power was inevitably abused. Herodotus portrayed Xerxes as an able administrator, a shrewd commander, and a man capable of a surprising degree of feeling for others. (Just before the invasion of Greece, Herodotus tells us, Xerxes was reviewing his troops, feeling deeply satisfied by his mighty army. Then suddenly, he began to weep. Asked what caused his change in mood, Xerxes replied, "I was reflecting on things and it occurred to me how short the sum total of human life is, which made me feel compassion. Look at all these people—not one of them will still be alive in a hundred years' time."[38])

Nonetheless, Xerxes was capable of acts of violence no less horrific than those of the mad Cambyses. The story of Xerxes's dealings with Pythius the Lydian vividly makes this point. The two met in Celaenae, a border town, when Xerxes was preparing to invade Greece. Pythius, a rich landowner, voluntarily offered to contribute a large sum of money to the war effort. Xerxes was so pleased with this patriotic act that he not only refused Pythius's money but gave him an even greater sum in return. Later, however, as the Persian army was on the verge of departing for Greece, omens warned Pythius that his five sons, all of whom had been conscripted, were in danger. Encouraged by Xerxes's earlier generosity, Pythius asked if his eldest son could remain behind, so that Pythius would have someone to take care of him and his possessions.

The strategy backfired. Pythius, Xerxes retorted angrily, was his "slave" and should follow him unhesitatingly, along with his whole household. Pythius's son would be left behind but not to look after his father. Just as Darius had done earlier, Xerxes ordered his soldiers to kill the boy. Adding insult to injury, he then had the body cleaved in two, placing one half on the left side of the main road out of town, and the other on the right. When the army finally marched out to Greece, the last thing the soldiers saw was the mutilated corpse of the dead boy.[39]

The story offers a poignant window onto the arbitrariness of autocratic rule. This idea was brought home not just by the sudden change in Xerxes's behavior and the horrible nature of the punishment but also by the very language Herodotus has his characters use. Pythius addressed Xerxes as "master," and Xerxes described Pythius as his "slave." As wealthy and well connected as Pythius was, the reality was that, like any chattel slave, his fate depended on the whim of his master, the king.

Other stories about Xerxes made the same point. Herodotus recounted how, on Xerxes's way home to Persia after the disastrous defeat at Athens, his ship encountered strong winds. The ship was overladen with the Persian army and royal entourage. Overcome by fear, Xerxes asked the captain what their chances were of surviving.

"None at all, master," the captain replied, "unless we get rid of this crowd of passengers."

On hearing this, Xerxes addressed his men. "My life is in your hands, it seems, gentlemen of Persia," he said. "Now you have an opportunity to show how much you care for the safety of your king."

In response, the men prostrated themselves before him and jumped into the sea. Lighter now, the ship reached Asia safely. As soon as he went ashore, Xerxes gave a golden garland to the captain for saving the king's life—then cut off his head for causing the deaths of so many Persians.[40] (Herodotus himself thought this story was probably untrue, but not because of Xerxes's callous disregard for human life or the strangely submissive attitude of his subjects. Rather, Herodotus believed that Xerxes would have sacrificed the ship's crew rather than the Persian passengers. The latter were, after all, not just ordinary Persians, but his close friends and relatives, the leading lights of Persian society.[41])

The pernicious effects of autocratic rule were not evident just at the top. The king's underlings, Herodotus made clear, often behaved as tyrannically as their masters. Under Darius's reign, for instance, Persian envoys were sent to the Macedonian court of King Amyntas, one of Darius's vassals, on a diplomatic mission. Amyntas received them with generosity and entertained them with a lavish banquet; however, this was not enough for the Persians. Although Macedonian custom kept men and women separate, they insisted on having the court women attend the banquet. Reluctantly, Amyntas granted this wish, because the Persians were, after all, his "masters." As the evening proceeded, the Persians, growing drunker, started to fondle the women's breasts and even tried to rape them. Amyntas was afraid to protest, but his son Alexander was so offended by this behavior that he ordered his soldiers to kill all the Persians. The story had a happy ending, of sorts: Alexander successfully covered up his crime by offering a large bribe, which included his own sister, to the Persian general who came looking for the missing envoys. Nevertheless, Amyntas's behavior painfully illustrated the servility and powerlessness expected from even royal subjects of the Persian king.[42]

The cumulative effect of Herodotus's portrayal of the Persian kings and their underlings made clear the dangers of autocracy. Life under an autocrat was precarious. Even a benign ruler could always turn around and kill sons or violate daughters. Not even power and social status could protect against the arbitrary whims of an autocrat. True personal security was therefore possible only in self-governing states such as Sparta and Athens.

Herodotus's own experience might have inspired his negative portrayal of autocratic rule. Tradition has it that he had to leave his hometown Halicarnassus after an altercation with Lygdamis, the local tyrant. He was then supposed to have moved to Samos, where he wrote the *Histories.* Eventually, though, he returned to Halicarnassus and helped expel Lygdamis. If this is true, Herodotus knew firsthand what it was like to live under autocratic rule. Moreover, it suggests that he was so opposed to the regime that he was willing to bear exile and risk armed rebellion to end it. (It should be noted, however, that this information comes from a Byzantine encyclopedia compiled in the tenth century AD, almost 1,500 years after Herodotus's putative date of birth, and we have no way of knowing whether it is true.[43])

Regardless, Herodotus's views were by no means idiosyncratic. On the contrary, the idea that a person's life and goods could be secure only under a popular government became commonplace in the Greek world. The Athenian tragedian Euripides, for instance, a contemporary of Herodotus, made much the same point. Without popular self-government, Euripides explained in the patriotic play the *Suppliant Women*, justice could not exist; the will of the ruler alone was law. Further, he felt that tyranny discouraged private enterprise and even procreation. Why work hard when all one's profits could be taken away at the ruler's whim? And why have children when they, and especially the girls, were always in danger of being molested if they caught the tyrant's fancy?[44] Similarly, the Athenian politician Pericles, in a public speech to commemorate those fallen in battle against the Spartans, celebrated Athenian democracy for the individual independence it offered its citizens. "We are open and free in the conduct of our public affairs and in the uncensorious way we observe the habits of each other's daily lives," Pericles said (as reported by Thucydides). "We are not angry with our neighbor if he indulges his own pleasure, nor do we put on the disapproving look which falls short of punishment but can still hurt."[45]

This point is worth emphasizing, because it is sometimes claimed that the ancient Greeks had no interest in individual independence, only in the collective freedom of the community to govern itself.[46] But writings by Herodotus and others let us see that they believed freedom—or the ability to control the way we are governed—was also crucial to the preservation of personal security and individual independence. Far from privileging collective freedom above personal security, the Greeks believed that one could not exist without the other. Under an autocrat, even a seemingly benign one, a person could never live a truly free life. Only democratic citizens could set their own goals and live life as they wanted, in dialogue with one another. The Greeks, in other words, believed that individual freedom could not exist without collective freedom.[47]

Greek Freedom: Mirage or Reality?

By the end of the Persian wars, Greek thinkers had come to embrace freedom as their most important political value, the characteristic that distinguished them from their neighbors to the east and west. The Persians and Egyptians might be richer and more sophisticated, and the Thracians and Scythians perhaps had fiercer warriors, but only the Greeks were free. Instead of kowtowing to an almighty ruler, they governed themselves and enjoyed a personal security and independence wholly out of reach for the subjects of the Great King.

Of course, these boasts need to be taken with a large grain of salt. From the perspective of adult male citizens, there is something to be said for the idea that the Greeks were uniquely free; that is, self-governing. This is immediately obvious when we compare them to the subjects of the Persian king, who were, at least in theory, completely subjected to the will of their ruler. The Great King explicitly presented himself as the supreme master, legislator, and judge of his subjects. As we know from official sources like Darius's Bisutun inscription (a gigantic inscription taking up an entire limestone cliff, discovered along an ancient road connecting the capitals of Babylonia and Media), the Great King saw himself as standing far above his subjects, whom he called his *bandaka* (meaning "dependents," or literally, "those who wear the belt of dependence").[48]

Visual representations of the Great Kings proudly advertised their absolute power. In sculptures found on their tombs and on the gates of the capital of Persepolis, the king is often represented seated on a throne that

The Great King supported by throne bearers at Persepolis, Hall of the Hundred Columns.

is literally supported by his subjects, who, in turn, are depicted with their hands above their heads, palms up, bearing the seat of command. The message of such images was unmistakable: subjects were to support and obey their kings, not the other way around. On his tombstone, Darius, for instance, bragged that his subjects did "whatever he told them to do, either by night or by day."[49]

Of course, such claims should not be taken too literally. The Persian Empire was enormous, even by modern standards: at its most extensive, it spanned two continents (Eurasia and Africa) and comprised millions of subjects. (Population estimates vary considerably, from 17 million to 35 million, but in any case, the number of people under the Great King's control was huge.[50]) We should therefore not imagine Darius or Xerxes personally controlling the lives of all of their subjects: the empire's sheer size made that impossible. Even the satraps, regional governors who did much of the actual ruling, interfered little in the lives of their Egyptian or Babylonian subjects, as long as they continued to pay the tribute due to the Great Kings.

Nevertheless, all inhabitants of the Persian Empire, even the wealthy and powerful, were, at least nominally, completely subject to the will of their ruler. Satraps and other potentates, such as military commanders, could lose their positions or even their lives if the king was either dissatisfied with the way they acquitted themselves of their duties or felt they were becoming too powerful. Their titles and power were seen as gifts from the king, gifts that could easily be revoked if an underling was perceived as disloyal. Provincial rulers had no right to take even the smallest military or diplomatic initiative without the king's approval. A Darius or Xerxes might take council from trusted advisers, but in the end he and he alone made all the important decisions.[51]

This was in sharp contrast with the way things were done in most Greek polities. After Cleisthenes's reforms, all major decisions in Athens were made by the popular assembly. All adult male citizens—regardless of financial status—had an equal voice in this assembly. Moreover, all key public offices were either elective, typically for short terms, or allotted through sortition. While access to these offices might (at least initially) have been restricted to the wealthier Athenians, our sources report no property qualifications for voting, which meant that all citizens had a say in who would govern them. Even Athenian generals—perhaps the most prominent public officers in a state engaged in constant warfare—were elected directly by the demos.[52]

Of course, not all Greek cities gave as much power to the demos. In Sparta elites had much more control. Since time immemorial, military power in Sparta had been exercised by two "kings." Although these generals, like their Athenian counterparts, were elected by the citizenry, they typically hailed from just two dynasties and were elected for life. Unlike the Persian Great King, however, Spartan kings could be held accountable for their leadership in battle, and often were: we know of several instances when a Spartan king faced exile after being convicted for failing to fulfill his duties adequately. As in Athens, moreover, one of Sparta's founding documents, the so-called Great Rhetra, or Great Speech, explicitly gave the demos the power to make the final decisions over important communal matters.[53]

In short, male Greek citizens had far greater control over their governance than their Persian counterparts. But from the perspective of marginalized groups, such as women and slaves, the idea that Greece was the land of the free must have rung quite hollow. Even in Athens, the most democratic of all Greek cities, a large majority of the population had no say in the way they were governed.[54] Women, resident aliens (called metics), and slaves had no political rights at all. And the number of slaves was very high—modern estimates put them at between 15 and 40 percent of the population. The number of metics was also substantial. Aristotle, who boasted so proudly of Greek freedom, could not participate in Athenian democracy, because he was not a citizen. He spent most of his adult life in Athens, but since he was born in Stagira, he was considered a metic.

Even today, of course, most states exclude resident aliens from participating in politics. More troubling, perhaps, was the exclusion of women and slaves. And these exclusions were rigorous. Women were not allowed to enter the Pnyx, the hilltop where political assemblies were typically held, let alone cast their vote or stand for election. Indeed, in the eyes of the Athenian state, women simply did not exist as independent human beings. In all their dealings with the public authorities, they had to be represented by a male relative or guardian. Even more strikingly, when an Athenian woman was mentioned in public, for instance in judicial proceedings, she was commonly referred to as So-and-So's wife or daughter rather than by name. The best thing that could happen to a woman was not to be talked about. As the Athenian politician Pericles told war widows in his famous funeral oration, "Your reputation is glorious if . . . there is the least possible talk about you among men, whether in praise or blame."[55]

Some women might have exercised political power behind the scenes: that seems to have been the case for Aspasia, a high-class prostitute whose advice Pericles relied on. Moreover, after Pericles's death, Aspasia helped her new lover, low-born sheep dealer Lysicles, become the most important politician in Athens. But this kind of female influence was probably limited; husbands were usually much older than their brides and unlikely to seek their advice or even discuss their affairs with them.[56]

The same was true for slaves. Like women, male slaves were forbidden to enter the assemblies or law courts. Even after their emancipation, slaves typically remained excluded from political power, as they were counted as metics, or resident aliens. There were exceptional cases, however, in which male slaves became citizens. Pasion was a slave who famously rose to become a wealthy banker and Athenian citizen. When his owners, two Athenian financiers, put him in charge of banking operations in the nearby port town of Piraeus, he quickly rose to chief clerk. After inheriting the bank from his masters, Pasion became enormously rich. Generous donations to the Athenian state eventually resulted in his being awarded citizenship. But Pasion's case was exceedingly rare: we know of only a handful of former slaves who managed to become full-fledged citizens.[57]

These exclusions were hardly ever questioned by Greek thinkers. The idea that slaves should participate in politics was not discussed even once, probably because it seemed so absurd. The exclusion of women from politics was addressed almost as rarely, with some notable exceptions. In the *Assemblywomen*, for instance, Aristophanes, known for his absurd flights of fancy, imagined Athens being taken over by women and turned into a gynocracy. Wearing false beards and their husbands' clothes, a group of disgruntled Athenian women sneak into an assembly meeting and succeed in voting women into political power, arguing that their experience as mothers and household managers makes them better qualified to govern than men.

There is no doubt that Aristophanes mainly played with the idea of female rule for laughs. One of the first measures the new rulers in his play implemented was the decree that all sexual favors be held in common, thus giving all women the right to sleep with all men. In order to make sure that this did not benefit only young, beautiful women, older, plainer women were granted the right to sleep with a man before he slept with the younger woman he actually desired. Hilarity ensued. In one of the final scenes, three old, unappealing women fight over a strapping young man who actually has his eye on a fourth woman who is young and beautiful. The old crones nearly rip him apart before he can get to her. "Our laws must be obeyed!" one of them shrieks as she drags the unwilling youngster to bed.[58]

But Aristophanes was not simply ridiculing female political participation. Praxagora, the female character who had come up with the plan to take the power from men, was represented by Aristophanes as an upright, decisive leader who was genuinely concerned with the public interest. By contrast, her husband and other male characters were portrayed as selfish and narrowly interested in their own private concerns, especially filling their bellies. These men's main objection to the women's rule was that they would no longer receive their stipend for attending the popular assembly. Praxagora responded to the objection with a speech intended to convince the men that the new regime would be in their interest as well, and by the play's end, the male characters seem wholly reconciled to the new political reality.

Aristophanes's play can therefore plausibly be read as a critique of female exclusion from power.[59] But such a critical attitude seems to have been shared by only a few. Far more common were the views Aristotle expressed in *Politics*. He described women as the "natural inferiors" of men, lacking the male ability to think rationally. The same was true, according to Aristotle, of "natural" slaves, who were born less intelligent than normal human beings. Just as children were under their parents' control and the body was under the control of the mind, women and slaves were to be ruled by men.[60]

In short, the Greek cult of freedom should not blind us to the fact that, in reality, self-government was limited to a relatively small proportion of the population—adult male citizens. At the same time, freedom was real for those individuals who experienced it. Not only were male Greek citizens freer than their Persian contemporaries, but they also, compared to inhabitants of modern democracies, seem to have had an extraordinary amount of control over the way they were governed. Whereas today most governing is done by impersonal bureaucracies or professional politicians, in many Greek cities, ordinary citizens were personally involved in all aspects of political life.[61]

The second main claim made by Greek thinkers—that they enjoyed greater personal security and individual independence because of their collective freedom—is harder to assess. It is nearly impossible to know if Herodotus was right in saying that Greek citizens enjoyed more personal security and independence than their Persian counterparts, although it should be noted that modern historians tend to view Herodotus's account of Persian tyranny as a caricature. The only major rebellions in the Persian Empire were around succession crises, which suggests a general acceptance of the Great King's rule. The empire, moreover, seems to have flourished economically, which casts doubt on Herodotus's frequent insistence that, in the Persian Empire, no one's life or possessions were safe.[62]

Conversely, recent research has made clear that life in Greek city-states offered very little personal independence or security to marginalized groups. The lives of Spartan slaves, called Helots, were precarious indeed.[63] Unlike the slaves in many other Greek cities, Helots were Greek—in fact they were the Spartans' neighbors until the Spartans subjected and enslaved them. It was their labor that let the Spartans devote themselves to military training. The Helots were not individually owned; they worked the land as public slaves, making them comparable to medieval serfs, although some did act as personal servants to individual Spartans.

We do not know exactly how many were held in this status, but sources agree there were many, as Sparta had the highest proportion of unfree persons of all Greek cities. The Helots' large numbers meant the Spartans lived in fear of revolt, which prompted them to treat the Helots with considerable brutality. Every year, Spartan officials would officially declare war on the Helots, allowing anyone to kill them with impunity. According to Thucydides, Spartan officials regularly sent out death squads to Helot villages. Composed of Spartan youngsters, the squads operated at night, ambushing and killing the sturdiest Helots, who were most likely to act as ringleaders in the event of a revolt. Helots were also abused in other ways. They were forcibly made drunk by Spartans and then paraded around the city to show young Spartans what drunkenness was like and, by implication, how a Spartan should not behave.

In Athens, slaves seem to have been treated somewhat better, and Athenian law prohibited their killing (although the fines levied for a dead slave were significantly lower than those for a free person). Remarkably, Athenian law even protected slaves against *hubris* or aggressive, abusive behavior. But apart from these two inhibitions, owners had almost complete freedom, both in law and custom, to treat slaves as they wished.[64]

Similarly, it should be emphasized that Greek women, even if free, had very little control over their own lives. Athenian women in particular were always under the guardianship of their fathers or husbands, and, especially if upper class, were rarely allowed to leave their homes; when they went outside, they were heavily veiled. Some Athenian women lived such secluded lives that they were rarely seen, even by their male relatives.[65] From the perspective of slaves and women, then, life under Greek popular government was just as, or perhaps more, oppressive than that under Persian autocracy.

In short, there are good reasons to doubt the reality of Herodotus's sharp contrast between Greek freedom and personal security, on the one hand, and Persian "slavery" on the other. At the same time, historians have made short shrift of another, equally stubborn myth: that Greek citizens were completely subservient to the state and lacked all individual independence. This idea was propagated, in particular, by the nineteenth-century French historian Numa Denis Fustel de Coulanges. In his extremely influential book the *Ancient City,* Fustel de Coulanges sketched a view of Athens and of ancient city-states more generally as communities in which the government regulated every detail of life and the state exacted complete obedience from its citizens. The antique city-state, as Fustel de Coulanges claimed, was "omnipotent," and hence, "the ancients had not known individual liberty. . . . The individual person counted but for little when compared to the holy, almost divine authority of the state or the fatherland."[66]

Such views, however, have little basis in fact. As Mogens Hansen has pointed out, Athenian citizens enjoyed robust protections against potential abuses by state officials. Thus, no citizen could be executed without due process, and the torture of citizens was likewise prohibited. Perhaps even more important, Athenian citizens had recourse against public officials who had harmed them. Any citizen could hold officials accountable for their behavior in office by means of a private suit. Since public officials were held to represent the polis, private citizens could effectively bring, and even win, suits against them. Athenian democracy also provided ways to hold magistrates publicly accountable; thus, every summer thirty officials sat for three days in the Agora to receive written complaints against public officials.[67]

Moreover, compared to other societies in the ancient world, classical Athens rarely imposed legal restrictions on private life. Behavior that affected only individuals, such as male homosexuality, was usually not prohibited. To the extent that the Athenian state did meddle with private behavior, it was typically to protect the general interest of the polis. Male prostitutes, for instance, ran the risk of losing their citizens' rights. But this was not on the grounds of immorality. Rather, their behavior indicated that they could be bought. Hence, it was thought they might endanger the safety of the city by selling their votes to foreign tyrants. Athenians also enjoyed considerable freedom of speech. They were free to praise the Spartan constitution, even though for much of its history, Athens was at war with Sparta. In short, as one scholar has put it, "as a day-to-day reality, Athens' democracy was remarkably tolerant."[68]

Regardless of how one evaluates the reality of Greek freedom, however, the importance of the Greek cult of freedom as an intellectual construct cannot be overstated, as its identification of freedom with democracy has had a long-lasting impact on Western political thinking. For centuries to come, as we shall see, political thinkers and activists would repeat the mantra that freedom could be enjoyed only in a popular regime in which the people governed themselves. The Greeks' valuation of freedom has had an equally long-lasting impact. The idea that personal security and individual independence could be enjoyed only within the context of free, self-governing states remained commonplace for centuries—even though it was challenged from within by influential Greek thinkers.

Freedom's Critics: Oligarchs and Sophists

The views expressed by Aeschylus and Herodotus were shared by many—but not by everyone. Especially as the memory of the Persian wars receded into the past, a powerful undercurrent that was more critical of the cult of democratic freedom began taking shape in Greece. In Athens, in particular, a growing number of intellectuals began to question whether popular self-government really did lead to freedom for all. Indeed, the cult of freedom came to be criticized by some of the most famous and influential Greek thinkers.

The first thinkers to develop a coherent critique of the cult of democratic freedom were the so-called oligarchs—those who opposed democracy in principle and propagated the idea that a small elite of wealthy and wellborn citizens should govern. As part of their campaign to delegitimize democracy, these thinkers also came to contest the democratic conception of freedom. Democracy, they argued, was not really the rule of all. Rather, it gave undue power to the poor, who in every society constituted a numerical majority over the rich. From the perspective of the wealthy few, in other words, democracy did not lead to freedom but rather to another form of tyranny—tyranny by the poor.

To a large extent, this oligarchic criticism of freedom can be understood as a backlash against the increasing democratization of the Athenian political regime in the wake of the Persian wars. After Cleisthenes's reforms in the late sixth century BC, Athens was one of the most democratic cities on the Greek mainland. But popular self-rule became even more entrenched in the immediate aftermath of the Persian wars, when a series of constitutional changes further increased the political power of ordinary Athenians.[69] Under Cleisthenes, for example, public officials were elected, but in the fifth century this system was replaced by selection by lot, which prevented a well-connected elite from dominating the elections and monopolizing offices. (An exception was made for public offices requiring specific skills, like the military and the treasury.) In addition, Athenian reformers went on to introduce pay for government service, which meant that even Athenians who worked for a living could take time off to serve in the day-to-day administration of their city.

As a result, political power came to be exercised by Athens' ordinary citizens, men whose names (such as Epicrates, Pandionis, Mantitheus) have been preserved in administrative decrees but whom we know nothing else about. In any decade of the late fifth and fourth centuries, between a quarter and a third of the citizenry over thirty (the age at which one became eligible for office) held public office.[70] Reforms were also introduced to increase the participation of ordinary Athenian citizens in the popular assemblies that made the most important political decisions. In 390 BC, attendance was rewarded by a small stipend, to ensure that even the poor could afford to attend to the often-daylong meetings. As a result, participation rates were relatively high: the best modern estimates show that about 6,000 citizens regularly attended the assembly, which roughly approximates a voter turnout of between 10 and 20 percent, making attendance comparable to voter turnout for referenda today.[71]

Finally, even the judiciary was democratized. Lawsuits were no longer brought before a specialized court, as they had been under Cleisthenes, but before juries drawn by lot from the overall population. These juries were typically several hundred strong, which meant that cases were heard by a true cross-section of the Athenian population. But that was not the only part ordinary citizens played in the justice system. Plaintiffs pled their own cases, so no professional lawyers were involved—indeed, lawyers simply did not exist. Nor were there judges to instruct the jury: it was up to the jurors to decide whether a case had merit.

A generation after the Persian wars, political power was firmly entrenched in the hands of the entire Athenian demos rather than a wealthy or wellborn elite. A relief sculpture from the late fourth century BC, when Athenian democracy was at its pinnacle, vividly illustrates this reality. It represents Demos as a bearded, adult man in the prime of his life, seated on a throne-like chair. A young woman, the goddess Demokratia, or "Democracy," holds a wreath—the symbol of power—above Demos's head.[72] The message was clear: in Athens, the demos was king.

The cult of freedom played an important role in legitimating these reforms. Athenian politicians argued that only full-fledged democracies like theirs counted as truly free regimes. They claimed that under an elite government, ordinary citizens were as unfree as they would be under a tyranny. As one Athenian orator put it, in oligarchic cities, "some inhab-

Demos being crowned by Demokratia, Athenian relief sculpture, fourth century BC.

itants look on the others as slaves, while the latter look on the former as masters." By contrast, the Athenians, he said, "do not think it right to be each other's slaves or masters. Equality of birth in the natural order makes us seek equality of rights in the legal and defer to each other only in the name of reputation for goodness and wisdom."[73] Hence, only cities in which all male citizens were treated as equals could be described as free.

But many of Athens' wealthier elite—who were also the most likely to put their thoughts on paper—were angered by their declining influence on the political process, and they became increasingly critical of the regime. One of the earliest examples of this ire is captured in an anonymous essay titled the *Constitution of Athens*. We know very little about the

author or his circumstances, although most scholars agree the piece
was probably written during the heyday of Athenian democracy—in
the second half of the fifth century BC—by a disgruntled member of the
Athenian elite. (Historians usually call the author the Old Oligarch.)
The essay's goal seems to have been to explain to outsiders how the
Athenian regime worked, but the author also made it abundantly clear
that he deeply disapproved of the Athenian constitution.[74]

In particular, the Old Oligarch made short shrift of the idea that democracies offered freedom for all. He identified Athenian democracy with
the rule of the poor and uneducated, those whom he described as the
"worst" people. ("Among the people there is a maximum of ignorance,
disorder, and wickedness; for poverty draws them rather to disgraceful
actions, and because of a lack of money some men are uneducated and
ignorant.") They ruled, he made clear, in their own interest, and thus to
the detriment of the rich. More specifically, Athens's poor majority had
turned the state into a system for redistributing money from the rich to
the poor, "so that they become wealthy and the wealthy poorer."[75]

The poor, the Old Oligarch complained, monopolized public office
and the corresponding salaries. They got the state to pay them for rowing
the triremes of Athens's navy. They ran the court system in their own interests. They even profited disproportionately from the city's religious
ceremonies, as it was they who feasted on the animals sacrificed at public
expense. No less telling was the fact that Athens had built many wres-
tling quarters, dressing rooms, and public baths at the state's expense.
"The rabble has more enjoyment of these things than the well-to-do members of the upper class," the Old Oligarch pointed out, since the rich had
their own private gymnasia, baths, and dressing rooms.[76]

Poor Athenians had even managed to monopolize less-tangible benefits of power, like prestige. They protested when common people were
spoken ill of in the state-sponsored theater festivals, but if a comedy writer
wanted to attack the elite, nothing prevented him from doing so. As a result, the Old Oligarch stressed, comedy writers singled out individuals
of wealth, high birth, or influence for mockery—yet another example of
anti-rich bias.

These claims, of course, can plausibly be construed as a critique
of Herodotus's celebration of democratic freedom. In the *Histories*,

Herodotus had argued that only the introduction of broad-based, inclusive political regimes protected individuals against the abuses that were inevitable when power was concentrated in the hands of a single person. But according to the Old Oligarch, democracy could be an oppressive regime, too—at least from the perspective of the rich and wellborn.

This is not to say that the Old Oligarch believed that freedom would be more secure under elite government. On the contrary, he made clear that all types of government involved the domination of one class by another. Hence his rather paradoxical conclusion: it was reasonable for the common people to prefer democracy, even though it led to "bad" government. As he put it, "The common people do not want to be slaves in a city with good government. They want to be free and hold power. Bad government is of little concern to them."[77] Or as he said elsewhere, "I pardon the people themselves for their democracy. One must forgive everyone for looking after his own interests."[78]

The Old Oligarch was not alone in making such claims. Thucydides, another disgruntled member of the Athenian elite, made similar arguments.[79] The scion of a prominent Athenian family, Thucydides was elected as a general during the Peloponnesian War, a decades-long conflict between Athens and Sparta. However, he bungled his mission, and his angry compatriots exiled him for his failure. He spent the remainder of the war outside of Athens, compiling notes and working on what would eventually become his life's work: a detailed account of the Peloponnesian War.

Like the Old Oligarch, Thucydides believed all politics was power politics. The Peloponnesian War was fought in the name of freedom, but it was really a struggle between two equally self-interested opponents. He saw the civil strife between democrats and oligarchs unleashed in many Greek cities in the wake of the battle between Athens and Sparta—often described as the second front of the Peloponnesian War—in the same way. There too, ideals like freedom were used to cover up the real source of strife: the self-interested pursuit of domination.[80]

Thucydides made this point at some length in his account of the outbreak of civil war in Corcyra. Corcyra was traditionally a democratic city and an Athenian ally. The struggle began when a hefty fine was imposed on a group of oligarchs. Refusing to pay the fine, they burst into the council

chamber and killed dozens of councilmen—probably emboldened by the
hope that they would get Sparta's support. The democrats, however, immediately mobilized, and heavy fighting broke out all over town. The
democrats soon gained the upper hand. There were more of them, and, as
Thucydides noted, they also had the enterprising support of their women,
who pelted the enemy with tiles from their houses. The Athenian navy
supported them as well.

The democrats showed no mercy, and the standoff ended, Thucydides
recounted, with a dramatic collective suicide. The defeated oligarchs fled
to a religious sanctuary, where they began to kill one another so as to
remain out of the hands of their opponents. But this was not enough to
slake the bloodlust of the victorious side. Under the pretext of executing
those who had conspired to subvert democracy, they started slaughtering
their compatriots for various reasons. Some were killed out of private hostility, including debtors who had not paid back loans. Death took every
imaginable form: "Fathers killed their sons; men were dragged out of the
sanctuaries and killed beside them; some were even walled up in the
temple of Dionysus and died there."[81]

The Corcyrian civil war was, in other words, a vicious fight in which
all human decency was thrown overboard. But during the fight, Corcyrian
democrats and oligarchs both invoked lofty ideals. They used, as
Thucydides put it, "fine-sounding terms," claiming espousal either of
"democratic rights for all" or of a "conservative aristocracy." But in reality,
both sides were driven by greed and ambition, leading, in turn, to the passions of the party rivalries thus established.[82] This template, Thucydides
explained, was followed throughout all the civil wars that erupted in the
course of the Peloponnesian War: even though men claimed to be fighting
for freedom and democracy, in reality they were just out to line their own
pockets and settle old scores.

In addition to the Old Oligarch and Thucydides, democracy's critics
also found support in a more unexpected place: among the sophists. The
sophist was a new type of intellectual—a professional educator who toured
the Greek world, offering instruction in subjects including politics and
ethics and conveying more practical skills like rhetoric. This new pro-
fession was a response to the social and political developments of the
period and, more crucially, to the growing political importance of the

demos, which led to a demand for instruction in political and legal oratory. At the same time, the increasing wealth and intellectual sophistication of Greek cities, especially Athens, created a demand for higher education, something beyond the traditional grounding in literacy, arithmetic, music, and physical exercise. As such, the sophists were in high demand and were paid well.[83]

As a group, the sophists did not propagate a particular political perspective, though some, including Protagoras, seem to have been committed democrats.[84] But their incisive questioning of all social and political norms brought some of them quite close to the position taken by Athenian oligarchs that all politics was power politics and that words like "just" or "free" were simply smokescreens invented by the powerful to legitimate their rule. The sophist Thrasymachus, active in Athens in the late fifth century BC, seems to have been associated with an argument of this kind. Little is known about Thrasymachus's life, and he left no record of his ideas, but some of his thinking was transmitted through Plato.

If Plato's report is correct, Thrasymachus seems to have claimed that every kind of government—not just monarchy—was intended to benefit those in power: "Democracy makes democratic laws, tyranny makes tyrannical laws, and so on with the others. And they declare what they have made—what is to their own advantage—to be just for their subjects, and they punish anyone who goes against this as lawless and unjust. This, then, is what I say justice is, the same in all cities, the advantage of the established rule. Since the established rule is surely stronger, anyone who reasons correctly will conclude that the just is the same everywhere, namely, the advantage of the stronger."[85]

There are some indications that, through sophists' influence on elite education, similar views became widespread among wellborn Athenian youngsters. Alcibiades—an Athenian politician who became infamous for his disdain for democracy—made much the same point as Thrasymachus in a conversation with the elder statesman Pericles, reported by the historian Xenophon. Alcibiades started with a seemingly innocent question: What is law? Pericles felt that this question could be easily answered: Law, he replied, was what the multitude had approved and proclaimed to be law. It stipulated what one should do and what one should not do. Unconvinced, Alcibiades asked if everything that was written down was law.

What about laws proclaimed by a small elite or a tyrant against the wishes of the population? These, Pericles replied, obviously were not law, since they were imposed through force. But then what about laws made by the democratic majority and imposed on the wealthy against their wishes? Were they, too, "violence rather than law?" At this point, the exasperated Pericles gave up: "We too were quite clever indeed at things of this sort when we were your age. For we too practiced such things and made precisely the sort of sophisticated arguments that you, in my opinion, are now practicing."[86]

These and similar attacks on popular government appear to have had an impact in the real world, as Athenian democracy was overthrown by oligarchic coups in 411 and 404 BC. The first coup gave power over the day-to-day administration to a council of elite citizens—the so-called Four Hundred—and limited full citizenship rights to 5,000 male Athenians. That regime quickly lost power due to infighting, however, and democracy was restored. Seven years later, in 404, power was seized by an even smaller group, the so-called Thirty. They were led by a wellborn Athenian named Critias, who was such an inveterate opponent of democracy that his grave monument reputedly featured a personified Oligarchia setting fire to Demokratia. The Thirty instituted an oligarchic regime in which a handpicked group of 3,000 Athenian men shared in governing. Less than a year after the coup, the regime was overthrown by pro-democratic forces.

Of course, these coups cannot be blamed only on antidemocratic arguments developed by intellectuals like Thrasymachus and the Old Oligarch. They took place at the tail end of the long and bloody Peloponnesian War that pitted Athens against Sparta. The pressures of this war, particularly the fact that Athens lost, might have been enough to delegitimize the democratic regime. In addition, the hope that replacing democracy with oligarchy would give Athens better peace terms with oligarchic Sparta probably helped bolster the oligarchs' case. Nevertheless, it seems clear that antidemocratic arguments like those formulated by the Old Oligarch had an impact on the coup's instigators. The historian Xenophon reported that Critias, the leader of the Thirty, defended their actions by saying that "for men like ourselves . . . democracy is an oppressive form of government."[87]

Ironically, the actual experience of oligarchic rule did much to restore the moral standing of democracy in Athens. The Thirty's regime quickly revealed itself to be a far greater danger to the property and lives of Athenians—rich and poor alike—than democracy had ever been. In his *Hellenica,* a continuation of Thucydides's *Peloponnesian War,* Xenophon made clear that the reign of the Thirty had been a vicious tyranny. As soon as they had gotten power, they had used it for their own gain. Supported by Spartan troops, they turned to arresting their personal enemies, then targeted wealthy individuals in order to confiscate their property. Most dramatically, the Thirty arrested and executed Theramenes, once a prominent supporter, when he began to voice his concerns about their policies. According to Xenophon, in eight months they killed as many Athenians as the Spartans had in ten years.[88]

Predictably, the regime quickly lost support even among the Athenian elites, and when the Spartans retreated, its army was roundly defeated by Thrasybulus, the general of the democratic party. In victory, as Xenophon made clear, the democrats behaved better than the oligarchs had. Instead of seeking revenge, they called for general amnesty, and they restored democracy and civic concord in Athens. Xenophon's negative assessment of the oligarchic coup was all the more remarkable because he was a cavalry officer and hence belonged to the elite; moreover, he was an admirer of the Spartan regime and, at least in theory, could be expected to favor oligarchy more than many other Athenians. Other sources also illustrate how much the reign of the Thirty discredited oligarchy. The Athenian orator Isocrates—by no means an ultra-democrat—remarked that the restored democracy was "a divine creation" compared to the Thirty's regime.[89]

Nevertheless, the arguments developed by the Old Oligarch and the sophists would continue to resonate. After all, it was not entirely wrong to say that Athenian democracy gave predominant power to one social group—the less well-off—thereby excluding others, particularly the wealthy, from power. Indeed, in revised form—as an argument about the danger of tyranny by the majority—this claim would feature prominently in cases made against democracy centuries after the demise of the Athenian democratic government.

Freedom's Critics: Plato

The Old Oligarch and Thrasymachus were not the only critics of democratic freedom. Even after the triumphant restoration of Athenian democracy in 403 BC, one of Greece's most brilliant thinkers—the philosopher Plato—continued attacking the regime under which he lived.[90] He made it clear that, in his view, the Athenian insistence that democratic freedom was the most important political value was misguided and even potentially dangerous. However, Plato also rejected the cynical defense of power politics made by the Old Oligarch and Thrasymachus. In his view, political ideals were important—but his contemporaries had adopted the wrong ones. Human happiness was more important than freedom and individual independence. Hence, the best possible regime was not democracy, but rule by the "best man"—the person most likely to lead his subjects to a good life.

Like Thucydides and Alcibiades, who were a generation older, Plato was born into a wealthy and influential Athenian family. He originally seems to have aspired, as most young men of his class did, to a political career serving the Athenian democracy. His family would probably have expected as much: his stepfather, Pyrilampes, was a close friend of the influential Athenian politician Pericles and such a staunch pillar of Athenian democracy that he named his son, Plato's stepbrother, Demos.[91]

However, as a young man, Plato had come under the spell of Socrates. Like the sophists, Socrates, the son of a stonemason, had devoted his life to the education of young Athenians, but unlike these itinerant teachers, Socrates had refused to accept pay for his teachings. He emphasized the difference between himself and the sophists by describing himself as a "philosopher"—a "lover of wisdom." Despite his relatively low birth and unprepossessing physique, Socrates exercised profound influence on his followers. Under his influence, Plato decided to devote his life to intellectual pursuits rather than to politics. Eventually, Plato founded his own philosophical school, the Academy, and devoted most of his time to writing philosophical treatises.

Plato's turn away from politics and toward a philosophical life was probably further encouraged by his experiences during the reign of the Thirty, who came to power when he was a young man. In the

Seventh Letter, an epistle written by Plato in later life and considered authentic by many scholars, Plato explained that he had been tempted to participate in the newly established oligarchic regime, despite his family's democratic leanings.[92] (Plato had friends and family members among the Thirty as well; Critias, its leader, was a cousin of Plato's mother.) But it quickly became clear to him that the Thirty were planning to unleash a reign of terror. "I thought that they were going to lead the city out of the unjust life she had been living and establish her in the path of justice," the *Seventh Letter* says, "so that I watched them eagerly to see what they would do. But as I watched them they showed in a short time that the preceding [democratic] constitution had been a precious thing."[93]

For Plato, however, the restoration of democracy only brought more heartache. In 399 BC, about four years after the Thirty's defeat, Socrates was tried and executed by an Athenian jury for impiety and for corrupting Athenian youth. The motivations for Socrates's conviction remain unclear. Perhaps ordinary Athenians were uncomfortable with his highly unconventional ideas about religion and other norms and values. But it is also quite possible that the charge of impiety was a pretext, and that Socrates's conviction was triggered by his supposed sympathies for antidemocratic forces. After all, the leader of the Thirty, Critias, had been Socrates's pupil, and many suspected that Critias had learned his hatred for democracy from his famous teacher. Even after the overthrow of the Thirty, Socrates was suspected of being a secret (or even not-so-secret) antidemocrat.

Whether these suspicions were true or not is still hotly debated, and the debate is particularly difficult to solve because Socrates left no written record of his teachings.[94] It is clear, however, that Plato was profoundly affected by his teacher's death. Socrates's trial and execution left Plato as disillusioned about democracy as he was about oligarchy. This disillusionment had a considerable impact on his political writings, which can be read as attacks on the democratic ideals that he had grown up with— including the concept of freedom—as well as attempts to come up with better alternatives.

The Republic, Plato's most well-known and influential contribution to political thought, is a case in point. Written as a dialogue between Socrates and a number of younger men, *The Republic* is wide ranging, full of outlandish ideas about the political danger of poetry and song, the importance of mathematical knowledge for political leaders, and the proper position of women in politics. (Plato was more positive about female leadership than most of his contemporaries.) But Plato's main goal was to come to a definition of the best possible political regime, which, to him, meant the political regime most likely to engender true human happiness. It was from this perspective—the question of human happiness—that he evaluated the key Athenian political value: freedom.

Plato began by rejecting the bleak power politics exemplified by the Old Oligarch and Thrasymachus. Politics was not just about power, he argued. The only legitimate regime was a regime that acted in the interest of both the rulers and the ruled alike. But he also rejected the idea that democratic freedom was an attractive ideal. In Book 8 of *The Republic,* in which he discussed the existing forms of government, Plato distinguished between four of those forms: timocracy (rule by a military class), oligarchy (rule by the wealthy few), democracy (rule by the poor), and tyranny (rule by a single person). He made clear that he believed, like most Greeks, that freedom could be equated with democratic self-government. A democracy, he explained, is "the only city worth living in for someone who is by nature free."[95]

Moreover, like Herodotus and others, Plato made clear that the collective freedom offered by democratic regimes was a necessary precondition for preserving individual independence; for only in free states were individuals given the opportunity to behave exactly as they wanted. A democratic city, Plato wrote, was "full of freedom and frankness—a man may say and do what he likes," which implied that "the individual is clearly able to order for himself his own life as he pleases."[96]

According to Plato, then, individual independence would necessarily result from democracy. If a city were not governed by a king or tyrant, people would become used to thinking of themselves as their own rulers and would thereby be encouraged to order their lives as they wanted. By degrees, this attitude of independence, in Plato's view, would move from the political sphere into private houses: fathers would grow accustomed to descending to the level of their sons and begin to fear them, whereas sons would come to think of themselves as equal to their fathers and mothers, thus losing respect and reverence for them. Similarly, metics or foreigners would begin to see themselves as equal to citizens, and citizens to believe they were no better than metics.

So good were democracies at fostering individual independence that, according to Plato, in democratic cities, slaves did not behave like slaves, and women acted as if they were on a par with men. Even domestic animals were affected, acting more freely in a democracy than they would in other kinds of states: "Horses and donkeys are accustomed to roam freely and proudly along the streets, bumping into anyone who doesn't get out of their way."[97]

Plato admitted that there was something attractive about this model. Democratic freedom and the individual independence it fostered, he explained, meant that in a free state "there will be the greatest variety of human natures." An observer might therefore see such a state as "the fairest of States, being like an embroidered robe which is spangled with every sort of flower." Indeed, for many, Plato said, this might seem to be the best kind of regime: "And just as women and children think a variety of colours to be of all things most charming, so there are many men to whom this state, which is spangled with the manners and characters of mankind, will appear to be the fairest of states."[98]

But ultimately, Plato did not share this positive assessment of democracy. Instead, he believed that the fact that democracy was so conducive to individual independence was problematic. Eventually, the licentiousness unleashed by a democratic regime would bring about its demise, as democratic freedom spilled over into anarchy, with "subjects who are like rulers, and rulers who are like subjects."[99] Paradoxically, this anarchical state of affairs would eventually lead to the opposite of freedom—namely, tyranny—for citizens would eventually grow tired of their unbridled freedom and call for a strong hand to restore order. An unscrupulous man would likely take advantage of this situation and establish his own personal rule—and this, Plato emphasized, was a highly undesirable outcome. After all, tyranny (which Plato defined as the rule of an unfit individual over everyone else) was the regime least conducive to human happiness.

Democratic freedom, in short, was self-defeating. It led to licentiousness rather than to good rule, and it was unsustainable in the long run. What should we think of this doctrine? First and foremost, it is hard to imagine that Plato expected his warnings about uncontrollable slaves and recalcitrant donkeys to be taken literally. This was hyperbole, but it was intended to make a deeper point. He was not just warning that democracies were inherently unstable (this was true, after all, of all the regimes he discussed in *The Republic*); rather, he was pointing out that the individual independence and freedom provided by democratic regimes was typically used to bad ends. Ordinary people, Plato said, could not be trusted to use their freedom wisely.[100]

Plato was convinced of this because he had a low opinion of most people's intellectual capacities. He made that opinion clear again and again throughout *The Republic*. In a famous passage, he compared democratic politicians to sailors who are reluctant to accept the guidance of a captain more knowledgeable than they about navigation and other indispensable skills. Yet, the sailors had no idea how to get anywhere. "They don't understand that a true captain must pay attention to the seasons of the year, the sky, the stars, the winds, and all that pertains to his craft, if he's really to be the ruler of a ship. And they don't believe there is any craft that would enable him to determine how he should steer the ship, whether the others want him to or not, or any possibility of mastering this alleged craft or of practicing it at the same time as the craft of navigation."[101]

However, Plato also rejected the obvious alternative to democracy: rule by the wealthy elite. Unlike many of his contemporaries, he did not believe that the wealthy were automatically better qualified to rule. They, too, were likely to be swayed by wanton passions. Indeed, Plato was just as scathing, if not more so, about oligarchy as compared to democracy. In his view, oligarchs were ruled by an all-consuming passion for lucre, a base passion for wealth that was even farther removed from true human happiness than democrats' lust for independence.

Thus, Plato proposed a very different regime: rule by philosopher-king. He wanted political power to be given to leaders who, from an early age, were rigorously trained in, among other subjects, martial arts, mathematics, and astronomy. After a long period in gaining practical experience as military commanders and in other official capacities, a select few—all over the age of fifty—would study philosophy. This rigorous education would ensure that the philosopher-kings were prepared for the warfare in which Greek cities were constantly engaged. More importantly, it would give them unique insight into what Plato called "the good life"—the only life that brought true human happiness. Unlike a tyrant, a philosopher-king could therefore be expected to reign not according to caprice but according to philosophical insight.

In the regime of the philosopher-king, citizens would have virtually no say over their government. There was no room for elections in Plato's system or, indeed, for any input from ordinary people. There would be no popular assembly, jury system, or selection by lot for administrative functions—rather, Plato envisaged that all decisions would be made by the elite philosophers or, perhaps, just the greatest of them. Rulers would then become a self-perpetuating caste, as the philosopher-kings in power at any given time would select their successors. (Interestingly, these successors could be men or women, so a select group of women would increase their independence under Plato's system.)

For Plato, the loss of democratic involvement was worth it, because "it is better for everyone to be ruled by what is divine and wise." In an ideal world, he asserted, everyone would have this "divine and wise" element within himself, but in the real world, that was not the case. Therefore, good rule should be imposed on individuals from the outside, "so that as far as possible we may all be equal, and all friends, since we are all under the guidance of the same commander." In the ideal regime of the philosopher-king, men would therefore be "the slave of the best person, since the best person has the divine ruler within him."[102] Plato may have expressed this view even more bluntly in another dialogue, *Clitophon* (although the authorship of this dialogue is disputed). According to this text, a foolish man who lived his life according to whim rather than rational thought was better off dead. If such a foolish man had to live, it would be better for him "to live as a slave than to be free, handing over the rudder of his mind, like that of a ship, to somebody else who knows the skill of steering men."[103]

In his later writings, Plato backtracked somewhat from his enthusiastic defense of political "slavery." In the *Laws*, which most scholars believe to be his most mature work, Plato substantially modified his views about the ideal regime.[104] He no longer argued that the best regime was that of a philosopher-king, admitting that there was very little chance of finding political leaders who could live up to that ideal. "Human nature," Plato now noted, in a remarkable echo of Herodotus, "is not at all capable of regulating the human things, when it possesses autocratic authority over everything, without becoming swollen with insolence and injustice."[105] Instead, he now argued that, in the best possible regime, people would live under the rule of laws rather than men.

Plato's change of heart may have been caused by a failed attempt to put the ideal of philosopher-king into practice. According to the *Seventh Letter,* at the age of forty, he was invited by Dion, a relative of the reigning tyrant Dionysius, to the Sicilian city of Syracuse to be Dionysius's tutor and make him into a philosopher-king. Initially hesitant—it would be a long, arduous journey—Plato eventually agreed. As he explained in the *Seventh Letter,* "If anyone ever was to attempt to realize these principles of law and government, now was the time to try, since it was only necessary to win over a single man and I should have accomplished all the good I dreamed of."[106]

The experiment, however, failed ignominiously. After only four months, Dionysius banned Dion for conspiring against the tyranny and held Plato in Syracuse against his will. Trying to make the best of a bad situation, Plato tried to make Dionysius see the light, but Dionysius resisted Plato's attempts to bring him to "the philosophic life." In fact, he had Dion killed on his return to Syracuse. If the *Seventh Letter* is to be believed, the whole experience so shook Plato that he gave up on the idea that a philosopher-king could be found, and he had to rethink his political philosophy.

But Plato never came around to democracy. Even in the *Laws,* he did not imagine a regime in which people lived under laws that they had helped to make. Instead, he envisaged a regime in which a legislator of near-divine wisdom provided a city with laws it continued to follow until the end of time. Plato provided readers with a detailed list of these laws. While the people were to elect the magistrates responsible for their implementation, the lawmaking process itself would not be under popular control. The people living under the regime Plato defended in the *Laws* are, in other words, best described not as free but as servants to the laws. As Plato himself put it, the people should not be the "master," but rather "the willing slaves of the laws."[107]

Plato's political philosophy, in short, was based on a wholesale critique of the Greek ideal of democratic freedom. In a remarkable reversal of values, Plato defended political subjection as more conducive to human happiness than democratic freedom—as long as one's rulers lived up to the demanding ideal of the philosopher-king. Plato's views would have a huge impact on political thought for centuries to come. In fact, his main argument against democratic freedom—that it inexorably led to anarchy and license—would be repeated for centuries. Likewise, his defense of political slavery, in which ordinary people submitted to the "best" or "wisest," would have profound impact on subsequent political thought.

In his own time, however, Plato's views gained little traction. Apart from his small coterie of disciples, very few contemporaries agreed that subjection to the "best man" was preferable to democratic freedom. Even those who agreed that Athenian democracy had become "extreme" shied away from Plato's radical conclusions. Isocrates, for instance, an Athenian speechwriter and one of Plato's most important rivals as an educator, also criticized the political regime under which he lived. Like Plato (and the Old Oligarch, for that matter), Isocrates believed that Athenian-style democracy, with its heavy emphasis on complete citizen equality, led to the rule of the least capable: the poor and the ignorant.[108]

However, the alternative Isocrates proposed in his influential pamphlet *Areopagiticus* was much less radical than Plato's. Rather than rule by a philosopher-king or a small, unaccountable elite, Isocrates proposed a return to the "original democracy" of Athens, in which political leaders were elected rather than selected by lot. Under such a regime, Isocrates argued, the most capable men would be in charge (because the demos could be relied on to choose the best among them for office), instead of a random selection of the population, while the people would continue to have supreme authority.[109]

Other indicators confirm that support for democratic freedom among Athenians—rich and poor alike—was robust. After the overthrow of the Thirty, the restored democracy remained in place, unthreatened, for another eighty-five years, until the Macedonian general Antipater installed an oligarchic puppet regime. This eight-five-year duration is evidence of widespread support, because a democracy, especially of the Athenian type, can hardly survive if a majority or even a substantial minority of citizens are opposed to it. In Greece as a whole, democracy likewise remained firmly entrenched. According to data compiled by historian David Teegarden, 40 percent of Greek cities for which we have regime-type information experienced democracy in the second half of the fifth century, as opposed to only 18 percent in the first half. And those numbers seem to have remained stable even into the second half of the fourth century, when 46 percent of Greek cities were democracies.[110] These statistics suggest that popular support for democracy and the ideals it was based on remained widespread, despite the criticism of elite thinkers like the Old Oligarch, Thrasymachus, and Plato.

After Chaeronea: The Turn to Inner Freedom

In the fourth and third centuries BC, Greek debate about freedom was affected by new political developments, notably the rise of Macedon. In 360, Philip II became king of Macedonia, a mountainous region to the north of Greece mainly populated by farmers.[111] Previously only marginally important, Macedon quickly became a great power thanks to Philip's military and organizational genius. He quelled the many rivalries among Macedon's noble families and turned them into a formidable army, specialized in combined infantry and cavalry operations. Next, he turned his attention to neighboring cities and states, conquering several Greek colonies in the northern Aegean.

While at first the Greeks were not overly worried about Macedon's rise, eventually Philip's expansionary ambitions became plain to all. The Athenian politician Demosthenes embarked on a tour of the mainland to rouse the Greeks to action. Appealing to the Greeks' age-old love of freedom, Demosthenes urged them to unite against Macedon's rise. Philip was no ordinary player on the international scene, Demosthenes said, but was a mortal threat to the freedom and self-government of Greek cities. "What is your object?" he asked the Athenian Assembly, before answering his own question. "Freedom. Then do you not see that Philip's very titles are utterly irreconcilable with that? For every king, every despot is the sworn foe of freedom and of law. Beware . . . lest, seeking to be rid of war, you find a master."[112]

Perhaps even more important in inciting the Greeks to action was Philip's attack on Byzantium in 340 BC, accompanied by the capture of a fleet of ships carrying grain. The attack directly threatened Athens, which regularly imported grain from the Black Sea. War had become inevitable. Although it took two more years of negotiations to put together a Greek alliance, the Greeks, led by the Athenians, finally came head to head with the Macedonians at Chaeronea in 338 BC. Philip's cavalry, now led by his son Alexander, obtained the decisive victory, with enormous casualties on the Greek side. A year later, the League of Corinth was formed, presided over by Philip and, after him, his heirs, essentially putting the Greek cities under Macedonian rule.

Philip was not to enjoy the fruits of his victory for long. Shortly after Chaeronea, he was murdered at a religious festival. (His assassin, a young man from the royal bodyguard, was also killed, and his motivation remains mysterious.) Philip was succeeded by his son Alexander, but the latter soon departed to conquer Persia, leaving Greece under the control of one of his generals, Antipater. In 323 BC, Alexander's sudden death in Persia created a power vacuum, and several Greek cities, including Athens, made a last-ditch attempt to regain their independence. But the revolt was quickly crushed by Antipater, who assumed full control over the Greek mainland. Angry at Athens's rebellion, Antipater installed a puppet regime that gave power to a small, pro-Macedonian elite. Demosthenes and other anti-Macedonian politicians were sentenced to death. Demosthenes managed to flee Athens, but, chased by a bounty hunter, he eventually killed himself (reportedly by putting a poisoned pen in his mouth).[113]

Yet, this was not the end of democracy in Greece.[114] For much of the Hellenistic period, many cities continued to be governed democratically by officials appointed through election and sortition, an assembly, and popular courts. Throughout the Greek-speaking world, citizens still passed laws and decrees, collected taxes, minted coins, and administered justice, much like they had done in the fifth and fourth centuries. Incessant warfare and competition between the different Hellenistic kings and pretenders even allowed Greek citizens some modicum of control over their foreign policy. This only changed around 150 BC, when Greek cities became part of the growing Roman Empire, and the last remaining democracies were abolished.

But while there was much continuity, things did change in important ways. In the centuries following Alexander's death, the center of power in the Greek-speaking world shifted from city-states like Athens and Sparta to the enormous empires that came out of Alexander's conquests. By 300 BC, after decades of warfare, the "big three" kingdoms of the Hellenistic period had been established: Egypt, Macedon, and Greater Syria (which consisted of the former Persian Empire minus Egypt). Greek cities remained nominally free and were not strictly parts of the kingdoms, but local kings and dynasts had considerable, if informal, influence. As the center of gravity shifted toward kings and their courts, the importance of the rich and powerful within Greek cities increased, because they were the only ones with access to the kings. As a result, the political influence of ordinary citizens gradually diminished even where democracy was nominally retained.

These changes had a profound effect on Greek political thought, although the impact was not immediately noticeable. To a large extent, the political debates of the fourth and even third centuries BC continued along the lines sketched earlier: for and against democracy.[115] Aristotle, Plato's most famous pupil, continued to think that Greek polis life was the natural locus of politics. In his best-known political treatise, *Politics*, Aristotle barely acknowledged the existence of large-scale monarchy, even though as Alexander's tutor he had experienced Macedonian political life up close. Instead, *Politics* can best be understood as a contribution to earlier debates about democracy and democratic freedom.[116]

Like Plato, Aristotle showed himself to be quite critical of democracy's key value—freedom.[117] Aristotle's most sustained discussion of the concept of freedom occurred in book six of *Politics*, in which he discussed different existing constitutions. Here, he explicitly identified freedom as the key value of Athenian-type democracies. In a democracy, he explained, people were commonly considered to be free, because rulers and ruled alternated, leaving no one man or group of men in charge of everyone else. Following convention, Aristotle also highlighted that such democratic freedom went hand in hand with individual independence, or the ability "to live as one likes": "This, they say, is the result of freedom, since that of slavery is not to live as one likes. . . . From it arises the demand not to be ruled by anyone, or failing that, to rule and be ruled in turn."[118]

In Aristotle's view, however, such democratic freedom had two major downsides. Much like Plato, he believed that there was a slippery slope leading from democratic freedom to licentiousness and anarchy. In democracies, everyone lives "'according to his fancy,' as Euripides says," Aristotle noted. But this was bad. It led people to rebel against the rule of law, and that was the most common cause for the demise of democracies.[119] Second, and perhaps somewhat contradictorily, Aristotle also objected to Athenian-style democracy because it gave too much power to the numerical majority—the poor. This would obviously lead to injustice, since, as Aristotle put it, "if justice is what the numerical majority decide, they will commit injustice by confiscating the property of the wealthy few."[120]

Unlike his famous master, however, Aristotle did not propagate subjection to a philosopher-king or divine lawgiver as the best alternative to Athenian-style or "ultimate," as Aristotle called it, democracy. Instead, he touted—much like Isocrates had done—a return to older, more moderate types of democracy, in which office-holders were not selected by lot but elected from among wealthy or distinguished citizens. "People governed in this way are necessarily governed well," Aristotle commented, "the offices will always be in the hands of the best, while the people will consent and will not envy the decent."[121]

Eventually, however, philosophers in the Hellenistic age began focusing on the new political realities. In the third and second centuries BC, an increasing number of treatises appeared with titles like *On Kingship*. Most of these have been lost, and their arguments are largely unknown. The few surviving fragments, however, as well as later works drawing on the same tradition, suggest that the ideals they defended were largely inspired by Plato. They started from Plato's assumption that government by a wise ruler was most conducive to human happiness. A true king was an almost superhuman being, possessed of greater wisdom than any of his subjects and thus capable of leading them to the good life. This ideal was sharply contrasted with tyranny, where the ruler governed in his own interest, without any concern for his flock. The main goal of those Hellenistic writers, then, seems to have been to exhort their putative audience (kings and future kings) to conform to the kingly rather than to the tyrannical template.[122]

These changes also affected the debate about freedom. While many Greek intellectuals continued to extol the importance of democratic freedom, others came to argue for a very different understanding of the term. Freedom, they argued, did not necessarily depend on the political institutions under which one lived. Rather, whether one could live a free life or not had more to do with the one's strength of character or self-control. A person could be free even when he was ruled by a tyrant, as long as he had the appropriate moral strength. Thus, Hellenistic thinkers came to propagate a wholly personal, inner kind of freedom, mirroring the growing disempowerment of ordinary citizens in Greek political life.[123]

Such a moralized conception of freedom had deep roots in Greek thought.[124] In the fifth century BC, Euripides suggested in his play *Hecuba* that most human beings were in thrall to their desire for money, lust for fame, or fear—and hence could not truly call themselves free.[125] Similarly, the idea that "true" freedom required complete control over one's passions seems to have been defended by Socrates. While Socrates's disciples left varying accounts of what their master taught, they all agreed that the identification of self-control and self-abnegation with freedom was one of his cardinal tenets. Xenophon, for instance, reported Socrates as having described those in thrall to gluttony, lechery, alcohol, or foolish and costly ambitions as "slaves" subjected to "hard masters." "We must fight for our freedom against them," Xenophon's Socrates warned a young disciple, "as persistently as if they were armed men trying to enslave us."[126]

Socrates seems to have put these ideals into practice in his own life as well. According to Xenophon, Socrates showed an admirable disregard for his appearance and personal comfort. Even more strikingly, he refused to accept money for his lessons. In this way, Xenophon explained, Socrates was "attending to his freedom." The sophists and others who accepted money for their teachings were, in contrast, "enslavers of themselves." They were not free to choose their students based on their own preferences but were bound to teach those who paid them.[127]

Other philosophers were even more extreme in their commitment to self-abnegation. Diogenes of Sinope, the founder of the so-called Cynic school, for example, deeply impressed his contemporaries with his single-minded devotion to paring down his life to the barest essentials. Stories about him circulated widely. It was reported, for instance, that one day, when Diogenes observed a child drinking out of his hands, he threw away his cup, exclaiming, "A child has beaten me in plainness of living!" Like Socrates, Diogenes seems to have identified his sober way of living with true freedom, asserting that he "preferred liberty to everything."[128]

But in the course of time, this moralized conception of freedom became associated, in particular, with the Stoic philosopher Zeno of Citium and his disciples. Indeed, the idea that "the wise man"—that is, someone in full control over himself and his passions—alone was free became one of the famous Stoic "paradoxes." These paradoxes were pithy sayings, usually attributed to Zeno, that turned common beliefs upside down and were meant to provoke thought and discussion. Allusions to paradoxes, along with short explanations of their meanings, abound in Stoic writings.[129]

Of course, the identification of freedom with self-abnegation and self-control was first and foremost an ethical doctrine. When philosophers like Socrates and Zeno argued that only those in full control of their passions were free, they were not necessarily making a political point. However, the Stoic paradox that "only the wise can be free" *might* be understood as a political statement, if it was meant to imply that people's freedom depended on their moral characteristics rather than on their political condition. Understood in this sense, the idea that "only the wise can be free" appears as a both criticism of and an alternative to the democratic theory of freedom, which held that free people were those who lived under a democratic constitution.

It is hard to tell whether Zeno intended to imply this when he talked about freedom as self-control, as none of his writings have survived. However, at least some later Stoic thinkers understood the claim this way, as suggested in an essay by Philo Judaeus in the first century AD. A thoroughly Hellenized Jew, Philo is best remembered for his endeavor to prove that Jewish scripture was in accordance with Greek philosophy (thus hinting that the Greeks had nothing more valuable to say than the Jewish prophets). But he also wrote, in what was probably a more youthful endeavor, an essay on the Stoic idea that "every good man is free."

(A companion piece, in which Philo elaborated on the idea that "every fool or bad man is a slave" has not survived.)[130]

Philo made it clear straightaway that he disagreed with those who identified freedom with popular self-government, describing this idea as "short-sighted."[131] The true hallmark of freedom, he explained, was not one's political position but one's moral status. Only a wise man could attain true freedom. Fools would always remain enslaved, no matter how exalted their position or how great their power over other human beings.

To prove his case, Philo explained that one must only consider the precise meanings of *free* and *slave*. To live in slavery meant to have "no power over anything, including oneself."[132] But the wise man would always have that power, even if he was legally a slave or subjected to an all-powerful ruler: "The good man always acts sensibly, and, therefore, he alone is free. One who cannot be compelled to do anything or prevented from doing anything, cannot be a slave. But the good man cannot be compelled or prevented: the good man, therefore, cannot be a slave."[133]

Philo offered the Greek philosopher Diogenes the Cynic as an example. At one point in his life, Diogenes had been captured by robbers, who then tried to sell him at a slave market. Diogenes was not in the least concerned about this turn of events. When a prospective buyer asked him what he was skilled at, Diogenes jokingly replied, "ruling men." He then tried to sell himself to another buyer, a visibly effeminate man, saying: "You should buy me, for you seem to me to need a husband." About Diogenes, then, Philo asked admiringly, "Must we apply the term slavery to such as him, or any other word but liberty, over which irresponsible domination has no power?"[134]

Greek philosophers were not the only people capable of true freedom, however. Another example admiringly held up by Philo was the Indian thinker Calanus, who stood up to no one less than Alexander the Great. When Alexander ordered Calanus, who had impressed him, to accompany him back to Greece, Calanus replied that he would not let himself be compelled, saying, "Bodies you will transport from place to place, but souls you will not compel to do what they will not do, any more than force bricks or sticks to talk. . . . There is no king, no ruler, who will compel us to do what we do not freely wish to do."[135]

In short, Philo left no doubt that freedom depended on a person's moral characteristics rather than on his political condition. Even someone who was enslaved, like Diogenes, or living under an autocrat, like Calanus, could be free—as long as he (women do not seem to have had this capacity in Philo's view; at least, none of his moral examples were female) was prepared to stand up for his own convictions and not let himself be cowed by fear or ambition. The implication was clear: even those who lived under an autocratic government, like Philo himself, could be free— as long as they had the proper moral spine.

Manifesting a truly free spirit could sometimes be more demanding, however, than simply speaking truth to power. Philo made this clear in a particularly gruesome anecdote about Zeno of Citium. According to Philo, Zeno was tortured by the authorities who wanted him to tell something he felt bound not to disclose. While being branded with fire and hot irons, Zeno undertook drastic action to prevent himself from disclosing his secrets. "He gnawed off his tongue and shot it at the torturer, lest under violence he should involuntarily utter what honor would leave unspoken."[136]

Philo himself, it seems, tried to live up to this ideal in his own dealings with the powers that be. Shortly before his birth, Philo's hometown Alexandria—a Greek city with a large Jewish population—was incorporated into the Roman Empire. Relations between the Alexandrian Jews and their Roman overlords became ever more strained. A crisis erupted when the Jews refused to allow statues of Emperor Caligula to be placed in their synagogues. Their refusal aroused the anger of the non-Jewish citizens, and riots broke out. The violence was silently condoned by the Roman governor, thus making a bad situation even worse. Philo, a prominent member of the Jewish community, was selected to lead a mission of Alexandrian Jews to Caligula to ask that he exempt them from his demand for worship.[137]

This mission was not without risk: Caligula's behavior had become increasingly erratic and violent. After waiting in Rome for months for an interview, the Jewish delegates were finally received by the emperor. The interview got off to a bad start: Caligula immediately rebuked the delegates for not recognizing his divine nature. Then he walked rapidly through gardens and buildings to inspect construction workers carrying out renovations, while Philo and the other delegates hurried to keep up with him. Suddenly Caligula stopped and asked the Jews why they did not eat pork and then walked rapidly away. As he walked, he told them, apparently over his shoulder, to speak on the Jewish ideas of justice. Philo tried to oblige, but he had to talk on the run to the constantly retreating back of the emperor, who continued conversing with the construction workers.

The story, as recounted by Philo, had a happy ending. Ever unpredictable, Caligula suddenly decided to give the Jews their exemption. "These men," Philo reported Caligula as saying, "appear not so much wicked as unfortunates and fools for not believing that I have been endowed with the nature of deity."[138] Nevertheless, it is clear from Philo's account that he and the other members of the legation had repeatedly feared for their lives. If this story is indeed true (we have only Philo's word for it), then it seems Stoic doctrine was capable of inspiring great moral courage in the face of absolute power.

At the same time, however, the shift from the traditional, democratic conception of freedom to a more moral understanding of freedom also encouraged political quietism. Stoic doctrine encouraged people to think of freedom as something to be achieved in the personal sphere, through character-building exercises, rather than something that entailed political or institutional reforms. Indeed, in none of his extensive writings did Philo question the legitimacy of one-man rule. In his view, the solution for the brutality of Caligula was hope for a better ruler. Philo acknowledged that autocratic rule could lead to arbitrary violence, but he looked to a better king, not to popular control over government, to solve this problem.

After Chaeronea, in short, the Greek cult of freedom changed slowly but profoundly. Greek intellectuals continued to attach importance to freedom, but evidence suggests that they now increasingly came to identify that condition with a moral disposition rather than a political condition. The story of democratic freedom, however, did not end in 338 BC. Indeed, in a way, it had only just begun. West of Greece, another power was emerging: Rome. And to the Romans, democratic freedom was just as important as it had been to the classical Greeks.

CHAPTER 2

The Rise and Fall of Roman Liberty

I n 509 bc, the Roman people took a first important step on the long road to liberty. Their city was 244 years old at the time and had been ruled by kings since its inception. Romulus, the city's founder, and his successors were mild and wise rulers. The city had flourished under their leadership. But Rome's seventh king, Lucius Tarquin, was made of a different cloth. Nicknamed "the Proud," he had become king of Rome by murdering his father-in-law, the aging Servius Tullius. In a dramatic showdown with Servius, Tarquin declared himself to be the rightful king and flung his father-in-law from the steps of the Senate house, where Rome's official business was conducted. Faint from loss of blood and half dead, Servius was making his way back home when the men that Tarquin had sent in his pursuit caught up with him, and he was killed.

The murder initiated a reign marked by violence and oppression. Tarquin began his rule by refusing to bury Servius's body—adding insult to injury. He then proceeded to kill off Servius's most important supporters. But his cruelty was not limited to those associated with the preceding regime. He executed, exiled, or fined anyone he suspected of being hostile toward his reign, along with those from whom he had nothing to gain but plunder. The poor, likewise, suffered dearly under his tyranny. Tarquin forced the Roman people to do backbreaking labor on prestige projects such as the new Temple of Jupiter and the *Cloaca Maxima*, or "Great Drain"—a sewer. When these projects neared completion and the laborers threatened to swell the mass of the unemployed, Tarquin simply banished them from Rome.

It was, therefore, no great surprise that Tarquin's reign ended as violently as it had begun. The final straw came when one of Tarquin's sons raped the beautiful and chaste Lucretia, the wife of a Roman officer. Unable to live with her shame, Lucretia killed herself but not until she had made her husband and father promise to avenge her memory. As soon as Lucretia died, Lucius Junius Brutus, a friend of Lucretia's husband, grabbed the dagger from her hands, which was dripping with blood, held it up, and swore to rid Rome of the Tarquins. As Lucretia's dead body was paraded through the streets, Brutus gave a stirring speech reminding the Roman people of Tarquin's brutality and the hard labor to which he had subjected them. The Romans became angry and rebelled, and the Tarquins were exiled.

Perhaps more unexpected was what followed these events. Instead of crowning himself the new king, Lucius Brutus, the leader of the revolt, decided to change the way power was exercised in Rome. From then on, he said, the most important Roman officials—who were henceforth called "consuls"—would be elected rather than being drawn from the royal house. Just as important, they would hold office for only short periods—no longer than one year—so as not to amass too much power. Consuls and other important officials also were not allowed to make decisions on their own; instead, they were expected to consult with a group of advisors, the senators, who were drawn from among Rome's most eminent men. In addition, the Roman people as a whole, or at least the adult male citizens, were given final approval over the most important decisions, as new laws had to be ratified by popular assembly.[1]

The overthrow of the monarchy and the founding of the Roman Republic, or *Respublica*, as the new regime came to be called, was a momentous occasion. *Respublica* literally means "public thing," but it was also understood as synonymous with *res populi* or "property of the people," thus suggesting a meaning like "popular government."[2] It was the first important victory, all Roman historians agreed, that put their city on a path to freedom for all. But the newly acquired liberty was fragile. First and foremost, the old order still posed a threat to the infant republic. A gang of young noblemen found it hard to adapt to the new, republican institutions. They thought it demeaning to kowtow to the masses or even to their fellow patricians in the Senate, and they longed for the days when all they needed for advancement was to be in the good books of the Tarquin family. A plot was hatched to restore the Tarquin dynasty, but the careless conspirators ran their mouths in front of a slave, who reported their plans to the authorities.

Lucius Brutus, who had been elected as one of the first two consuls, acted quickly and decisively: he gave orders for all the conspirators to be rounded up and put to death. To his dismay, his own sons were among those involved in the conspiracy. Brutus refused to make an exception for his own flesh and blood, even though some of his friends tried to convince him otherwise. He presided in person over the judicial proceedings and witnessed the executions of his sons. According to one historian, Brutus watched as his sons were put to death "without a tear, without a groan, without once shifting his gaze; he bore his calamity with a stout heart."[3] After these events, the Romans were so in awe of his devotion to the republic that they erected a bronze statue of Brutus on the capitol. He was immortalized wielding a sword, ready to chop off the heads of the statues of Rome's early kings.[4]

But even after the final defeat of the old order, much remained to be done. Freedom had not been established for all. Even though the monarchy had been overthrown, political power continued to be controlled by a small and increasingly hereditary elite—the patricians. The patricians monopolized the Senate and the most important public offices, like the consulate, while ordinary Romans, or plebeians as they came to be called, were prohibited from standing for office or joining the Senate. The plebeians soon began to complain that they were just as unfree as they had been under the Tarquins. As one exasperated plebeian politician put it, "Does the ultimate power belong to the Roman people or to you [the patricians]? Did the expulsion of the kings give the power of domination to you, or did it give equal liberty to all men?"[5]

For the next 200 years, ordinary Romans continued to struggle for their freedom, now against the patricians.[6] While the Conflict of the Orders (as this struggle came to be known) was occasionally marked by violence and bloodshed, the plebeians eventually managed to break patrician power through peaceful collective action. In 494 BC, riled up by an economic crisis, they staged the first of several mass walkouts (called "secessions" by our sources) from the city, leaving Rome largely defenseless against its many enemies and creating panic among patricians. During the following decades, they repeated this tactic several more times, with success. The patricians were forced to grant a series of concessions, which gradually eroded all the significant differences between themselves and plebeians and gave the latter equal access to political power.

A first series of reforms created public offices open only to plebeians. The most important of these offices were the tribunes, officials who were elected by the plebeians and who had the specific mission of defending their interests. Thus, new avenues opened up for plebeians to exercise political power. But the plebeians' ultimate goal was to make every office, including that of the consulship, accessible to plebeian candidates. According to a later historian, plebeian reformers believed that the consulship was "the pillar, the stronghold of their liberties." Only by abolishing patrician control over this office would "monarchy" be "completely banished" from the city and "their freedom securely established."[7] The plebeians eventually succeeded. In 367 BC, after decades of dogged refusals by conservative patricians, plebeian candidates were allowed to compete for the consulship.

Just as important were reforms that increased plebeian control over the lawmaking process. As with the creation of the tribunes, first, a special assembly was created for the plebeians, in which patricians were not allowed to participate—the Tribunal Assembly. Laws made by this assembly were originally binding on the plebeians alone. But in 247 BC the Lex Hortensia laid down that votes of the plebeians were binding on the whole people. In addition, the Senate's power to veto laws made by popular assemblies was abolished. This was generally thought to have given the plebeians equal footing with the patricians, thus ending the Conflict of the Orders.

Freedom in the Early Republic

This, in a nutshell, was the standard account of Rome's early history, as told by Titus Livius (known as "Livy" in English), Dionysius of Halicarnassus, and other historians; it was the story every Roman boy absorbed with his mother's milk. It made clear that freedom was extremely important to the early Romans, a point brought home most poignantly, perhaps, in the story about Lucius Brutus who executed his own sons when they conspired against the republic. But the plebeians' centuries-long struggle for *libertas* suggested that ordinary Romans attached no less importance to freedom. Moreover, the historical accounts left no doubt about the nature of the freedom the early Romans were prepared to fight and die for: it was the liberty to govern themselves, rather than to be governed ("enslaved") by haughty kings or arrogant patricians.

The early Romans, at least as they were portrayed by later historians, sounded very much like the Greeks. Like the Greeks, they valued freedom more than any other political ideal, and like the Greeks, they identified this ideal with popular self-government. And that is not where the similarities end. Roman historians also suggest that the early Romans valued freedom for pretty much the same reasons as the Greeks had. Like the Greeks, the Romans seemed to believe that popular self-government was necessary for individual security and personal independence. The experience of Tarquin's reign convinced them that monarchy was always in danger of shading into tyranny. Similarly, complaints about the tyrannical behavior of the patricians, particularly their disregard for the lives and interests of the plebeians, played a crucial role in the plebeian push for democratic reforms.[8]

It is hard to know, however, to what extent this account corresponds to historical reality. Were the first few centuries of Rome's existence indeed characterized by a protracted fight for freedom or popular self-government? This question cannot be answered conclusively. All the stories we have about Rome's earliest history were written by individuals who lived centuries after the events they recorded. Livy, the most celebrated historian of the early Roman republic, wrote his account in the final decades of the first century BC, more than 500 years after the purported overthrow of the Tarquin dynasty. He had access to the now-lost work of earlier annalists and historians, such as Quintus Fabius Pictor, who was born around 270 BC, which means that, at least for the third century, Livy's narrative was based on living memory rather than on legend. But Livy did not consult documentary evidence or do any of the fact-checking that modern historians see as the very basis of their craft.

Unsurprisingly, therefore, modern scholars tend to be skeptical of many aspects of Livy's narrative.[9] The lurid story of Lucretia's rape was almost certainly an invention, if only because it mirrors, to a suspicious degree, the story of the fall of the Peisistratids in Athens (which had also supposedly been triggered by a sex scandal, albeit one involving unwanted homosexual advances rather than heterosexual rape). Moreover, the year Tarquin supposedly was overthrown—509 BC—was the same year the Athenian tyrant Hippias was deposed. This likewise suggests that Roman historians deliberately sought to create a parallel with Athenian history and molded their narratives about early Rome accordingly. The creation of the republic, in all likelihood, took much longer and involved a much slower transformation of the political system than the abrupt transition imagined by later historians. Similar doubts can be raised about the stories of the Conflict of the Orders. Rome's earliest consul lists, for instance, contained several plebeian names. This casts doubt on ancient historians' claims that Rome's highest office was closed to plebeians until the reforms of 367 BC.

It is even more difficult to know to what extent fifth- and fourth-century Romans thought of the overthrow of the monarchy and the subsequent democratization of the political system as a fight for freedom. Did the call for *libertas* play any role in early Roman political debate? Supposing that there was indeed a man named Junius Brutus who abolished the monarchy, did he do so under the cry of liberty? Did the plebeian reformers think of their struggle as a movement for liberation? We do not know, although it seems highly unlikely that the speeches attributed to reformers by later historians were based on any historical record. Instead, the rhetoric attributed by Livy and other historians to the plebeian reformers probably reflects the popular political ideology of later times more than it does the Conflict of the Orders.

Nevertheless, it seems plausible that the basic outlines of the story had at least some basis in fact. Even if later historians got many, or even most, of the details wrong, they were probably right in presenting the transition from monarchy to a system with elected officials as a major turning point in Roman history—there are, after all, various archeological and other sources that confirm that Rome was indeed ruled by kings during its earliest history. It seems equally likely that the fifth and fourth centuries BC were characterized by a prolonged political struggle between a privileged, hereditary minority and the rest, a struggle which eventually resulted in at least a partial victory for the latter. After all, the distinction between plebeian and patrician survived into the historical period, even though, by that time, it had lost all of its practical and political relevance.

And finally it seems plausible that, at some point, Romans began to think of their fight for popular self-government as a fight for liberty, even if it is impossible to know when exactly this happened. (The earliest surviving reference to freedom in a political context occurred in 126 BC, on a coin issued by Lucius Cassius Longinus Ravilla, but the term may have also been used in earlier sources that are now lost.[10]) In view of the remarkable similarities between Greek and Roman freedom-talk, however, it is tempting to conjecture that Romans started talking about their struggle for self-government as a struggle for freedom fairly late; and more specifically, that they started doing so after contact with Greece was intensified. Greek influence on early Roman intellectual development was, after all, quite considerable, in particular from the third century BC, when Roman power expanded toward the east and contact with the Greek world increased. The very first Latin plays, for instance, written around 240 BC, were modeled on Greek examples. Similarly, the very first history of Rome was written in Greek by a historian keen to argue that Rome was, for all intents and purposes, a Greek city.[11]

Of course, by portraying early Roman history as a long but ultimately successful fight to gain freedom for all, Roman historians conveniently overlooked the fact that large swathes of the population—notably, women and slaves—remained largely excluded from the political process. Like the Greeks, Romans thought of slaves as property, the equivalent of human livestock. Hence, their exclusion from politics was accepted without debate, again just as it had been in Greece. (It should be noted, however, that the Romans gave emancipated slaves—with the exception of certain categories involved in dishonorable pursuits, such as gladiators—full citizenship rights. Freedmen and their descendants, in other words, could vote, even if conservative politicians frequently attempted to restrict their electoral influence.[12])

Just as in classical Greece, moreover, Roman men thought it perfectly natural for their wives, mothers, daughters, and sisters to be excluded from the political process.[13] Compared to Athens, however, where respectable women were supposed to stay indoors, Rome's matrons were less secluded, and this gave them more opportunities to get involved in politics. One of the most dramatic episodes involving female political action came in 195 BC, when women pushed to repeal the Lex Oppia, an austerity measure introduced twenty years earlier to raise money for the wars against Hannibal by restricting women's finery. Repeal was supported by vigorous women's demonstrations. According to Livy, the demonstrations grew so large that the matrons blocked all the streets and approaches to the Forum, in direct defiance of their husbands' orders to stay home.[14]

Traditionalist politicians were aghast. Cato the Elder, a staunch conservative, opposed the repeal of the law by delivering a long and passionate speech. Giving into the women on this issue, he warned male citizens, would ultimately result in men losing their control over the political system and, hence, their freedom. "If they win in this, what will they not attempt?" Cato asked his audience. The women would want to abolish all the laws that traditionally subjected them to their husbands. And things would not end there. If women were allowed to "wrench themselves free" and to place themselves on "a parity with their husbands," they would not long be content with that situation. "The moment they begin to be your equals, they will be your superiors."[15]

Not all male politicians shared these anxieties. Those who supported the women in their demand for repeal of the Lex Oppia, however, can hardly be described as protofeminists. Rather, these male supporters argued that women were weak and vain creatures, whose feelings were hurt by the prohibition on finery. In their view, when Roman matrons saw women in neighboring towns adorned with gold and other baubles that they themselves were not allowed to wear, they understandably became angry. "A thing like this would hurt the feelings even of men," one proponent of repeal argued. "What do you think is its effect upon weak women, whom even little things disturb?"[16]

More important, defenders of repeal made short shrift of the idea that abolishing the Lex Oppia would create a slippery slope leading to domination by women and the subjection of men. They mocked the idea that women could pose a threat to male power. Cato compared the women's advocacy to the secessions of the plebeians that ultimately democratized the Roman political system. But that comparison, proponents of repeal argued, was ludicrous: in reality the frail nature of women meant they would always remain subjected to men—and willingly so. "Never while their males survive is feminine slavery shaken off," Lucius Valerius argued, "and even they abhor the freedom which loss of husbands and fathers gives."[17]

As this debate suggests, in Rome, greater opportunities for women's collective action raised more questions about female political participation than it had in ancient Greece, or at least in Athens. At the same time, however, the debate also made clear that most men thought female subjection was perfectly natural, something that women themselves wanted. Not that many male Romans shared Cato's anxieties—as is suggested by the fact that the Lex Oppia was eventually repealed. In short, Roman politicians believed, much like Aristotle, that women should not be seen as fully independent beings. Hence, by being disallowed participation in politics, women were not rendered any more unfree than they already had been.

But the stirring rhetoric about the early Romans' fight for freedom did not just overlook the exclusion of women and slaves. It also ignored the fact that the outcome of the Conflict of the Orders was a political system heavily slanted in favor of the rich.[18] The struggle of the plebeian reformers had not resulted in a democracy in the Athenian mold. Instead, a new governing class, consisting of both rich patricians and plebeians, was created. Even after the consulate was opened up to plebeians, only the wealthy could run for office. The exact amount needed to qualify is not known, but sources suggest that it was set at the very highest level—limiting public office to the upper 10 percent of the population. Unsurprisingly, this meant that Rome's rulers were typically drawn from a tiny elite: indeed, it has been computed that about half of all Romans who filled the role of consul, the most important public office, came from but a handful of ancient wealthy families.[19]

Despite their elite provenance, public officials were accountable to the population at large. All adult male citizens could vote, regardless of their wealth. Short terms meant that Roman politicians constantly had to campaign for reelection, which made them more responsive to popular pressure. But the voting system, too, was stacked in favor of the wealthy. In Rome's exceedingly complex electoral system, senior public officials, including consuls, were chosen by the Centuriate Assembly. In this assembly, citizens were divided into voting units—called "centuries"—based on wealth. The rich were far fewer in number than the poor, yet they were assigned more voting units, so the number of voters in those units would have been comparatively small compared with those in the centuries of the least well-off. As a result, the vote of a wealthy Roman weighed more heavily than that of his poorer compatriots. Moreover, the wealthiest centuries got to vote first, and as soon as a majority was reached, voting was halted. If the rich centuries were united, they could determine the result of an election without the poorer centuries even having the chance to vote.

Control of the well-to-do over the Roman political system was further entrenched by the existence of the Senate. Senators were not elected but were chosen from among former office-holders and appointed for life, which meant that, unlike consuls and other magistrates, senators could ignore the popular will without fearing repercussions. Their powers were vast. The Senate supposedly "advised" the consuls but, in reality, made many of the most important decisions, particularly with regard to foreign policy. For instance, the Senate—not the citizenry, as in Athens—received embassies and concluded treaties with foreign powers. The Senate also controlled the treasury and was responsible for prosecuting criminals who posed a threat to public safety.

Yet elite control over the Roman political system should not be exaggerated.[20] The votes of the poor could be essential to political success or failure, especially in closely contested elections. As a result, the concerns of ordinary people played, at least on some occasions, an important role in Roman politics. Anecdotes illustrate this quite clearly. Valerius Maximus, in his *Memorable Deeds and Sayings*, told the story of Publius Scipio Nasica, a descendant of one of the most illustrious Roman families. At the beginning of his career, Scipio was standing for the aedileship, an office that would have given him responsibility for public works in Rome and for the organization of public festivals. While he was canvassing among potential voters, Scipio shook the rough, calloused hand of a peasant farmer. Scipio jokingly asked whether the man was used to walking on his hands. The honest Roman peasant took this as an insult, and Scipio lost the election—rightfully so, Valerius commented, since it was an "offensive joke."[21]

Roman politicians could also be held accountable to the public after their term in office. If elected officials did not fulfill their functions properly, they could be prosecuted. Originally, former magistrates were tried in front of the popular assembly for cowardice, incompetence, and corrupt behavior. Later on, they were tried in front of a jury of about fifty Roman citizens. These procedures were not always effective: bribery was rampant, and apparently drunkenness among the jurors was also a problem. However, all proceedings were public, so the weight of public opinion also played an important role in holding officials accountable. In addition, Roman citizens had a right to appeal against officials when they threatened to interfere with their property or lives. They could then invoke the right to be tried by the people as a whole.

Perhaps even more important, ordinary Romans were in a position to exercise considerable power over lawmaking. Laws were voted on by the Tribal Assembly, which was more equitable than the Centuriate Assembly that elected public officials. Because the Tribal Assembly was based on geographical "tribal" divisions, not on wealth, in principle the votes of rich and poor weighed the same. Unlike Athens, however, Rome did not pay its citizens for attendance in the Tribal Assembly, which privileged wealthier citizens, who would have had the leisure to travel the often-long distances from Rome's ever more far-flung territory to the city. Nevertheless, if poorer citizens felt their interests were at stake, they at least had the possibility to express their views. There is some evidence that they were, in fact, prepared to travel great distances when it was really necessary. Tiberius Gracchus's agrarian bill, for instance, which promised to redistribute land to ordinary citizens, "caused people to flock into Rome."[22]

Voting assemblies were often preceded by *contiones*, or discussion meetings, in which rival officials tried to win over the people to their point of view. We have no way of knowing how frequent and well attended they usually were, but there are several hints that they provided a forum for the passionate exchange of political views. On one occasion, in the first century BC, it was said that the crowd shouted so loudly to silence a speaker they disagreed with that a crow, which had the bad luck to be flying past, fell to the ground, stunned, as if struck by lightning. The existence of these discussion meetings again illustrates that Roman politicians could not simply push new laws through but needed to win over the people if their proposals were to succeed.[23]

In some ways, the Roman political system was markedly more democratic than the Athenian one. Unlike Athenians, Romans freely gave citizenship, including voting rights, to freed slaves and, after 88 BC, to the adult males of allied Italian cities. (This was a hard-won concession, which was granted only after Rome's allies, disgruntled about their lack of power, turned against it in the so-called Social War.) The result was a citizen body vastly more numerous than that in Athens, not just in absolute but also in relative terms. While there were never more than 40,000 male citizens in Athens, sources report no fewer than 300,000 Roman citizens even before the expansion of citizenship to the entire Italian peninsula. In 70 BC, in the wake of the Social War, the citizen body had expanded to something over a million.[24]

In short, while the Romans' claim that their political system provided freedom or self-government for all should be taken with an even larger grain of salt than similar Greek boasts, that claim was not entirely untrue either. Under the Roman constitution, ordinary citizens had considerable sway over both the selection of their political leaders and the framing of the laws under which they lived (as long as they were adult males). For all its differences with Athenian democracy, Rome was still much closer to that model than to the Hellenistic monarchies founded in the wake of Alexander's conquests, in which kings claimed absolute power over the decision-making process.

This point was also emphasized by one of the earliest and most astute observers of the Roman political system, the Greek historian Polybius.[25] Born into a prominent family, Polybius was in his thirties when Greece was subjected by the Romans in 168 BC, and he was one of 1,000 Greek hostages taken to Rome to ensure continued compliance of the defeated enemy. After his arrival in Rome, Polybius became close to some of the most important Roman statesmen of his day and therefore had the opportunity to observe the Roman political system closely. Fascinated by his hosts, Polybius then wrote one of the earliest—and quite possibly the earliest—analysis of the Roman political system. He described it as a "mixed" constitution, in which a monarchical element (the consuls) and an aristocratic element (the Senate) were balanced with an important democratic element (the assemblies). Despite the formidable power of the consuls and the Senate, Polybius emphasized, in the end they could not act without the people: they had "to pay particular attention to the masses in the political sphere and to defer to the people."[26]

Fighting for Freedom: From the Middle to the Late Republic

Freedom remained a central concern of the Romans even after the Conflict of the Orders had died down.[27] In the third century BC, Rome enjoyed a period of internal peace and social harmony. It was during this time that the Romans expanded their realm and transformed themselves from a regional power into a world empire. They did so first and foremost by defeating Carthage, their main rival in the Mediterranean Basin. The Roman victory was not a given: at one point, the Carthaginian general Hannibal, by crossing the Alps and attacking Rome from behind, as it were, managed to nearly destroy the city. But Roman armies snatched victory from the jaws of defeat, mainly because of their superior manpower. After three long wars, Carthage was decisively defeated. Romans continued to expand their power to the east and west, with campaigns bringing Spain, Greece, and Macedonia under their control.

But the internal harmony did not last. In the second century BC, discord between elites and ordinary Romans again flared—now even more violently than during the Conflict of the Orders. Disaffection was triggered by various causes; among them, poor Romans objected to the fact that the spoils of their many victories had overwhelmingly gone to a few wealthy citizens who, as a result, had amassed huge agricultural land-holdings exploited by slaves. Meanwhile, small landholders were driven off their farms. The increasing grip of elites on the political system only caused further resentment.

A small group of politicians, most of them elected tribunes who soon became known as the *populares*, or "popular" politicians, tapped into this discontent.[28] The *populares* did not comprise a party in our sense of the word: they neither voted together in the Senate or popular assemblies nor campaigned together. They, nevertheless, shared a number of demands, notably for land redistribution, and they pleaded for reforms that would make the political system more responsive to ordinary Romans. They also looked to the same charismatic leaders for inspiration. In this regard, the brothers Gracchi were the most important.

The *populares* movement took off when Tiberius Gracchus, the eldest of the Gracchi, was elected as a tribune in 133 BC on his promise of land redistribution. Gracchus's agrarian bill was first and foremost an attempt to do something about widespread poverty. But fierce opposition by the Senate soon turned the debate about Gracchus's bill into a power struggle between popularly backed politicians and the Senate. As a re-sult, Gracchus—and, even more, the successors he inspired—began to campaign for political reforms. They struggled to introduce the secret ballot, to make it more difficult to use bribery and elite influence to sway elections. They pilloried the widespread corruption of the ruling classes and tried to reform the judiciary to make it easier to punish dishonest politi-cians. When their opponents struck back by trying to dismantle or even abolish the tribunal office, the *populares* played a key role in the campaign to maintain and enhance the power of the tribunes.

The *populares* left no doubt that they thought their political reforms enhanced the freedom of the Roman people. Their speeches, as reported by later historians, make this abundantly clear. (Note, however, that while historians' renderings of these speeches should not be thought of as ac-curate, verbatim reports, they are very likely to reflect the overall tone and rhetoric of the speeches, much more so than reports of the earlier plebeian campaign did, since the historians who rendered the *populares* speeches lived much closer in time to the men who delivered them.) Rome, *populares* politicians emphasized again and again, was in danger of succumbing to the "mastery of a few men." Ordinary Romans had become so used to the elite's arrogance that they had come to believe they had "ample freedom," simply "because your [ordinary citizens'] backs are spared, and because you are allowed to go hither and thither by the grace of your rich masters." But nothing was less true; the ruling elite's grip on power threatened to turn all citizens into slaves. Only by fighting back—that is, by supporting *populares* reforms—could ordinary people regain their freedom. "The common people are treated as vanquished," one orator exclaimed, "and this will be more so every day, so long as your oppressors make greater efforts to retain their mastery than you do to regain your freedom."[29]

Other genuinely contemporary sources—namely, coins minted by a number of *populares* politicians—confirm that the *populares* identified freedom with popular self-government. In 126 BC, for instance, a silver denarius was issued to celebrate a law introduced by the tribune Lucius Cassius Longinus Ravilla, which instituted the secret ballot at public trials, a pet cause of the *populares*. On one side of these coins, we see a female charioteer holding the reins to four horses in one hand and a small conical cap in her other, with the legend "C. Cassi" underneath. The charioteer is the goddess Liberty, as we know from the cap, which referred to the conical cap slaves received when they were emancipated. On the other side of the coin, we see the helmeted head of Roma, the representation of Rome, and a voting urn. The coin's message was clear: increasing popular political influence made men more free.[30]

Some of the *populares* seem to have held more radical views about what it meant to live a free life. If Cicero—who was not a friend of the movement—is to be believed, some of the reformers claimed that Rome's much-vaunted "mixed government" left too little room for popular participation and that, hence, ordinary Romans were free in name only. "They vote, they entrust commands and offices, they are canvassed and asked for their support," Cicero reported the *populares* as arguing. "But they . . . are asked to give what they do not have themselves. They

A silver denarius minted by C. Cassius in 126 BC.

have no share in power, in public deliberation, or in the panels of select judges, all of which are apportioned on the basis of pedigree or wealth." Instead, these "democrats" looked to Athens as an example and argued that "in no other state than that in which the people has the highest power does liberty have any home."[31]

Such hyperdemocratic views, however, do not seem to have been very widely shared. The *populares'* main goal was to reform the existing system by giving poor Romans a greater say over the way they were governed. Most of them did not aim to transform the Roman system into an Athenian-style democracy. In their rhetoric (as reported by the historians), the Conflict of the Orders was invoked far more often than the Athenian example. They presented this conflict as a successful struggle for liberation on the part of ordinary Romans against elites, and they encouraged their audience again and again to take a leaf from their ancestors' playbook. "Your forefathers," one orator thundered, "to assert their rights and establish their sovereignty, twice seceded and took armed possession of the Aventine; will you not exert yourself to the utmost in order to retain the liberty which they bequeathed to you?"[32]

The *populares* were savagely opposed by the so-called *optimates* or "best men." *Optimates*, in essence, were defenders of the status quo who opposed any attempt to democratize the political system and were prepared to go to extreme lengths in this effort. Shortly after he had been reelected as a tribune, Tiberius Gracchus and 300 of his supporters were clubbed to death by elitist hardliners, and their bodies were thrown into the Tiber. A few years later, Tiberius's brother Gaius, together with about 3,000 of his supporters, met a similar end when he tried to continue Tiberius's legacy. And this was not the last of it: several more *populares* politicians were murdered by the *optimates*. The Senate, meanwhile, legitimized these political murders by giving consuls the power to act in any way they liked—including killing elected politicians—to preserve the state during purported states of emergency.

With their implacable opposition to democratizing reforms, the *optimates* bear a clear resemblance to Athens's antidemocrats, such as the Old Oligarch and Critias. Unlike the Athenian oligarchs, however, who rejected not just democracy but also the very idea that freedom was an important political value, Roman *optimates* claimed that they were fighting for freedom rather than against it. In their view, the Gracchi and the other *populares* were merely trying to enhance their own personal power; by appealing to the people against traditional elites, they were trying to take over power for themselves. Tiberius Gracchus, in particular, was accused of having royal aspirations: it was rumored that he wanted to make himself a king. But even ancient historians thought this was unlikely. As Plutarch dryly commented, "The combination against him would seem to have arisen from the hatred and anger of the rich, rather than from the pretexts which they alleged."[33] Still, the accusation would be repeated after every new murder: by killing their political opponents, the *optimates* claimed, they were merely trying to preserve Rome's freedom from power-hungry individuals.

These arguments were, of course, self-serving. But they do suggest that freedom, understood as communal self-government, remained a no less important ideal for the *optimates* than for their *populares* opponents. That point is also confirmed when we turn to Cicero's writings.[34] As an ambitious young politician from a wealthy but relatively obscure family, Cicero sympathized with the *populares* in the beginning of his career. But after he climbed the political ladder, becoming a quaestor and then a consul, he converted to the cause of the *optimates*. In the 50s BC during a lull in his political career, Cicero used his spare time to write a treatise on the best form of government, called *The Republic*. It was followed by a companion volume, *The Laws*, which set forth the specific statutes that should govern the ideal state. These writings offer a unique window into the mindset of the more philosophically minded *optimates*. Cicero's works confirm that Roman *optimates* remained more committed to freedom as a political value than did Athenian antidemocrats such as the oligarchs or Plato.

In *The Republic*, Cicero expressed considerable admiration for Plato and quoted the Athenian philosopher frequently. Nevertheless, the differences between the thinkers were vast: whereas Plato defended subjection to a philosopher-king as the best form of government, Cicero maintained that a good political system must provide freedom for all, albeit of a "moderate" kind. He cited, as a legitimate objection against both monarchy and aristocracy, that these forms of government completely excluded the people from decision-making, hence turning them into slaves. "The people that is ruled by a king lacks a great deal, and above all it lacks liberty, which does not consist in having a just master, but in having none," Cicero explained. And the same thing was true for an oligarchy. When people were ruled by an elite, even if these ruled with "the greatest justice," he maintained, their condition could still be described as "a form of slavery."[35]

At the same time, Cicero rejected democracy on the grounds that it gave too much freedom to ordinary people. "Excessive" freedom, he claimed—quoting Plato extensively in support of this view—could lead only to licentiousness and, hence, back to tyranny. A pure democracy was not workable. The only acceptable kind of government provided moderate freedom. Cicero argued for the traditional, mixed constitution of Rome, in which ordinary male citizens had some say in government, but in which their power was balanced by the "monarchical" consuls and "aristocratic" Senate.

This was not a reactionary vision. Cicero explicitly identified his ideal commonwealth with the Roman Republic as it had existed since the end of the Conflict of the Orders—the same system, in other words, the *populares* claimed to defend. Indeed, as *The Laws* makes clear, Cicero did not hesitate to support some of the institutions and reforms most cherished by the *populares*. He argued that the tribunate was a necessary part of the Roman constitution because it gave the Roman people "real liberty" rather than the "nominal one" they had enjoyed before the Conflict of the Orders.[36] He even supported the secret ballot, an institution excoriated by other *optimates,* even though his defense was based on instrumental reasons rather than on any real enthusiasm for the institution. In practice, Cicero pointed out, the law had not really diminished the power of the "best men," because ordinary people respected their opinion and continued to follow their lead anyway. So having the secret ballot as an "appearance of liberty" was harmless and kept the people happy.[37]

In short, as Cicero's writings illustrate, the political ideals of the *optimates* and *populares* were not that divergent—this despite the very real violence to which both parties resorted. Both parties agreed that the preservation of freedom, understood as communal self-government, was of key importance, and both agreed that the Roman Republic, in the shape it had taken in the wake of the Conflict of the Orders, was the embodiment of that freedom. They differed, however, over the best way to maintain that freedom. According to the *populares,* incremental reforms were necessary to prevent the elite from once again becoming a closed, hereditary ruling caste, as it had been after the expulsion of the Tarquins. The *optimates,* on the other hand, feared that giving ordinary Romans too much political power would eventually make the rise of tyrannical demagogues inevitable.[38]

This ideological consensus, however, could not avert the downfall of the republic. After a drawn out and often bloody process of political change, the republic eventually gave way to a very different political regime—the principate, or the empire. Why this happened remains much disputed.[39] Unsurprisingly, the *optimates* blamed the *populares* for the breakdown of the republic. By whipping up hatred against the elite, it was argued, the Gracchi and their followers were responsible for the discord that eventually led to the civil wars and the collapse of the regime in the 50s and 40s BC. Modern historians tend to dismiss this explanation as a self-serving justification on the part of the elites. After all, during the Conflict of the Orders, Rome had been far from harmonious, so it was not as if discord had been fostered first by the *populares.* If anything, it seems more likely that it was the behavior of the *optimates*—their extreme opposition to the *populares* and their frequent recourse to political violence—that did much to delegitimize the republic, at least in the view of lower-class citizens.

Other factors were at least as important in the republic's demise. The growing influence of the Roman armies over political life—which was itself, in all likelihood, a result of the democratization of the armed forces—played a crucial role in the republic's eventual destruction. In 107 BC, the Roman consul Marius opened up the army for landless citizens, thus swelling the army's ranks with individuals who were dependent on their generals for booty and, therefore, their livelihoods. This, in turn, strengthened the power of military commanders and made it possible for them to use their armies for their own ends rather than for the good of the Roman state. The stability of Rome's political system was further undermined by the wealth pouring into the republic's coffers. By 50 BC, the Roman Empire had come to span much of the then-known world, and the riches to be reaped from the far-flung empire had increased manifold. Politicians and military men were increasingly tempted to try to monopolize these rewards.

A first ominous sign of the increasing fragility of the republic occurred in 88 BC. In that year, the military commander Lucius Cornelius Sulla invaded Rome to avenge a personal slight. It was the first time since the mythical Coriolanus (who had supposedly sided with the Volsci against Rome) that a Roman general had turned his troops on Rome itself. Sulla then went on to establish himself as Rome's dictator. Ordinarily, this was a short-term office that gave men extraordinary powers to deal with emergency situations, but Sulla appointed himself dictator without a time limit. His reign quickly turned violent. His henchmen drew up lists of "proscriptions" containing the names of thousands of men, including about a third of all senators, whom Sulla considered enemies of the state. These names were posted throughout Italy, and a generous price was placed on their heads. As a result, as one ancient historian put it, "husbands were butchered in the arms of their wives, sons in the arms of their mothers." The majority of the proscribed men had not been enemies of Sulla but were killed for their property, which was confiscated and auctioned off, making Sulla a very wealthy man.[40]

After three years, Sulla—who was a traditionalist at heart—unexpectedly resigned his dictatorship, disbanded his legions, and reestablished regular elections. He eventually retired to his country house in the Bay of Naples, with his young wife and male lover, where he devoted his time to writing his memoirs and stayed out of politics. He died in his bed of natural causes in 78 BC. It was a surprisingly peaceful end for a military man, though the disease from which he died seems to have been particularly grisly: Sulla was literally eaten by worms. As one ancient historian vividly explained, his flesh was infested with maggots that multiplied so quickly, they could not be removed, no matter how often he bathed and scoured his skin.[41]

But Sulla's invasion of Rome and his dictatorship were just a harbinger of worse things to come. The final breakdown of the republic happened a good forty years later and was occasioned by another ambitious general, Julius Caesar. A politician from an impeccably pedigreed but impoverished family—he boasted that his family was descendent from the goddess Venus herself—Caesar began his career with *populares* leanings, playing on the socioeconomic grievances of veterans and the poor. But it soon became clear that he was no Tiberius or Gaius Gracchus. He was more interested in furthering his own career than in democratizing the Roman political system. In 59 BC, Caesar achieved one of his most important ambitions when he was given command over the armies in Gaul, a rich province to be conquered. But he wanted more. Ten years later, as a victorious general at the head of seasoned troops, Caesar famously crossed the Rubicon, the river that marked the northern boundary of Italy.

In doing so, Caesar effectively turned his armies against Rome, exactly like Sulla had. In response, the Senate asked Pompey, one of Rome's most talented military commanders and a one-time friend and collaborator of Caesar, to defend the republic. A civil war ensued, which saw Roman armies pursue each other throughout the Mediterranean Basin. Caesar eventually managed to defeat Pompey and all his other enemies. Upon his return to Rome, it quickly became clear that Caesar aimed to concentrate power in his own hands. Like Sulla, he was appointed as a dictator, initially for a short term. In 48 BC, after another important military victory, the Senate again made him dictator for a year, and then in 46 for ten years. Finally, by the start of 44 BC, he had become dictator for life.

Caesar's power grab galvanized opposition among the *optimates*, and they rallied against him under the banner of liberty. Their rhetoric was strongly reminiscent of the arguments used by earlier *optimates* against

Tiberius Gracchus and other *populares* reformers.[42] Just as Publius Cornelius Scipio Nasica (the politician who murdered Tiberius Gracchus) had done, Caesar's enemies accused him of aspiring to kingship. In Caesar's case, however, such accusations might have held more water. While Caesar's ultimate motivations and goals continue to be much disputed by historians, there are some indications that, especially toward the end of his life, he had wanted to do away with the republic altogether.[43] Thus, on formal occasions, he took to wearing the costume of the kings of Alba Longa, a dynasty from which his family claimed descent, which notably included calf-length boots in red leather. To these, Caesar added a laurel wreath—an honor symbolizing military victory that had the additional benefit of hiding his growing baldness. It seems that, in 44 BC, he even began wearing a gold version of the boots.

It remains unclear, however, how serious Caesar was about becoming a king. On one famous occasion, at the time of a popular religious festival, his loyal lieutenant Mark Antony offered him a diadem with a wreath of laurel tied around it—a symbol of royal power. According to Caesar's biographer Plutarch, Antony's offer of the diadem elicited some applause. But there was not much of it, and it did not sound spontaneous. When Caesar pushed the diadem away from him, however, there was a general and much louder ring of applause. Antony then offered him the diadem for the second time, and again only a few applauded. When Caesar again rejected it, there was applause from everyone. The whole incident was obviously carefully staged, although its meaning remains disputed. Some commentators believe that Caesar wanted to accept the crown and would have done so if only the crowd had seemed more enthusiastic. But it is equally probable that he wanted the glory of refusing such an offer and perhaps also hoped to put an end to the talk about his royal ambitions.

Even if Caesar had no ambition of wearing a crown, his position as perpetual dictator gave him king-like power. Under the terms of his dictatorship, Caesar had the right to directly nominate some candidates for "election," and he controlled the other elections behind the scenes. He also severely curtailed the power of the Senate: he increased the number of senators, thus packing the Senate with his own followers. Many decisions that fell under the traditional purview of the Senate were now made behind closed doors by Caesar and a few of his associates, without any consultation with the senators. Moreover, Caesar gave no indication that he was planning on voluntarily relinquishing his dictatorship, as Sulla had done.

From the start, Caesar's growing power was resisted by a number of prominent *optimates*. One of Caesar's earliest and most stubborn opponents was Cato of Utica, a politician who prided himself on his stern devotion to the republic and Rome's traditional institutions. His inflexibility in defense of what he believed was right sometimes led even his closest allies to despair. Cicero famously commented that Cato "in the best spirit and with unquestionable honesty . . . does harm to the commonwealth: the resolutions he puts forward are more fitting for Plato's ideal Republic, than the cesspit of Romulus."[44] Cato had played a crucial role, together with Cicero, in exposing a conspiracy by Catiline, a patrician who had attempted to gain absolute power in Rome by presenting himself as a champion of the lower classes. Soon after, Cato used his political influence to oppose the designs of Caesar and his allies, warning his fellow senators and everyone else who would listen that Caesar's ambition was out of control and that he needed to be taken down a peg.

After the rout of Pompey's army, Cato refused to accept defeat and took command over the Senate's army together with other die-hard opponents of Caesar. But Cato's continued opposition led to naught: the armies he and his associates managed to raise were eventually crushed by Caesar. Upon learning that Caesar had vanquished his allies and was marching toward Utica, where he had fled, Cato chose to commit suicide, reportedly because he preferred to die rather than to be at Caesar's mercy.

But Cato's death did not end the opposition. Soon after Caesar's triumphant return to Rome, a small group of senators hatched a plot to assassinate him. Their motives were varied—many of the conspirators had supported Caesar during the civil wars but had come to resent his ever-growing power, while others nursed personal grievances against the dictator. But there can be no doubt that the two leading conspirators—Marcus Junius Brutus and Gaius Cassius—were primarily motivated by "a sense that to have one man possessing as much permanent power as Caesar was incompatible with a free Republic."[45] Brutus idolized his uncle Cato (who was also his father-in-law) and had fought with Pompey. (He had surrendered to Caesar, however, when Pompey was beaten, rather than continuing the fight as Cato had done.) Moreover, Brutus's family prided itself on being descendent from Lucius Brutus, the legendary founder of the republic. According to Brutus's biographer Plutarch, he was prodded into action by anonymous graffiti writers who daily reminded him of the deeds of his illustrious ancestor by covering Rome's walls with slogans like "Brutus, are you asleep?" and "You are not really Brutus."[46]

The plot was carried out on March 15, the famous Ides of March, in 44 BC.[47] Around 11 AM, Caesar arrived in the Senate house, as usual, to conduct business, and he seated himself on his golden chair. One of the conspirators went to present Caesar with a petition, and the others crowded around him, touching and kissing Caesar's hands as if to beg for his support. Then one of them gave the agreed-upon signal, and the conspirators started stabbing Caesar with daggers they had concealed in their pencil cases. At first, Caesar tried to resist. But according to some accounts, when he realized Brutus (for whom he had a particular fondness) was involved in the plot, he drew his toga over his head and allowed his assailants to butcher him. There were so many of them and they were so eager to participate in the killing that they ended up wounding each other with their daggers. Caesar's body ended up lifeless on the Senate floor. He had been stabbed twenty-three times.

The conspirators believed Caesar's murder to be a tyrannicide, an act of liberation. After Caesar died they marched, spattered with blood, to the capitol, carrying on a pole the cap traditionally worn by freed slaves, as a symbol of the liberty they had regained for Rome. Along their way, they told everyone who would listen that they were trying to restore the republic, just as the first Brutus had done. In the wake of Caesar's murder, during a debate in the Senate, several senators expressed their support for the conspirators, and some even wanted to officially designate them "tyrannicides." Subsequently, Marcus Brutus tried to officialize this narrative by issuing coins, which depicted the cap of liberty between two

A silver denarius issued a year after the murder of Caesar. The cap of liberty is featured between two daggers, while the legend below reads, "EiD MAR," short for "the Ides of March," the day Caesar was murdered. The other side of the coin shows Marcus Brutus's image.

daggers, to celebrate Caesar's death. Ordinary Romans, however, seem to have been less than enthusiastic about the attempt to "liberate" them from Caesar's "tyranny." Despite his disregard for the traditional constitution, Caesar had been an able administrator, and fear for a return to the civil wars was deep-seated.

Moreover, it quickly became clear that Caesar's murder had been to no avail. New contenders for the throne immediately stepped into the power vacuum, among whom Mark Antony, Caesar's closest ally, was the most dangerous—or so many believed. With Brutus and Cassius gone from Rome (they had left the city, fearing for their safety after a man mistakenly held to be one of Caesar's murderers had been ripped apart by an angry mob), the aging Cicero came to play a prominent role in the opposition.

Cicero was sixty-two at the time.[48] After a brilliant career in politics—in his early forties, he had been elected consul, the highest public office in Rome—he had become sidelined in his old age. And as Rome had become increasingly plagued by political strife and civil wars, Cicero had retreated to his villa in the suburbs. He had become absorbed in philosophy, writing on ethics and theology; he also wrote an influential treatise on the art of oratory. Private worries absorbed much of his time. The death of his beloved daughter Julia in February 45 BC left him devastated. For months, he was unable to think and talk about anything else.

But as his despair slowly lifted, Cicero believed that he needed to enter the fray one last time. He had not participated in Caesar's murder—indeed, he had not even known the assassination was planned. But now he took advantage of the occasion to express his support for the killers and to warn against Mark Antony's designs. Over the next few months, Cicero kept repeating this message, giving no less than fourteen speeches on this theme in the Senate. His speeches were so admired by his contemporaries and later generations that they came to be known as the Philippics, after the powerful anti-Macedonian orations by the legendary Athenian orator Demosthenes.

Again and again, Cicero called upon his fellow senators to defend— with their lives, if need be—Rome's "freedom" against Mark Antony's attempts to overthrow the republic and introduce one-man rule. "There is nothing more detestable than disgrace; nothing more shameful than slavery," Cicero told his audience. "We have been born to glory and to liberty; let us either preserve them or die with dignity." Or, as he put it in another speech, "Peace is liberty in tranquility; slavery is the worst of all evils—to be repelled, if need be, not only by war, but even by death." All in all, Cicero invoked *libertas* more than sixty times in the course of his fourteen orations, and he warned against "slavery" no fewer than twenty-six times.[49]

In the short term, Cicero's eloquence was effective: he managed to persuade the Senate to brand Mark Antony as a public enemy. But even this failed to quell the growing political and military ascendancy of Antony and his associates—Octavian, Caesar's adopted son, and Lepidus, another Caesarian loyalist. When the trio began to purge Rome of their enemies, just as Sulla had done, Cicero's name featured among the hundreds of senators and ordinary citizens on the dreaded proscription lists. Cicero retreated to one of his villas, but Mark Antony's men managed to find him in December of 43 BC. They apprehended Cicero as he was being carried away in a litter, in a last-ditch attempt to flee to Macedonia. He was decapitated on the spot. His head and right hand were sent to Rome, where they were nailed to the speaker's platform in the Forum.[50]

Less than a year later, Brutus and Cassius were also finally defeated, at the battle of Philippi. After they had left Rome, both men took up official duties in the East. But the growing power of Mark Antony and his associates encouraged them to take up their arms again. They managed to raise an army and march to Rome. However, at Philippi, a town in the north of Greece, they were intercepted by the combined forces of Mark Antony and Octavian and were defeated. Following Cato's example, both men committed suicide, Cassius reputedly killing himself with the knife he had used on Caesar.

Philippi marked the final attempt of the *optimates* to regain control of the situation and to put a stop to the growth of autocracy in Rome. Of course, one can wonder what the regime that men like Cato, Brutus, Cassius, and Cicero wanted to "restore" would have looked like and how much room it would have left for the input of ordinary Romans. As the writings of Cicero show, these men claimed to want to go back to the republic as it existed right before Sulla's time. But at the same time, they always seemed more intent on restoring power and independence to the Senate rather than to the tribunes and the assemblies. However, this will always remain an open question, as the *optimates* of the late Republic never even came close to putting their ideals into practice.

After Augustus: Freedom in the Early Imperial Period

Following their victory at Philippi, Mark Antony, Octavian, and Lepidus divided power among themselves and ruled as military dictators, the so-called Triumvirate. The alliance was eventually torn apart by the competing ambitions of its members. After a decade of further civil wars, Lepidus was driven into exile and stripped of his position. Mark Antony committed suicide following his defeat by Octavian at the Battle of Actium in 31 BC. Having amassed sole power, Octavian ended up creating a new form of government—the principate, or empire. Thus, he put an end to the republic and to the last remains of freedom for the Roman people.

Or did he? Octavian actually spared no effort to make it seem as if he were the restorer rather than the gravedigger of the republic and Roman freedom.[51] On January 16, 27 BC, three and a half years after his victory at Actium, Octavian appeared before the Senate and formally left his office as consul. In his autobiography, he later explained that he had thus "given back" political power to the Senate and the Roman people. Ever after, he did his utmost to avoid giving the impression that he desired royal power. He objected to being acclaimed publicly as *dominus*, or "master." While he did accept the title of *Augustus*—literally "Illustrious One"—this was an honorific with religious rather than political overtones. In 28–27 BC, the same year that he "restored" power to the Senate and the people, Augustus issued coins bearing the inscription "vindicator of the liberty of the Roman people."[52] He declared in the opening sentences of his autobiography that he had "freed" the republic from the "domination of a faction"—a reference, in all likelihood, to Mark Antony and his supporters.[53]

Augustus's immediate successors adopted the same strategy. They refrained from calling themselves *rex*, or "king," and officially carried only titles fitting of a republic. And they invoked the slogan of "freedom" even more enthusiastically than Augustus had. Claudius, Augustus's great-nephew, was the first emperor to issue coins featuring the goddess Liberty, recognizable by her association with the cap of liberty. Under the emperor Galba, Nero's successor, "public liberty" (*libertas publica*) became a very common legend on imperial coins. Overall, more than thirty emperors issued coins that featured the goddess Liberty, holding the cap of liberty in her hand or on a rod.[54]

Many Romans, however, seem to have taken Augustus's claim to have restored republican freedom with a large grain of salt.[55] That much becomes clear from Appian's *Roman History*. Appian, an Alexandrian who lived in Rome in the middle of the second century, wrote a history of his adoptive city in which he devoted considerable attention to the civil wars and the subsequent changes to the Roman political system. He had no doubt that Rome had become a monarchy under Augustus and his successors; however, Romans refrained from referring to their emperors as kings, Appian explained, "out of respect, I believe, for the ancient oath" (an oath that all Roman officials traditionally had to take, renouncing monarchy). "Yet they are very kings in fact."[56]

Other Roman intellectuals were equally critical of the idea that the regime created by Augustus and his successors could be called free. Cassius Dio, a Roman senator of Anatolian extraction who wrote the eighty-volume *Roman History* in the early third century, made it perfectly clear that he believed freedom had come to an end during the battle of Philippi, when Brutus's and Cassius's troops had been defeated by Octavian and Mark Antony. Philippi, Dio wrote, had not been simply a battle between competing strongmen, the way later struggles between Octavian and Mark Antony had been. Rather, freedom had been at stake, as the Romans fought to decide whether they would go in the direction of autocracy or popular self-government. After Philippi, the Roman people definitively lost their liberty, as the democratic element in the constitution was defeated and the monarchical element became dominant. Dio hastened to add, however, that this was not necessarily a bad thing, for the Roman Empire had simply become too extensive to be ruled by a democracy. It was therefore inevitable that this situation would end either in "slavery" or "ruin"—and the former was obviously much preferred over the latter.[57]

Appian and Dio certainly had a point. While Romans continued to hold elections until the third century, candidates for public office were now put forward by the emperor, and when he "recommended" a candidate, their election was all but assured. The choice of the most prestigious office, that of consul, was always made based upon the recommendation of the emperor. For lower functions, in the beginning, there was still an element of electoral competition; however, voting now took place within the Senate rather than before the Roman people at large. And even that process eventually disappeared. Senators were likewise appointed by the emperor, although the picture was complicated by the fact that the office of senator was also made hereditary by Augustus, which gave senators, at least in theory, greater independence from the emperor than other office-holders. Finally, adult male citizens lost their long-established rights to participate in making laws and to act as jurors. It was now the emperor who made law and who spoke justice. In short, the Roman Empire functioned, for all intents and purposes, like a Hellenistic monarchy, in which the ultimate decision-making power was in the hands of a single person.[58]

Of course, we can ask ourselves whether life under the empire was really all that different for the bulk of the population than life under the republic. For women and slaves, the demise of the republic did not make that much of a difference, and arguably the position of some selected women and slaves improved under the empire. Because of their proximity to the emperor, women in the emperor's household (typically the emperor's wife and mother) might come to wield considerable power. According to the historian Tacitus, Augustus's wife Livia became the real power behind the throne when Augustus became old and infirm. She, more than anyone else, made sure that her husband was succeeded by Tiberius—her son from a previous marriage—rather than by Augustus's own flesh and blood. Her great granddaughter Agrippina the Younger was even more formidable. As the wife of the emperor Claudius (who was, incidentally, her uncle), she exercised a power that Tacitus described, disapprovingly, as a "masculine despotism." She reportedly bragged that she was a "partner" in the empire that her ancestors had won, on equal footing with her husband. She also apparently tried to bring that message across by innovating imperial seating arrangements: again according to Tacitus, she was the first empress to sit on a throne next to her husband, where she received homage just like Claudius.[59]

Slaves and freedmen in the imperial household could also gain great power and influence. The philosopher Epictetus, for instance, himself a freed slave, related an amusing anecdote illustrating just how much even the lowliest slave's status could be raised by proximity to the emperor. A certain Epaphroditus (so Epictetus tells us) owned a slave, Felicio, a cobbler by training, whom Epaphroditus sold off for being no good at his job. The man then happened to be bought by one of the members of Caesar's household and became the emperor's cobbler. "You should have seen how Epaphroditus paid court to him," Epictetus sniggered. "'What is the good Felicio doing, I pray you?' And then if anyone asked us, 'What is Epaphroditus doing?' he was told, 'He is in consultation with Felicio.'"[60]

Nevertheless, from the perspective of adult male citizens, things did change substantially in the wake of the Augustan Revolution. Whereas previously their votes had been solicited and their opinions taken into account by politicians, they now lost any role whatsoever in the political process. Augustus's rise to power had a momentous impact on the self-understanding of Roman citizens. For centuries, Romans had congratulated themselves on being a free people. They were, in their own view at least, a people that governed itself and was not subjected to the arbitrary whims of an autocrat. With the establishment of the empire, however, this self-image became increasingly difficult to sustain. The Romans, many started to worry, were reverting to the condition they had been in under Tarquin the Proud: subjects instead of citizens, submitting to an all-powerful and often harsh ruler. Even the most nobly born Romans, those descended from long lines of consuls and other public servants, were now at the beck and call of the emperors and their cronies. The elite, in other words, were no better off than slaves.

Some Roman intellectuals responded to the new, disquieting reality with a flight to the greener pastures of the republican past.[61] Livy provided the most famous example of this retreat into nostalgia.[62] A native of Padua, a city about 300 miles north of Rome, Livy had moved to the capital when he was still a young man, which allowed him to witness the turmoil of the civil wars up close. He began writing a history of his adoptive city during the civil wars and continued working on this project for as long as he lived. Although the larger part of his history has now been lost, we know that he covered the entire history of Rome, *ab urbe condita,* "from the founding of the city" until Augustus's reign. But the most celebrated part of his work (and hence, unsurprisingly, the section that has survived until today) focused on the first few centuries of Rome's existence.[63]

Many of his readers, Livy acknowledged in his preface, would probably want to skip ahead to their own times. He nevertheless decided to devote his creative energies to an account of the city's founding and the period immediately following it. Doing so allowed him, Livy wrote, to "avert his gaze" from the troubles that plagued his own times and to absorb himself in the recollection of "the brave days of old."[64] There was much to be admired about the ancient Romans. They had been more morally upright, more devoted to the good of the city, less greedy, and less corruptible. All of these qualities, Livy made clear, allowed them to preserve their liberty against tyrants or would-be tyrants.

In particular, the earliest part of Livy's *History*—the first "decade," as the initial ten chapters of his book were called—was a celebration of the early Romans' successful fight for freedom against both foreign invaders and would-be autocrats from within. Livy made it clear that the Romans had become a "free people" only after they had gotten rid of their kings and given the main decision-making power to annually elected magistrates. This was a moment of great consequence, he emphasized, akin to a second founding of Rome. Likewise, the Conflict of the Orders was given ample space in Livy's narrative, with a starring role for plebeian reformers. In speech after speech, Livy had these reformers argue that the institutional changes they demanded were essential for freedom. (Livy himself was probably much less democratically minded than the reformers whose words he scripted so eloquently. Certain remarks in his own authorial voice suggest that, like Cicero, he was wary of the "excessive" freedom of pure democracies like Athens.[65])

Livy's main interest, however, was not in institutional history but in the men who had shaped these institutions. Nearly every page of his *History* contained descriptions of people fighting for what Livy called "the sweets of liberty." The story of Lucius Junius Brutus, for instance, was given a prime place in Livy's narrative. Brutus was depicted by Livy as a model freedom fighter: he was introduced as "the great soul who was to free the Roman people."[66] By contrast, Livy had no sympathy whatsoever for Brutus's sons, who, in his view, had betrayed not just their father but also their newly liberated country when they became involved in the coup to overthrow the republic. He therefore wholeheartedly approved of Brutus's execution of his own sons. (Not all ancient commentators shared this view: Plutarch chided Junius Brutus for being "hard by nature" and called the execution of his sons a "dreadful act."[67])

Livy was not the only historian to keep the memory of republican freedom fighters alive. Under the early empire, a veritable cult was established around Caesar's opponents.[68] The lives of men like Cato and Brutus were celebrated by several different authors. This tradition had already started during their own lifetimes. After Cato's suicide, both Brutus and Cicero wrote eulogies of the dead man. (Caesar responded with a vilification titled *Anti-Cato*.) A few years later, Cicero continued to celebrate

Brutus's deeds in the *Philippics.* The hagiography went on undiluted during the early empire. A contemporary of Livy, Cremutius Cordus, wrote a history celebrating the memory of Brutus and his coconspirator Cassius. A generation later, the poet Lucan, whose epic *Pharsalia* focused on the civil wars, portrayed Caesar as a vicious tyrant and commemorated Cato as the only righteous man of his time. Even Nero's tutor and unofficial adviser, the philosopher Seneca, shared this republican nostalgia. Especially in the moralizing essays and letters he wrote in retirement, after Nero had thanked him for his services, Seneca depicted the fall of the republic as the end of freedom and an unmitigated disaster, condemning Caesar and celebrating Cato's role in the civil wars. The famous line "Cato did not survive liberty, nor did liberty survive Cato" elegantly summarized Seneca's views.[69]

Republican hero worship was given its most influential form by Plutarch. Like Livy, Plutarch was from the provinces, albeit from even farther afield than Livy.[70] He was born and bred in Chaeronea, a Greek-speaking city about seventy miles from Athens. Although he traveled widely, he remained there his whole life and was very active in local politics. Plutarch was, in other words, Greek through and through, but his mental horizon was shaped just as much by Rome and its history as by his Greek heritage. (When Plutarch was born, Chaeronea had been part of the Roman Empire for over two centuries.) His fascination with Rome and its history comes through clearly in one of his earliest books, the *Lives of the Roman Emperors,* a now-lost work that focused on the biographies of Augustus and his successors.

Plutarch's most famous work was the *Parallel Lives,* a series of joint biographies of Greek and Roman men. (Plutarch did not think it necessary to devote even a single biography to a woman.)[71] The scope of this work was broad: the men it featured ranged from mythological heroes like Theseus (supposedly the founder of Athens) to historical figures like Mark Antony. One of Plutarch's goals was to compare Greek and Roman cultures, which is why every Greek hero or villain was paired with a Roman figure of comparable stature. But the Roman lives could also be read independently, as a contribution to Roman historiography. When approached that way, Plutarch's predilection for the republican past, and especially for the freedom fighters of the late republic, is unmistakable. Plutarch's biographies of Cato of Utica, Cicero, and Marcus Brutus are much longer than the other lives. The men are presented as admirable examples, reflecting the importance Plutarch attached to them.

Cato of Utica, in particular, was depicted as a man among men, a true patriot who selflessly devoted his life to fight for Rome's freedom against an ever-changing cast of would-be kings.[72] Even as a young boy, Plutarch explained, Cato manifested a fearless hatred of tyrants such as Sulla. As a fledgling senator, he opposed all demagogues who tried to undermine the republic and did not flinch even when they used violence to try to silence him. Eventually, after Caesar started a civil war, Cato put himself at the head of the Senate's armies to fight him. The only negative thing Plutarch had to say about this great hero was that he was occasionally too scrupulous. For instance he rejected a marriage alliance with Pompey, one of Caesar's main rivals, because he wanted to retain his freedom to act according to his own exacting principles. As a result, Pompey allied himself with Caesar rather than with Cato, thus hastening the end of the republic.

But more than the admirable way he lived his life, what made Cato Rome's freedom fighter par excellence, in Plutarch's view, was the manner of his death. Cato famously committed suicide after his armies had been defeated by Caesar. He died in a particularly gruesome manner, described in loving detail by his biographer, whose account would inspire dozens of painters over the centuries. A first attempt to kill himself by his sword failed: Cato's son and attendants found him lying in a pool of his own blood, with a large gaping wound in his stomach from which his intestines dangled—but he was still alive. A physician stuffed the intestines back into Cato's stomach and tried to sew his wound back together. But when Cato became aware of this attempt to rescue his life, he pushed the physician away, tore open the wound, and ripped his own innards apart with his bare hands.

Cato killed himself not because he was afraid to die by Caesar's hand, Plutarch emphasized. He knew that he could probably count on Caesar's mercy, provided he would be prepared to go into exile, as this would enhance Caesar's own reputation. But Cato was not prepared to do that. Never, he had repeatedly told his friends and associates, would he con-

Death of Cato of Utica by Jean-Paul Laurens (1863).

sent to live under the yoke of a tyrant. Cato's suicide was therefore motivated by his desire to remain a free man, by his refusal to be subject to
another's authority. His sword, Plutarch told us, allowed Cato to remain
his "own master" rather than to submit to Caesar's power.[73]

Marcus Brutus was depicted as a self-sacrificing freedom fighter in
much the same mold as his uncle. Plutarch's account of Brutus's life focused on the conspiracy against Caesar and the subsequent campaign
against Caesar's heirs, Antony and Octavian. Plutarch made a considerable effort justifying Brutus's murder of Caesar, though he had always
behaved with the greatest magnanimity toward the younger man. But
this did not mean, Plutarch argued, that Brutus should be accused of
ingratitude and other moral failings. Rather, it showed how "disin-
terested and sincere" his opposition against Caesar had been, "since
without any private grievance against Caesar he risked his life for the
common liberty."[74] Cicero's character was described in less glowing
terms. (Perhaps this had something to do with the fact that Cicero's life

and thoughts—warts and all—were already so much better documented than that of other important actors of the late republic.) While Plutarch recognized Cicero as a "true patriot," he also dwelled upon Cicero's many character faults—in particular, his considerable vanity. But his death, at the hands of Antony's odious henchmen, was, like Cato's, suitably heroic.[75]

By celebrating the lives and deaths of famous republican heroes like Junius Brutus, Cato, Marcus Brutus, and Cicero, writers like Livy, Lucan, and Plutarch were keeping the cult of liberty alive under the empire. They made clear that, to earlier generations, freedom was about having the ability to rule yourself and to answer to no master. And they were not afraid to highlight that such freedom had been lost under the empire. Further, their narratives showed that to many admirable men, such freedom was worth dying for, thus bringing home the message that living in slavery could be worse than death.

Retreat into republican nostalgia was not the only possible response, however, to the new political realities. Cornelius Tacitus, perhaps the most talented of the imperial historians, adopted a very different approach. Instead of focusing on the republic and its heroes, Tacitus produced a detailed and decidedly unflattering account of life in the first few decades of the empire, which allowed him to highlight the pernicious consequences of the Romans' loss of liberty. Under the emperors, as he spelled out in lurid detail, the Romans had lost all personal security, and Rome's elite had been transformed into cringing, debased slaves.[76]

Born in the mid-fifties as a member of the provincial elite, Tacitus ended up in the inner circles of Roman power: he was appointed a senator under Domitian and eventually even became a consul and then the proconsul, or governor, of the wealthy province Asia—an extraordinary feat for someone of his background.[77] But it was his literary output that would bring him lasting fame. He first wrote a biography of his father-in-law, the Roman general Agricola, followed by an ethnographic account of the German tribes living on the border, both fairly conventional works. His third book, the *Histories,* an account of life under the Flavian emperors, was more ambitious and innovative. However, it is hard to form a judgment of its main message because the work has been largely lost: out of a total of twelve books, only the first four have been preserved, those dealing with the social and political upheaval of the disastrous year 69 AD, when Rome was ruled in quick succession by no fewer than four emperors.

But Tacitus's masterpiece was undoubtedly the *Annals,* his final book.[78] In the *Annals,* Tacitus went back even further in time than in the *Histories.* A massive work, which must equal about one thousand modern pages in its complete version (roughly half of the original text has been preserved), it focused on Augustus's final years and on the reigns of Augustus's earliest successors: Tiberius, Claudius, and Nero. Tacitus had chosen this subject matter, as he explained in his introduction, because the history of the republic had already been adequately served by "famous historians," while the reign of Augustus had also been described by "fine minds"—at least until growing "obsequiousness" made them go silent. But historians had treated Tiberius, Claudius, and Nero far from objectively: their reigns had provoked considerable hatred, and existing accounts were violently hostile. Tacitus would therefore be the first to try to give the Julio-Claudian dynasty its due, writing "without rancour or bias."[79]

For all his emphasis on impartiality, however, Tacitus did not hesitate to deliver an extraordinarily harsh judgment of Rome's earliest emperors. The rule of Tiberius, the first emperor whose career Tacitus discussed in full, began promisingly. But things changed for the worse after the death of Tiberius's son Drusus, his heir apparent. Tiberius succumbed to the influence of Lucius Aelius Sejanus, the prefect of the praetorian guard (the emperor's bodyguard). Sejanus managed to persuade Tiberius to retreat from Rome to Capri, Tacitus explained, and so became the de facto ruler of Rome, behaving like a real tyrant. After Sejanus lost Tiberius's favor, he and his followers were murdered in a massacre, with Tiberius's silent approval. Even Sejanus's small children were not spared. Tacitus recounted, in a horrible vignette, how Sejanus's daughter, a mere child, was first raped by the public executioner before being hanged, because custom prohibited the execution of virgins.[80]

Tacitus went on to describe Tiberius's final years, during which the aging emperor began behaving ever more erratically and despotically. The account of Tiberius's reign closed with a ghoulish laundry list of people being accused of treason and killing themselves or being executed. One prominent citizen, Tacitus reported, poisoned himself on the Senate floor, while his accusers were summing up the charges against him. He was then hurried to prison and strangled, even though he was already dead.[81]

Claudius was not much better. While admittedly a good and capable administrator, Claudius was also depicted as the plaything of his wives and freedmen. But Tacitus preserved his real fire for Nero. Nero was a moral monster, who murdered his own mother and both of his wives for no good reason. He drove men to commit suicide simply because they were descendants of Augustus, even when they posed no real threat to his power. No one was safe under his reign. As a young emperor, he had the habit of roaming around Rome at night with his companions, drunken, beating up innocent bystanders for fun. When a Roman citizen attacked by the gang retaliated and gave Nero a good beating (not knowing it was the emperor), he was forced to commit suicide. The discovery of a conspiracy against Nero's life resulted in an orgy of killing the guilty and innocent alike. His tutor Seneca was among the victims. Even some of Nero's closest friends, like the poet Petronius, were driven to suicide.[82]

No matter how powerful, how wealthy, how well connected, anyone's life could be snuffed out on the emperor's whim. Even the cover of obscurity could not keep one safe. That point was made clear by the fate of the Christians. At the end of his reign, Nero embarked upon a cruel persecution of the Christians to distract attention from the rumor that he had set fire to Rome. Nero inflicted on them the most exotic punishments: he had them dressed up in the hides of wild beasts to be ripped apart by dogs, and he hanged them on crosses that were then burned to provide lighting at night. "As a result," Tacitus commented, "guilty though these people were and deserving exemplary punishment, pity for them began to well up because it was felt that they were being exterminated not for the public good, but to gratify one man's cruelty."[83]

Much like Herodotus, Tacitus showed that there could be no personal security under imperial rule and indicated that this was a structural problem. The lack of security under the empire was caused by the unchecked nature of autocratic rule rather than by the personal qualities of Tiberius or Nero. Tacitus made it crystal clear in the first few pages of

the *Annals* that he believed that the reign of Augustus had marked a constitutional change in which "freedom"—that is, popular government—had been replaced by autocracy. At several points in his subsequent story, he emphasized that elections had become a charade, in
sharp contrast to those of the old republic. The fact that the power of
Augustus's successors knew no bounds had greatly contributed to their
crimes and moral degradation. This was perhaps best illustrated by Tiberius's reign: Tiberius had started out as a good ruler, until he was led
astray by evil councillors like Sejanus.[84]

Herodotus had of course made very similar claims in the *Histories*, although Tacitus, describing his own rulers rather than those of a foreign
enemy, inflected his story with a bitterness and moral outrage never
matched by Herodotus. But Tacitus did not just echo his Greek predecessor. In his description of the vicious effects of autocracy, Tacitus went
beyond Herodotus's focus on personal security. An equally pernicious result of imperial rule, Tacitus made clear, was that it bred servility, destroying the moral character of the Roman people.

In Tacitus's narrative, the moral effects of the disappearance of freedom
were most visible in the behavior of Rome's elite.[85] Most senators portrayed in the *Annals* acted with repulsive servility toward their masters,
the emperors. In one episode, a hapless young man, Libo, tried to rebel
against Tiberius. He was found out and committed suicide. After his
death, several senators pretended to be so overjoyed that the emperor's
life had been spared that they tried to make Libo's date of death into a
national holiday. In another anecdote, a Roman knight ordered silver din-
nerware decorated with Tiberius's image, presumably to showcase his
admiration for the emperor. But he was accused of treason by some of his
peers, who pretended to be scandalized by the fact that he ate his meals
from the emperor's image. Indeed, the senators' sycophancy was so bla-
tant and exaggerated that it even irritated Tiberius himself, Tacitus
claimed: "The story goes that, whenever he left the Senate house, Tiberius
was in the habit of declaring, in Greek: 'Ah, men ready to be slaves!'
Clearly, while he objected to the freedom of the people, he was also sick-
ened by such abject submission from his 'slaves.'"[86]

By the time Nero rose to power, things had gotten even worse. The
senators offered praise when Nero murdered his own mother, Agrippina,

in an elaborate plot involving a self-sinking boat. They applauded again when he had his blameless first wife Octavia killed and showed off her head on a stake to please his new wife, Poppaea. After Nero accidentally killed her too, in a fit of rage, the senators acquiesced in the deification of this scheming and villainous woman. But perhaps the lowest point of all, in Tacitus's view, was when several members of Rome's oldest and most illustrious families accompanied the young emperor as actors and singers on stage, even though such jobs were typically the preserve of the lowest of the low.[87]

Not all senators behaved in such an abject manner, however. Tacitus's discussion of the life and deeds of Thrasea Paetus showed that some senators tried to keep the spirit of liberty alive. One of the few honorable men left under Nero's reign, Thrasea opposed the mad emperor whenever he could. When one of his colleagues was threatened with execution for reciting irreverent verses about Nero, for instance, Thrasea courageously spoke up and secured a milder punishment.

But Thrasea received precious little support from most of the other senators, and he eventually withdrew from public life. Nero, however, continued to hold a grudge, and instigated a trial against Thrasea on trumped-up charges. Our text of the *Annals* breaks off with an emotional scene in which Thrasea, rather than subject himself to the humiliation of a trial, prepared to commit suicide like his role model Cato of Utica. Like Cato, Thrasea made it clear that he preferred to die rather than to live in slavery, declaring that he was making a libation to Jupiter the Liberator when he opened up his veins. The moral of this story was clear: a truly free spirit could not coexist with imperial rule.[88]

Tacitus's *Annals* provided a chilling analysis of what a lack of freedom did to the moral character of a people. It should be noted, however, that Tacitus was not as scathing about the emperors of his own time as he was about those in the Julio-Claudian dynasty. From his early work, it is clear that he considered the political situation to have become much better with the accession of Nerva, who became emperor in 96, when Tacitus was about forty years old. Tacitus was even more enthusiastic about Nerva's successor, Trajan, the first emperor of provincial rather than Roman descent. In his very first book, the *Agricola,* Tacitus even suggested that, under a good ruler, individuals could enjoy some form of freedom, at least in the sense of having personal security. By restoring peace and order, he wrote, Nerva and Trajan had accomplished a feat that had previously seemed impossible: they had "mingled what had been for ages irreconcilable things, the principate and liberty."[89] This was an isolated remark, however. On the whole, Tacitus's writings brought home the opposite message: that a robust sense of freedom could not coexist with imperial rule.[90]

As the works of Tacitus, Livy, and Plutarch make clear, in short, the cult of freedom had by no means disappeared after Augustus. Historians like Livy and Plutarch celebrated the heroes of the republican period who had fought for freedom, thus drilling home the message that, to some exemplary men at least, freedom was more important than life. Tacitus, for his part, laid bare the effects of political slavery. Life under imperial rule, he made clear, was precarious at best. In addition, lack of freedom had a terrible impact on the moral fiber of the Roman people. He showed how the once-proud senators had been transformed into a despicable bunch of sycophants and, as a result, had lost all their dignity.

Unsurprisingly, the emperors and their advisors worried about the subversive effects of the cult of republican freedom and made life quite difficult for some of the historians and poets who tried to keep the memory of the republic alive. A few intellectuals even paid with their lives. Cremetius Cordus, for instance, who had celebrated Brutus's and Cassius's murder of Caesar, starved himself to death after being condemned for treason and having his book burned. The poet Lucan, another admirer of the tyrannicides, died as a result of his participation in a plot to overthrow Nero. (Although Tacitus claimed that Lucan's enmity toward Nero stemmed from the fact that Nero, jealous of Lucan's success, had blocked his poetical career rather than from Lucan's republican sympathies.)[91]

Such harsh measures were probably superfluous. In the real world, the survival of the cult of freedom seems to have had little impact. After 27 BC, the empire remained firmly in place. Just one serious attempt was made to turn back the clock to the republic, and that attempt quickly proved abortive. In 41 AD, a group of disaffected praetorians killed the emperor Caligula, Tiberius's successor. In the power vacuum that opened up, the Senate attempted to put an end to imperial rule. A number of senators called a meeting and hailed Caligula's murderers as heroes and tyrannicides in the mold of Brutus and Cassius. Notably, Gnaeus Sentius Saturninus called upon his peers to seize the moment to put an end to political slavery once and for all and to reclaim the liberty of their ancestors.[92]

But the senators' talk was to no avail. Back in the imperial palace, the praetorian guard had already picked a new emperor, Caligula's hapless uncle Claudius, who went on to reign unchallenged until his death thirteen years later. The whole episode only underscored the point that the old system of government was gone for good. After Caligula, many other emperors were to lose their lives and thrones, but these events were always palace coups, engineered to replace one ruler with another. Never again was the empire, as such, challenged.[93]

Indeed, there is plenty of evidence that even republican-minded intellectuals like Livy, Plutarch, and Tacitus, despite their enthusiastic paeans to liberty and bitter denouncements of political slavery, were resigned to maintaining the empire. In their view, the demise of the republic, however much it was to be regretted, had been all but inevitable in the face of the mounting corruption of the elites and the growing discord of the citizens. The more probable alternative to the empire than the reestablishment of freedom, they realized, was a return to civil war. This explains why Livy was on friendly terms with Augustus and why Tacitus wholeheartedly supported the Antonine dynasty under which he lived. Similarly, Plutarch described the late republic in his *Life of Julius Caesar* as a sick body and Caesar as its healer.[94]

Nevertheless, by immortalizing the freedom fighters of both the early and late republic and by denouncing the effects of political slavery on the Roman people, historians like Livy, Lucan, Plutarch, and Tacitus made a hugely important contribution to the history of freedom. They immortalized a cast of freedom fighters even more appealing than Herodotus's Sperthias and Bulis, as well as villains more colorful than Cambyses or Xerxes. They developed a veritable treasure trove of moralizing tales about the corrupting influence of political subjection. And their stories would inspire readers for centuries to come.

Demise of the Cult of Freedom in the Later Imperial Period

Not all Roman or Romanized intellectuals of the early empire, however, were intent on keeping the cult of republican freedom alive. Plenty of them came to think, as Plato had, that there was nothing wrong with living in slavery—as long as this meant living under the reign of the best person. Dio Chrysostom, for instance, a contemporary of Tacitus, had come of age during the violent reign of Domitian. But instead of bemoaning the advent of the empire and Rome's loss of liberty, as Tacitus had done, Dio praised Domitian's successors, Nerva and especially Trajan, as wise and beneficial rulers. Subjection to such rulers was no disaster; it was the best thing that could possibly happen to a person.[95]

A wealthy citizen of Prusa in Bithynia (modern Turkey), Dio was a frequent guest of Rome during the reign of the emperor Vespasian. He appears to have been some sort of society figure and was friendly with members of the emperor's inner circle. When Domitian ascended the throne, however, Dio's charmed life was over. He was banned from Italy and his native province, probably because of his association with a Roman patrician suspected of attempted treason. During his exile, Dio's interest in philosophy was sparked. Cut off from his funds, he tried to make the best of a dire situation by traveling through the empire as a philosopher-sage. He soon acquired a reputation for his oratorical skills and was given the nickname Chrysostomos or "Golden Voice." In 96 AD, when Domitian was assassinated, Dio's life again took a turn. Domitian's successor Nerva recalled Dio from exile, and Dio settled back in Prusa. His fortune restored by the new emperor, Dio became an influential man in his hometown, and his fellow citizens sent him as an ambassador to Rome. Here, he was expected to defend Prusa's interests before yet another emperor, Trajan, who had succeeded Nerva after his unexpected death just sixteen months into his reign.

Wanting to make his embassy a success, Dio came armed with a creative gift for the new emperor: the *Kingship Orations*. These immensely influential orations, four of which have survived, drew on Plato's idea that to be ruled by a wise king was the best kind of government men could hope for. While Dio's ideas were by no means original, he did enliven Plato's views with extravagant metaphors. Dio compared a good king with a shepherd tending lovingly to his flock and with a ship's captain who alone knew how to steer his crew safely back home. Indeed, in Dio's view, the emperor could be compared with the sun itself, who brought warmth in summer, which was necessary for life, but who also permitted cold in winter, because the earth needed rain. Like the sun, the good emperor made sure everything under his care was just right. "With such perfect nicety of adjustment does he [the sun] observe his bounds with respect to our advantage that, if in his approach he got a little nearer, he would set everything on fire, and if he went a little too far in his departure, everything would be stiffened with frost!" Dio exclaimed.[96]

Dio, of course, realized that not all rulers lived up to this ideal. He was willing to admit that life under a bad ruler was precarious at best and entailed horrible suffering at worst. But the difference between a king and a tyrant, he made clear—much like Hellenistic thinkers had done—was not institutional. Kingly power was just as unchecked and unbounded as the power of a tyrant. The difference was in their moral character. A king could avoid becoming a tyrant by reading Homer (Homer's poetry alone was "truly noble and lofty and suited to a king, worthy of the attention of a real man," Dio wrote), by avoiding flatterers, and by working on his self-control and moral rectitude.[97]

In the centuries following Trajan's accession to power, Dio's enthusiastic embrace of kingly rule became more and more the norm. As the memory of the republic dimmed, the cult of freedom kept alive during the empire's first century and a half by Livy, Tacitus, and Plutarch slowly faded away. Drawing on Hellenistic kingship theory, which was based, in turn, on Plato's vision, imperial writers celebrated monarchy as the best regime imaginable. No longer was the main contrast being drawn between tyranny and freedom; rather, it was between tyranny and kingly rule—a distinction that hinged on a ruler's moral character and superior wisdom rather than on institutional differences.[98]

A telling indication of these changes can be found in the nomenclature used to address the emperors. The term "dominus," when used in public address, meant "lord" or "master" and was used, in particular, to describe the relation between a master and his slaves. The autocratic associations of the term made it inappropriate for the early Roman emperors, and refusal of the title became a conventional marker of the "good" emperor. Augustus, Tiberius, and Claudius had all made a great show of rejecting the title of "dominus," whereas "bad" emperors like Caligula and Domitian were accused of insisting on it. By the late second and early third centuries, however, the term started becoming commonplace for addressing emperors, who thus declared themselves to be the masters of their slave-subjects.[99]

This shift in thinking was further encouraged by a very different cultural development: the rise of Christianity.[100] By the middle of the first century, there were enough Christians in Rome for the public authorities to be aware of them, as illustrated by the fact that Nero tried to blame them for the destruction of Rome in 64 AD. But their growth proceeded at a glacial pace, and, for a long time, Christianity remained a marginal sect. In the second half of the third century, however, the number of Christians seems to have increased rather dramatically, while worship at pagan altars declined. This might have spurred the persecutions of the third century and of the first decade of the fourth century. During the so-called Great Persecution instigated by the emperor Diocletian in 302, hundreds, perhaps thousands, of Christians were executed when they refused to sacrifice to the traditional gods.

But eventually, of course, Christianity won the day and became established in the corridors of Roman power. This was largely the work of Constantine, Diocletian's successor. Constantine did not turn Christianity into the official religion of the empire, as is often mistakenly claimed, nor did he prohibit polytheism—a step that would have proved almost impossible to enforce anyway, since the majority of the population remained pagan until well into the fifth century, at least. But under Constantine's reign, imperial hostility toward Christianity turned into enthusiastic support, backed with money and patronage. In retrospect, Constantine's reign proved to have been an important turning point—all of his successors but one (the short-lived Julian) followed Constantine's example and supported Christianity, which thus became an increasingly important cultural and political force.

Early Christian attitudes toward political power were ambivalent.[101] Some of the church's first leaders, most notably the apostle Paul, held that secular authorities had been appointed by God and that, hence, Christians should obey them at all times. As Paul famously put it in a letter to a Christian community in Rome: "Let every person be subject to the governing authorities; for there is no authority except from God, and those authorities that exist have been instituted by God. Therefore whoever resists authority resists what God has appointed, and those who resist will incur judgment."[102] Others, however, had a more negative attitude toward the empire. In the book of Revelations, an apocalyptic text which was probably written in the wake of Domitian's persecution of the Christians, Rome was described as the "whore of Babylon," and her downfall was prophesied.[103]

After Constantine's providential-seeming conversion, however, such ambiguities were smoothed over, and Christian thinkers came to wholeheartedly support the empire. In doing so, they drew, to a certain extent, on earlier, pagan philosophers like Plato. Thus, Eusebius, bishop of Caesarea in Palestine and the emperor's biographer, depicted Constantine as being worthy of the throne because he was truly a master of himself and a wise man—much like Plato's philosopher-king. In an oration written to celebrate the thirtieth anniversary of Constantine's ascent to the throne, Eusebius described the emperor as a "true king"—"above the thirst of wealth, superior to sexual desire; victorious even over natural pleasures; controlling, not controlled by, anger and passion." These were all key virtues of the Hellenistic kingship tradition, of course, but Eusebius deviated from that tradition by stressing Constantine's devout Christianity as his main qualification for the throne, deeming it more important than all his other assets.[104]

Christian doctrine also provided defenders of the empire with new arguments to defend one-man rule. Christian thinkers made much out of the fact that there was but one God and that, hence, monarchy mirrored the rule of the deity. As Eusebius wrote, "There is one God, and not two, or three, or more: for to assert a plurality of gods is plainly to deny the being of God at all. There is one sovereign; and his word and royal law is one."[105] Another popular argument was that God had signaled his approval of the empire by allowing his son to be born under Augustus, the first emperor. Eusebius explained, in his influential work

Preparation for the Gospel, that the advent of the empire had been divinely ordained. By purposely making Augustus "sole ruler," God had put an end to the endless wars and strife that had plagued the pre-imperial period, thus heralding an age of peace and prosperity that enabled the spread of the gospel throughout the world.[106]

A very different, but equally influential, defense of imperial rule was developed by Augustine.[107] A citizen of Thagaste—a Romanized town in north Africa—who became a bishop and Christian apologist, Augustine lived during a particularly turbulent period in Roman history. In 410 AD, when Augustine was fifty-six, Rome was sacked by the Visigoths, an event that profoundly shook elites throughout the Roman world. In order to rebut pagan claims that this disaster had resulted from the spread of Christianity, Augustine wrote an apology designed to show that things had been far worse under pagan rule. But the *City of God,* as the work became known, expanded far beyond its original goal, evolving into a more general statement of Augustine's worldview, including his views on politics.

Augustine rejected the Platonic-Eusebian justification of kingly rule. It was wrong to expect that a political leader could guide his subjects to happiness, because true bliss could only ever be achieved through the grace of God in the afterlife. Life in the here and now could only ever bring misery and pain. Even the establishment of the empire had not been able to do away with the perennial violence and strife plaguing humanity. The very making of the empire, as Augustine explained, had come at a horrific cost: "All those terrible wars, all that human slaughter, all that human bloodshed!"[108] Moreover, the peace it brought remained precarious at best: the Romans had no lack of foreign enemies, and the empire continued to be beset by internal strife, which was even more devastating than foreign war.

In Augustine's view, humankind had been brought to this miserable condition not by God's design but by our own sinful nature. The suffering to which humans were subjected was a direct consequence of the fall of Adam and Eve, the earliest humans. As explained in Genesis, the first humans had lived happily with God in paradise, where they were free from sin, pain, and even death. However, seduced by a snake, Adam and Eve had transgressed God's only command: that they refrain from eating the fruit of a particular tree. As a result, God expelled them from paradise, and they and their descendants continued to live hard, painful, and finite lives, plagued by sinful urgings.

In Augustine's reading, the story of the Fall also helped to explain how political power had come into being in the first place. God had originally created men as equals and given them control over irrational creatures but not over other humans. "By nature, then," Augustine wrote, "as God first created man, no one is a slave either to man or to sin." Hence, political subjection was unnatural. It was only in the wake of the Fall that men had become beset by the lust to dominate one another, and that was how political power had come into being.

This was a wholesale rejection of Plato's and Eusebius's exaltation of kingly rule as a path to human happiness. Political authority was not merely powerless to guide individuals to the good life; it was also unnatural, a product of human sinfulness rather than part of God's original plan for mankind. Nevertheless, Augustine endorsed subjection to imperial rule just as strongly as Eusebius did. Augustine asserted that political authority had to be obeyed, not because a ruler was capable of guiding his subjects to the good life but because it was God's will: God had introduced political subjection to punish human beings for their sins. As Augustine famously put it, "The first cause of slavery, therefore, is sin, with the result that man is made subject to man by the bondage of this condition, which can only happen by the judgment of God, in whom there is no unrighteousness and who knows how to assign different punishments according to the merits of the offenders."[109]

This enthusiastic embrace of political subjection as divinely ordained colored Christian conceptions of freedom. Probably as a result of its original rootedness in slave communities, the concept of freedom played an important role in Christian doctrine.[110] Early Church documents— especially Paul's pastoral letters—abound with references to the liberating function of Christianity. In a letter to the Christian community in Galatia (a region in modern-day Turkey), Paul wrote that all Christians were "one in Christ Jesus," so that there was "neither slave nor free" in a Christian community. At the same time, however, Paul made it very clear that the freedom he was talking about was strictly of the inner, spiritual kind.

By emphasizing that all men were equal in Christ, he simply meant to say that Christ had liberated them from false gods.[111]

Paul made this even clearer in his letter to the Corinthians, where he advised slaves not to rebel against their lot: "Were you a slave when called? Do not be concerned about it. Even if you can gain your freedom, make use of your present condition now more than ever. For whoever was called in the Lord as a slave is a freed person belonging to the Lord, just as whoever was free when called is a slave of Christ. You were bought with a price; do not become slaves of human masters. In whatever condition you were called, brothers and sisters, there remain with God."[112] On this view, freedom had a central role in Christian doctrine, but Paul also made it clear that the promise of Christian freedom did not entail criticizing the existing social order, in which many men and women, sold and bought as slaves, were deprived of their most basic liberties. Christian liberty did not entail a plea for changes in the political sphere.[113]

Later Church fathers, such as Ambrose of Milan, brought home the same message.[114] Ambrose was a powerful bishop during the late fourth century, a time of considerable political upheaval in Italy, exacerbated by religious strife. (By this time, however, the main conflict was no longer between pagans and Christians but between different Christian sects.) In a long pastoral letter to his friend and fellow clergyman Simplician, Ambrose set out to explain the meaning of Paul's views on freedom, as articulated in the first letter to the Corinthians; more specifically, he elucidated the meaning of Paul's warning, "You were bought at a price; do not become slaves of human beings."

Ambrose's interpretation of this dictum paralleled the classic Stoic doctrine that "every wise man is free and every fool a slave." According to Ambrose, Paul's words implied that "our liberty consists in the knowledge of wisdom."[115] Ambrose went on to explain, "The wise man is free, since one who does as he wishes is free. Not every wish is good, but the wise man wishes only that which is good; he hates evil for he chooses what is good. Because he chooses what is good he is master of his choice and because he chooses his work is he free."[116] Ambrose was careful to emphasize that this Stoic idea had first been articulated in the Bible: Esau's father, for instance, had made Esau subject to his brother Jacob, because

Esau had not been intelligent enough to stand on his own two feet. "The foolish man cannot rule himself," Ambrose wrote, "and if he is without a guide he is undone by his own desires."[117]

Ambrose also made a more innovative point. If only the wise were free, because they truly followed their own will, then only God-fearing people were free, because only true Christians could be called wise. "He alone is wise, then, who uses as his guide God to search out the lair of truth," Ambrose wrote.[118] By emphasizing the importance of Christian faith, rather than purely intellectualized wisdom, as the hallmark of a truly free individual, Ambrose changed Stoic doctrine in an important way. Stoic thinkers believed that freedom was a condition reserved for very few—an elite group of male philosophers. Ambrose, by contrast, opened up the ranks of the free to a much larger group. Like Philo Judaeus, Ambrose invoked the examples of wise individuals who had been able to remain free—that is, in control of themselves—in the face of considerable pressure. The example he dwelt on most extensively was not a male philosopher, however, but three young, martyred girls who had gone singing to their deaths, strong in their faith. "Among us [Christians]," Ambrose exulted, "even maidens climb the steps of virtue mounting to the very sky with their longing for death."[119]

Yet, overall, Ambrose's conception of Christian freedom remained very close to the Stoic idea of freedom. Like Philo, Ambrose believed true freedom was a purely inward-looking condition and not affected by power relations in the outside world. As such, true believers—the truly wise— would always remain free, even if enslaved or subjected to the authority of cruel masters and tyrannical rulers. In that sense, the Christian conception of freedom, just like its Stoic counterpart, encouraged political quietism rather than revolution or reform.

In the later imperial period, in sum, the cult of freedom so characteristic of the republic and the early days of the empire slowly faded away, as Roman intellectuals came to accept imperial rule not just as a necessary evil but as an intrinsic good. This development was further encouraged by the rise of Christianity, which provided imperial intellectuals with new arguments to buttress the superiority of monarchy. Moreover, to both pagan and Christian imperial thinkers, freedom was an inner, spiritual quality that could be achieved through the cultivation of wisdom and faith rather than political change.

After Rome: Freedom in the Middle Ages

The idea that freedom was an inner, spiritual quality remained even after the slow collapse of the western half of the Roman Empire in the fifth century. During the third and fourth centuries, the empire had become too unwieldy to be governed by one man, and Roman emperors had experimented with various schemes to divide their work. This eventually resulted in a division of the empire into an eastern half, governed from Constantinople or "the new Rome," and a western half—although, legally, the empire remained one state. In the fifth century, the Western Empire increasingly came under pressure and eventually ceased to exist. But in the Eastern Empire imperial power continued to function much as it had since the late fourth century.

It is therefore unsurprising that in the east, political thought continued to be deeply influenced by Eusebius and other defenders of imperial rule.[120] Like Eusebius, Byzantine thinkers (as they were labeled by later historians) routinely depicted the eastern emperors as the embodiment of wisdom, virtue, and faith—men who were truly worthy of the throne because they alone could guide their subjects to true happiness. And Christian arguments for imperial rule, such as the godly nature of the empire, continued to circulate. In the time of Justinian, the monk Cosmas Indicopleustes described the Roman Empire—which he considered identical to the regime he lived under—as a divine creation: "While Christ was still in the womb the Roman Empire received its authority from God as the agent of the dispensation which Christ introduced, since at that very time began the never-ending line of the successors of Augustus. The empire of the Romans thus participated in the majesty of the Kingdom of Christ, for it transcends, so far as an earthly realm can, every other power; and it will remain unconquered until the final consummation."[121]

Occasionally, dissident voices could be heard. Ioannes Lydos, a professor of Latin in sixth-century Constantinople, lamented in a treatise discussing the history of Roman magistracies that the establishment of the empire brought about the loss of Roman liberty.[122] But such voices remained isolated and were muted by censorship. On the whole, Byzantine thinkers echoed their predecessors from the third and fourth centuries, even after the empire had shrunk to a small remnant of its former size. As a result, Eusebius's political philosophy, as one historian put it, went "almost unchallenged in its essentials for over 1,000 years" in the East.[123]

In the West, the fifth and sixth centuries brought more fundamental changes.[124] Here, the Roman Empire ceased to exist after the last emperor, the aptly named Romulus Augustulus ("Little Augustus"), was overthrown by the "barbarian" military leader Odoacer in 476. This was not a sharp rupture: Odoacer continued to exercise political power in the name of the eastern emperor. But Odoacer styled himself "king," which meant that after 476, there was no Roman emperor in the West—at least until Charlemagne was crowned emperor by Pope Leo III in 800, more than three hundred years later.

By 500, a completely new political landscape had taken shape in the West. A patchwork of new states understood themselves to be different from the Roman Empire, evidenced by the fact that they started issuing their own coins. These successor states diverged, in some ways quite fundamentally, from their Roman predecessor. In particular, the new political elites were increasingly unable to collect direct taxes from landowners, due to the demonetization of the economy. Hence kings were unable to pay for a standing army; instead, they rewarded their men with land—a strategy that led to the rise of vassals, who were often as mighty as the kings themselves.

Despite these very real changes, there were important elements of continuity. Most notably, the successor states all adopted the monarchical template.[125] The influence exercised by the Roman example, including both the memory of the defunct Western Empire and the "new Rome" on the Bosporus, undoubtedly played a crucial role in this development. True, on the fringes of Europe, some communities did not recognize royal authority. In Iceland, for example, power was located in the island-wide assembly, the Althing. But these communities were the exception rather than the rule, and Iceland's experiment in popular rule came to an end in 1262, when the island's inhabitants invited the king of Norway to take control. As a result, by 1300, most people in western Europe were—in one way or another—ruled by kings or queens.

In this context, late imperial justifications for kingly rule continued to exercise profound influence.[126] Augustine's views, in particular, were echoed repeatedly. Isidore of Seville, a Visigoth and probably the most widely read author of the early Middle Ages, also traced the origin of slavery and government to the fall; like Augustine, he argued that the subjection of man to man was both the penalty for Adam's sin and the divinely authorized remedy for its consequences. Others relied directly on biblical authority to make the same point. Thus, Archbishop Hincmar of Rheims, an adviser of the Carolingian emperor Charles the Bald, invoked Paul's letter to the Romans to argue that all power was divinely authorized and, hence, to be obeyed. In addition, after the "restoration" of the Roman Empire in the West, first by Charlemagne and later by Otto I, imperial spokesmen again began to tout the idea that the regime they lived under was identical to the "divine" Roman Empire.[127]

This is not to say that intellectuals in the Latin-speaking West were wholly uncritical or submissive toward the powers that be. Bitter denunciations of tyranny were by no means uncommon. Some political thinkers were even willing to admit that a tyrant, if duly identified, could be rightfully deposed by his subjects. But the proposed alternative to tyranny was always monarchy; that is, rule by a good king. The idea that a free state—in other words, popular self-government—was the best alternative to tyranny was rarely floated during the course of the Middle Ages. The key distinction in medieval political thought was between a good king and a tyrant, rather than between tyranny and freedom.[128]

Like earlier defenders of kingly power, most post-imperial commentators held that the difference between a king and a tyrant was temperamental rather than structural or institutional.[129] A king differed from a tyrant because of the way he governed. He did not pillage or oppress his people but used his power to enhance their well-being. Thus, post-imperial thinkers hit upon much the same view of kingship as Plato had, even though *The Republic* had disappeared from collective memory in the Latin-speaking West after the demise of the Roman Empire. (There were, of course, important differences as well: whereas Plato had emphasized superior wisdom as the most important attribute of the ideal king, medieval thinkers put much more emphasis on a king's moral virtues, such as clemency and generosity.)

It should therefore come as no surprise that the most popular genre of political thinking in this period came in the form of so-called mirrors for princes.[130] These moralistic, educational treatises were either dedicated to or written at the request of some reigning prince. They held up a metaphorical mirror that allowed their recipients to see how they should behave if they wanted to be a good king and not a tyrant. Their authors used different strategies to bring their messages home. Some focused on the biographies of exemplary princes, emphasizing their ethical qualities and admirable deeds; others listed a set of practical rules, principles, and norms for princely conduct. But what they all had in common was that they laid great stress upon a ruler's personal virtues. It was his moral character that determined whether the people were ruled benevolently or groaned under tyranny.

During the course of the eleventh and twelfth centuries, this universal embrace of kingly rule in the West came to be challenged by two very different developments. First, the Church, energized by the leadership of dynamic popes such as Gregory VII, began to assert its independence from worldly authority.[131] During the investiture controversy, popes and kings sparred about who had the final say over the appointment of bishops, who were not just spiritual leaders but often exercised considerable secular power as well. Equally contested were the boundaries between lay and clerical jurisdiction. Could criminal clergymen, for instance, be punished in royal courts, or were they subject to papal jurisdiction alone? Finally, by the late thirteenth century, the fiscal obligations of clergymen to secular authorities and, conversely, of laymen to the pope, became a matter of intense dispute.

During these controversies, papal spokesmen frequently invoked the concept of liberty to defend their position. The pope's advocates acknowledged that secular authority had been instituted by God and that kings and emperors should therefore be seen as the representatives of God on earth. But, they claimed, God had given a different kind of power to the pope—spiritual power. Hence papal authority was not subordinate to, but on a par with, secular authority. This doctrine had far-reaching implications, the pope's supporters argued: it meant that the Church should be free from secular authority; that is, it should be able to appoint clergy without outside interference and to collect taxes—a position often described as *libertas ecclesia* or the "freedom of the Church."[132]

Thus, the investiture controversy and similar debates revived the idea of freedom or self-government in the Latin-speaking West, albeit limited to self-government for one specific sector of society: the Church. However, many of the pope's spokesmen ended up defending a position in which the idea of freedom did not figure at all. Indeed, quite a number of papal spokesmen came to argue not just that secular power should be distinguished from spiritual power but that the former was actually subordinate to the latter. As the soul's goal (eternal happiness in heaven) was superior to the body's (material well-being on earth), the body's goal must be directed toward the attainment of the soul's goal; and since material well-being on earth must be ordered toward the attainment of eternal happiness in heaven, the power responsible for the soul (the spiritual power) must supervise and direct the power responsible for the body (the temporal power). Just like their secular opponents, in other words, many defenders of papal authority came to defend autocratic rule, albeit by a theologian-king rather than a philosopher-king.[133]

A second and perhaps even more important challenge to the kingly ideal was posed by the growth of urban power in Italy and other parts of Europe.[134] From the eleventh century onward, amid growing economic prosperity, many Italian cities shook off the authority of the local bishops and counts that had governed them and eventually created forms of government that resembled, in key aspects, the city-states of ancient Greece and Rome. Initially, power had remained in the hands of a noble elite, but especially in the thirteenth century, during the so-called era of the people, several Italian cities, especially in the north, had come under control of a broader number of citizens. Even then, large numbers of the population remained excluded: in addition to women and the clergy, most cities continued to exclude those who worked with their hands as well as the poor. The Italian communities, in other words, can hardly be qualified as genuine democracies; nevertheless, they involved a much broader swathe of the population than any regime since the ancient city-states.

There was an awareness that these governments were not like the monarchies of the rest of Europe. In describing the differences, some commentators used words like "freedom" and "free government." While traveling through Italy in the 1150s, the German bishop Otto of Freising was struck by how differently power was organized south of the Alps. Italian cities, he reported, "so much love liberty" that they wanted to be ruled by elected consuls rather than by governors sent by their nominal overlord, the Holy Roman emperor.[135] About a century later, Ptolemy of Lucca, an Italian monk, noted with patriotic pride that the Italians had always been "less able to be subjected than others"; this was why they did not have despotic governments like the other Europeans.[136]

Nevertheless, these developments had a limited impact on medieval political thought. Popular government in medieval Italy was characterized by considerable violence and civic strife. Civic life in many of these cities was marred by protracted and violent internal conflicts, often sparked by blood feuds between different families. Vendettas were so common that many cities introduced legislation specifically to forbid them (albeit unsuccessfully). Conflict between rich and poor was also rampant: in Florence, for instance, laborers and craftsmen, whose situation had deteriorated substantially thanks to ongoing wars, overthrew the existing government and briefly seized power during the Ciompi Rebellion in 1378. These internal conflicts were often exacerbated by the ongoing strife between Guelphs and Ghibellines, two factions who fought for control over the Italian peninsula ostensibly in the name of the pope and the Holy Roman emperor.[137]

The political instability of the Italian popular governments by and large prevented them from being seen as attractive models. That much is suggested by Thomas Aquinas's influential treatise *On Kingship*. Born and bred in southern Italy, Aquinas later moved to France, where he became affiliated with the University of Paris, first as a student and then as a professor. He therefore spent a substantial part of his life as a subject of the French king Louis IX, a devout Christian who died en route to the Holy Land and who was later canonized. *On Kingship*, however, was dedicated to a more obscure personage, the "King of Cyprus," which probably referred to Hugh II of Lusignan, who appears to have had a particular affection for the Dominican order.[138]

The opening chapters of *On Kingship* defend monarchy as the best and most natural form of government. After rehearsing some of the more traditional arguments for monarchy—"There is one king among the bees, and in the whole universe one God, maker and rector of all"—Aquinas appealed to experience to buttress his case. "Provinces and cities that are not governed by one," he wrote, "labor under dissentions and are tossed about without peace, so that what the Lord bewailed through the prophet seems to be fulfilled: 'Many shepherds have demolished my vineyard.'" It seems highly likely that what he had in mind were the Italian city-states, with which he was personally familiar.[139]

Eventually, the constant violence led to the demise of popular self-government in Italy. In the thirteenth century, many Italian cities invited salaried outsiders, called *podesta,* to take control over government and, in particular, the local militia, in order to control internal dissent. Over time, many of the *podesta* turned into strongmen who used force to undermine the elected governments that had initially appointed them and to take over power for themselves. By the late fourteenth century, most of the Italian city-states had been turned into principalities governed by hereditary rulers, as was the case in the rest of Europe.[140]

In short, in the centuries that followed the demise of the Roman Empire in the West, political thinkers continued to take their cues from Augustine and other late imperial writers rather than from Cicero or Tacitus—in the same way that the successor states that emerged from the ruins of the empire were modeled after the empire rather than the republic. But the demise of the cult of freedom was by no means permanent. The cult reappeared, centuries later and in a very different political context, when Renaissance admirers of Greek and Roman popular self-government invoked the concept of freedom to attack the regimes under which they lived.

PART II

Freedom's Revival

CHAPTER 3

The Renaissance of Freedom

I N THE *INFERNO,* the first and most celebrated part of his *Divine Comedy,* the Florentine poet Dante Alighieri outlined his vision of hell: it was populated by the souls of a multitude of sinners from all times and places, including the biblical figure Cain, who slew his brother Abel and became the world's first murderer. Also in hell were Muhammad, the founder of Islam (whom Dante believed to be a Christian heretic), as well as more humdrum evildoers, such as Fra Alberigo, a contemporary of Dante's who'd had his brother and nephew killed during a banquet at his home. The sinners received horrible punishments, tailored to fit their particular crimes—punishments that Dante described in lurid detail. Thus atheists, who denied the resurrection of the body, were trapped for all eternity in their tombs. And fortune-tellers had their heads twisted around on their bodies so that they had to walk backwards for eternity, tears streaming down their buttocks.

But the very lowest rung of hell, the place reserved for the worst sinners, was occupied by just three individuals. That one of them was Judas Iscariot is unsurprising. One of Jesus's original twelve disciples, Judas betrayed his teacher to the Romans in exchange for thirty pieces of silver. He was thus responsible for Jesus's crucifixion, and in the Christian world this made him the embodiment of evil. Dante envisioned a special punishment for Judas: he spent eternity in the jaws of Lucifer, hell's master and (as Dante described him) a gigantic, dragon-like creature with three heads. This fearsome beast gnashed Judas's head to bits while flaying and shredding his victim's back with his claws.

The identity of Judas's two companions, however, might raise some eyebrows. Also in Lucifer's jaws were Marcus Brutus and Gaius Cassius, Caesar's murderers—antiquity's most famous tyrannicides. What were they doing next to Judas? They were killers, but so were others that Dante met on his descent into hell, and they did not incur such horrible punishment. This was all the more puzzling because the man killed by Brutus and Cassius was a pagan and a military man, who had ample blood on his own hands. Why suggest that his murder was on a par with Judas's betrayal of the savior of the world?[1]

From Dante's perspective, Brutus's and Cassius's fate was well deserved. He explained as much in *On Monarchy*, a learned political treatise he wrote while also working on the *Divine Comedy*.[2] Dante thought that by turning against Caesar, the founder of the Roman Empire, Brutus and Cassius had turned against God himself. To Dante, the establishment of the Roman Empire was divinely ordained, a fact demonstrated by Jesus's birth under its authority. Paradoxically, even the fact that Christ was crucified on the authority of a Roman emperor highlighted the God-given nature of the regime. After all, Christ had died to atone for man's sins. But, Dante argued, Jesus's death would not have been a true punishment if the crucifixion had not been legally valid—which implied that the authority demanding that act was legitimate in the eyes of God. By killing Caesar, Brutus and Cassius had killed one of God's most important instruments.

Dante did not rely only on sacred history to buttress this claim; "the light of human reason, no less than scripture, taught that Caesar's authority had been a boon for mankind.[3] While the ultimate goal of man was, of course, eternal beatitude, human beings also needed to achieve happiness in the here and now. For that they needed strong and unified leadership. Hence, Dante concluded, it was only under a monarchy that mankind could live "in its ideal state."[4] In murdering Caesar, the founder of what Dante considered the first true monarchy, Brutus and Cassius had endangered the well-being of all of humanity.

Judas Iscariot (middle), Marcus Brutus, and Gaius Cassius (right and left) in the pith of hell, being chewed by the mouths of Lucifer.

By placing Brutus and Cassius in the very pith of hell, Dante was making a clear political statement: monarchy was the only legitimate regime. Those who tried to subvert imperial authority were abominations who would meet their just punishment in the afterlife. (Incidentally, as Dante made clear in *On Monarchy*, this was true not just of tyrannicides but also of those who challenged secular authority on religious grounds. The pope's pretension to be above the emperor, Dante explained, was just as contrary to scripture and human reason as Brutus's and Cassius's attempt to subvert Caesar's rule.)

In making these claims, Dante drew on a long-established tradition in Western political thought. As we have seen, in the last centuries of the Roman Empire, monarchy had come to be embraced as the only acceptable political ideal, and this belief continued to echo throughout the medieval period. The legitimacy of one-man rule was supported by a wide range of arguments, some inspired by the Hellenistic kingship tradition and others by the Christian worldview. Dante used many of them in the *Divine Comedy* and *On Monarchy*.[5]

A century later, however, this fervent embrace of monarchy was weakening, as suggested by Leonardo Bruni's *A Dialogue Dedicated to Pier Paolo Vergerio*.[6] Like Dante, Bruni was a citizen of Florence, a self-governing city-state in the north of Italy. The *Dialogue*, from around 1400, was one of his earliest works, written when Bruni was about thirty. In this brief tract, Bruni evaluated how "modern" Italian writers, including Dante, compared with their ancient predecessors. He rebutted the charge that Dante was an ignorant man who had made many factual mistakes. But Bruni found it less easy to excuse Dante's treatment of Caesar's killers. Bruni was clearly dumbfounded by Dante's opinion of them. Marcus Brutus, in particular, was celebrated for his moral character, his sense of justice, and his magnanimity. Why place such a man in hell? Further, why consign him to the same level as Judas—the betrayer of God's very own son?

Even more importantly, Caesar was a heinous tyrant, and murdering him was not a crime. Rather, the act of Brutus and his associates was patriotic, an attempt at "reclaiming freedom" for the Roman people, "taking it from the robber's jaws." The only way Bruni could make sense of Dante's Brutus was by attributing the character to poetic license. "Painters and poets have always had the same ability to dare anything," Bruni concluded. Dante's Brutus—a "seditious, trouble-making criminal"—was a literary "invention," with little or no relation to the historical Brutus, who had been "the best and justest man, the recoverer of liberty."[7]

Dante's and Bruni's views, in short, could not have been more different. How should we understand their disagreement? What prompted Bruni to take such a radically different view from Dante on Rome's tyrannicides and the value of freedom they symbolized? This is all the more puzzling because the two authors had a lot in common. Both were citizens of Florence, a self-governing city-state. They both came from a relatively modest background—Dante's family was comfortable but by no means rich; Bruni's father was a grain merchant. Finally, both made names for themselves as men of letters—Dante as a poet and philosopher; Bruni as a translator and prose writer.

To grasp how Dante and Bruni, for all their similarities, came to such different views, we need to consider the broader evolution—perhaps even revolution—that occurred in political thought during this time. While less than half a century had passed between Dante's death in 1321 and Bruni's birth in 1370, this period was characterized by one of the major cultural upheavals of the modern period: the Renaissance. The Renaissance changed Europe's culture and political thinking, sparking a long-lasting revival of the ancient cult of freedom. This revival began in Bruni's homeland—the city-states of northern Italy. Eventually it would affect the whole of Europe and its overseas colonies.

Ancient Freedom in Renaissance Italy: The Humanists

When historians talk about the Renaissance, they can mean two very different things. One meaning goes back to the work of the nineteenth-century Swiss historian Jacob Burckhardt, whose *Civilization of the Renaissance* was a foundational text. Burckhardt defined the Renaissance as the period in history when first Italy and then the rest of Europe became modern—a sea change linked to the discovery of the individual.

Medieval men had thought of themselves as members of social groups, families, or corporations that were defined by faith and tradition. By contrast, fourteenth- and fifteenth-century Italians saw men as distinct individuals, capable of fashioning themselves and their environments in any way they wanted. In Renaissance Italy, we first witness the "development of free personality"—as Burckhardt put it—that is characteristic of modernity.[8]

This conception of the Renaissance still has some currency today.[9] Most historians, however, now dismiss Burkhardt's view of the Renaissance as a myth.[10] In social and cultural terms, they point out, there was considerable continuity between the late medieval period and the period usually denominated as the Renaissance. Thus it seems highly unlikely that medieval Italians thought any less of themselves as individuals than their fourteenth- and fifteenth-century descendants. More important, to the extent that Renaissance men and women thought and acted differently, it was not because they had suddenly become "modern." Rather, they had become interested in reviving certain aspects of the Greco-Roman heritage. The Renaissance, in short, should not be seen as the beginning of modernity but as a centuries-long campaign to recreate (parts of) the long-lost world of the ancients—a renaissance of antiquity.

In what follows, the term *Renaissance* is used in the second, more literal sense of the term. In other words, when attributing a central role to the Renaissance in the history of freedom, I do not mean to suggest that fourteenth- and fifteenth-century Europeans suddenly broke the chains of faith and tradition that had shackled their medieval predecessors. Instead, Renaissance thinkers, spurred by a newfound passion for antiquity, rediscovered and came to admire a political tradition very different from the one they had inherited from late antiquity and the medieval period—a tradition that celebrated freedom, not obedience to kings and princes, as the most important political value.[11]

A key role in this process was played by a small but influential group of scholars, the so-called humanists.[12] Humanists were convinced that the culture of the ancient world was both very different from and far superior to their own. They embarked upon an ambitious campaign to revive the study of the classics. They hunted for copies of ancient writings that had been lost, editing and disseminating them—an effort that was helped by the invention of a revolutionary new means of communication, the printing press—and they ensured that the study of these texts became the centerpiece of a new kind of "humanist" education.

Of course, medieval civilization had also depended heavily on its inheritance from antiquity. This is amply illustrated by the fact that throughout the Middle Ages, Latin was used almost exclusively for all serious thought. Moreover, classical authorities such as Augustine and—from the twelfth century onward—Aristotle continued to exercise a profound influence on medieval thought and schooling, while classical literary texts were read and admired throughout the Middle Ages. Dante, for instance, venerated the Roman poet Virgil, modeling many passages of the *Divine Comedy* on Virgil's masterpiece, the *Aeneid*. Even more strikingly, Virgil was a major character in the *Divine Comedy,* acting as Dante's guide through hell and up the mountain of purgatory. (Pagan Virgil obviously could not guide Dante into heaven.)

The humanists' attitude toward the classical past, however, differed fundamentally from that of their medieval predecessors, whose appreciation of classical authorities was essentially ahistorical. Medieval thinkers believed the works of ancient writers contained timeless wisdoms that could be extracted and appropriated effortlessly. One of the reasons for Dante's particular devotion to Virgil, for instance, was that he believed, like many of his contemporaries, that Virgil had foretold the birth of Christ. By contrast, humanists believed that their own age was distinct from that of antiquity. They venerated the ancients precisely because their wisdom was different from that of their own time. Learning from the classics, therefore, entailed the painstaking and difficult labor of reconstructing a lost world in all its historical particularity.[13]

The humanist movement was sparked, to a large extent, by the enthusiasm of one man: the Italian poet and scholar Francesco Petrarch.[14] A younger contemporary of Dante's—Petrarch's father had been Dante's friend and compatriot before both were exiled from Florence—Petrarch seems to have been born with a passion for ancient writers and ancient history. Even as a young boy, he idolized the authors of the so-called golden age of Latin literature, from the late republic to the early empire, during which the Latin language was perfected as a literary medium. Petrarch was particularly fond of Cicero, admiring him both for his superior style and his moral outlook. Petrarch extolled the "radiance" of antiquity, calling his own age an era of darkness, characterized by an inferior culture and the lack of great personalities that had proliferated in the ancient world.[15]

His main goal became to rouse his contemporaries from their "sleep of forgetfulness" (as he put it in his great Latin poem *Africa*) by reviving interest in the classics.[16] During his travels through Europe, Petrarch began collecting crumbling Latin manuscripts, in the process discovering long-forgotten copies of classical texts such as Cicero's personal letters. Petrarch also busied himself with the less glamorous, but perhaps more important, work of correcting copies that had been rendered unintelligible by bad transcriptions. Petrarch put together different "decades," or chapters, from Livy's *History of Rome,* which had survived in different manuscripts, making the text accessible again to a broader audience. But Petrarch's engagement with antiquity was not just scholarly. He tried to imitate and emulate his classical models as well. Thus he wrote letters modeled on Cicero's. Another work, the epic *Africa,* told the story of Roman military hero Scipio Africanus, Hannibal's nemesis.

Petrarch's enthusiasm proved infectious. Soon, hunting for dormant manuscripts in Europe's musty monastic libraries became a favorite pastime of educated Italians. Here were books that had not been opened for centuries, containing texts that had all but disappeared from the collective memory. Among them were histories by Herodotus, Tacitus, and Plutarch, all of which, as we have seen, played a key role in the development of the idea of freedom. In addition, Petrarch's disciples began modeling their own literary output on classical models. Collucio Salutati, one of Petrarch's most famous and influential followers, was known as "Cicero's ape" for his uncanny ability to mimic Cicero's style—and this was meant as a compliment, not a rebuke.[17]

But the rediscovery of antiquity influenced not only the humanists' literary style; it also had a substantial impact on their political imagination.

Petrarch and his heirs saw that these ancient writers valued freedom—the ability to set one's own goals and agenda—above all other political principles. They came to realize that, for these ancient writers, a free way of life could be enjoyed only under a popular government, or a republic, as was the case in Athens or Rome, where people ruled themselves rather than being under the sway of a king or prince.[18]

In the wake of these discoveries, a number of humanists, first and foremost in Italy, adopted this way of thinking as their own. They wrote treatises extolling the virtues of living in liberty and bemoaned its absence in their own world, as their predecessors Livy and Tacitus had. The most radical among them even argued that to end the "slavery" to which they and their contemporaries were subjected, the republics of antiquity needed to be recreated in the modern world. They came up with detailed manuals on how to do this, based on their examination of Athenian, Roman, and other ancient governments, and they reflected on the socio-economic and cultural conditions that enabled popular self-government in the ancient world.

This is not to say that all humanists turned into freedom fighters. In the courts of Renaissance princes, many humanists used their new knowledge to support their master's rule by comparing him, for instance, with Augustus or Plato's philosopher-king.[19] Reading ancient texts, in other words, did not automatically turn one into a defender of Athenian- or Roman-style popular government. But quite a number of humanists did embrace liberty as the key political value. Between 1330, when Petrarch embarked on his campaign to wake his contemporaries from their "sleep of forgetfulness," and the 1550s, when northern Italy came under the thumb of the Spanish monarchy, Italian humanists produced a stream of texts glorifying ancient liberty and the ancient freedom fighters.

Petrarch himself is a case in point.[20] He used his deep knowledge of the classics to support the movement of Cola di Rienzo, a charismatic popular leader, who, in 1347, overthrew baronial and papal authority in Rome. Petrarch, who had met Cola di Rienzo a few years earlier, became an immediate and ardent advocate of the revolutionary regime. In a series of public letters addressed to the people of Rome, Petrarch described Cola as the "third Brutus," a new liberator of the Romans. "Without liberty life is a mockery," Petrarch told his readers. "Keep your past servitude constantly before your eyes. . . . In this way, if at any time it should become necessary to part with one or the other, there will be no one who will not prefer to die a freeman rather than to live a slave."[21]

Cola was eventually defeated by the barons, but Petrarch continued to support Roman freedom. In 1351, the pope created a commission to replace the unpopular baronial rule and give the Romans a new form of government. The commissioners turned to Petrarch for advice, and he rose to the occasion, sending two long letters to persuade them to exclude the barons from office and restore Rome's popular republic. With extensive references to Livy's account of Rome's early history, Petrarch argued that non-noble Romans should be given access to office, just as the plebeians in ancient Rome had. "Christ orders you to reestablish [Rome's] freedom," he concluded dramatically. The commissioners ignored him, but Petrarch's case would go on to inspire later thinkers.[22]

An even more important contribution to the revival of ancient freedom was made by Florentine humanists such as Leonardo Bruni.[23] Florence was one of the wealthiest and most powerful cities in northern Italy, and Petrarch's most influential disciples lived and worked there. In addition, Florence's peculiar political situation made its humanists especially receptive to the freedom-centric message of ancient thinkers. Around 1400, when the humanist movement began to hold sway among Italy's educated elites, Florence was one of the few self-governing republics left in Italy. It was by no means a democracy, as a handful of elite families exercised a disproportionate influence over appointments to the priorate (the chief executive body), but they never achieved full control of the political process. There was ample room for contestation by ordinary Florentines, especially over contentious matters like wars and taxes. Indeed, through the early decades of the fifteenth century, Florentine oligarchs frequently complained about the excessively democratic nature of the regime.[24]

At the same time, however, Florentine self-government was increasingly under threat. External foes, such as the papacy and neighboring Milan, threatened to end its independence. More important, Florence's communal government was endangered by internal developments, notably the growing power of the ultrarich Medici family. Cosimo de' Medici and his successors tolerated the machinery for communal self-government, but they wielded an enormous amount of informal power. They slowly turned the Florentine state from a relatively broad-based communal government into an autocracy. Cosimo was described by contemporaries as "king in all but name."[25] The trend toward autocracy was punctuated by intermittent attempts to curb the Medicis' power and restore more democratic government. But these attempts failed, and in 1532 Alessandro de' Medici became the hereditary duke of Florence, definitively ending the republic.

The political situation in fifteenth- and early sixteenth-century Florence resembled, in some crucial aspects, that of the late Roman Republic and the early empire. It is hardly surprising that a number of Florentine humanists began to echo, with increasing insistence, the claims of writers like Cicero, Livy, Plutarch, and Tacitus.[26] In 1479, Alamanno Rinuccini wrote *On Freedom*—the first treatise to appear under this title in the post-classical world and a powerful indictment of Medici rule. He described Lorenzo de' Medici as the "Florentine Phalaris"—a reference to the Sicilian tyrant from the sixth century BC, famous for roasting his enemies alive and eating infants. But Rinuccini also made clear that the Florentines' loss of freedom was caused not only by bad leadership; it also resulted from profound institutional changes. A people simply could not be free, Rinuccini emphasized, unless it governed itself and kept everything "under its own control."[27]

In making these claims, Rinuccini drew, in part, on his personal experiences. The scion of a wealthy Florentine family, he had played a prominent political role in his hometown for much of his adult life, until he got on the bad side of Lorenzo de' Medici. But Rinuccini's arguments were also inspired by his reading of ancient authors. He buttressed his claims with extensive quotes from Cicero, Demosthenes, and Aristotle and extolled ancient Athens, Sparta, and Rome as models of free government. Even the format he adopted was classicizing. Like antique philosophical texts, such as those by Plato and Cicero, *On Liberty* was written as a dialogue between *Eleutherius* ("the Lover of Liberty") and two companions, *Alitheus* ("the Truthful") and *Microtoxus* ("the Straight-Shooter").

Niccolò Machiavelli, a younger contemporary of Rinuccini's, was even more dejected by Florence's loss of liberty.[28] Today, Machiavelli's name more readily evokes wily authoritarianism than a devotion to freedom. This reputation rests on the *Prince,* a slim booklet containing Machiavelli's groundbreaking advice on how to take and keep power. But he had another side, as well, shown in his *Discourses on the First Ten Books of Livy.* In this larger and more substantial work, Machiavelli bemoaned, much like Rinuccini, the "slavery" that Florentines, and indeed all "modern" peoples, were subjected to.

Like Rinuccini's, Machiavelli's interest in ancient freedom was sparked by both his humanist education and his personal experiences.[29] Though raised in a family of relatively modest means, Machiavelli had received a good classical education. His father owned Livy's massive work on Rome's early history, and he nurtured his son on stories of daring Roman heroes fighting rapacious kings and patricians to preserve or enlarge their freedom and that of their fellow citizens.

Machiavelli's exposure to autocratic rule must have reinforced these lessons. He came of age during a charmed moment in Florence's history: when he was in his early twenties, the Medici were expelled in the wake of military disaster, and communal government was restored. Machiavelli did well under this regime, holding important posts in the Florentine Republic and essentially acting as its ambassador. But in 1512, when he was in his early forties, a military coup overthrew the popular government and installed Cardinal Giovanni de' Medici as the city's new ruler. The cardinal immediately fired Machiavelli from his post.

But worse was to follow a few months later, when a conspiracy to assassinate the cardinal and restore popular government was discovered. The conspiracy had gone nowhere—just two people were involved—but they had made the mistake of writing down twenty names that they thought were sympathetic to their cause. The cardinal acted decisively and had everyone on the list, in addition to the instigators, arrested. This included Machiavelli, who was imprisoned and tortured "with the rope"—a treatment that entailed being hoisted up by a rope attached to a pulley that hung from the ceiling and then dropped suddenly, stopping just short of the floor. Despite the intense pain he must have suf-

fered—the torture typically left its victims with dislocated shoulders—
Machiavelli denied involvement, and after twenty-two days, he was
released due to lack of evidence.

Machiavelli wrote his *Discourses* shortly afterward. In his view, not
just Florence but the entire world had become the easily dominated plaything of wicked men. In this regard, modern peoples compared unfavorably
to the ancients. "All peoples of ancient times," Machiavelli pointed out,
"were greater lovers of liberty than those of our own day." He attributed
the difference to long-term changes—including the rise of Christianity—
that undermined the "ferocity" necessary to fight for freedom against
would-be tyrants.[30]

Yet Machiavelli—unlike Rinuccini—was not content with simply di-
agnosing the problem. Freedom could be restored by reaching back to
the political models of antiquity. Machiavelli wanted his *Discourses,* as
he explained in the preface, to rekindle enthusiasm for ancient political
models. In the same way that others had propagated the imitation of the
ancients in sculpture or in medicine, Machiavelli wanted to encourage
emulation of their political art. For Machiavelli, the main model was
Rome. More even than Athens, Sparta, and Carthage, republican Rome
epitomized a successful free government. It had maintained its liberty
for half a millennium, while conquering the whole of Italy and large
swathes of the rest of the world. If one wanted to live freely, one could
do no better than to imitate the Romans. In investigating the secrets of
Rome's success, Machiavelli turned primarily to Livy, the main authority
on early Roman history.

So what lessons did Livy and other Roman authors offer? Machiavelli's answer attributed a key role to the popular institutions created in the
wake of the Conflict of the Orders. Throughout Rome's early history, he
explained, the plebeians had successfully transformed the Roman constitution so that it protected them from the domination of kings and patricians. This was not to say that Rome had ever been a pure democracy;
its constitution had always retained monarchical and aristocratic elements
along with its popular, democratic institutions. Nevertheless, Rome had
eventually become "a government of the people," and Machiavelli left no
doubt that this was why it was a free state.[31]

Machiavelli did not limit his analysis to Rome's institutional frame-work. He also devoted considerable attention to the social and cultural characteristics that had allowed Rome to flourish in freedom. He praised the Romans' religiosity, which had instilled in them a respect for the law and their leaders, which prevented their freedom from turning anarchical. Equally important, Roman citizens did not hire mercenaries but always bore arms themselves. This meant they never became dependent on war-lords for their protection, thus staving off the danger of foreign domina-tion. Last but not least, Romans had also maintained socioeconomic equality by keeping "the public treasury rich but their citizens poor." This, too, had been instrumental for the preservation of freedom, because extreme differences in wealth created civic strife, which ultimately led people to turn to authoritarian government. "Where no equality exists," Machiavelli warned, "a republic cannot be created."[32]

With his analysis of the Roman model, Machiavelli made a highly orig-inal contribution to the history of freedom. The most vocal defenders of freedom in the ancient world had been historians rather than students of politics per se; they had narrated the histories of their polities and cele-brated individual freedom fighters. Machiavelli's approach was more an-alytic: he investigated how institutions, customs, beliefs, and social con-ditions helped maintain freedom. He drew on ancient examples but saw them as models, offering principles of liberty that could be implemented in his own time. As we shall see, his precepts would have considerable impact on subsequent thinking about the institutionalization of freedom.

Ancient Freedom in Renaissance Italy: Beyond the Humanists

The humanist movement initiated by Petrarch was the project of a small group of scholars; men (and some women) who predominantly wrote in Latin, the language of the learned, and whose interests typically ran to the highbrow and esoteric. If it had continued like this, humanism's im-pact on Italian and European political culture might have been fairly limited. But instead, in the decades after Petrarch's death, the new pas-sion for antiquity spread beyond the rarified circle of his disciples—with very visible results. New buildings, for instance, began to dot the Italian landscape—buildings that had more in common with the temples of

classical antiquity than with the Gothic style of the thirteenth and
fourteenth centuries. But the Renaissance's effects were noticeable in
less tangible ways as well. Clerics in the courts of humanist popes such
as Julius II and Leo X began to refer to God as Jupiter Optimus Maximus, to call churches "temples," and to introduce classical forms into
the Catholic liturgy.[33]

Why did the passion for antiquity catch on? How did humanism
become a major cultural movement and not just a pastime of a few
learned individuals? These questions are difficult to answer; however,
historians agree social changes helped foster an obsession with all
things ancient.[34] During the twelfth and thirteenth centuries, northern
Italy had become the most urbanized and wealthiest region of Europe.
Italian society was not dominated by nobles and clerics as were the
lands north of the Alps. Instead, the tone of society was set by the
cities and their merchant elites. The most important educated groups
were the lawyers and notaries who drew up the contracts that made
trade possible. These men sought examples to model their lives upon
and readily found them among the secular elites of ancient Greek
and Rome.

If social changes can help us understand why the humanist project
caught on, changes in communication techniques can explain how it became entrenched, first in Italy and later in the rest of Europe.[35] The arrival of printing disseminated ancient texts and knowledge far beyond the
narrow circle of humanist scholars. Although the invention of movable
type originated in Germany, German printers versed in the new techniques were quick to move to the more populous cities of northern Italy,
where they started printing the antique manuscripts that humanist
scholars had collected. Many print editions catered to traditional tastes;
for example, Quintus Curtius Rufus's romanticized biography of Alexander the Great, which had been all the rage in the Middle Ages, was reprinted several times. But the newly rediscovered works of Herodotus,
Livy, Tacitus, and Plutarch were also on the bestseller lists.[36]

Educational reforms also played an important role in perpetuating the
humanist passion for antiquity. In late medieval Italy, secondary education focused on arithmetic and Latin grammar. Humanist pedagogues
revolutionized the curriculum, especially from the fifteenth century

onward. They focused on the study of original classical texts for their superior eloquence and because they believed these texts would instill a higher moral outlook in students. In actual practice, of course, humanist schools often fell short of the pedagogues' exalted ideals. Many students never advanced beyond the slow and tedious reading of a tiny number of books. Nevertheless, the new curriculum instilled some knowledge of and reverence for ancient texts and ancient history, thus engraining humanist attitudes in generations of students.[37]

As a result of these developments, the newly ardent attachment to freedom quickly spread beyond the small circle of humanist scholars. Renaissance visual artists translated the humanists' message into images that reached a much broader audience than that of Latin texts. Italian painters and sculptors—in particular, those who worked for the few surviving republics such as Florence (during its intermittent republican phases) and Siena—decorated their cities with frescoes, statues, and paintings that glorified the ancient republics and their love of liberty. Roman history was a particularly popular subject.[38]

One of the earliest examples of such "republican" art can be found in Siena, a city about forty miles south of Florence that was ruled by a broad-based oligarchy. In 1413, Siena's leaders commissioned Taddeo di Bartolo, a local artist, to paint a fresco cycle in the antechapel of the Palazzo Pubblico, the seat of the communal government.[39] Completed the following year, the frescos glorified Roman republican heroes and the freedom they defended. The individuals portrayed ranged from those of the early republic to those in the period of its demise—from Lucius Junius Brutus to Cato and the second Brutus. The Roman heroes are introduced by Aristotle, depicted on the arch connecting the antechapel to the Sala del Consiglio. He holds a scroll making it clear that the depicted Roman heroes are presented as exemplary freedom fighters: "As civic examples," reads the scroll, "I show you these men; if you follow in their sacred footsteps your fame will grow at home and abroad, and liberty will always preserve your honor."[40] On the wall opposite Aristotle are Caesar and Pompey, two of the gravediggers of the republic. As the inscription accompanying these two figures explained, they served as negative illustrations of the consequences of the "blind ambition" that

Taddeo di Bartolo, *Allegories and Figures from Roman History* (1413–1414).

plunged the republic into a civil war and eventually caused "Roman liberty" to "perish."[41]

The message of the frescoes was in line with that of humanists like Bruni, Rinuccini, and Machiavelli—indeed, it was probably directly inspired by Bruni's pioneering work on Rome's history.[42] Similar messages can be found in other works of art from this period. Sandro Botticelli's set of oil paintings, created around 1500—the *Tragedy of Lucretia* and the *Story of Virginia*—depicted antimonarchical episodes from Livy's *History of Rome*. A few decades later, the Renaissance's most famous artist, Michelangelo Buonarotti, was asked by his friend Donato Giannotti, a staunch opponent of the Medicis, to sculpt a bust of Marcus Brutus. Although Michelangelo never finished the work, his *Brutus* is a heroic, resolute, and defiant figure that has been described as "one of the most stirring images of the republican hero in the history of Western art."[43]

Ironically, after Michelangelo's death, the Medicis acquired the bust. They added a Latin epigram beneath it, reading "While the sculptor shaped this effigy from the marble he called to mind [Brutus's] crime

Michelangelo, Brutus bust (1540–1542).

and ceased," thus reinterpreting the work as an advertisement against tyrannicide rather than a glorification of it.[44] The true reason the bust remained unfinished is probably more prosaic. In the years following Giannotti's commission, Michelangelo was frequently ill. He was also given various other and more lucrative commissions that distracted him from working on the Brutus bust.

The revival of the ancient cult of freedom was not just a literary and artistic affair; it also inspired real-life imitators. In Florence in particular, a veritable Brutus cult grew up among the more excitable of the humanists' pupils. Throughout the fifteenth and sixteenth centuries, quite a few of these "Tuscan Brutuses" attempted to end Medici rule by killing the dynasty's reigning scion. These efforts usually had results as minimal as did the original Brutus, but that did not seem to dampen the enthusiasm for tyrannicide held by the Medici opponents.[45]

In 1478, a group of disgruntled Florentines led by members of the Pazzi family hatched a plot to dislodge the Medici government, attacking Lorenzo and Giuliano de' Medici during High Mass at a crowded duomo. In full view of the congregation, they stabbed Giuliano nineteen times, killing him. Lorenzo—the head of the Medici family—was severely wounded, but he survived and quashed the rebellion. The perpetrators of the Pazzi conspiracy were hunted down and hanged.

The conspirators' motives were varied, but disgruntlement at the increasingly authoritarian Medici regime was certainly one of them. Immediately after the attack, one accomplice attempted to rally the crowd to his side with cries of "*popolo e libertà*."[46] Unsurprisingly, the conspirators were quickly likened to ancient tyrannicides like Brutus and Cassius. A year after the attack, Rinuccini lauded the attempted murder of Lorenzo as a "glorious deed, an action worthy of the highest praise" in *On Liberty*. In his view, the Pazzis had tried "to restore their own liberty and that of their country," therefore their actions were as laudable as those of the famous ancient tyrannicides.[47]

The Pazzis were the first of many Brutus imitators. In 1513, Pietro Paolo Boscoli and Agostino Capponi attempted a plot against Guiliano, Giovanni, and Giulio de' Medici. The conspirators, however, were betrayed and condemned to death. The night before his execution, Boscoli reportedly confessed to the historian Luca della Robia that his actions had been inspired by the Brutus myth. "Ah! Luca," Boscoli is supposed to have exclaimed, "pluck Brutus from my mind, that I may pass from this world a perfect Christian."[48]

But the most famous of the tyrannicides was undoubtedly Lorenzino de' Medici. In 1537, Lorenzino, the black sheep of the Medici family (he was also known as Lorenzaccio or the "bad Lorenzo") stabbed and killed his kinsman Alessandro de' Medici, the ruler of Florence. It is still unclear what motivated Lorenzino, who by all accounts had been close to Alessandro—indeed, they often showed up in public mounted on the same horse. However, the friendship was perhaps less genuine than it appeared: Alessandro had sided against

A coin issued by Lorenzino de' Medici to celebrate his assassination of
Alessandro de' Medici (1537).

Lorenzino in a legal dispute about an inheritance, which might have
given Lorenzino cause for resentment.

Whatever may have driven him, Lorenzino was quick to depict himself as a freedom fighter in the mold of Brutus and Cassius rather than
as a common murderer. He wrote a public defense of his actions—the
Apologia—in which he compared Alessandro to Nero and Caligula and
himself to Timoleon, a Greek tyrannicide who had killed his own
brother. "If I had to justify my actions," the *Apologia* began, "I should
use all my powers to demonstrate, to give reasons (and there are many)
why men should desire nothing beyond the civic life, that is to say, liberty."[49] Lorenzino also issued a coin to celebrate his deed, an almost
exact replica of the coin issued by Marcus Brutus in the wake of his assassination of Caesar. Like the original Brutus coin, Lorenzino's prominently featured the Roman cap of liberty between two daggers, with a
portrait of Lorenzino in Roman dress on the reverse.

Lorenzino's *Apologia*, however, was one of the last important contributions to the revival of ancient liberty in the Italian context. Between
1494 and 1559, Italy became a near-permanent battleground as French and
Habsburg armies, supported by mercenaries from all over Europe, fought
to control the northern half of the peninsula. The wars caused enormous
physical damage and brought normal life more or less to a halt. In 1559,

France and Habsburg Spain signed a peace treaty that ended the sixty-year struggle. Habsburg Spain now controlled most of the principalities of northern Italy, with only the Papal States and the Republic of Venice remaining independent polities. The Habsburg victory brought peace and stability, reviving Italy's population and economy, but Habsburg dominance left little room for anything but unconditional acceptance of monarchical rule.[50]

As a result, the cult of freedom that had been so vibrant in fifteenth-century Italy slowly faded away.[51] A symbolic ending came in 1559, when the Habsburg emperor Charles V, supported by his Medici allies, finally defeated a group of Florentine and Sienese exiles who had barricaded themselves in the town of Montalcino. Fighting under a banner reading "LIBERTAS," they made a last-ditch attempt to resist the inevitable. As earlier generations of freedom fighters had done, the exiles (or their biographers) emphasized that their struggle for freedom was inspired by classical examples: their leader, Piero Strozzi, supposedly tried to relax himself on the eve of battle by translating Latin classics into Greek. For the surrender, they dressed in mourning.[52]

After Montalcino, there was much less talk of freedom in Italy. Of course, Italians still read ancient authors like Livy, Tacitus, and Plutarch. But sixteenth- and seventeenth-century Italians read these texts in new ways. Claudio Monteverdi's opera, the *Coronation of Poppea*, is a case in point.[53] The opera, which premiered in Venice in 1643, was the first to treat a historical rather than mythological theme. The libretto, written by the Venetian poet Giovanni Busenello, borrowed from various ancient sources on Nero's rule, including Tacitus's *Annals* and Suetonius's *Twelve Caesars*. These sources described how Nero became enamored with the villainous and scheming Poppea. Set on becoming Nero's empress, she encouraged him to divorce and banish his blameless wife Octavia. Eventually, on Nero's orders, Octavia was murdered.

Busenello took many artistic liberties with his sources; for instance, compressing events that Tacitus had described as taking place over years into one day. But above all, Busenello changed the story's moral. In Tacitus's account, Octavia's banishment and Nero's marriage to Poppea were evidence of the corrupting effects of absolute power. But

Busenello's libretto had a completely different message: that love has more influence on mankind than either virtue or fortune. The opera ends with the entirely un-Tacitean message that love conquers all. As Nero and Poppea finally get married, they celebrate their love in a duet: "I adore you, I embrace you, I enchain you, no more grieving, no more sorrow, o my dearest, o my beloved / I am yours. . . . O my love, tell me so, you are mine, mine alone. / O my beloved, o my dearest."[54]

Even in Venice, the last surviving republic, there was a growing emphasis on order and stability after 1559 rather than on freedom.[55] Yet, Montalcino by no means signaled the end of freedom's revival in Europe, more broadly speaking. While Italian enthusiasm for ancient liberty was muzzled by war weariness and Habsburg dominance, Europeans on the other side of the Alps began talking about their desire to "live a free life" like the ancient Greeks and Romans. While this happened a good deal later than in Italy, this revival proved much more durable.

The Revival of Ancient Freedom Across the Alps

As in Italy, the revival of freedom across the Alps was first and foremost a product of the Renaissance. In France, Poland, the Netherlands, England, and other European countries, the new humanist knowledge of antiquity sparked an interest in ancient ideals of freedom—as well as a growing sense that the modern world was worse off for lack of them. And again, like in Italy, the more radical among the northern humanists took these complaints about the "slavery" to which modern Europeans were subjected to a revolutionary conclusion. As Machiavelli had done, they propagated a return to the republics of antiquity—also described as "popular governments," "commonwealths," "mixed governments," or, more seldom, "democracies"—as the only way to free their contemporaries.[56]

Humanist knowledge was transmitted in many ways from Italy to northern Europe.[57] Personal contacts established by traveling scholars and soldiers played an important role, as did the frequent invasions of Italy, which brought looted Italian art and books as well as Italian humanists and artists across the Alps. By the early 1500s, an indigenous humanist movement began to take shape in northern Europe. The likes of Desiderius Erasmus, Johann Reuchlin, Guillaume Budé, and Thomas More began to rival and even surpass their Italian predecessors in technical skill and linguistic abilities.

Print and pedagogy were important vectors in disseminating Renaissance ideas. In the sixteenth and seventeenth centuries, the new humanist curricula were introduced in secondary schools in several European countries. Scholars started translating the classical canon into the vernacular, making that heritage accessible to a far broader audience. By 1600, the overwhelming majority of ancient texts were available in at least one European language, and Gutenberg's invention put them into more hands than ever before. A guesstimate has put the number of copies of ancient history books (in both the original Latin or Greek and in translation) in circulation between 1450 and 1700 at 2.5 million. (By way of comparison, scholars estimate that about 5 million copies of the Bible were sold during the sixteenth century.)[58]

In northern Europe, humanist knowledge found a very different context from the Italian one. States like France and England bore much less resemblance to the ancient republics than did Italian cities like Florence.[59] These northern states were also far larger and more populous and were usually ruled by kings and queens. Unlike many Italian city-states, they had no history of popular self-government or even of oligarchic rule. That is not to say that the power of Europe's kings and queens was absolute. Many European kingdoms had consultative assemblies—variously known as parliaments, estates, *cortes*, or diets—that began to play an increasingly important political role in the late Middle Ages. Nevertheless, these parliaments and estates were subordinate to the king: their members were advisors, not co-rulers. What power they had also waxed and waned throughout the early modern period. The French Estates General, for instance, did not meet at all between 1484 and 1560.

In the Low Countries, Europe's most urbanized region apart from northern Italy, many towns had a proud history of self-government. But even these were not really comparable to the Italian city-states. Towns like Antwerp and Ghent—which had a good bit of autonomy—had always recognized the lordship of princes like the dukes of Burgundy or the Habsburg emperors. They did not think of themselves as independent political entities but as parts of a larger whole. Consider the conflicts that erupted in the Duchy of Brabant in the early fifteenth century. The duke, the towns, the barons, and the three estates (nobility, clergy, and commons) faced repeated standoffs during a period of weak ducal government between 1415 and 1430. It ended with the duke conceding that the estates could choose a new regent if he infringed on any of the rights or privileges of the estates or their members. However, none of these conflicts challenged the principle of kingship itself; on the contrary, in the rebellious cities, barons and estates always claimed that they acted in the prince's name.[60]

There were some exceptions. In the middle of Europe, tucked behind the Alps, Swiss peasants and cities had combined into a confederation, the Swiss Republic.[61] They were ruled by representatives from the thirteen cantons that made up the confederation, itself created by a series of treaties concluded among the cantons between 1291 and 1513. But the Swiss Republic was small and marginal, with a population of only 600,000 in 1500. It was also poor. Throughout the early modern period, mercenaries were the Swiss Republic's main export product. In the sixteenth and seventeenth centuries, large, powerful monarchies like France were the norm in Europe.

In these circumstances, the self-governing communities of the ancient Greeks and Romans must have seemed far more alien than they had in Italy. It is not surprising then that many European humanists ignored the political message of the ancient authors they so admired. Justus Lipsius, one of the most famous humanists of the sixteenth century, was fiercely devoted to bringing antiquity back to life. His motto was *"Moribus antiquis"* or "According to ancient habits." He prepared what became the standard editions of Tacitus's *Annals* and *Histories*. But Lipsius by no means shared Tacitus's abhorrence for political slavery. In his major political treatise, the *Six Books of Politics or Political Instruction,* Lipsius preached complete submission to the king's will, equating freedom with licentiousness and anarchy and marshaling his considerable knowledge about antiquity to strengthen his case for kingly rule. Lipsius repeatedly quoted Tacitus out of context to make it seem as if the latter was a staunch supporter of absolute monarchy rather than the reverse. Lipsius also wrote a book on the "Greatness that Was Rome," which depicted the Rome of the Caesars as the apex of human development.[62]

Still, the radical message of Italian humanists like Machiavelli—that popular government à l'ancienne could and should be revived if modern Europeans wanted to live in liberty—in due course came to be echoed on the other side of the Alps. Expression of these ideas was often muffled and oblique, not least because all European states practiced some form of censorship. But in moments of crisis, when the state's ability to control the circulation of ideas broke down, European humanists and their disciples often seized the occasion to express their love of ancient liberty.[63]

This happened first in France, where, in the final decades of the sixteenth century, monarchical authority was undermined by a prolonged succession crisis combined with a severe economic downturn and religious strife.[64] The crisis was sparked in 1559 by the untimely death of Henri II, when he was just forty, in a jousting tournament. His young son, Francis II, ascended to the throne and reigned for less than a year before he died and was succeeded, in turn, by his brothers Charles IX and Henri III, who each reigned for relatively short periods. The instability this created was exacerbated by a subsistence crisis: after a long period of economic growth, France was repeatedly struck from the 1520s onward by widespread famine, as the cold winters and wet summers of Europe's "Little Ice Age" made crops ripen late or rot early.

Added to this volatile mix were the religious tensions caused by the Reformation. In France, the Reformation had been an immediate success. In particular, Jean Calvin's *Institutes of the Christian Religion* quickly became the most forceful and successful exposition of the new, reformed religion. From Geneva, where he fled from France's anti-Protestant violence, Calvin sent out trained ministers to organize the burgeoning French Protestant population. These soon came to be called Huguenots, after the legendary ghost Huguet, or Hugon, who was said to haunt the vicinity of Tours at night. The Protestants, too, typically met under the cover of darkness, to escape scrutiny by the authorities.

By the 1560s, the number of Protestants in France had exploded: they made up an estimated 10 percent of the population. Conflicts over liturgy (the Huguenots were especially dismissive of Catholic doctrine of tran-substantiation; they accused the Catholics of worshiping a "god of dough") and religious iconography soon became violent. A particularly harrowing episode, the so-called Saint Bartholomew's Massacre, occurred in 1572, when Catholics in Paris and several other cities, provoked by fears of a Protestant uprising, murdered hundreds, perhaps thousands, of Hugue-nots. As terrified refugees streamed into the Calvinist stronghold of Ge-neva, the situation appeared even worse than it was, with some reporting about 50,000 dead. The Huguenots suspected that the massacres had been instigated by King Charles IX himself.

All of this led to an outpouring of political treatises and pamphlets. Many of these contained attacks—often of the scurrilous kind—on the person of the monarch. Charles IX and Henri III were vilified and ac-cused of the most heinous crimes, including sodomy and murder, as was their mother, Catherine de' Medici, who acted as a regent for her young sons. But some of the Huguenot writings contained a more systematic critique of the principle of kingly authority—a critique in the name of freedom, inspired by the humanist embrace of antiquity.

One of the earliest and most impassioned outcries against the political slavery under which the French lived came from a young nobleman named Étienne de La Boétie. Born into an up-and-coming aristocratic family, La Boétie had received an excellent humanist education under the tutelage of Niccolò Gaddi, the bishop of Sarlat (La Boétie's home-place) and a learned Italian scholar. From boyhood, La Boétie had de-voured classics of antiquity like Plutarch's *Lives*. Reading these texts in-spired him to try his hand at writing, and in the 1540s, still in his teens, he produced a short but powerful essay titled *On Voluntary Servitude*, in which he took stock of his age and the political conditions under which modern Europeans lived.[65]

La Boétie intended his essay for private circulation; he sent copies of the manuscript to friends and colleagues but never tried to publish it. Then shortly after his death, his essay came into the hands of the French Huguenots. Through their efforts, the text was published in 1574 under the title *Contr' Un*, or *"Against One,"* gaining a much broader audience and, to the horror of La Boétie's good friend Michel de Montaigne, be-coming part of the Huguenot assault on royal authority—even though La

Boétie himself seems to have been a staunch Catholic. It would continue to be reprinted until well into the nineteenth century.[66]

It is not hard to see why La Boétie's essay appealed to Charles IX's Huguenot opponents. Just like Rinuccini's *On Liberty*, *On Voluntary Servitude* is a powerful indictment of one-man rule as a form of slavery. La Boétie began by quoting a line from Homer's *Iliad* in praise of monarchy: "I don't see any good in having several lords; let no more than one be master, and let only one be king," Homer had written. This view, La Boétie thought, was "completely contrary to reason." It was always an "extreme misfortune" to be subject to a master. When one man had power over all others, his subjects could never be sure that he would be a good or mild ruler. Life under a king was so precarious that personal security was impossible to preserve. From this perspective, the political condition of sixteenth-century France was bleak. The vast majority of La Boétie's contemporaries lived under kingly rule and, hence, were no better off than "slaves."[67]

La Boétie lamented that his contemporaries compared unfavorably to ancient peoples for whom liberty was the highest good. The Greeks had proved as much in their valiant battles against the Persians. Taking his cue from Herodotus, La Boétie emphasized that the Greco-Persian wars had not been between two enemy nations but between freedom and domination. Anecdotes like the altercation between the Spartan envoys Sperthias and Bulis and the Persian satrap Hydarnes—a story La Boétie recalled with "pleasure"—made that clear.[68] La Boétie also extolled the tyrant slayers of antiquity: Harmodius and Aristogeiton, who had slain Hippias; Lucius Junius Brutus, the founder of the Roman Republic; and Cato of Utica, who even in his youth had stood up to the dictator Sulla.

La Boétie, it should be noted, ended his essay on a pessimistic note. He was doubtful that the political situation in France would ever change, given the immense power of custom. Dynasties were typically founded by clever men who took advantage of the gullibility of ordinary people to elevate themselves. Initially their subjects might chafe at the yoke, but with time they ceased to feel the weight of their shackles. Tyrants also recruited the upper classes to their cause with favors and kickbacks, and elites tended to support kings to further their own interests and enrich themselves (which was stupid, La Boétie commented, because a tyrant's subjects could never really call their property their own). La Boétie, therefore, counseled resignation, not revolution, as he thought it unlikely the situation would change.[69]

Other French humanists, however, were less easily reconciled to the status quo, as illustrated by François Hotman's *Francogallia.*[70] The scion of an old family of lawyers, Hotman was appointed professor of Roman law at the Sorbonne in 1546. He published extensively on early French legal and constitutional history and soon made a name for himself as a humanist scholar. His life changed dramatically, however, in the wake of the Saint Bartholomew's Massacre of 1572. A Protestant convert, Hotman fled with his family to Geneva, where, like many other Huguenots, he started questioning the principle of one-man rule. Unlike La Boétie, Hotman did not simply mourn the lost liberty of the French. Instead, in *Francogallia,* he used his vast humanist erudition to sketch a political model for the French that would liberate them, much as Machiavelli had done for the Florentines in his *Discourses* about half a century earlier.

Francogallia repeatedly extolled the government of the ancient Greeks and Romans. The Romans, Hotman explained, had had a "mixed government," meaning that they reserved "the highest authority" neither for the king nor his senate but for the people themselves and their assemblies.[71] This political system had made the Romans a free people. But there was no such freedom in France. Indeed, Hotman compared the French to the Turks, who were ruled "by the will and pleasure of a single king." To be ruled this way was degrading, dehumanizing: the subjects of a single ruler were treated like "cattle and beasts, as Aristotle rightly observes in his *Politics.*"[72]

Unlike Machiavelli, however, Hotman did not recommend that the French adopt the Roman model to escape their predicament. Instead, he said they should restore the ancient constitution of Francogallia— that is, France as it had been under the Merovingian kings—which the growth of royal power had subverted. Hotman's understanding of what this "ancient constitution" entailed was clearly informed by his knowledge of the ancient republics. Like the Romans, Francogallia had a "mixed government" in which the supreme authority was not the king but was, rather, "the formal public council of the nation," in which the king, the people, and aristocratic elements were represented.[73] In fact, according to Hotman, originally the French kings had been elected—just as the Roman consuls had been. Hotman's message was clear: if the French wanted to be free, they needed to reject monarchy and revert to the mixed constitution of their ancestors, which was much like that of the Roman Republic.

As La Boétie and Hotman illustrate, the breakdown of political order in France in the final decades of the sixteenth century led to a radical attack on monarchy as a form of slavery. But the crisis of the French monarchy was relatively short-lived. In 1589, the accession of the Bourbon prince Henri IV restored political order and monarchical authority. Raised as a Protestant, Henri succeeded in reconciling the two warring factions by converting to Catholicism while imposing a degree of toleration of Protestants with the Edict of Nantes in 1598. While royal authority was again challenged in 1648, when France descended into civil war, this did not lead to a renewed criticism of the monarchy as an institution, possibly because the conflict now lacked a religious dimension. After the accession of Louis XIV, the monarchical order grew ever stronger. Influential French thinkers like Jacques-Bénigne Bossuet, the bishop of Meaux, argued with renewed emphasis, as their antique and medieval predecessors had, that political obedience was the will of God.[74]

In other European countries, however, humanists also began to talk about freedom. In the Polish-Lithuanian monarchy, a succession crisis combined with religious disagreements led to the introduction of an elective monarchy in 1572. Under the new constitution, the Polish king was to be elected for life by an assembly of all nobles, who made up about 6 to 8 percent of the population and held the final say over all important decisions, such as the right to wage war. In addition, the king was to be assisted by a council of self-styled "senators" drawn from the high nobility, who held their posts for life.[75]

Polish humanists were quick to compare their new regime—the Republic of the Two Nations, as it came to be called—to the Roman

Republic. Apart from Venice, they argued, the Polish-Lithuanian state was the sole *respublica libera*, or "free republic," in Europe. Unlike other Europeans, Poles were not ruled by a single ruler; they governed themselves, just like the ancient Romans. But their newfound freedom did not make the Poles complacent. Throughout the seventeenth and eighteenth centuries, they continued to worry about possible encroachments of royal power on Polish freedom. In the view of many Poles, kings— even elected ones—were ever ready to turn despotic; eternal vigilance was required to keep their ambitions in check. Freedom became the key word in Polish political culture until the demise of the independent Polish-Lithuanian state in the 1790s.[76]

Something similar happened in the Netherlands. In the 1570s, several provinces in the Low Countries rebelled against the Spanish-Habsburg king, Philip II.[77] Opposition to Philip's reign was provoked by increasing taxation and by anger at the policy of harsh repression of Protestants. In 1567, Philip II sent his crack general, the Duke of Alva, to the Netherlands to restore order and bring the population back into the Catholic fold. The "Iron Duke," as Alva soon was known, created a tribunal, the Council of Troubles, which tried more than 12,000 people and executed 1,000. More than 50,000 people went into exile. These exiles started a rebellion led by William of Orange, a prominent Protestant nobleman. Although the war would not officially end until 1648, by the 1580s it had become clear that the breakup of the Habsburg Netherlands into a Catholic section, which remained under the control of the Habsburg kings, and an independent Protestant section was inevitable. By the 1590s, after several attempts to find a new and more pliable king had failed, the newly independent Dutch provinces decided to go through life as the Republic of the United Netherlands.

As in the Polish-Lithuanian Republic of the Two Nations, in the Dutch Republic, freedom was key to political discourse.[78] Dutch pamphleteers never tired of describing their country as one of the few free states in Europe; they also left no doubt that the Dutch considered themselves free because they governed themselves like the ancient Greeks and Romans, or like their own supposed ancestors, the legendary Batavians. According to the Dutch legal historian Hugo Grotius—who had carefully read Hotman's *Francogallia*—the constitution of the ancient Batavians had been quite similar to that of the Spartans. The Dutch Revolt had restored this ancestral Batavian freedom.[79]

Again, however, as in Poland-Lithuania, Dutch humanists continued to worry about the return of monarchy and political slavery. Even after the establishment of the republic, the Dutch political system had retained a king-like figure with the stadholder, the commander of the republic's armies, which quickly became a hereditary function exercised by princes of the House of Orange. Throughout the seventeenth and eighteenth centuries, anti-Orangists like the humanist Rabo Herman Scheels protested these kings by another name, warning that their arbitrary power would eventually put an end to Dutch freedom. In his 1666 essay "Public Liberty," Scheels took his cues from Herodotus, Tacitus, and Cicero, making clear that liberty could exist only in a commonwealth where rulers and ruled frequently changed places.[80]

Ancient Freedom in England

In England, the uptick in freedom talk came somewhat later than in France, Poland-Lithuania, or the Netherlands. But when it did emerge, English attachment to ancient liberty became particularly acute and long-lasting. From the 1620s until the 1690s, England underwent a prolonged and often violent political crisis, which led to a wholesale breakdown of the monarchical order, culminating in the execution of Charles I in January 1649 and the proclamation of the English Republic or Commonwealth a few months later. The underlying causes of this crisis have been much debated. While some historians put more emphasis on the effects of long-term social changes triggered by inflation and population growth, others tend to see the crisis—and, in particular, the English Civil War—as the last manifestation of the religious wars provoked by the Reformation. In addition, some scholars have pointed to the importance of new political ideas introduced by the spread of humanist knowledge.[81]

Whatever were the conflict's deeper causes, however, the kindling was clearly provided by the precarious fiscal situation of the Stuart kings. Compared with, for instance, their French neighbors, the English kings had far more difficulty obtaining the necessary funds: they had no access to permanent taxes, even as military innovations had made warfare ever more expensive. In addition, by the end of the sixteenth century inflation had decreased the real value of the royal income from taxation. Attempts by James I and Charles I to get Parliament to agree to new and more permanent taxes were met by counterdemands for more influence over decision-making, which led to frequent political crises in the early decades of the seventeenth century.

Things came to a head in 1639, when Scottish troops invaded England. The Scots were unhappy that Charles I was trying to impose the Anglican book of prayer on them. Charles needed money to strengthen the army and convened Parliament to raise the funds. However, the strategy backfired and Parliament refused to pay for the defense of the realm, instead issuing the Grand Remonstrance, which demanded parliamentary authority to approve all royal counselors. Charles exploded in rage and left London in 1642, declaring war against Parliament. The English Civil War, as the conflict came to be known (although it also involved Ireland and Scotland) was won by the Parliamentarians, who under Oliver Cromwell's leadership first defeated the armies of Charles I and subsequently those of his son, Charles II.

After the defeat of Charles I's armies in 1648, Parliament put the king on trial and executed him—an unprecedented act that sent shockwaves through Europe, scandalizing even the republican Dutch. After Charles's death, England was transformed into a republic, but the new regime was met with mounting opposition. In 1660 monarchy was restored under Charles II, Charles I's son and heir, who had sat out the interregnum in France. This, however, did not spell the end of England's troubles. The restored Stuart kings continued to encounter much resistance from old commonwealthmen and from Protestant hardliners who suspected the Stuarts of being crypto-Catholics. Stability was achieved only when the Glorious Revolution of 1688 brought an end to the Stuart dynasty and installed William and Mary, and later the Hanoverians, on the throne.

As a result of this prolonged political crisis, England became the locus for the revival of the ancient cult of freedom in transalpine Europe, though this was not immediately apparent. Initially, the conflict between king and Parliament was articulated in terms of a defense of traditional rights and liberties. But in the course of the 1630s and 1640s, talk about ancient rights and liberties turned into complaints about the political slavery to which the English had been subjected by their kings.[82] When, in 1649, Parliament took the unprecedented step of executing their king in order to create a republic—or a "free commonwealth," as they called it—they justified the act by arguing that experience had found government by a single person to be incompatible with liberty. Invoking the examples of the Romans, Venice, Switzerland, and the Netherlands, Parliament explained that, in commonwealths, "a just freedome of their consciences, persons and estates, [was] enjoined by all sorts of men." By contrast, under kingly rule, the English people had suffered "injustice, oppression and slavery." Hence, "the representatives of the people now assembled in Parliament, have judged it necessary to change the government of this nation from the former monarchy, (unto which by many injurious incroachments it had arrived) into a republique, and not to have any more a king to tyrannize over them."[83]

In the decades that followed the execution of the king, English commonwealthmen continued to loudly reject one-man rule, claiming it to be incompatible with liberty.[84] It was the "basis of the government of the state of Lacedemon," the London newspaper *Observations* reminded its readers in 1654, using another term for Sparta, "that all should be free, that all should be able to govern."[85] Another writer drew on the "Romane histories" to argue that the "people never had any real liberty, till they were possess'd of the power of calling and dissolving the supreme assemblies, changing governments, enacting and repealing laws."[86] Thirty years later, Algernon Sidney, a fierce opponent of the restored Stuart dynasty, made much the same point. "It has been hitherto believed in the world," he explained in *Discourses on Government,* "that the Assyrians, Medes, Arabs, Egyptians, Turks, and others like them, lived in slavery, because their princes were masters of their lives and goods: Whereas the Grecians, Italians, Gauls, Germans, Spaniards, and Carthaginians, as long as they had any strength, virtue or courage amongst them, were esteemed free nations, because they abhorred such a subjection. They were, and would be governed only by laws of their own making."[87]

The message was clear: if the English wanted to be free, they needed to get rid of their kings and govern themselves like the ancient Greeks and Romans. But how was this to be done in practice? How could the free regimes of antiquity be recreated in the wildly different context of seventeenth-century England? This question generated a lot of debate among commonwealthmen. The most influential contribution to this debate was made by James Harrington. A landed gentleman, Harrington belonged to the upper echelons of English society—indeed, he seems to have been friendly with Charles I and may have even attended to the latter on the scaffold. Nevertheless, after Charles I's execution and the creation of the English commonwealth, Harrington became a committed republican and produced several political treatises detailing how the popular governments of antiquity might be resurrected in the modern world. The *Commonwealth of Oceana,* first published in 1656, was the most famous of these works.[88]

As Harrington stated in the introduction of *Oceana,* his goal was to revive, as Machiavelli had done, "ancient prudence," or statecraft, because that was the only way to establish freedom. Harrington's Oceana was inspired by ancient examples—he claimed to have drawn from Rome, Athens, Sparta, Carthage, Israel, the Achaeans (Greeks)—and three modern republics: Venice, Switzerland, and the Dutch Republic.

What Harrington took from these examples was that a people could be free only under what he alternatively described as "popular government" or "democracy."[89] He was, of course, aware that such a type of government might be more difficult to introduce in seventeenth-century England than in the city-states of antiquity, which were thought to be quite a bit smaller. But he believed that these differences should not keep modern Europeans from imitating ancient institutions. First and foremost, the size discrepancies had been much exaggerated. Most ancient commonwealths, Harrington pointed out, covered relatively large territories that included several different cities. "Lacedemon," he noted, "consisted of thirty thousand citizens dispers'd throout Laconia, one of the greatest provinces in all Greece." Moreover, the principle of representation—which Harrington, through a creative interpretation of his sources, managed to trace back to antiquity—meant that the people could participate in politics without having to assemble in one place.[90]

Harrington proposed the creation of two representative bodies—a popular assembly and a senate, both elected indirectly by all adult males except servants, and with only the wealthier eligible to serve in the senate. These representative bodies would make the laws and choose the public officials responsible for the executive and judicial functions of government. Once a representative or public official had completed his term, he would be ineligible for reelection for a specified period. In Harrington's view, this latter principle—the "rotation of offices"—was crucially important for keeping all office-holders accountable. It was the only way, he explained, to make sure that the nation remained "king PEOPLE" rather than having to rely on "the dole or bounty of one man."[91]

But political institutions were not enough. Harrington also emphasized that the preservation of liberty required a certain measure of socioeconomic equality; in particular, equality of landed wealth. A careful study of history showed that power depended on the balance of property; or, as Harrington expressed it, the "superstructure" of politics depended on a "foundation"—on the distribution of property and, in particular, of landed property, the main source of wealth.[92] If all land belonged to a single man, the state would become an absolute monarchy, as was the case in countries like Turkey. If the land was monopolized by a small elite, the state would automatically turn into an aristocracy or limited monarchy, as it had in England during feudal times. A more or less equal division of property gave rise to the creation of a "popular government" or "commonwealth." As Harrington put it, "Where there is equality of estates, there must be equality of power: and where there is equality of power, there can be no monarchy."[93]

Harrington's discovery that the political superstructure depended on the distribution of property made him optimistic about the prospects of popular government in his own day and age. In feudal times, the concentration of land in the hands of a small class of noblemen had made limited monarchy the most appropriate form of government. But in the past few

centuries, various circumstances had brought about a more equal distribution of property in England. The revolt of Parliament against the Stuarts had been the inevitable result of these socioeconomic changes. As
Harrington put it, "Wherfore the dissolution of this government caus'd
the war, not the war the dissolution of this government."[94]

Nevertheless, Harrington thought it prudent to create a legal
framework—what he called an agrarian law—that would help prevent the
growth of economic inequality in the future.[95] The necessity of such a
legal framework was illustrated most clearly by the example of the Romans. In the early days of their republic, they had divided conquered land
equally among the people, in accordance with their agrarian laws. But
they had allowed these laws to lapse, and a patrician elite had come to
monopolize all newly conquered lands. As a result, a number of these
patricians had grown ever richer and ended up overthrowing the republic.
Thus, the Romans had "forfeited the inestimable treasure of liberty for
themselves and their posterity."[96]

More specifically, Harrington stipulated that in a free republic, inheritance laws should promote the distribution of property, first and foremost by making the equal division of large landed estates among one's
children obligatory. Wealthy families would, in other words, be prohibited from leaving the bulk of their estate to one child only, as they typically did in Harrington's time. In addition, men would be prohibited
from acquiring land above a certain value. He believed both these measures, in the long run, would result in a more or less equal division of
landed property.[97]

In arguing that an agrarian law was indispensable for maintaining
popular government, Harrington drew on Machiavelli, who had likewise
suggested that a well-functioning republic required "equality," and on several other ancient sources that made suggestions to the same effect. But
Harrington gave this proposal a far more prominent place in his writings
than either Machiavelli or any ancient author.[98] Indeed, Harrington considered an agrarian law to be as fundamental for the preservation of the
republic—and hence liberty—as institutions designed to bring about
political equality. Harrington's novel emphasis on economic equality as
essential for preserving democratic freedom would have a huge impact,
as we will see, on subsequent debates about how to introduce a free

regime, which took place in the context of the American and French Revolutions.[99]

In summary, between 1500 and 1700, the ancient cult of freedom came roaring back to life in transalpine Europe. Much like in Renaissance Italy, the humanist passion for all things Greek or Roman led to a new emphasis on the value of freedom, understood as popular self-government. This was especially the case in countries such as France, Poland, the Netherlands, and England, which had been confronted with a breakdown of the monarchical order. Here, humanists like La Boétie, Scheels, and Sidney denounced the slavery under which they lived, much as Rinuccini had done in fifteenth-century Florence. Even more radical thinkers, such as Hotman and Harrington, took a leaf from Machiavelli's playbook and developed detailed descriptions for recreating the popular governments of antiquity.

At the same time, we need to be aware of the fact that the humanists' devotion to freedom had clear limits. While the humanists talked a great deal about their desire to create free regimes in which the people were king, they often defined such regimes in rather narrow terms. The polities that many of them held up as exemplary free regimes tended, in fact, to be highly elitist. Thus, Polish, Dutch, and (more briefly) English humanists celebrated their respective republics as exemplary free governments. Yet, political participation in all of these republics was limited to a small slice of the population: in Poland-Lithuania, only nobles (who made up about 6 to 8 percent of the population) were allowed to vote in the assembly; the Netherlands was ruled by a small and self-perpetuating oligarchy called the regents (literally "rulers"). Similarly, the short-lived English Republic restricted the franchise to adult males who owned substantial property, and it excluded Roman Catholics and known royalists.[100]

These exclusions often went unacknowledged. Polish humanists seemed to think it was self-evident that the "nation" that was supposed to govern itself included only nobles.[101] Dutch republicans had much the same attitude. Thus, Rabo Scheels, in his paean to liberty, described the House of Orange as the only threat to freedom in the Netherlands, while never once discussing the power monopoly established by the regent elite. Similarly, when discussing free regimes more generally, he included both aristocratic and democratic governments under this category without ac-knowledging that, under the rule of an elite, most people were just as much excluded from self-government as under a monarchy.[102]

In England, where political strife was fiercer and things remained unsettled for much longer, there was more debate about who was to be included in the political nation and why. Here, elitist commonwealthmen often pointed out that giving power to the "rude multitude" would only bring back monarchy—and hence put an end to liberty. According to the poet and republican propagandist John Milton, the example of the Roman Republic highlighted the dangers of giving too much power to the people. In his view, Roman popular leaders, the tribunes in partic-ular, had been responsible for fomenting dissension and unrest, so that eventually the republic collapsed, giving Sulla the opportunity to estab-lish his dictatorship. In order to preserve freedom, Milton concluded, power had better be located in the hands of those "who are rightly qualified."[103]

Yet republican elitism should not be overstated. In the course of the sixteenth and seventeenth centuries, a number of republican thinkers also condemned oligarchic regimes as no less detrimental to freedom than monarchy. In 1572, the Polish scholar Andrzej Wolan (or Andreas Wolanus, as he called himself) published the treatise *On Political or Civil Liberty,* in which he heaped praise on the Polish-Lithuanian state as the epitome of freedom because it was ruled by laws made with the consent of the people. At the same time, Wolan was also critical of the oligarchic tendencies of the Republic of the Two Nations. Without reforms, he warned, "liberty for all" would be replaced by the domination of "the power of a few."[104]

Even more radical were the Dutch brothers Johan and Pieter de la Court.[105] Successful cloth merchants, the de la Courts were among the wealthiest men in the Netherlands, and they had strong ties with the pa-trician elite who ruled the country. Nevertheless, they were extremely critical of the oligarchic nature of the Dutch Republic. They made this particularly clear in their *Considerations of State or Political Balance,* a work written in 1660 in which they compared three forms of govern-ment: monarchy, aristocracy, and democracy. After dismissing, in classic humanist fashion, monarchy as nothing more than slavery, they went on to make a more exceptional claim. Aristocracies, they explained, would always end up ruling in the interests of the elite, hence reducing the large majority of the people to slavery, just as kingly rule did. The de la Courts therefore concluded their book with a strong plea for Athenian-style democracy, in which all adult males had the right to participate in a general assembly to declare war and peace, to promulgate new laws, and to appoint magistrates to execute those laws.[106]

But the critique of elite rule was probably most vibrant in revolutionary England.[107] The exclusionary nature of the short-lived English Republic was sharply criticized by Marchamont Nedham, who—in an exact inversion of Milton's argument—invoked Roman history to argue against elite government. Roman history showed, Nedham contended, that the people were only secure in their liberty "as long as the popular interest continued regular and more predominant than the other." By contrast, as soon as the Senate had succeeded in "worming the people out of power," Rome had "lost her liberty," and the decline toward the tyranny of Caesar began.[108] Similar claims were made by a host of equally populist commonwealthmen. John Streater, for instance, emphasized that the people alone could be counted upon to protect their liberty, whereas nobles tended to have a strong preference for monarchy: "A people are the best guard of those in power, and the best guardians of their own liberty."[109]

Of course, even such democratically minded thinkers as Nedham and the brothers de la Court had their limits. While they developed powerful arguments for the participation of nonelite men, they continued to exclude substantial categories of people—notably, women and servants—from participating in politics. Like their ancient predecessors, they argued that these individuals were not really independent to begin with; hence, by subjecting them to political slavery, nothing was lost. Women, the de la Courts explained, were more subject to passions than men, suffered from debilitating monthly indispositions, and were physically dependent on the help of men. Their subordination to the male sex was perfectly natural, just like children were naturally subordinate to adults.[110]

Despite the obvious limits of their political vision, northern humanists and their disciples played a crucial role in the story of freedom. Just
like their Italian predecessors, they claimed that living a free life was
the highest political good; they also made clear that such a free life
could be enjoyed only in the context of self-governing republics *à
l'ancienne*. They came up with innovative ideas, including the argument that a free state required socioeconomic equality. Some developed
a powerful critique of elite rule as a form of slavery. These ideas, as we
shall see, would come to play an important role in late-eighteenth-
century debates about freedom, particularly in the context of the Atlantic Revolutions.

Rethinking Freedom? The Impact of the Reformation

It is clear that Renaissance humanism had a major and long-lasting impact on European political thought and, in particular, on thinking
about freedom. Contemporaries recognized as much. Thomas Hobbes
famously complained in 1651 about what he thought was the pernicious
influence of Greek and Roman writers. "In these westerne parts of the
world," Hobbes grumbled, "we are made to receive our opinions concerning the institution, and rights of commonwealths, from Aristotle,
Cicero, and other men, Greeks and Romanes." These Greek and Roman
authors "living under popular states" had believed "that they were free-
men, and that all that lived under monarchy were slaves"—an opinion
that most of his contemporaries had uncritically accepted, Hobbes concluded. Indeed, Hobbes believed that the humanist association between monarchy and slavery was so firmly and widely established that
it could be held partly responsible for the violent overthrow of the
Stuart monarchy.[111]

But the Renaissance was not the only major cultural transformation
that affected European political debate in the sixteenth and seventeenth
centuries. Equally crucial were two other intellectual developments: the
Reformation and the emergence of natural-rights doctrine. It is conventional to say that these developments steered the freedom debate in a
more "modern" direction. But is that really the case? We can assess this
claim by tracing the genesis and development of these movements and

exploring their impact on early modern debates about freedom. As we shall see, there are good reasons to think that the impact was much less significant than traditionally thought.

According to a narrative established in the nineteenth century—mostly by Protestant historians—the Reformation caused a radical cleavage between modernity and the mental worlds of antiquity and the Middle Ages. In this view, medieval Catholicism was an oppressive religion that subjected laymen to priestly authority and prevented them from thinking for themselves. The Reformation emancipated Protestants, making the laity equal to priests (creating, as Luther put it, a "priesthood of all believers") and encouraging lay people to read and interpret scripture for themselves. This religious freedom led to a new appreciation for personal freedom—the ability to act and think as one wanted without state interference—that differentiated the modern world not just from the Middle Ages but also from classical antiquity, which privileged collective freedom above that of the individual.[112]

This view still has wide currency, especially in the Anglophone world. But it is based on a number of questionable assumptions. First and foremost, scholars of antiquity have shown that ancient thinkers did not privilege collective freedom above individual freedom. Rather, as we have seen, writers like Herodotus firmly believed that individual security and personal independence existed only in the context of a free or self-governing state. This was also true of their humanist heirs. When men like Machiavelli or Harrington advocated freedom or self-government in the collective sense, they did so because they believed it was the only way people could control their own lives. Both the ancients and their humanist admirers pointed to being able to speak one's mind or choose one's life plan as one of the main benefits of living in a free state (that is, popular government).[113]

There are other reasons not to assign the Reformation a starring role in the history of freedom. In the twentieth century, the rosy assessment of nineteenth-century scholars was countered by revisionist historians like Ernst Troeltsch, a liberal Protestant theologian who painted the Reformation in a darker hue. For all their revolt against papal authority, the major reformers, as Troeltsch and others pointed out, propagated authoritarian views. They insisted not on religious freedom but on subjection to the word of God, and they advocated not freedom of conscience but the extirpation of heresy. To the extent that the Reformation propagated freedom, it was an inner, irenic kind of freedom, compatible with an individual's submission to the word of God and to the king or other political authority. The Reformation, as Troeltsch pointed out, could actually be said to have prolonged the Middle Ages, not brought it to an end.[114]

Examining the writings of the most influential reformers shows the persuasiveness of Troeltsch's view. Martin Luther's advocacy of Christian freedom, for instance, can by no means be construed as a defense of religious diversity or the right of Christians to believe or congregate according to their own convictions. Derived from the teachings of Paul, especially his letter to the Galatians, this theological concept designated a purely spiritual and inward freedom. For Luther, it essentially meant an acceptance of the doctrine of justification and redemption through faith in Christ alone. True Christians were free in the sense that they accepted their salvation was in the hands of God and could not be achieved by doing good works or obeying manmade rules such as papal decrees.[115]

Similarly, when Luther talked about freedom of conscience, he did not simply mean that men should think whatever they wanted or be allowed to worship God in their own manner. For Luther, a conscience was free when it was "captive to the Word of God," and that word—as expressed in the Bible—was unambiguous.[116] He could not conceive of legitimate religious disagreements or interpretations. ("There exists on earth no clearer book than Holy Writ."[117]) When others understood biblical passages differently than Luther, he thought they had either been misled or were willfully flouting God's orders, and deviations from true belief—that is, from Luther's interpretation of scripture—should be combatted. Initially reluctant to call in the aid of secular authorities—who, after all, were sinners like everyone else—to punish heresy, by the 1530s, he had come to believe it was the duty of rulers and public authority to suppress the Catholic Mass as an abomination, a blasphemous crime. He gave no weight to Catholic appeals to freedom of conscience, since their conscience, unguided by scripture, was merely "a conscience in appearance."[118]

Other reformers agreed. Like Luther, Calvin defined Christian freedom as an essentially spiritual condition. It did not mean that one could do or believe as one wanted, nor was it, Calvin noted sternly, to be equated with the freedom of gluttony or sloth. A Christian was free in the sense that he or she should "willingly obey God's will."[119] Calvin also agreed with Luther that the secular authorities had a duty to maintain religious orthodoxy. In the *Institutes,* he made clear that the foremost duty of Christian rulers and magistrates—God's deputies on earth—was the care of religion and the church. This meant protecting the outward worship of God and defending sound doctrine, as well as suppressing idolatry, sacrilege, and blasphemy.

Of course, the Reformation was not solely the work of Luther and Calvin. Since the 1962 publication of G. H. Williams's influential study *The Radical Reformation*, historians have paid more attention to the emergence, alongside these "magisterial" reformers (so called because their reforms had the support of secular rulers) of movements seeking to implement religious change from the bottom up. These "radical" reformers were, unsurprisingly, far more willing to question the legitimacy of existing religious and political arrangements. For instance, unlike Lutherans and Calvinists, Anabaptists favored a truly voluntary church, hence their refusal of pedobaptism, which forced children to join the religious community before they could decide for themselves. Some argue that Anabaptists and other radical reformers were the modern face of the Reformation, genuinely committed to freedom of conscience.[120] At the same time, it should be kept in mind that the Radical Reformation was a fringe movement with limited impact on religious and political debate in the early modern period.

In recent years, historians have also taken a fresh look at what Luther's and Calvin's heirs—later generations of mainline Protestants who had lived through the religious wars—contributed to the debate about freedom and, more specifically, freedom of conscience. As religious fractures became permanent and Protestants began fighting among themselves (in, for instance, the Netherlands and England), some mainline Protestant thinkers came to acknowledge that the word of God was not as unequivocal as Luther and Calvin had believed; that is, reasonable people really could disagree on the interpretation of scripture. These thinkers' conception of freedom of conscience was further from Luther's and Calvin's and closer to ours. Since no one could be certain about the best way to salvation, individuals should be able to follow the dictates of their own conscience.

Perez Zagorin has recently argued that such Protestant defenders of freedom of conscience played a major role in the advent of religious toleration in the West. Other simultaneous developments, like the rise of religious skepticism and the growing realization that violence could not restore religious unity, played an important role as well. But by themselves, these developments do not fully explain the eventual embrace of religious toleration. Religious skepticism remained the preserve of a tiny elite—and the true skeptic had little motivation to make a principled case for toleration. Similarly, the grudging compromises reached by warring religious factions were too unstable to provide religious freedom in the long term. Without the ethical arguments of the Protestant toleration thinkers, freedom of conscience might not have emerged.[121]

That does not mean, however, that we have come full circle or that we should credit the Reformation with introducing a new, more modern appreciation of individual freedom and autonomy. As John Dunn and other historians have reminded us, the defense of freedom of conscience by Luther's and Calvin's heirs remained predicated on a decidedly unmodern worldview: the idea that religious salvation was crucial. Freedom of conscience was, in other words, precisely that—the freedom to follow one's conscience. It by no means implied the freedom to think or say whatever one wanted; this is why even the most radical Protestant defenders of freedom of conscience had no qualms about prohibiting atheism or blasphemy: atheists and blasphemers could not claim to be following their consciences. Nor did freedom of conscience automatically lead to a commitment to individual autonomy in the nonreligious sphere. There was no sense whatsoever that even a radical defender of freedom of conscience like John Locke recognized a general right to think whatever one happened to think, let alone express those views.[122]

The role of the Reformation in the history of freedom, in short, was much more modest than traditionally assumed. Major reformers like Luther and Calvin frequently invoked the concept of freedom and presented their movement as a liberating force, but they also made it clear that the freedom they envisioned was of a purely spiritual, inner kind. As a result, their advocacy of Christian freedom was compatible with religious and political authoritarianism. A radical fringe of mostly Protestant reformers did play an important role in propagating the idea that secular authorities should refrain from interfering with their subjects' religious beliefs. But even the most insurgent among them refrained from advocating freedom of thought and speech more generally. There is no direct line from the Reformation to the idea that freedom consists of private independence requiring protection against overweening state power.

Freedom and Natural Rights

While much ink has been spilled about the Reformation's impact on the history of freedom, historians have also paid considerable attention to another, more highbrow, intellectual development—the emergence of natural rights doctrine. In the seventeenth century, so the story goes, Locke and others adopted a new and more enlightened way of thinking about politics. They rejected the prevailing view that authority was God-given or natural. Instead, they argued that men were free by nature; that is, that they had certain inalienable individual rights, such as the right to property. Only governments that respected the natural liberty of individuals—their natural rights—could be seen as free and legitimate.

As such, natural rights thinkers such as Locke are often credited with inventing a new conception of how to be free in a society or as a society. In the wake of the invention of natural rights thinking, it is argued, freedom came to be equated with limited government—the kind of government that preserved order but did not otherwise interfere with men's natural rights. This new way of thinking about freedom reflected the rise of modern, commercial societies in the course of the seventeenth century, in which the protection of individual rights—notably, property rights—against state authority became increasingly important.[123]

Like the story about the Reformation, this narrative still has wide currency, even though historians have largely revealed it to be a myth. First and foremost, the emergence of natural rights thinking, we now know, had little to do with the rise of capitalism or modern market societies. Major tenets of the natural rights tradition—the idea that men were free by nature and that such freedom meant they had individual rights—were articulated in medieval political debate.[124] And while these ideas did gain more traction in the seventeenth century, this was not because of new economic developments. Instead, the growing popularity of natural rights thinking in the seventeenth century must be understood as a reaction to the moral and political skepticism engendered by the Reformation and the resulting religious wars. The Reformation made previously accepted ways of grounding legitimacy—notably the appeal to biblical authority— increasingly untenable. In this context, natural rights doctrine became a seemingly attractive alternative.[125]

Second, the emergence of natural rights thinking by no means led to the identification of freedom with a set of inalienable individual rights that needed protection against government interference. The major proponents of natural rights thinking were both more conservative and more radical than has typically been argued.[126] Most of them supported royal absolutism—not surprising, since natural rights doctrine emerged from the need to ground political obligation non-scripturally. Even though they insisted on man's natural freedom, they did so not to question the legitimacy of royal absolutism or the political status quo but to argue that the state of nature was so anarchical that everyone could see that political authority was necessary and desirable.

Hugo Grotius—a Dutch jurist who is generally thought of as the founder of modern natural rights doctrine—is a case in point. While he grew up in the Dutch Republic, Grotius had been forced to flee the country after becoming embroiled in an internal conflict, and he ended up on Louis XIII's payroll.[127] His seminal treatise, the *Rights of War and Peace,* was dedicated to his patron, and many have read it as a defense of royal absolutism. Grotius emphasized that man was naturally free and that, hence, political subjection had an essentially voluntary character. But he made it equally clear that it was perfectly legitimate for this subjection to be absolute. The state of nature, after all, was an undesirable, anarchical condition in which men's rights were precarious. If men wanted to renounce their natural liberty in exchange for the greater security offered by strong royal authority, this was rational and therefore legitimate. Even slavery, Grotius explained, was better than death: "Right reason suggests . . . that life is far preferable to liberty."[128] Similar claims were made by Samuel Pufendorf, a philosophy professor at the University of Lund and one of the most influential natural rights thinkers of the seventeenth century. As Pufendorf said bluntly in his seminal *On the Law of Nature and of Nations,* the main natural law textbook at universities throughout Europe, "One who enters into the state sacrifices his natural freedom and subjects himself to sovereignty."[129]

Of course, not all natural rights thinkers supported royal absolutism; some of them were opposed to the political status quo. They rejected Grotius's view that men would voluntary relinquish their natural freedom in exchange for security, even if this meant living in slavery. After all, life under the arbitrary will of a king or prince was bound to be just as precarious as in the state of nature; it would be irrational for men to consent to their subjection to absolute monarchy. Hence, it was more plausible to argue that a state could be legitimate only if it allowed men to enjoy freedom—albeit civil or political, rather than natural, freedom. But as radical natural rights thinkers made clear, such civil freedom could flourish only under popular self-government, not minimal government.

Thus, Benedict de Spinoza, an influential Dutch radical and freethinker, argued that only a democracy could be legitimate, because that was the only kind of government in which man's natural liberty was preserved. In the *Theological-Political Tractate,* published in 1670, Spinoza described democracy as "the most natural form of state, approaching most closely to that freedom which nature grants to every man. For in a democratic state nobody transfers his natural right to another so completely that thereafter he is not to be consulted; he transfers it to the majority of the entire community of which he is a part. In this way all men remain equal, as they were before in a state of nature."[130] One hundred years later, Jean-Jacques Rousseau, in his even more influential contribution to modern political thought, the *Social Contract,* similarly argued that a government could be legitimate only if it allowed man "to obey only himself" and hence "remain as free as before"—which required democratic control over power.[131]

Even Locke, traditionally held to be the paradigmatic proponent of a new rights-based way of thinking about freedom, held similar views.[132] Like Spinoza (and, later, Rousseau), Locke denied that absolute monarchy, in which there was no recourse against the prince's decisions, could ever be a legitimate form of government. Complete subjection to the arbitrary will of another person would make one's life just as precarious as in the state of nature; nay, even more precarious. Hence, no reasonable man would voluntarily subject himself to that kind of government. Men were not so foolish that they would take care to avoid "what mischiefs may be done them by pole-cats or foxes," only to allow themselves to be "devoured by lions."[133]

Locke, in other words, strenuously rejected Grotius's view that slavery could ever be a legitimate political condition. A state could be legitimate only if it allowed men to continue to be free. But, as he also made clear, the freedom men enjoyed as members of a political community—what Locke called civil freedom—had nothing to do with an absence of state interference. It had been said, Locke wrote, that freedom was "a liberty for every one to do what he lists, to live as he pleases, and not to be tied by any laws." But this was quite wrong. Civil liberty—the liberty one enjoyed as a member of a political community—was not about being able to do whatever you wanted without outside interference. Instead, Locke explained, "freedom of men under government" was "to have a standing rule to live by, common to every one of that society, and made by the legislative power erected in it."[134]

If we want to understand what Locke meant by this somewhat enigmatic formula, we need to keep in mind that he believed that "standing rules," or laws, should be made with the consent of the people or of their expressly appointed representatives. As Locke explained elsewhere in the *Second Treatise,* a law could be a law in the full meaning of the word only if it was made with "the consent of the society, over whom no body can have a power to make Laws, but by their own consent, and by Authority received from them." The people could only be bound by laws "such as are enacted by those, whom they have chosen, and authorised to make laws for them."[135]

In short, natural rights philosophers came up with two strongly divergent views on freedom. On the one hand, conservative natural rights thinkers such as Grotius and Pufendorf invoked the doctrine of natural liberty to justify complete subjection to political authority, thus rejecting the value of freedom altogether. On other hand, radical natural rights thinkers such as Spinoza, Locke, and Rousseau identified freedom (or at least civil liberty) with the ability to live under laws of one's own making. The latter point of view was, of course, quite close to the definition of freedom advocated by the humanists and their ancient sources, who had likewise identified freedom with the ability to exercise control over the way in which one was governed.

There was one important exception to this rule: Thomas Hobbes, perhaps the most famous and controversial natural rights thinker of the seventeenth century. A staunch supporter of the Stuart dynasty, Hobbes used the doctrine of man's natural liberty to argue, like Grotius and Pufendorf, for the legitimacy of royal absolutism. Without political authority to keep them in check, Hobbes argued, men were wont to abuse their natural freedom. In the state of nature, men were in a condition of war of all against all. Hence, they had good reasons to abandon their natural liberty in return for the security offered by the emergence of a sovereign power— even if that sovereign power held absolute control over their lives and goods.

Unlike Grotius and Pufendorf, however, Hobbes explicitly argued that, after the transition to civil society, men retained a form of liberty, the "liberty of the subject." This liberty entailed that men keep certain rights vis-à-vis the sovereign—most notably, the right to defend their own lives against the authorities. In addition, and more important, the liberty of the subject meant that men retained the freedom to do whatever the laws were silent about. As Hobbes put it in *Leviathan*, "The greatest liberty of subjects dependeth on the silence of the law, since in cases where the sovereign has prescribed no rule, there the subject hath the liberty to do, or forbeare, according to his own discretion."[136]

Hobbes therefore came up with a new understanding of freedom that was very different from the ancient conception revived by the humanists. As Quentin Skinner has pointed out, Hobbes did so quite deliberately. By offering his own alternative understanding of freedom, Hobbes aimed to replace what he saw as the dangerously democratic definition of freedom offered by the humanists and other aficionados of antiquity. Whereas the humanists believed that a person could be free only if he lived under laws of his own making, Hobbes said that freedom, properly understood, depended on the absence of law. Hence, his novel understanding of freedom allowed him to argue that absolute monarchy offered just as much freedom as popular government. To rebel against monarchical authority in the name of freedom was therefore nonsensical. As Hobbes put it, "Whether a common-wealth be monarchicall, or popular, the freedome is still the same."[137]

However, it is important to emphasize that Hobbes's attempt to replace the ancient definition of freedom with a new and very different understanding of the term was largely unsuccessful. An extensive investigation into the impact of the *Leviathan* in seventeenth-century English political debate found just one writer using Hobbes's arguments about freedom.[138] Instead, royalist thinkers and pamphleteers typically put forward very different arguments. Robert Filmer, for instance, spoke for many when he denounced the doctrine of natural liberty as new and dangerous, arguing instead that subjection to a king was both natural and beneficent; his *Patriarcha* was subtitled, revealingly, *A Defense of the Natural Power of Kings against the Unnatural Liberty of the People.*[139]

All this means that commonly accepted narratives about the emergence of more modern ways of thinking about liberty—narratives typically centered on the political impact of the Reformation or the emergence of more enlightened ways of thinking about politics—should be viewed with skepticism. There was no huge break; when early modern Europeans thought about freedom, they thought, much like their ancient predecessors did, of the ability to govern oneself. In order to determine whether someone was free, the relevant question remained: Who governs? And it remained clear to early modern thinkers that only a people that governed itself could be called free (even if they, too, were more than ready to exclude large swathes of the population on the grounds that they had never been free to begin with).

The continued predominance of the ancient, democratic understanding of freedom through the sixteenth and seventeenth centuries is also attested by sources usually ignored in textbook histories of freedom: early modern dictionaries and emblem books. Throughout the Middle Ages, scholars compiled word lists in various European languages, in which the meaning of difficult or technical words was clarified by listing one or more synonyms. But in the early modern period, lexicographers became more ambitious. They started creating dictionaries that explained the meaning of conventional words via definitions and exemplary phrases or quotations from classical texts.

An analysis of several of these dictionaries clearly shows that ancient definitions of freedom remained predominant in the late seventeenth century. One of the earliest examples of this new genre was the *Dictionary of the French Academy*. Compiled under the auspices of the Académie française, founded in 1630 by Cardinal de Richelieu, this dictionary took half a century to complete, with delays caused by deaths and squabbles. (Reportedly, the Académiciens hurled dictionaries at each other when passions ran high.) But the result was worth the effort: published in 1694, the dictionary had considerable impact on the French language, and foreign dictionaries proudly invoked its authority. It has remained in print throughout the centuries; a ninth edition is currently being prepared.[140]

When readers opened the heavy folio pages, they encountered a definition of freedom (*liberté*) quite similar to that espoused by Herodotus or Tacitus. The Académiciens started by acknowledging that liberty was a central term in moral and theological debate about the freedom of the will; in that sense, freedom was defined as "the power of the soul to choose one thing or another." But this definition was immediately followed by two very different ones. In legal terms, the Académiciens explained, liberty was the opposite of servitude. In addition, liberty "in relation to the State," should be understood as "a form of government in which the people has sovereign authority." This final meaning was immediately followed by an exemplary phrase referring to Roman freedom: "As long as Rome enjoyed its liberty."[141]

Other dictionary-makers agreed with these definitions. The next most influential French dictionary, Antoine Furetière's *Dictionnaire universel*, published in 1690, a few years before the *Dictionary of the French Academy*, included a definition of liberty as something said of "states where a popular administration and magistrates are established." This meaning was illustrated with the phrase, "The Greeks and Romans have long battled for their liberty."[142] In England, Ephraim κατ' ἐξοχὴν Theriacum vocamus. Quæ quidem commemorare libuit, vt non immeritò tot numiſmata cuſa exiſtimemus, quæ ſerpentem habent cum inſcriptione, SALVS. veluti eſt ille nummus in ſpiram collectum ſerpentem habens, cuius inſcriptio, SALVS ANTONINI AVG. In alio eiuſdem nummo ſerpens eſt tractu ſinuoſo tortiliq; obrepens virgæ, quam ſignum ibidem adiectum dextera humi applicat. Atq; in alio Dea ipſa læua virgam gerit, dextera poculum angui porrigit, inſcriptio eſt, SALVS AVG. COS. III. In aliis ipſe ſella ſedens pateram porrigit angui ſuo de loculo exeunti, caputq; pateræ admouenti, inſcriptione adiecta, SALVS AVG. In nummo verò M. Aurelii Seueri Alex. ſedenti ſimulacro pateramq;

porrigenti aſſurgit anguis, cum inſcriptione, SALVS PVBLICA In nummo Antiochi Soteris, SALVS Dea Romanis habita pingebatur forma mulieris, habitu regio ſedentis pateram tenentis, iuxta quam erat ara, & ad aram inuolutus anguis caput attollens. Sed ne ſingula commemorem, quæ quidem ſunt innumera, Commodi, Criſpinæ, & aliorum, per angues deniq; omnes Salutem intellexerunt. Pleriq; noſtra ætate viri eruditi coniiciunt, ab Alciato hic tacitam eſſe factam alluſionem ad Ambroſianum illum anguem, qui Mediolani viſitur in marmorea columna erectus ipſa æde D. Ambroſii. Sed ſatis, vt auguror, anguibus inuoluti hæſimus, age ad libertatem aſpiremus.

[margin left: Cuius liquor ſeruant nos fer... ... .]

[margin right: Anguis Ambroſianus Mediolani.]

Reſpublica liberata.

EMBLEMA CLI.

Ss   CAESARIS

Chamber's 1728 *Encyclopaedia*—directly inspired by the *Dictionary of the French Academy* and the first modern English-language dictionary—defined "free" in the abstract as the opposite of being "constrained, confined, necessitated," and it went on to note that a "free state" was defined as "a republick govern'd by magistrates elected by the free suffrages of the inhabitants."[143]

Emblem books likewise attest to the widespread identification of freedom with ancient-style popular government. In the wake of the print revolution, which made the reproduction of text and images ever cheaper, these books became amazingly popular among the European reading public. These books consisted of pictorial representations ("emblems," from the Greek *émblēma*, meaning "embossed ornament") of abstract concepts or principles, explained in verse. Representations of the notion of freedom in such emblem books leave little doubt that the ancient definition of freedom was uppermost in their makers' minds. Andrea Alciato's best-selling *Emblems*—over two hundred editions were published in the sixteenth and seventeenth centuries alone—illustrated the concept of a free state (*respublica liberate*) with an image of Brutus's famous coin, accompanied by the following explanation: "When Caesar had been destroyed, as a sign of liberty regained, this coin was struck by the leaders, Brutus and his brother. In chief are daggers, beside which there also stands a cap, such as slaves receive when set free."[144] Similarly, Cesare Ripa's *Iconologia*, the most famous book of emblems from the seventeenth century, depicted freedom as a young woman holding the cap of liberty.[145]

Freedom in the Early Eighteenth Century

In the wake of Petrarch's invention of humanism, the ancient cult of freedom was revived, first in Renaissance Italy and later in other parts of Europe. Even though the debate about freedom was complicated by other important intellectual transformations, notably the Reformation and the emergence of natural rights doctrine, ultimately these did not steer European thinking about freedom in a different direction. By the late seventeenth century, the notion that one could be free only if one did not depend on the will of another—meaning that individual freedom could exist only amid collective freedom—was so well established that dictionaries confirmed it.

Throughout the eighteenth century, the revival of the ancient cult of freedom continued unabated in parts of Europe. Stanisław Staszic, one of the most famous Polish thinkers in the late eighteenth century, reminded his countrymen that freedom could exist only where the nation had control over legislative power: "Where lawmaking does not belong to the nation, there is no society, only a lord and his herd of cattle."[146] In the Dutch Republic, similar views were echoed by Lieven de Beaufort in his 1737 *Treatise on Liberty in Civil Society*. Under one-man rule, only the prince was free, Beaufort explained, while all his subjects were "slaves."[147]

In England, political debate evolved somewhat differently. Here, renewed religious and political tensions again led to the overthrow of the Stuart dynasty in 1688. But now, the leaders of the revolt carefully avoided any hint that theirs was a revolution for freedom. Parliament made William of Orange sign, as a condition for his becoming the new king, a bill of rights, listing a series of "rights and liberties," the violation of which was "illegal." But the text did not mention the word "freedom."[148] Similarly, the Act of Settlement of 1701 repeatedly referred to Parliament as "We Your Majesties most dutifull and loyall subjects."[149]

But if Parliament was reluctant to embrace the concept of freedom, other political actors were less so. After the Glorious Revolution, a new generation of commonwealthmen emerged. True, they took pains to avoid any hint that abolishing monarchy as such was their goal—the memory of the short-lived English Republic had left little appetite to renew that experiment. But they left no doubt that they wanted to enhance popular control over government by increasing the frequency of elections for the House of Commons and combating the crown's influence over it. In making these claims, the post-1688 commonwealthmen invoked the authority of ancient freedom fighters like Cato and of their seventeenth-century predecessors, like Sidney and Harrington.[150]

It is important to note, however, that outside Poland, the Dutch Republic, and England, freedom-talk remained relatively muted. That changed dramatically in the 1770s and 1780s, when Europe and its Atlantic colonies became engulfed by revolution. Suddenly it seemed as if the whole world was talking about the sweetness of liberty and the pernicious effects of slavery. Most spectacularly, even in France—Europe's most powerful monarchy—royal authority was overthrown in the name of freedom. The Atlantic Revolutions were the apogee of the Renaissance cult of ancient liberty; the crowning achievement, so to speak, of Niccolò Machiavelli and other humanists who had tried to rekindle the ancient love of liberty in the postclassical world. Yet this triumph would also spark a powerful backlash against democratic freedom.

Freedom in the Atlantic Revolutions

O N MARCH 23, 1775, Patrick Henry, a thirty-nine-year-old attorney, gave an impassioned speech at St. John's Church in Richmond, Virginia. Representatives of the colony of Virginia had assembled there to debate what position they should adopt in the conflict between the American colonies and Britain—a conflict that had started with a dispute about import duties but quickly escalated into a struggle for the colonies' independence vis-à-vis the metropole. Should Virginians prepare to join with Massachusetts and other colonies in armed rebellion against George III? Or should they wait and see what happened? In a short but ardent address, Henry urged his fellow Virginians to join the uprising.

Henry acknowledged that war carried huge risks for the American colonists. But he believed these risks were well worth taking. As he explained to his fellow Virginians, the issue was "of the most awful moment to this country." It was "nothing less than a question of freedom or slavery." To back off now, to allow Britain to impose tariffs without following proper consultation procedures, was to be reduced to slavery: "There is no retreat but in submission and slavery!" Henry exclaimed. "Our chains are forged! Their clanking may be heard on the plains of Boston!" Even death was preferable to such a fate, he concluded: "Is life so dear, or peace so sweet, as to be purchased at the price of chains and slavery? Forbid it, Almighty God! I know not what course others may take; but as for me, give me liberty or give me death!"[1]

Henry's stirring words had a tremendous effect. At the end of his oration, many in the audience were repeating the same "liberty or death" cry. Henry's resolutions passed, albeit by a narrow margin. With the entry of Virginia—one of the wealthiest and most populous American colonies—into the war, the revolt against Britain was definitively transformed. A rebellion with limited aims now became a full-fledged war for independence—a war that would last another seven years and result in a completely new political order on the eastern seaboard of the American continent.[2]

The American rebellion against Great Britain signified the beginning of a general conflagration that eventually engulfed the whole of the Atlantic world. In the Netherlands, a civil war broke out in 1787 between the Patriots, who wanted to democratize the oligarchic Dutch political system, and the Orangists, defenders of the status quo. While this rebellion was quickly put down by the Prussian army, the blaze next reached France, where a fiscal crisis triggered revolt against the regime of Louis XVI in 1789. From France, revolutionary fervor spread east to Warsaw, where a revolt broke out in 1794 against the Russians, who had occupied large swathes of Poland the year before. It also spread west, back across the Atlantic, where in 1791 the largest slave revolt in history broke out in the French colony Saint-Domingue. Finally, when French armies overthrew the Spanish king Ferdinand VII in 1808, revolution spread to Latin America as well, as colonists used the power vacuum in Spain to declare independence.[3]

The Atlantic Revolutions were triggered by many different factors. An important cause was fiscal pressure owing to the ever-increasing costs of warfare. The Seven Years' War, fought between 1756 and 1763, had brought England and France to the brink of default. In both countries, the imposition of new taxes, which was necessary to solve the fiscal crisis, sparked revolt. Another important factor was demographic growth. As it became more difficult to feed the population, urban citizens in many European countries became increasingly discontent with the status quo. When extreme weather led to bad harvests, discontent easily turned violent. In the spring of 1788, a drought struck France, while a powerful hailstorm caused additional damage in parts of the country, leading to a poor grain harvest and subsequent famine. And the relatively harsh winter of 1788 and 1789 made the already bad situation even worse. While none of these events caused the revolution as such, high food prices definitely contributed to its outbreak in the summer of 1789.[4]

But while fiscal policy and demographic pressures were important proximate causes of rebellion, it is important to emphasize that the Atlantic revolutionaries themselves did not think they were fighting simply for lower taxes or for bread and other foodstuffs. Instead, they made it clear again and again that they were struggling for something more abstract and exalted: freedom. The fighting words with which Patrick Henry ended his 1775 speech—liberty or death—were soon adopted as the semi-official slogan of the American revolutionaries. In August 1775, soldiers of the First Virginia Regiment adopted as their flag the image of a coiled rattlesnake with Henry's famous words on either side.[5] Flags carried by the New York and South Carolinian regiments in the Continental Army were decorated with the same words or, alternatively, with the motto *Vita potior libertas* ("Liberty above life.")[6]

These and similar watchwords soon began to be repeated all over the Atlantic world.[7] In France, the revolutionaries repeatedly proclaimed their willingness to die for freedom. Members of the National Guard—a militia created in July 1789 to defend the achievements of the revolution—took an oath pledging their willingness to "die if need be in order to defend liberty."[8] Similarly, in the Netherlands, Patriot citizen militias marched under banners decorated with a personified liberty, typically depicted as a young woman carrying a freedom staff and a Dutch freedom hat.[9] In Poland, the maxim *Dulce et decorum est pro patria mori* ("Sweet and honorable it is to die for the fatherland") was continually reiterated throughout the 1794 revolt against Russia, Prussia, and Austria—the great powers that had partitioned the Polish Republic among themselves.[10] A few years later, in 1804, when the former French colony Saint-Domingue became independent and adopted the name Haiti, its new leader, general Jean-Jacques Dessalines, made it plain that the Haitians would rather die than lose the liberty they had fought for. To bring "the empire of liberty" to their homeland, Dessalines, in a speech marking Haiti's newly established independence, explained, "we must take any hope of re-enslaving us away from the inhuman gov-

Jean Baptiste Regnault, *The Genius of France between Liberty and Death* (1793).

ernment that for so long kept us in the most humiliating torpor. In the end we must live independent or die."[11]

Such revolutionary slogans also inspired some of the most talented artists of the late eighteenth century. Probably the most famous example was Jean-Baptiste Regnault, one of France's preeminent classical historical painters. Regnault dramatized the choice between liberty and death in an allegorical painting finished in 1793 and first exhibited during the Salon of 1795. In his depiction, a winged and naked young man, the personified genius of the French people, was confronted with the choice of either Liberty (represented as an attractive young woman holding a liberty cap) or Death (a skeleton holding a scythe).[12]

This sudden explosion of freedom-talk did not come out of nowhere. As we have seen, throughout the preceding centuries, the ancient cult of freedom was slowly but surely revived in Europe as Renaissance humanists and their pupils familiarized themselves with the long-lost world of antiquity. But the discourse at the end of of eighteenth century was nonetheless unprecedented. Never before had Europeans and their colonial offspring invoked the concept so frequently. Between 1775, when the American Revolution began in earnest, and 1815, when revolution made way for restoration in Europe, the whole of the Atlantic world talked constantly of freedom.

The freedom fought for by the Atlantic revolutionaries was of a particular kind: it was the antique freedom to govern themselves. The Atlantic revolutionaries executed kings and toppled oligarchic elites, replacing them with governments that were, at least by their own lights, popular or democratic. They also adopted laws meant to promote economic equality; like Harrington, they believed economic equality a necessary condition for popular self-government. The revolutionaries were inspired by their reading of classical sources as well as by modern adaptations of these sources. And while the revolutionaries also talked a lot about their desire to reassert man's natural rights, this meant, first and foremost, the right to popular sovereignty.

Democratic Freedom in the Atlantic Revolutions

In 1776, a year after Patrick Henry's speech at St. John's Church, Richard Price, a Welsh clergyman and enthusiastic supporter of the American Revolution, published a short treatise titled *Observations on the Nature of Civil Liberty, the Principles of Government, and the Justice and Policy of the War with America,* which became an instant bestseller. It went through fourteen editions in 1776 alone and sold over 60,000 copies within the first few months of publication, while also being translated into French, German, and Dutch. *On Civil Liberty* made Price—a Unitarian minister previously known only within a small circle of theologians and other intellectuals—famous overnight. He became a hero to both the American colonists and their British supporters. In 1778, the newly established American Congress even passed a motion requesting that Price move to North America so that he could help the new state with its finances. (Price politely declined.)[13]

In *On Civil Liberty*, Price set out to explain why he sided with the rebellious colonists. The British were wrong for many reasons, Price made clear. The British constitution expressly forbade raising taxes without representation, therefore their resort to war was unconstitutional. Sending troops across the Atlantic would cost much more than the colonies would ever produce in revenue, so it was also bad policy. But above all, Price maintained, the British stood condemned on grounds of "the principles of liberty." By arrogating the right to impose taxes on the American colonists without consulting them—the declared cause of the war—the British were threatening to impose "slavery" on the colony.[14]

Price realized that this claim might seem overblown to at least some of his readers. After all, compared to actual slaves, whose plight was just starting to attract attention in Britain, the American colonists were well off. George III was by no means introducing white bondage in the colonies. Neither could British rule in the American colonies be described as overly oppressive. The proposed taxes on the American colonists were not onerous relative to the levies imposed on average Britons.

But, as Price underscored, describing George III's policies as potentially enslaving was not so strange if one had a clear view of what liberty meant. As Price explained, there were many seemingly different kinds of freedom. You could speak of being free in a physical sense; that is, being able to act on your own initiative. On a more abstract level, you could be morally free if you had the power of following, in all circumstances, your sense of right and wrong. Or you could be said to have religious freedom if you had the ability to choose the religion you thought was best. But in the end, all these different freedoms were, in essence, based on the same principle: self-government. In each instance, an agent was free to the extent that he was able to follow his own will or to the extent that he was "self-directed." Conversely, one was unfree or "a slave" when one was under the will or direction of "a force which stands opposed to the agent's own will."[15]

This was also true of civil or political liberty (Price used these terms interchangeably). For if freedom consisted of self-government, it followed that a state could be free only when it was self-governing; that is, when its government was exercised by the people themselves or their representatives. Just as an individual was free only to the extent that he was guided by his own will and did not depend on the will of another, so a state could be called free only when guided "by its own will; or, (which comes to the same) by the will of an assembly of representatives appointed by itself and accountable to itself." Conversely, a state in which the legislature was not elected by the people was "in slavery."[16]

It followed that the Americans were rightly worried about the imposition of new taxes by the British Parliament. Not because these taxes were so high but because they were introduced without the prior approval of the colonists who had to pay them. By claiming that "this kingdom has power . . . to make laws and statutes to bind the colonies, and people of America, in all cases whatever," Parliament had arrogated itself a "dreadful power" over the colonists. "I defy any one to express slavery in stronger language," Price concluded dramatically.[17]

Price's claim that the British government was out to enslave the American people was based on a specific understanding of freedom: that you could be free only in a self-governing state. In Price's view, being free in a society or as a society had nothing to do with the extent to which government interfered with one's life. Rather, one was free as long as one had a say in the direction of one's country. This was not because the act of governing in and of itself set one free. Price carefully avoided such claims. Rather, in Price's view, self-government was necessary for the robust enjoyment of liberty. Under a despotic government, private men "might be allowed the exercise of liberty; . . . but it would be an indulgence or connivance derived from the spirit of the times, or from an accidental mildness in the administration."[18]

Price's understanding of freedom was widely shared among American, Dutch, French, and Polish revolutionaries.[19] In 1774, Thomas Jefferson, a young lawyer and member of the Virginia House of Burgesses, drew up a strongly worded statement in which he laid out the colonists' various grievances against Britain, such as the imposition of high tariffs on trade. But Jefferson also had a more fundamental complaint: the colonists were being turned into slaves. In recent years, a "series of oppressions" had been initiated by the British Parliament that "plainly prove[d] a deliberate and systematical plan of reducing us to slavery." More specifically, Parliament was undermining the American colonists' liberty by imposing new laws without consulting the Americans themselves. "Can any one reason be assigned," Jefferson exclaimed in frustration, "why 160,000 electors in the island of Great Britain should give law to four million in the states of America, every individual of whom is equal to every individual of them, in virtue, in understanding, and in bodily strength?" He continued, "Were this to be admitted, instead of being a free people, as we have hitherto supposed, and mean to continue ourselves, we should suddenly be found the slaves, not of one, but of 160,000 tyrants."[20]

Dutch Patriots agreed. "You cannot be said to be free if you do not govern yourself, your property, and your happiness," wrote Pieter Vreede—a Dutch wool merchant who played a prominent role in the Patriot movement—in 1783. Hence, the large majority of Dutch people, who had no say in government at all, were just as unfree as the subjects of the French or Spanish kings—unless the regent elite was overthrown.[21] In France, a similar claim was made in the abbé de Mably's *On the Citizen's Rights and Duties*. Although this treatise had originally been written in 1758, it remained unpublished until 1789 when it was printed in three different editions. Mably provided a stinging judgment of the French monarchy, which, in his view, had turned all Frenchmen into slaves. "We are perfectly aware of the fact that we have a master, we experience that every day," he wrote, adding that only a people that was "its own legislator" could be called free.[22] A few years later, the leaders of a Warsaw revolt against Russian domination made clear that they were fighting to be a "self-ruling people," and therefore to be "free."[23]

Eighteenth-century revolutionaries were quick to point out that such freedom or self-government required, first and foremost, the eradication of monarchy. But like their sixteenth- and seventeenth-century humanist predecessors, they also generally agreed that the ability to live a free life depended on more than the mere abolition of royal power. It also required the introduction of a broad-based, popular government. Price made that crystal clear in *On Civil Liberty*, when he explained that not only

American colonists but also the majority of the English lived in slavery. After all, the British Parliament did not really represent that many Britons. According to Price's calculations, half of the members of the House of Commons were chosen by fewer than 6,000 voters, and a further one-ninth of all representatives were in effect chosen by 364 individuals. Therefore, most Britons could likewise be said to be unfree; or, as Price put it, it was "an abuse of language" to say that they possessed "liberty." The existence of Parliament was rather "disguising slavery, and keeping up a form of liberty when the reality was lost."[24]

Other revolutionary thinkers and actors agreed. As a result, most revolutionary movements throughout the Atlantic world had a stated goal of increasing popular control over their respective governments. While they used different terms to designate their preferred form of government—republic, popular government, or (more rarely) democracy—these were all typically used to refer to regimes in which the most important public officials were chosen through relatively broad-based elections. When American revolutionaries talked about their preference for republican government, they made it quite clear that this meant government subjected to popular control. This was true both during the initial phase of the revolution, when the different state constitutions were created, and during the late 1780s, when the federal constitution was drafted.[25] For instance, in a speech delivered to his fellow Pennsylvanians very early in the ratification debates, James Wilson made the case that the Constitution was "purely democratical" because the "supreme power . . . [was] vested in the people."[26]

Other framers were more wary of the word "democracy"—which, in the late eighteenth century, connoted mob rule and anarchy—preferring "popular government" or "republic." In *The Federalist Papers,* the Virginia politician James Madison famously denied that the new, federal constitution was "democratic," insisting instead that it instituted a "republican" government. But Madison meant something very specific by these terms. By "democracy," he meant direct democracy—"a society consisting of a small number of citizens, who assemble and administer the government in person." By "republic," in contrast, he meant "a government in which the scheme of representation takes place," and he made clear right away that such representation was to be of "the people."

Elsewhere in *The Federalist Papers,* the new constitution was repeatedly described as establishing a "popular government."[27]

Likewise, Dutch Patriots made clear that the "true republicanism" they fought for meant a regime based on broad-based representation. Later on, they started using the term "representative democracy" to describe their preferred form of government.[28] The leaders of the Polish revolt similarly emphasized that they were fighting not just for their homeland's independence from the great powers that had overrun it but also to restore and enlarge republican self-government, which was now meant to include not just the nobles but also a much larger swathe of the population. The Poles, as one revolutionary put it, were "striving for the freedom they have always enjoyed, which they want to set aright and extend to all residents."[29]

In France, the revolution started out on a more moderate note. Here, the goal was initially to introduce what the revolutionaries described as "constitutional monarchy." Influential revolutionary thinkers like the abbé de Sieyès believed that republicanism was undesirable in France and that a strong monarchy remained necessary; hence, in the new constitution of 1791, King Louis XVI was given executive power. Nevertheless, even at this early stage, revolutionaries made clear that the constitutional monarchy was to be based on the "general will" of the people at large—which meant that legislative power was to be assigned to the people's chosen representatives.[30] After Louis XVI's flight to Varennes in June 1791 revealed his lack of commitment to the new order, the revolutionaries' goal became to establish what they described as a "democratic republic." And even though the word "democracy" became less popular in the wake of the Terror, French revolutionaries continued to make clear that they were in favor of broad-based popular government—until Napoleon Bonaparte put an end to the republican experiment.[31]

In short, there are good reasons to describe the late-eighteenth-century revolutions as "democratic" revolutions, as the historian Robert Palmer did in his classic overview *The Age of the Democratic Revolution.*[32] But the democratic fervor of the Atlantic revolutionaries did not manifest itself just in their enthusiasm for popular government. In addition to introducing more democratic political institutions, quite a few revolutionaries also propagated measures aimed at enhancing economic equality—in the vein of James Harrington.[33] Economic measures, it was argued, were just as necessary for maintaining freedom as were representative institutions and frequent elections. If wealth disparity became too great, an oligarchy would form and take control of political power, and freedom would disappear. As one American revolutionary put it, "The great fundamental principle on which alone a free government can be founded and by which alone the freedom of a nation can be rendered permanent, is an equal distribution of property."[34]

This is not to say that, apart from a tiny, radical fringe, Atlantic revolutionaries had any enthusiasm for a wholesale redistribution of property, let alone for the introduction of communism. One of the main benefits of republican government vis-à-vis absolute monarchy, after all, was that it was supposed to offer personal security—including security of property. To reach the desired goal of greater economic equality, then, Atlantic revolutionaries focused on changing the laws that regulated inheritances. They argued that inheritance laws that fostered the concentration of property in the hands of a few—for instance, by creating entails or by favoring the eldest son—should be abolished, thus promoting the equal division of property between all natural heirs. This way, property rights would be respected, but in the long run, greater economic equality could be achieved.

In the American context, the outbreak of revolution immediately sparked a campaign to change the nation's inheritance laws. During the colonial period, law dictated, at least when there was no will, that real property went to the eldest son—a practice called primogeniture—or, alternatively, that the eldest son receive a double portion of the inheritance. Laws of entail existed in many colonies as well. An entail is a testamentary condition that says property can be passed only onto particular people; for example, only onto an oldest son. The goal of such a condition is usually to make sure that a testator's property remains concentrated in a particular branch of the family. In Virginia, for instance, even slaves could be entailed, so as to make sure that a plantation would be transmitted in its entirety from generation to generation.[35]

But soon after the Declaration of Independence, American revolutionaries set out to change these laws. Thomas Jefferson, in particular, played a key role in this campaign, successfully proposing to abolish both entails and primogeniture in Virginia. Jefferson did not hesitate to make the Harringtonian provenance of these proposals explicit. As he explained in his autobiography, repeal of entail laws was necessary to "prevent the accumulation and perpetuation of wealth in select families." These reforms were "the best of all agrarian laws," Jefferson said. They were "a foundation laid for a government truly republican," and in enforcing them "no violence was necessary, no deprivation of natural right."[36]

Jefferson's example was followed by many other American revolutionaries. As a result, by 1800, laws repealing entails and promoting the equal division of estates had been adopted in almost every state in the Union. There were some exceptions: in Connecticut, for instance, the eldest son continued to receive a double share of intestate estates. But overall, the postrevolutionary inheritance laws encouraged the equal division of property among heirs.[37] Like Jefferson, the proposers of these bills made their political goal quite explicit. A revision of North Carolina's inheritance laws in 1784 was undertaken on the grounds that "to promote . . . equality of property" was "the spirit and principle of a genuine republic" and that, therefore, "the real estates of persons dying intestate should undergo a more general and equal distribution than has hitherto prevailed in this state."[38] Similarly, the preamble of a 1794 statute adopted in Delaware stated that "it is the duty and policy of every republican government to preserve equality amongst its citizens, by maintaining the balance of property as far as it is consistent with the rights of individuals."[39]

In continental Europe, and in particular in France, revolutionaries were equally invested in the idea that staving off economic inequality was necessary for the preservation of liberty. This idea was vigorously defended by, for instance, the abbé de Mably in a number of writings published at the outbreak of the French Revolution of 1789. In his more radical treatises, Mably propagated the abolition of private property, and his name is now mainly associated with the defense of communism. However, Mably recognized that such measures were probably too utopian; his main emphasis was, therefore—just like that of Harrington, whom Mably read with admiration—on inheritance laws meant to ameliorate the unequal division of property in the long run. Thus, in his *On Legislation,* Mably defended inheritance laws that would compel the division of landed property among a number of actual or adopted heirs, with property reverting to the state for division among poor families when there were no heirs.[40]

As the French Revolution unfolded, legislators readily adopted such proposals. As early as 1790, several articles appeared in the *Moniteur Universel,* the main French journal of the time, linking "a truly free constitution" with "equal inheritance."[41] In April 1791 the Constituent Assembly made a first effort to foster greater economic equality with the adoption of a "Decree Relative to the Distribution of Intestate Successions." This decree provided for equality between heirs in intestate cases. Some of the more radical deputies also proposed, unsuccessfully, to make equal inheritance obligatory even in cases where there was a will. Maximilien de Robespierre, for instance, favored such a stringent law, arguing that "the too great inequality of fortunes is the source of political inequality [and] of the destruction of liberty."[42] Although this proposal was not adopted in 1791, in 1793 the Jacobin-dominated National Convention did make equal inheritance in all cases obligatory.

Indeed, the Jacobin-sponsored rewriting of France's inheritance laws went considerably further that of the American revolutionaries, who had focused solely on intestate cases. Subsequent laws made the equal division of inheritance even more stringent. Heirs had to return all dowries and other gifts to the succession. Only a small portion of the estate, known as the "disposable portion," was left free to be assigned by will, and it could be left only to nonheirs—to charity, for example. Finally, equal inheritance was made retroactive to July 14, 1789, the date on which the New Regime was supposed to have begun. The Jacobin inheritance laws, it should be noted, created a surge of protest, particularly among rural landholders who complained their estates were too small to be subdivided. But the Convention stood firm and refused to retract the new laws.[43]

Nevertheless, the radicalism of the Jacobins should not be exaggerated: they were just as opposed to the forcible redistribution of property as were their predecessors in the Constituent Assembly—or, for that matter, as were the American revolutionaries. Thus, while the Jacobin-dominated National Convention supported the rewriting of France's inheritance laws to foster economic equality in the long run, its members simultaneously banned proposals for the redistribution of property in the here and now. On March 18, 1793, the Convention even decreed the death penalty for anyone introducing such a measure.[44] As this again reminds us, the Jacobins—like Jefferson—were keen to foster economic equality not as an end in itself, but because they believed it was a necessary precondition for democratic self-government, and hence, for the freedom of all.

The Limits of Democratic Freedom

The Atlantic revolutionaries believed that the liberation of mankind demanded a radical reordering of their societies toward greater political and economic equality. But their radicalism had clear limits. Many eighteenth-century revolutionaries, while loudly protesting the metaphorical slavery to which they were subjected by haughty kings and arrogant patricians, either owned actual slaves or were involved in the slave trade. This was most glaringly the case in the American colonies, where in 1776 about half a million slaves lived. In Europe itself, slavery was nominally prohibited in many countries, including France. But thousands of slaves lived in France's overseas colonies, notably in Saint-Domingue, the richest and most prosperous French colony in the West Indies. The Dutch, for their part, also had slave colonies, notably the plantation colony Surinam, and in addition, their merchant ships played a crucial role in the transatlantic slave trade. In Poland-Lithuania, the peasants' status held some resemblance to that of serfs; thus the law forbade Polish peasants to move without seignorial permission.[45]

The discrepancy between the ideals of liberty professed by eighteenth-century revolutionaries and the persistence of chattel slavery and serfdom in the Atlantic world is not just evident in hindsight. Quite the contrary, contemporaries vehemently criticized the revolutionaries for failing to live up to their ideals. "How is it that we hear the loudest yelps for liberty among the drivers of negroes?" the British Tory Samuel Johnson remarked acerbically in 1775.[46] Similarly, in 1778, the Scottish philosopher John Millar condemned the American colonists for their inconsistency. While the Americans talked excitedly about their "political liberty" and "the inalienable rights of mankind," Millar lamented, they deprived "a great proportion of their fellow creatures" of "almost of every species of right." If anything, this showed "how little the conduct of men is at the bottom directed by any philosophical principles."[47]

But it was not just opponents of the Atlantic revolutionaries who remarked on this hypocrisy. Many revolutionaries and revolutionary sympathizers wrestled with it.[48] In a 1785 letter to Thomas Jefferson, Richard Price pointed out that the existence of slavery in the newly independent American states fundamentally compromised the revolution's promise. If "the people who have been struggling so earnestly to save themselves from slavery are very ready to enslave others," Price wrote, American independence would devolve into "aristocratic tyranny and human debasement," and "the friends of liberty and virtue in Europe" would be "mortified."[49] In the former colonies, too, revolutionaries pointed out to one another that the existence of chattel slavery was incompatible with their struggle for freedom. As the *Pennsylvania Journal* remarked in 1781, "A good whig should consider how inconsistent to the people of Europe the citizens of these states must appear, who, tho' enlightened to their own rights, are still blind to the case of the poor Africans."[50]

These were not just words. During a brief moment in time, it seemed as if the general fervor for freedom might lead to the eradication of chattel slavery in the revolutionary parts of the Atlantic world. In 1775, Philadelphia formed the first antislavery society in the world.[51] In the wake of the revolution, a number of Southern slaveholders voluntarily emancipated their slaves. But abolitionists made progress particularly in the North, where slavery was less entrenched. All states from North Hampshire to Pennsylvania took steps toward emancipation—which was, as one historian of the American Revolution remarks, "the first time in recorded history that legislative power had been invoked to eradicate slavery."[52] Moreover, slaves themselves turned the rhetoric of freedom against their masters. In the 1780s and 1790s, slaves in the North invoked the principle that "all men are born free and equal"—which had been written into many of the new state constitutions—in order to wage a legal battle against slavery. In some such cases, they were able to persuade the courts to release them from bondage.[53]

In France and its overseas colonies, revolutionary actors likewise campaigned to abolish slavery. Initial attempts by the Society of the Friends of the Blacks, founded in Paris in 1788, to abolish the slave trade led to naught in face of opposition by the planters, who were represented by a powerful and well-funded lobby in Paris. But in 1791, slaves rebelled against their masters in Saint-Domingue and formed an army that managed to take over a large part of the island. In 1793, a representative of the French government on the island, faced with the threat of either the Spanish or the British making use of the situation to take over Saint-Domingue, promised to abolish slavery in return for military assistance against France's enemies. A few months later, the Jacobin-dominated National Convention abolished slavery in the other French colonies as well.[54]

In the United States, however, neither the slaves nor their revolutionary sympathizers succeeded in eradicating slavery. Entrenched economic interests and deep-rooted racism proved a powerful bulwark against the revolutionary fervor for freedom. The abolitionist movement had but limited impact in the South; in fact, there were considerably more slaves in North America at the end of the revolutionary era than at the beginning. In 1790, the half million slaves of the 1770s had increased to some 700,000.[55] Moreover, by the 1790s it became clear that these trends would not change anytime soon, as the framers of the federal constitution explicitly rejected the example of the North. Madison assured delegates to the Virginia Ratifying Convention that the new constitution offered slavery "better security than any that now exists."[56]

Similarly, in France the abolition of chattel slavery was reversed by Napoleon in 1800, and slavery continued to be legal in France's colonies until 1848. The only exception to this rule was Saint-Domingue. Under the leadership of Jean-Jacques Dessalines, the former slaves managed to defeat the French army sent by Napoleon to reconquer the island and declared the independence of Haiti 1804. Half a million people were liberated from slavery. Yet the newly independent Haitians had to pay a heavy price for their freedom—and literally so. France refused to recognize Haitian independence until 1825, and then it did so only in return for a large indemnity (nearly 100 million francs), which was to be paid at an annual rate, rendering the Haitian government chronically insolvent. Meanwhile in the Netherlands, revolutionaries refused to even discuss the abolition of slavery. Emancipation came only in 1863.[57]

The failure to eradicate chattel slavery was not the only inconsistency in the Atlantic revolutionaries' campaign to liberate the world. For all their talk about handing over power to the people, most revolutionaries were perfectly happy to exclude large swathes of the population—most notably women—from their democracies and popular governments. In addition, many revolutionaries wanted to exclude the indigent or even the merely poor from political participation, along with certain other categories of people, such as servants. Thus, the French constitution of 1791 barred about 40 percent of adult males from voting, in addition to women and free blacks. In the United States, voting rights differed quite substantially from state to state: whereas in New Hampshire and Pennsylvania, about 90 percent of adult males could vote, around 40 percent were barred in Virginia and New York. Nationwide, about 20 percent of adult white males were excluded from voting for the House of Representatives by the 1790s. (Free black men were typically enfranchised on the same terms as white men.)[58]

Many Atlantic revolutionaries believed that these exclusions by no means undermined their adherence to the democratic theory of freedom. Women, they claimed, were unfree to begin with, since their lack of intellect and their passionate natures made them dependent on men in their day-to-day lives. Hence, nothing was lost by depriving them of the power to participate in government; this did not make women any more unfree than they already were. "Women," as one Dutch revolutionary put it, "are human, but, as they are under the supervision and protection of men, they are not citizens."[59]

Similar arguments were used to defend the exclusion of servants and the poor, who were deemed too dependent on the wealthy. During debates in the French National Assembly, for instance, several speakers asserted that servants should be prevented from "active" citizenship because their dependency on their masters ensured that their votes would not express their free wills.[60] In addition, some revolutionaries pointed out that the enfranchisement of servants and the poor was not merely superfluous; it was also, paradoxically, dangerous for the preservation of democratic freedom. Thus, during the Constitutional Convention of 1787, Gouverneur Morris introduced an amendment that would limit the right to vote to freeholders, arguing that this was necessary to prevent the creation of an overbearing "aristocracy." If the poor were given votes, Morris explained, they would surely sell them to the highest bidder. Votes should, therefore, go only to "secure and faithful guardians of liberty"—men whose property assured the independence necessary to vote according to their own will.[61]

Such claims were fiercely contested by more radical revolutionaries. For instance, Olympe de Gouges, a French playwright and pamphleteer, turned the revolutionaries' own arguments against them to plead for female suffrage. In her 1791 *Declaration of the Rights of Woman and of the Citizen*, written in reply to the 1789 Declaration of the Rights of Man and the Citizen, de Gouges accused the National Assembly of hypocrisy. They played at being revolutionaries and claimed their own right to equality, but women still suffered under the "perpetual tyranny of man." She closed her *Declaration* by urging women to wake up and demand their rights. Men had invoked "reason" to justify revolution; now it was up to women to extend that reasoning to combat the injustice of male hegemony. "Woman is born free," she wrote, "and remains equal to man in rights."[62] These arguments were picked up in different contexts: when Dutch revolutionaries issued a Declaration of the Rights of Man and the Citizen in 1795, an anonymous pamphlet appeared in reply. *An Argument that Women Should Participate in Public Government* accused the revolutionaries of establishing male "tyranny" and female "slavery."[63]

Even more contentious was the exclusion of poor white males. In France, the introduction of census suffrage was combatted in the National Assembly by a small but assertive group of deputies including Maximilien de Robespierre. According to Robespierre, any provision establishing a pecuniary condition for voting or eligibility would establish not freedom but an aristocracy; indeed, it would create the most unbearable of all aristocracies—that of the rich. If large numbers of adult males were excluded from the vote, the nation would remain "a slave" because it would be forced to obey laws it did not approve of.[64] Similarly, in America, the Constitutional Convention overwhelmingly rejected Gouverneur Morris's proposal to limit the franchise for the

House of Representatives to freeholders, on the grounds that this would create an odious tyranny. Benjamin Franklin warned that, in Britain, a similar limitation of suffrage had allowed Parliament to subject the disenfranchised "to peculiar labors and hardships."[65]

Overall, however, the Atlantic revolutionaries remained wedded to a less expansive vision of democracy. For all of de Gouges's eloquence, the possibility of female suffrage was not even debated in the National Assembly. In 1793, after the downfall of the monarchy, the issue was raised during debates about the new republican constitution in the Jacobin-dominated convention. However, no more than a few *conventionnels* argued in favor of female suffrage, and the issue was never put to a vote. In addition, even the most democratically minded revolutionaries continued to argue for the exclusion of certain categories of adult white males, notably servants. In France, new voting laws enacted in 1792 by Robespierre's Jacobins gave the right to vote to all adult males who had maintained a residence for one year and who lived off their own income or labor, thus coming close to the establishment of universal male suffrage. But even the laws of 1792 continued to exclude domestic servants from suffrage, as well as the unemployed and sons still living under their father's roof.[66]

In short, the political vision of the Atlantic revolutionaries was riddled with inconsistencies. They fought for freedom—but they owned slaves and failed to eradicate slavery. They wanted freedom for all—but many were just as excluded from political power as they had been in the monarchies and oligarchies of the ancién regime. Radical revolutionaries pointed out these inconsistencies, but they were belittled and ignored. However, despite the limits of their political imagination, in the context of their time, the Atlantic revolutionaries were undeniably radical, as Gordon Wood has recently argued with respect to the American Revolution.[67] Compared to the world in which they lived, in which power was concentrated in the hands of a infinitesimally small number of elite individuals, the reordering of power hierarchies—both political and economic—that Atlantic revolutionaries envisioned was a real challenge to the status quo. This is why their example continued to inspire future revolutionaries and even, as we shall see, those who had remained largely excluded from the promise of 1776 and 1789.

Triumph of the Ancient Cult of Freedom

Waged in the name of democratic freedom, the Atlantic Revolutions can be seen as the culmination of a long tradition going all the way back to antiquity. After all, when eighteenth-century revolutionaries referred to themselves as slaves robbed of their freedom by haughty kings or selfish elites, or when they talked about the introduction of republican government or democracy as a prerequisite for freedom, they were by no means making original claims. Rather, they echoed antique writers like Herodotus, Livy, and Tacitus as well as early-modern humanists like Machiavelli, Étienne de La Boétie, and James Harrington.[68]

This is hardly surprising. In the eighteenth century, elite education remained based on humanist principles, much as it had in the sixteenth and seventeenth centuries. Hence, many of the most prominent revolutionaries enjoyed good, classical educations. When John Adams entered Harvard in the 1750s, he was expected to be able to read Cicero, Virgil, and other common classical authors along with Greek texts, such as the New Testament. As a rhetorical strategy, moreover, the invocation of antiquity had obvious benefits. The Atlantic revolutionaries were engaged in a novel and risky political experiment. By making a show of their ancient intellectual inheritance, they downplayed the radicalism of their goals and made them more acceptable.[69]

Consider the symbolism and narrative strategies used by the Atlantic revolutionaries to undergird their fight for freedom. In the sixteenth and seventeenth centuries, as we have seen, the Roman symbol of freedom—the so-called liberty cap—reappeared on coins and in emblem books. By the end of the eighteenth century, there was a huge upsurge in the popularity of this antique symbol of freedom. In the American colonies, the liberty cap first appeared in the 1760s. In New York, colonists erected a wooden pole to celebrate the repeal of the Stamp Act and crowned it with a liberty cap. When the pole was cut down by British soldiers, the colonists resurrected it again. All in all, the colonists erected five different poles, the last of which was taller than any other structure in town.[70]

The liberty cap had a long shelf life in the American political imagination. In 1814, John Archibald Woodside produced a painting to commemorate the war of 1812 against the British. The painting, titled *We Owe*

Raising the Liberty Pole, 1776. Painted by F. A. Chapman, engraved by John C. McRae (c. 1875).

John Archibald Woodside, *We Owe Allegiance to No Crown* (c. 1814).

Jean-Jacques Le Barbier, *Declaration of the Rights of Man and the Citizen* (1789). The allegorical figures of France, breaking her chains, and Fame sit atop the declaration. The two stone tablets are decorated with a red liberty cap, a snake biting its tail, and a laurel wreath, representing liberty, eternal unity, and glory respectively.

Allegiance to No Crown, shows a sailor holding the American flag, while trampling a crown and broken chains underfoot. To the left is a young woman in classical garb, the personification of freedom, holding a pole topped with a red liberty cap in her right hand and a laurel wreath (symbolizing military victory) in her left.

In France, the liberty cap first appeared in 1789 in engravings and paintings commemorating the Declaration of the Rights of Man and the Citizen; for example, Claude Niquet's engraving *The Declaration of the Rights of Man and the Citizen* (1789) and Jean-Jacques-François Le Barbier's more famous painting on the same subject.

In the wake of the overthrow of the monarchy in 1792, the symbol became ubiquitous. The official seal of the First Republic featured a personified liberty with a liberty cap and fasces. The liberty cap made its appearance on the streets as well. In 1792, wearing the cap became a popular fad in Paris. The cap also became red, a color associated with the laborer's cap and hence with the democratic aspirations of its wearers.[71]

The Atlantic revolutionaries made their classical inspiration clear in many other ways as well. American, Dutch, French, and other revolutionaries explicitly modeled themselves on Greek and Roman freedom fighters. Cato of Utica, who had opted to kill himself rather than submit

A French Revolutionary–era liberty cap, patched with a red, white, and blue cockade.

to Caesar, was a particular favorite among American revolutionaries. Cato's popularity in the colonies was stimulated by the success of the play *Cato: A Tragedy,* which dramatized Plutarch's account of the last days of the Roman hero's life. Written by the eighteenth-century British playwright Joseph Addison, *Cato* was first performed in the American colonies in 1735 in Charleston, South Carolina, some twenty years after its opening performance in London. It quickly became one of the most popular plays in pre-Revolutionary America.[72]

When Patrick Henry spoke his famous line "give me liberty or give me death," he was probably quoting from Addison's play, in which Cato declared, "It is not now a time to talk of aught / But chains, or conquest; liberty, or death." Addison's play was also performed at Valley Forge where, in 1777, the American army had set up its winter quarters. Evidently, George Washington and other military leaders hoped to inspire their soldiers with Cato's example.[73]

Greek freedom fighters likewise functioned as models for the American revolutionaries. John Adams, in a letter to his friend James Warren, compared the American rebels with the Athenians and Spartans in their struggle against Persian and Macedonian invaders. "The Grecian Commonwealths were the most heroic confederacy that ever existed," Adams wrote, claiming American colonists should take heart and borrow from their admirable example. "Let us not be enslaved, my dear friend, by either Xerxes or Alexander."[74] The Virginian politician George Mason similarly praised "the little cluster of Greek republics" for having resisted and ultimately defeated the "Persian monarchy."[75]

French revolutionaries also liked to identify with ancient freedom fighters, although their preferred role model was not Cato but Lucius Brutus, the Roman hero who, according to Livy, had played an instrumental role in overthrowing the monarchy and establishing the Roman Republic. Voltaire's play *Brutus,* which was relatively unsuccessful after its premiere at the *Comédie française* in 1730, was revived in 1790 and became a breakout hit.[76] Set in the early days of the Roman Republic, right after the downfall of the Tarquin dynasty, the play revolves around the relationship between Lucius Brutus, Rome's first consul, and his son Titus. Titus is shown as the headstrong and victorious leader of Rome's armies. Frustrated in his political ambitions and blinded by his love for

Tullie, Tarquin's daughter, Titus decides to join a conspiracy against the republic—and, therefore, against his father. The conspiracy is uncovered, and Titus is condemned to death by his own father. The play ends with Brutus's refusal to be consoled. "Rome is free," he declares, and "that suffices, let us give thanks to the gods."[77]

In the heady atmosphere of 1790, the play's stirring rhetoric about freedom proved inflammatory. On November 17 and 19, 1790, the first two performances of Voltaire's *Brutus* took place at the National Theatre. The royalists in the audience applauded those lines favoring Tarquin. The revolutionaries—who were in the majority—applauded Brutus and other members of the resistance. When Brutus exclaimed, "Gods! Give us death rather than slavery!" the applause and shouts were "so deafening and the dust so thick that several moments were needed to restore order."[78] Seven months after the revival of *Brutus*, King Louis XVI made an abortive attempt to flee the country, and it was discovered he was conspiring to invade France with foreign support. He was immediately labeled a "Tarquin."[79]

Visual artists, too, contributed to the burgeoning Brutus cult in France. In 1787, Jacques-Louis David, one of France's most prominent classical painters, started working on a huge canvas that depicted the moment when the bodies of Lucius Brutus's executed sons were returned to him. It was completed in August 1789 and exhibited in the Salon in September 1789. The first commentaries did not reflect on its political message, possibly because of censorship or because it simply went undetected. But as the revolution radicalized, David's painting was increasingly read along the same lines as Voltaire's *Brutus*. David himself contributed to this new interpretation by designing sets for the revival of Voltaire's play. The play ended with a *tableau vivant*, in which the actors brought David's painting to life.[80]

As the revolution became more violent, some activists came to identify with different and more sanguinary Roman freedom fighters, such as Marcus Brutus. During the trial of Louis XVI, Louis-Antoine de Saint-Just called upon his fellow revolutionaries to take heart from the example of the second Brutus, who had killed the tyrant Caesar "with no law but the liberty of Rome."[81] In 1793, Charlotte Corday, a Girondist sympathizer, assassinated the Jacobin journalist Jean-Paul Marat, whom she

Jacques-Louis David, *Lictors Returning to Brutus the Bodies of His Sons* (1789).

considered a threat to the republic. When she set out on her mission, she reportedly carried a copy of Plutarch's *Lives*. Before her execution, she wrote that she looked forward to enjoying her "rest in the Elysian fields with Brutus and some ancients."[82]

In addition to modeling themselves on the ancient tyrannicides, the Atlantic revolutionaries looked to ancient lawgivers for inspiration, ransacking history books for examples of how to create free regimes. In the wake of the Declaration of Independence, most American colonies drew up new constitutions, a process eventually resulting in the drafting of the US Constitution. Classical antiquity functioned as an important reference point in the accompanying debates. John Adams, for instance, congratulated himself in 1776 on being born "at a time when the greatest lawgivers of antiquity would have wished to live."[83] Ten years later, during the ratification debate surrounding the federal constitution, America's founding fathers still identified with the ancient legislators. Thus, the authors of the *Federalist Papers* signed it together as *"Publius"*—a reference to Publius Valerius who, together with the first Brutus, established the Roman Republic after the last king of Rome had been expelled in 509 BC.[84] The ratification debate was conducted largely between pamphleteers with pen names like Cato and Brutus and, to a lesser extent, Solon and Lycurgus, the legendary Greek lawgivers.[85]

In Europe, references to classical models abounded during the constitutional debates. In the early stages of the French Revolution, as Harold Parker has shown, the example of antiquity was used especially by the more radical revolutionaries. During the debates of the Constituent Assembly in 1789 and 1790, the so-called *monarchiens*, who were proponents of limited reforms that would have left considerable power to Louis XVI, typically invoked the examples of antiquity only to argue against imitating them. By contrast, radical revolutionaries such as Honoré-Gabriel Riqueti (better known under his noble title, the Comte de Mirabeau), Antoine Barnave, and Bertrand Barère frequently called for the imitation of the classical republics.[86]

After the execution of the king and the establishment of the First Republic in 1792, the ancients were invoked ever more enthusiastically. When the first republican regime moved into its new hall in the Tuileries in May 1793, its members found themselves seated in a room decorated with full-length statues of Solon and Lycurgus, Plato and Demosthenes, Junius Brutus and Cincinnatus, all made from imitation marble. Thus, France's new, republican constitution was framed under the watchful eyes of ancient lawgivers and politicians.[87] This changed after 1794, as French revolutionaries became somewhat more hesitant to identify with the ancients in the wake of the Terror. But even then, ancient political models continued to be invoked, as the very names of successive regimes and governing institutions—the Consulate, the Tribunate, the Council of Edlers—illustrated.[88]

In the Netherlands, revolutionaries likewise sprinkled their speeches and pamphlets with references to the ancients. During debates about the new Batavian constitution, radical reformers explicitly invoked ancient examples to plead for a thorough democratization of the Dutch political system. In the so-called *Manifesto of the Twelve Apostles*, revolutionaries declared their ambition to turn "Batavians" into "Greeks or Romans."[89] Similarly in Germany, the poet and would-be revolutionary Friedrich Schlegel held up ancient Athens as a model for his own country, noting that "no state has reached a greater degree of freedom and equality than the Attic." Schlegel was convinced that "the moderns" still had "much to learn from the ancients."[90]

In light of such comments, it is hardly surprising that conservative commentators were quick to blame the era's revolutionary fervor on the inflammatory influence of the classics, much like Thomas Hobbes had more than a century earlier. Thus, the arch-Tory Jonathan Boucher was convinced that "an abundance of men, of liberal, generous and cultivated minds" had been "lost and undone by the habit, first acquired at school, of reading only the classics."[91] Similarly, Christoph Martin Wieland, a German writer living in Weimar, blamed the outbreak of the French Revolution on the influence of the classics. "At an age when sensitive souls still have an unblemished sense for the ethical, the beautiful and the great," Wieland wrote, the revolutionaries "became acquainted with the most excellent republicans of Greece and Rome, imbibing their love of republican liberty, their hatred of tyranny and monarchy, and their weakness for popular forms of government."[92]

Yet not all eighteenth-century revolutionaries shared in this uncritical admiration for classical antiquity. Some of the more sophisticated thinkers among them held the classical past at a greater distance; they also put more emphasis on their own originality by emphasizing that the republics they were creating were very different from classical predecessors. The world had changed so much since Cicero's day, they argued, that the knowledge of the ancients was no longer all that relevant. Alexander Hamilton, confessed to feeling nothing but "horror and disgust" when reading the histories of "the petty republics of Greece and Italy." Those were not examples the Americans ought to imitate. Instead, the "enlightened friends to liberty" should do their thinking for themselves. Thankfully, Hamilton noted, the "science of politics" had received "great improvement" in modern times.[93]

Such claims must be understood in light of the Enlightenment's impact on the development of political thought. Whereas sixteenth- and seventeenth-century political thinkers considered antiquity the pinnacle of human civilization, by the early eighteenth century, many enlightened thinkers had begun to argue that their own day and age was at least equal—nay, superior—to that earlier golden era. Such arguments were first developed in the context of the so-called Battle of the Books—a heated and long-ranging debate between European literati about the respective qualities of "ancient" and "modern" playwrights and poets—and ultimately created greater awareness of the achievements of postclassical Europe in other domains, too, such as politics.[94]

Yet even those revolutionaries most eager to emphasize their distance from classical precedents continued to embrace the antique, democratic conception of freedom. That much becomes clear when we turn to the debate about representative government. In ancient democracies, the people exercised legislative power directly. Laws were made by the demos as a whole, assembled for that express purpose in the marketplace or in specially designated public areas such as the Pnyx in Athens. But that was, of course, impracticable in the republics created by the Atlantic revolutionaries, which were far larger and more populous. Hence, the founders of the American, French, and other republics introduced representative institutions, notably elected legislatures. Laws were now made not by all adult male citizens but by a select group of representatives. If this was popular self-government, it was definitely very different from that of the ancients.

The introduction of representative institutions sparked considerable debate among the Atlantic revolutionaries. Some were anxious that this deviation from the ancient examples would undermine popular self-government and, hence, liberty. Such worries had first been articulated in 1762 by Jean-Jacques Rousseau. In his *Social Contract,* Rousseau warned that by handing over legislative power to representatives, citizens made themselves unfree, since the laws under which they lived would be made not by themselves but by a small group of people. He pointed to the English example, in particular, to buttress his case. The English believed themselves to be free, but in Rousseau's view, they were "greatly mistaken." Rather, Rousseau claimed, they were free only during the election of Parliament members; but "as soon as they are elected, [the English people] is enslaved, it is nothing."[95]

Some Atlantic revolutionaries shared Rousseau's worries. In his *On Civil Liberty,* Richard Price agreed with the Swiss thinker that freedom "in its most perfect degree" could be enjoyed only in "small states," where every individual was capable of giving suffrage in person and of being chosen for public office.[96] Price's own experience with the workings of the British Parliament only increased his concern. The House of Commons, he noted, claimed to represent the people, but it was in fact not accountable to the population at large due to the long terms in office of Members of Parliament and the small proportion of the population they actually represented.

Price, unlike Rousseau, made peace with representative institutions; direct democracy would not have been possible in large, modern states, after all. But Price did recommend that representatives be elected for short terms and that they be held accountable to their constituents. Only by keeping strict control over their elected representatives could the people counteract the downsides of representative government. "If the persons to whom the trust of government is committed hold their places for short terms," he wrote:

> If they are chosen by the unbiassed voices of a majority of the state, and subject to their instructions, liberty will be enjoyed in its highest degree. But if they are chosen for long terms by a part only of the state; and if during that term they are subject to no controul from their constituents; the very idea of liberty will be lost and the power of chusing representatives becomes nothing but a power, lodged in a few, to chuse at certain periods, a body of masters for themselves and for the rest of the community.[97]

Yet other revolutionaries took a more positive view of representation. Thinkers such as Alexander Hamilton talked about "the great principle of representation" as one of the most brilliant inventions of "modern Europe."[98] James Madison, Hamilton's co-author in the *Federalist Papers,* concurred. In his view, representative government had several intrinsic advantages over direct democracy. Most notably, through elections, legislative power would ideally be handed over to a "chosen body of citizens," who would be wise enough to discern "the true interest of their country." "Under such a regulation," Madison optimistically concluded, "it may well happen that the public voice, pronounced by the representatives of the people, will be more consonant to the public good than if pronounced by the people themselves, convened for the purpose."[99]

It is important to note, however, that even these modernists believed that representative institutions were problematic from a freedom-centric perspective. While Madison thought that the representative system was more likely than direct democracy to lead to good government, he also conceded that it might easily lead to oligarchic oppression. There was always a danger, Madison noted, that representatives would "betray the interests of the people." Hence, frequent elections were absolutely necessary to prevent the legislature from becoming oligarchic. Demanding that representatives subject their actions to regular scrutiny by the public would hopefully prevent them from working in their own interests rather than in the interests of their constituents.[100]

In short, in the fledgling American republic, even those revolutionaries most eager to talk about their republics as "new" and "modern," continued to think about freedom as equivalent to a government in which people kept direct and active control over the way they were governed. Madison made this quite explicit. "The genius of republican liberty," he wrote in the *Federalist Papers,* "seems to demand . . . not only that all power should be derived from the people, but that those intrusted with it should be kept in dependence on the people by a short duration of their appointments; and that even during this short period the trust should be placed not in a few, but a number of hands."[101]

Across the Atlantic, enlightened revolutionaries expressed similar views. Nicolas de Condorcet, a philosopher and deputy to the National Convention, was just as eager as Hamilton and Madison to emphasize the superiority of modern republics vis-à-vis their ancient counterparts. The Greek republics, he explained, were not entirely suitable examples for the "great nations of the modern age," because they were based on slavery and did not know the representative system. At the same time, Condorcet warned against the danger of "indirect despotism" posed by representative institutions. If representatives could not be held accountable by the people on a regular basis, representative government was just as likely to slide into tyranny as one-man rule. Hence, electoral procedures that kept deputies dependent on the people were very important for maintaining liberty.[102]

All this means that there are good reasons to think of the Atlantic Revolutions as the "last great act of the Renaissance," as the historian John

Pocock famously labeled it.[103] In many ways, the struggle for freedom in the late eighteenth century can be seen as the culmination of a centuries-long revival of ancient political thought initiated by Renaissance humanists such as Petrarch, Leonardo Bruni, and Niccolò Machiavelli. The ancient texts they rediscovered and popularized (and that were subsequently given a central place in school curricula) helped to shift decisively the political imagination of European elites. While these texts, of course, cannot be held directly responsible for the outbreak of the Atlantic Revolutions (*pace* conservatives such as Boucher or Wieland), they did do much to turn these revolutions into struggles for democratic freedom rather than into rebellions with more limited aims.

At the same time, it is important to emphasize that the Atlantic Revolutions were the Renaissance's curtain call. After 1800, freedom fighters, by and large, stopped invoking the ancient models and slogans that had played such a prominent role in European and American political thought. In the course of the nineteenth and twentieth centuries, reformers and would-be revolutionaries turned to the examples of the Atlantic revolutionaries themselves rather than to the increasingly distant world of the ancients. Thus, the examples of Harmodius and Aristogeiton, Cato of Utica, or the two Brutuses, were no longer invoked. Instead, when they wanted to support their fight for democratic freedom by invoking historical precedents, nineteenth-century radicals, suffragists, and abolitionists referred to examples from the more recent past, notably the American founders, the National Assembly, or the Jacobins.

This transition had much to do with the very real achievements of the Atlantic revolutionaries in transforming their political world. In many places, the revolutionary upheaval of the late eighteenth century caused a profound break with what had come before. This was, of course, most visible in the United States, where revolutionaries created an entirely new country that was far more democratic than any other in the world. Just as spectacularly, their French counterparts succeeded in destroying one of the mightiest monarchies of Europe. And even though the French Republic eventually succumbed in turn, the ancien régime was never restored in France, despite the best efforts of reactionary forces.

As a result, when radicals and revolutionaries continued the fight for democratic freedom in the nineteenth and twentieth centuries, they did so without the classical garb of the Atlantic revolutionaries. Even when ancient symbols were still invoked, they received an entirely new meaning. Thus, though the cap of liberty continued to be an icon of freedom in the nineteenth century, the symbol was no longer understood as a reference to the classical past. Instead, the liberty cap became almost exclusively associated with the French revolutionaries, in particular the Jacobins, and hence was depicted as it had been in the heyday of the French Revolution: in red.[104]

Natural Rights and Freedom in the American Revolution

The Atlantic revolutionaries did not turn only to the authority of the ancients to justify self-governance. They also frequently invoked concepts such as natural liberty and individual rights. Both in North America and in Europe, revolutionaries legitimated rebellion against their lawful sovereigns by arguing that these sovereigns had infringed on their subjects' natural rights and liberties. Subsequently, most of the new, revolutionary governments issued official declarations listing man's natural rights, signaling their intent to do better than their predecessors. The French Declaration of the Rights of Man and the Citizen and the American Bill of Rights are the most well-known examples of this trend.

Much has been made by scholars of the prominence of rights-talk in the context of the Atlantic Revolutions, notably the American Revolution. More specifically, historians such as Joyce Appleby and Isaac Kramnick have seen rights declarations as evidence for a "Lockean" influence on the American revolutionaries, wholly different from and indeed opposed to the classical legacy. The American Revolution, therefore, can be seen not just as the last act of the Renaissance but also as the beginning of a new way of thinking about freedom. In this interpretation, late-eighteenth-century revolutionaries, while building on ideas of seventeenth-century thinkers such as Locke, were the first to identify the free state with limited government rather than with democracy. Under this conception of freedom, a government could be called free if it recognized and respected its citizens' natural rights and refrained from infringing upon them—regardless of who was in power.[105]

The supposed emergence of this new understanding of freedom is often explained with reference to the fact that the American Revolution coincided with the tail end of another revolution in the West: the creation of market societies. In the seventeenth century, the argument goes, market exchanges in goods and labor slowly replaced the traditional direct-consumption society, both in Europe and its colonies. Observation of this phenomenon led to a new idea: that of a natural social order, created without compulsion but, as it were, through an "invisible hand." This idea sparked the imagination of the American revolutionaries and led them to think of government as an entity whose sole responsibility was to protect individual rights. Hence they came to redefine a free government as one that stuck to the task of protecting these rights—and notably, the right to property.[106]

There are several reasons, however, to reject the argument that the Atlantic revolutions were responsible for popularizing the understanding of freedom as the preservation of individual rights. First, this interpretation is based on a mistaken interpretation of the so-called Lockean tradition. Locke, as we have seen, at no point suggested that freedom be equated with the protection of natural rights by a limited government. He explicitly denied that "civil liberty" entailed freedom to do what you want. Instead he argued that liberty was the product of living under laws made with common consent. Locke's emphasis on natural liberty and natural rights was, in other words, perfectly compatible with the classical, democratic conception of freedom—or, to put it differently, Locke's understanding of freedom was pretty much indistinguishable from that of Jean-Jacques Rousseau's, even though the latter is usually seen as an exponent of a very different and more democratic tradition.[107]

The American revolutionaries themselves made it perfectly clear that they understood Locke's writings as pointing toward a Rousseauvian, democratic conception of freedom rather than as merely propagating limited government. Hence, when they invoked Locke's authority, they usually did so to signal their adherence to the democratic conception of freedom. Richard Price, as we have seen, identified freedom with popular self-government; he also argued that his principles were "the same as those taught by Mr. Locke, and all the writers on civil liberty, who have been hitherto most admired in this country."[108] Critics of the American

Revolution agreed. Josiah Tucker, a Welsh clergyman and an inveterate opponent of the American rebels, described Price as a "follower of Locke." Tucker also maintained that "honest, undissembling Rousseau" was the man who "clearly saw, where the Lockian hypothesis must necessarily end"—namely, in extreme democracy.[109] Similarly, the Scottish philosopher Dugald Stewart attributed the democratizing tendencies of the American Revolution to "the mistaken notions concerning political liberty which have been so widely disseminated in Europe by the writings of Mr Locke."[110]

Second, an analysis of the most important "Lockean" documents produced by the American revolutionaries—their various declarations of rights—clearly shows that their authors by no means meant to challenge the classical, democratic understanding of freedom or to introduce a new conception of liberty as the protection of individual rights. After the outbreak of war with Britain, many of the newly independent American colonies, while creating new constitutions, issued declarations of rights. In several of these declarations, freedom was identified with popular self-government. The Declaration and Resolves issued by the First Continental Congress in 1774, stated "that the foundation of English liberty, and of all free government, is a right in the people to participate in their legislative council" and that, hence, the American colonists had the right to legislate in their own assemblies.[111]

The federal Bill of Rights ratified seventeen years later, in 1791, did not contain such explicitly democratic language. Instead it listed a series of individual rights, such as the right to freedom of worship, the right to bear arms, and the right not to have soldiers sequestered in one's home. The Bill of Rights therefore is sometimes described as embodying a new vision of the free state—as a limited, rights-based state rather than a popular government. After 1776, the argument goes, experience with democratic or semidemocratic regimes at the state level convinced many American political actors that the main threat to liberty in a republican regime came from majoritarian tyranny, not from executive overreach. Hence, in the 1780s, the notion of liberty underwent a crucial change. As one historian of the American Revolution put it, "The liberty that was now emphasized, was personal or private, the protection of individual rights against all governmental encroachments, particularly by the legislature, the body which the Whigs had traditionally cherished as the people's exclusive repository of their public liberty and their surest weapon to defend their private liberties."[112]

There is little evidence, however, to support the idea that the introduction of the federal Bill of Rights signaled a shift away from the democratic conception of freedom toward a new, rights-based conception of liberty. That becomes clear when we take a closer look at the debate surrounding the introduction of the Bill of Rights in the summer of 1789. At this time, American political elites had divided into two rival factions. Federalists, on the one hand, supported a strong, national government. They were opposed by the Antifederalists, who believed that the main power should remain with the states. In addition to disputing the new constitution, these two groups debated the idea of a bill of rights. Federalists were adamantly opposed to the introduction of a federal bill of rights, while Antifederalists were strongly in favor. However, throughout this discussion, both Federalists and Antifederalists continued to argue from the same, democratic conception of freedom.

Federalists opposed the idea of a bill of rights, mainly because they believed a bill of rights was superfluous for the protection of liberty in a democratic republic. In monarchies such as Britain, it might be necessary to list a people's rights in order to dissuade the king from trampling upon them. But in a republic such as the United States, where the people ruled itself, government did not pose a threat to freedom. As one Federalist politician put it, in America, a bill of rights was "insignificant since government is considered as originating from the people, and all the power government now has is a grant from the people."[113] Similarly, Hamilton remarked in the *Federalist Papers* that bills of rights "have no application" in popular republics. "Here, in strictness, the people surrender nothing; and as they retain everything they have no need of particular reservations."[114]

By contrast, the Antifederalists—the opponents of the new, federal constitution—strongly supported the introduction of a bill of rights; several of them had actually voted against the new, federal constitution in 1788 because it did not contain a bill of rights. But their support for a bill of rights was by no means motivated by an adherence to new and more modern ways of thinking about freedom. Instead, they remained firmly committed to the idea that a people could be free only to the extent that it kept control over the way it was governed. The new constitution, they feared, would establish an "aristocracy" that would eventually renounce "all dependence on the people by continuing themselves, and their children, in the government."[115] They hoped therefore to make the new constitution more democratic by doubling the size of the House of Representatives, shortening the terms of the senators, making the senators subject to recall, and reducing the formal powers of the Senate. A bill of rights was likewise meant to be part of this democratizing agenda. Through this instrument, Antifederalists hoped to enhance public awareness of popular rights and thus to encourage the people to spring into action if and when the federal government infringed on these rights.[116]

A different view was expressed by Madison. Madison was one of the Federalists' most prominent spokesmen, and like most Federalists, he initially rejected the idea of a bill of rights, arguing that such "parchment barriers" had proven time and again to be entirely useless against despotism.[117] However, in 1789, he changed his mind, largely because he was convinced that a bill of rights would take the wind out of the Antifederalists' sails. Congressional action on a bill of rights, Madison hoped, would defeat the call for a second constitutional convention by diehard Antifederalists. Madison subsequently played a crucial role in shepherding the Bill of Rights through Congress.

When trying to persuade his colleagues of the necessity of a bill of rights, Madison added an important new perspective to the debate. Unlike the Antifederalists, Madison did not present such a bill as an instrument to enhance popular control over government; instead, he depicted it as a protection against majority tyranny. As he explained to the House of Representatives on June 8, 1789, in the United States, executive power did not pose the same threat to liberty as it did in Britain, so a bill of rights might seem superfluous. Yet it could prove useful to protect individuals against another danger: "the abuse of the community." A bill of rights, as Madison explained, might be "one mean to control the majority from those acts to which they might be otherwise inclined."[118]

Yet it would be a gross overstatement of the available evidence to see Madison's stray remark as evidence for a larger shift in thinking about freedom as the protection of individual rights against majority tyranny. None of Madison's Federalist colleagues, after all, endorsed his particular interpretation of the Bill of Rights. Neither did the Antifederalists. Moreover, Madison's own support for a bill of rights as a way to protect liberty always remained lukewarm. His speech introducing the bill to the newly elected House of Representatives was remarkably unenthusiastic: he described it as "neither improper nor altogether useless"—not exactly a ringing endorsement.[119]

More generally, Madison's writings show that a bill of rights was never his preferred solution to majority tyranny. In his most influential writings of the 1780s—his contributions to the *Federalist Papers*—Madison reflected extensively on the danger of majoritarian tyranny. But here, he did not refer to a bill of rights as a solution; instead he maintained that the tyranny of the majority could best be avoided by creating "extended" republics. In large republics, the number of interests, and therefore the number of factions based on these interests, was multiplied. Hence, it became "less probable," Madison argued, that "a majority of the whole will have a common motive to invade the rights of other citizens; or if such a common motive exists, it will be more difficult for all who feel it to discover their own strength and to act in unison with each other."[120]

In short, by issuing declarations of rights, American revolutionaries were by no means signaling that they had come to adopt a different way of thinking about freedom than humanists such as Rinuccini, La Boétie, or Harrington. Rather, they continued to think about freedom as something that could be established only through the imposition of popular control over government. The declarations they issued contained democratic language emphasizing that the right to participate in government was the foundation on which all other rights and liberties were based. Even the Bill of Rights was not intended to express a novel conception of freedom as limited government. Rather, it was designed to give people the wherewithal to rebel against their governments, should those governments overstep their rights.[121]

The French Declaration of the Rights of Man and the Citizen

The same can be said, mutatis mutandis, about the French Declaration of the Rights of Man and the Citizen. Unlike the American founders, who issued the Bill of Rights as something of an afterthought, the French revolutionaries almost immediately set about drawing up a declaration of rights. The declaration was promulgated on August 26, 1789, less than three months after the Third Estate had started the revolution by transforming itself into the National Assembly—and more than two years before the new constitution itself was adopted.[122]

Debates show little evidence that French revolutionaries thought of the declaration as gesturing toward a new understanding of freedom. The working draft of the declaration, presented on August 17, 1789, by a committee headed by the Comte de Mirabeau, was far more abstract and philosophical than the American Bill of Rights. Rather than enumerating key individual rights, it laid out the principles on which any legitimate constitution must be based. The first article stipulated that all men were born free and equal. This statement was followed by a number of articles outlining the basic principles of legitimate government—that is, the kind of government suitable for free and equal individuals. These principles held that all political communities were founded on a social contract and that all power came forth from the nation. Office-holders had authority only to the extent that it was delegated to them by the nation.[123]

Like Spinoza, Locke, and Rousseau, Mirabeau made clear that man's natural liberty could be preserved only in a specific kind of institutional context; namely, in a government based on the sovereignty of the nation. Article 6 of the draft declaration made this point even more explicit by stating that "the liberty of the citizen consists in being subject but to the law."[124] Article 4 declared, "A nation should recognize no other laws than those that were expressly approved and consented to by the nation itself or by its legally elected representatives."[125] To be free, in other words, was to live under laws of one's own making rather than under the arbitrary will of a king or prince.

Mirabeau's draft, however, was rejected by the Constitutional Assembly for reasons that remain somewhat mysterious. The declaration that was eventually adopted at first sight seemed to embody a very different logic. The first two articles seem to suggest that French revolutionaries had come to think of freedom as the protection of individual rights against governmental interference: "1. Men are born and remain free and equal in rights. Social distinctions may be founded only upon the general good. 2. The aim of all political association is the preservation of the natural and imprescriptible rights of man. These rights are liberty, property, security, and resistance to oppression." Also, individual rights are enumerated in articles 4 (the right to personal liberty), 7–9 (the right to fair trial), 10 (freedom of religion), 11 (freedom of speech), and 17 (property rights).

Yet, upon closer consideration, the declaration continued the Rousseauvian logic of Mirabeau's draft. All of the articles enumerating individual rights contained a disclaimer explaining that these rights could be limited by law, whereas article 6 stipulated that "law is the expression of the general will" and that, hence, "every citizen has a right to participate personally, or through his representative, in its foundation." In short, the declaration argued that individual rights had to be upheld but that the precise nature and limits of these rights could be determined by the lawmaker—the political community as a whole. The declaration also made it clear that national sovereignty was a key right. Thus, article 3 stipulated that "the principle of all sovereignty resides essentially in the nation. No body nor individual may exercise any authority which does not proceed directly from the nation."

The Rousseauvian nature of the declaration is confirmed when we look at the debate following the Declaration of Rights, notably the pamphlet wars sparked by Edmund Burke's *Reflections on the Revolution in France* in 1791.[126] In this book, Burke rejected the very idea of natural rights as fictitious and "metaphysical." He was scandalized, in particular, by the notion that men could have a natural right to participate in government. "As to the share of power, authority, and direction that each individual ought to have in the management of the state," he wrote, "that I must deny to be among the direct original rights of man in civil society."[127]

Burke's impassioned attack on the Declaration of the Rights of Man and the Citizen provoked several equally impassioned responses. Most notable was the long reply by Tom Paine, a British-born political thinker and enthusiastic supporter of the Atlantic Revolutions. In his bestselling treatise *Rights of Man*, Paine set about defending the principle of natural rights against the Burkean emphasis on prescription and convention.[128] Paine also made clear that he thought of these rights in a Rousseauvian manner. In his view, the main goal of both the American and French rights declarations was to proclaim popular control over government: "Monarchical sovereignty, the enemy of mankind, and the source of misery, is abolished; and sovereignty itself is restored to its natural and original place, the Nation."[129]

Similar views were put forward by other critics of Burke. James Mackintosh, a young Scottish lawyer, penned his *Vidiciae Gallica* to, as the subtitle explained, "defend the French Revolution and its English admirers against the accusations of the Right Hon. Edmund Burke." After praising the French for having begun their revolution with "a solemn declaration of these sacred, inalienable, and imprescriptible rights," Mackintosh made it clear that he conceived of the declaration as an instrument to establish popular control over government. Much as the American Antifederalists had done, he described rights declarations as "perhaps the only expedient that can be devised by human wisdom to keep alive the public vigilance against the usurpation of partial interests."[130] Mackintosh also argued that, according to natural law, "men retain a right to a share in their own Government" and that "the slightest deviation from [this principle] legitimates every tyranny."[131]

The Rousseauvian interpretation of the Declaration of the Rights of Man and the Citizen was not universally accepted; some commentators understood the declaration as a more libertarian document. But the latter interpretation was mainly pushed by opponents and critics of the French Revolution, such as the legal philosopher Jeremy Bentham. Bentham had initially welcomed the outbreak of the revolution, which he saw as a long-awaited opportunity to put his proposals for legal reform into practice. But in the wake of the Terror, Bentham—like so many others—changed his mind. The execution of Louis XVI, in particular, made a deep impression, and Bentham began to violently denounce the revolution.

His new, hostile view of the revolution is evidenced in the short treatise *Anarchical Fallacies*, written in 1795 (though not published until much later), denouncing the Declaration of the Rights of Man. (His original title, *Pestilential Nonsense Unmasked*, left even less to the imagination.) In this treatise, Bentham famously argued that natural rights did not exist. In his view, natural rights were "nonsense upon stilts." And natural rights doctrine was not just absurd; it was also dangerous. Belief in these rights, Bentham warned, would undermine all political authority. Natural rights were "the rights of anarchy—the order of chaos."[132] When taken seriously, after all, such rights should be thought of as trumps against state power—trumps individuals could use to flaunt all laws if they believed them to infringe upon their rights.

Bentham's critique was to have a long shelf life. But his reading of the Declaration of the Rights of Man and the Citizen, it must be emphasized, was a hostile one. The French revolutionaries themselves, as well as their Anglo-American admirers, did not think of natural rights as circumscribing a private sphere never to be infringed upon by state power, let alone as a license to do whatever one wanted. Instead, they thought of the Declaration of Rights as a document propagating popular sovereignty, which was the basis of both legitimacy and freedom. They remained close, in other words, to radical natural-rights thinkers like Spinoza, Locke, and Rousseau. Like these thinkers, they claimed that civil liberty, the kind of liberty one enjoyed in society, consisted in the right to be governed solely by laws made with common consent.

In sum, the Atlantic revolutionaries' invocation of natural rights did not point in the direction of a new way of thinking about freedom. But this is not to say that the influence of Locke and Rousseau added nothing at all to the debate about freedom during the Atlantic Revolutions. While talk about natural liberty and natural rights did not steer the debate in an entirely new direction, it did allow for the radicalization of freedom-talk. The self-governing Greeks and Romans served as a powerful indictment of the old monarchies and oligarchic republics. But these examples could be less easily invoked to criticize racialized or gendered forms of oppression: the ancients, after all, had held slaves, and they had excluded women from political participation. By contrast, natural rights doctrine, with its appeal to reason rather than historical precedent, allowed radical revolutionaries to criticize these forms of oppression as purely conventional and thus illegitimate.

Hence, during the Atlantic Revolutions, the most radical challenges to the political status quo were typically couched in natural rights language rather than in quotes from Herodotus or Livy. When revolutionary women (aided by a more limited number of male revolutionaries) challenged their exclusion from the political sphere, they typically argued that such exclusions violated the natural equality between the sexes. Olympe de Gouges, for instance, pointed out that, among animals, and indeed among "all living organisms," the sexes were "intermingled" and "cooperating harmoniously." "Only man," de Gouges continued, "has cobbled together a rule to exclude himself from this system." But the exclusion of women, "a sex that is blessed with every intellectual faculty," was "bizarre" and "blind," an "expression of the crassest ignorance."[133]

At the same time, the Atlantic Revolutions also clearly highlight the limits of this radical potential. For the authority of nature could just as easily be used to argue *against* the inclusion of marginalized groups—that is, to create new hierarchies of race and gender based on nature rather than convention. Thus de Gouges's arguments were countered by male revolutionaries who claimed that woman's nature made her unfit to exercise political power. As one French revolutionary put it, "Since when is it permitted to give up one's sex? Since when is it decent to see women abandoning the pious cares of their households, the cribs of their children, to come to public places, to harangues in the galleries, at the bar of the senate? Is it to men that nature confided domestic cares? Has she given us breasts to breast-feed our children?"[134]

The invocation of natural rights doctrine by no means necessitated a "cascade" of rights. There was no inner logic inexorably leading from the Declaration of the Rights of Man to the abolition of slavery or to female suffrage.[135] Moreover, as we shall see, in the nineteenth and twentieth centuries, the role of rights-talk in political debate changed fundamentally. In the postrevolutionary period, the idea that human beings had individual rights was increasingly invoked to argue against any extension of democracy. Political actors came to insist that popular government, instead of being an indispensable foundation for rights such as religious freedom and property, posed a major threat to them. Hence protecting rights—and the sphere of freedom they demarcated—required constraining democratic control over government.

In the decades following Patrick Henry's speech to the Second Virginia Convention, in sum, revolutionary movements all over the Atlantic world contested the political status quo in the name of freedom. Inspired by their reading of classical sources, as well as by modern adaptations of these sources, revolutionaries in Philadelphia, Amsterdam, Paris, and Warsaw argued with increasing insistence that anyone subjected to the arbitrary power of hereditary monarchs or oligarchic elites was no better off than a slave. The only way to be free, they emphasized, was to maintain control over the way one was governed. Hence, the Atlantic revolutionaries executed kings and toppled oligarchic elites, replacing them with governments that were, at least by their own lights, popular or democratic. The revolutionaries also adopted laws meant to promote economic equality, which they believed to be a necessary precondition for popular self-government.

The ideals propagated by the Atlantic revolutionaries would continue to inspire revolutionaries for decades to come. Throughout the nineteenth and twentieth centuries, radicals in Europe and the United States fought for manhood suffrage in the name of freedom. At the same time, the arguments of the most radical revolutionaries were picked up by new and increasingly vocal movements. Abolitionists came to insist with greater vehemence that the ideals of 1776 and 1789 could be realized only by eradicating slavery and extending full political and civil rights to blacks. Similarly, suffragists took up Olympe de Gouges's fight against the "enslavement" of women and argued that their full emancipation required extending to them the right to vote.

Yet, the late eighteenth century was not just a crucial time for the dissemination of the democratic theory of freedom; the outbreak of the Atlantic Revolutions also sparked a powerful backlash against democracy. This backlash led to the conceptualization of a wholly new way of thinking about freedom, in which liberty had nothing to do with establishing popular control over government. Rather, a person was free if they could peacefully enjoy their lives and goods—and that condition was, if anything, threatened rather than secured by the introduction of democracy. Thus, as we shall see, the concept of freedom was gradually transformed from being a weapon to fight *for* democracy into an instrument that could be used to battle *against* it.

PART III

Rethinking Freedom

CHAPTER 5

Inventing Modern Liberty

In 1784, Johann August Eberhard published the essay *On the Liberty of the Citizen and the Principles of the Form of Government*. A philosophy professor at the University of Halle, Eberhard was mainly known for his enlightened religious views. He had caused a minor scandal in 1772 by arguing that salvation did not depend on revelation and that, hence, a heathen could go to heaven. But, as his 1784 essay showed, Eberhard also had a keen interest in moral and political questions. The essay, he explained, was a contribution to the ongoing debate about what it meant to be free in a society or as a society. He wanted to correct the "young republicans" who believed that freedom was to be found only in democracies and not in monarchies. While Eberhard did not specify who these young republicans were, it seems plausible that at least some of them had been inspired by the example of the American Revolution.[1]

Indeed, since the outbreak of the War of Independence, the American fight for freedom had generated considerable enthusiasm, and the struggle between Great Britain and its recalcitrant colonies was extensively reported in the German-language press. In 1783, the widely read journal *Berlinische Monatsschrift* celebrated American victory against the English with the poem "America's Liberty." But some Germans went further, not just celebrating American victory against the British, but also arguing that Europeans should likewise try to liberate themselves by getting rid of royal absolutism. In 1782 Johann Christian Schmohl, a resident of Halle—and, like Eberhard, a subject of the Prussian king Frederick the Great—published *On North America and Democracy*, in which he praised the Americans for their fight for "popular sovereignty" and expressed the hope that Europe too would soon throw off the yoke of "tyranny" and thus gain "liberty."[2]

Eberhard strongly disagreed with such views. It was an "unfounded prejudice," he wrote, to believe that liberty was to be found only in democratic republics. The subjects of Frederick the Great already were free—hence, they needed no liberating—but they were free in a different way from the citizens of popular republics. To clarify, Eberhard explained that, when talking about "the liberty of the citizen," one should distinguish between two very different kinds of liberty: civil liberty and political liberty. A people had political liberty when it participated in government. Hence political liberty existed only in republics, and it was most extensive in democratic republics. In contrast, individuals who had the right to act as they wished, insofar as such acts were not restricted by law, enjoyed civil liberty. This type of liberty did not depend on the form of government; it could exist as easily in a monarchy as in a republic.

Eberhard's distinction between civil and political liberty was quite novel. As we have seen, some thinkers in the seventeenth century had begun to distinguish between natural liberty (the liberty one enjoyed in the state of nature) and civil liberty (the liberty one could enjoy in society).[3] Throughout the seventeenth and most of the eighteenth century, the terms "civil liberty" and "political liberty" were typically used interchangeably. By sharply distinguishing between these two types of liberty, Eberhard was not just trying to achieve greater conceptual clarity. He was attempting to subvert the theory of freedom defended by the Atlantic revolutionaries, who argued that a people could be free only if it had control over the way in which it was governed.

Eberhard claimed that political and civil liberty were not only different from each other but often inversely related. Experience taught that when a people enjoyed more political liberty, it had less civil liberty, whereas a people living under royal absolutism often had a great deal of civil liberty. In Sparta, for instance, citizens were not allowed to educate their children according to their own insights. Similarly, in the Swiss Republic, people enjoyed less freedom of thought than in an absolute monarchy such as Frederick the Great's Prussia. And in Great Britain, tax burdens were heavier and punishments more severe than in continental monarchies. This helped to explain why citizens of so-called free countries often left their fatherlands "to seek liberty in a country ruled by an unlimited monarch."[4]

How to make sense of this "curious phenomenon," as Eberhard called it? The power of absolute monarchs, he pointed out, was typically less secure than that in republican governments, which could count on more broad-based support. Hence, kings and queens were inclined to leave their subjects more freedom to act, so as not to provoke discontent. By contrast, in republics, the restriction of civil liberty was more easily accepted, because such restriction was balanced by citizens' awareness of their control over government. At the same time, in a democracy, the sovereign people was often swayed by passions and ignorance to take measures that undermined the common good and harmed individual liberties. Thus, popular governments often governed despotically, whereas in an enlightened monarchy like Prussia, the king and his civil servants acted on the basis of knowledge and reason. So if one wanted to be free, introducing democracy—as the American revolutionaries and their radical German admirers wanted to do—was not a good strategy. Rather, one had better put one's hopes in "unlimited monarchy." Civil liberty was best preserved not by the government of the ignorant multitude but under the rule of a wise and enlightened ruler like Frederick the Great.[5]

Eberhard was by no means alone in these views. During and after the Atlantic Revolutions, his distinction between civil and political liberty became increasingly and widely shared. This was not just the case within in the German-speaking world, where his essay was broadly read. All over Europe and North America, voices went up to criticize the democratic conception of freedom as misguided or insufficiently sophisticated. The introduction of this new way of thinking about freedom must be understood as part of a general backlash against the Atlantic Revolutions that first gained steam in the second half of the 1770s. Over time, an ever louder chorus of British loyalists, Dutch regents, French monarchists, and other counterrevolutionaries attempted to mobilize public opinion in defense of the political and social status quo.

In the wake of this backlash, a flood of pamphlets, treatises, and newspaper articles appeared in Europe and North America, with titles such as *Some Observations On Liberty, Civil Liberty Asserted,* or *On the Liberty of the Citizen.* These works dissected and criticized the revolutionary democratic conception of freedom. Like Eberhard, the authors of these broadsides defended the idea that liberty, or at least civil liberty, had more to do with being able to live one's own life in peace and quiet than with exercising control over the way in which one was governed. These authors also repeated Eberhard's stronger claim that political liberty was not just distinct from, but a potential threat to, civil liberty.

The impact of the counterrevolutionary critique would be long-lasting. This was not primarily because of the intellectual cogency of the counterrevolutionary theory of freedom; rather, it was the result of a continued backlash against democracy. As we shall see, the campaign against democracy was continued not just by hardline counterrevolutionaries but also by new intellectual movements, such as liberalism in continental Europe and Federalism in the United States. While the political goals of these movements differed in many crucial ways from those of the counterrevolutionaries, they were nearly as hostile toward democracy—and hence toward the democratic theory of freedom—as were men like Eberhard.

Freedom and the Counterrevolution, 1776–1815

Many welcomed the Atlantic Revolutions as the beginning of a new era. The English poet William Wordsworth, who traveled through France in the 1790s when he was in his twenties, expressed such sentiments most memorably in his autobiographical poem *The Prelude.* "Bliss was it in that dawn to be alive," reads a famous passage from book eleven. "But to be young was very heaven!" Young Wordsworth's blissful feeling might have had something to do with the fact that, while in France, he experienced his first great love affair. But excitement about revolutionary politics also contributed to his outburst of enthusiasm. By giving power to the people, Wordsworth hoped, the French Revolution would bring "better days to all mankind."[6]

Yet the introduction of new and more democratic political regimes in America, France, the Netherlands, and other countries also sparked an immediate backlash. The publication of Edmund Burke's *Reflections on the Revolution in France,* which appeared in 1791, is often seen as marking the birth of this counterrevolutionary movement, but in fact, it had begun over a decade earlier, when the American Revolution provoked a torrent of publications by British loyalists defending the political and social status quo. Similarly, the Dutch Revolt of the 1780s was combated not just by Prussian armies but also by a host of conservative writers, who defended the existing order with their pens rather than the sword.[7]

Opponents of the Atlantic Revolutions were motivated by many concerns. Some conservatives found fault with revolutionary attempts to remake governments according to human reason rather than tradition. Others were perturbed by efforts to separate church and state, which, they feared, would set society on a path to godlessness. But above all, counterrevolutionaries objected to the democratic turn. As one historian of the movement has put it, "Whatever else it may have been—Catholic or Protestant, secular or theocrat, Anglophile or Anglophobe, for or against intermediary bodies, moderate or extreme—counter-revolutionary thought . . . was always profoundly anti-democratic."[8]

Counterrevolutionary thinkers took a dim view of the political capabilities of ordinary people. They saw the masses as akin to children, utterly incapable of governing themselves. At best, popular rule would bring the ignorant and dim-witted to power; at worst, it would lead to violent savagery. As François-René de Chateaubriand, a French conservative, put it, "The people are children; give them a rattle without explaining the cause of the noise it makes and they will break it in order to find out."[9]

Hence, while they defended very different political regimes (British loyalists were in favor of constitutional monarchy, Dutch regents wanted to hold on to their oligarchic republic, and French and German royalists supported absolute monarchy), counterrevolutionaries were all equally opposed to democracy.

A key component of the counterrevolutionary attack on democracy was the call for a new understanding of freedom. All over the Atlantic world, revolutionaries had argued that their political reforms would set men free. But that promise, their opponents countered, was hollow. Being free had nothing to do with popular self-government; at best, participation in government offered an inferior "political" freedom. Instead, people were free—that is, they possessed "civil" liberty—if they and their property were secure; if they were able to enjoy their lives and possessions in peace and quiet. Hence, American colonists, Dutch burghers, and French subjects were already free under their existing political institutions—and the revolutionary attempts to democratize these institutions threatened to undermine liberty rather than enhance it.

The publication of Price's *Observations on Civil Liberty* lit a fire under opponents who sought to sever the link between freedom and democracy.[10] In the 1770s and 1780s, conservatives wrote at least forty pamphlets directly criticizing Price's views. Many of the pieces were commissioned by the British government, which felt threatened by Price's powerful rhetoric. Price's opponents tried to undermine his credibility by attacking his factual claims—his argument that the war in America would bankrupt Great Britain, for instance, elicited angry denials. But to a large extent, the response to Price's pamphlet focused on his more philosophical claims about the definition of freedom. Freedom, his critics argued again and again, had nothing to do with popular self-government; rather, it consisted in the peaceful enjoyment of one's life and goods.

Thus, John Wesley—an influential theologian with Tory sympathies—agreed with Price that the American colonists had an "undoubted right" to freedom. But they already enjoyed complete freedom under British rule—"because they enjoy religious liberty (the liberty to choose their own religion) and civil liberty (a liberty to dispose of our lives, persons and futures, according to our own choice, and the laws of our country)."[11]

The Scottish philosopher Adam Ferguson agreed. "Civil liberty," Ferguson explained, consisted in the "security of our rights" rather than in the ability to exercise control over the way we are governed. And from that perspective, the Americans already were free, since, as all agreed, British subjects experienced "more security than was ever before enjoyed by any people."[12]

These arguments soon came to be echoed across the channel as well. As revolutionary fervor—and the accompanying cry for freedom—spread from the American colonies to the Netherlands and other countries, counterrevolutionaries in continental Europe were quick to call for a new way of thinking about liberty. Like their British counterparts, they were apt to emphasize that freedom was indeed valuable and worth fighting for—but they also felt that it should be understood differently, as the quiet enjoyment of one's life and property, rather than as the freedom to rule oneself. The Atlantic revolutionaries were therefore harming rather than serving the cause of liberty with their attempts to democratize the political regimes under which they lived.

In the German-speaking world, as we have seen, such arguments were voiced by defenders of royal absolutism, such as Johann Eberhard. But the counterrevolutionary call for a new understanding of liberty sounded even more loudly in the Netherlands. Orangist supporters of the status quo were scandalized by the Patriots' identification of freedom with popular self-government. "To see so many publications on liberty while it is actually being raped: to see all this in our days! Who would have believed it!" exclaimed Adriaan Kluit, a professor of history at the University of Leiden and a staunch antidemocrat. The Patriots used "the splendid name of civil liberty" to argue for "sovereignty . . . of the people." But this was a malicious perversion of the language of liberty. Kluit therefore called upon all "true lovers of noble liberty" to defend the existing constitution, which had preserved Dutch freedom for hundreds of years.[13]

In the 1790s, with the outbreak of the French Revolution, debate about the nature and meaning of freedom became even more heated. Early fascination among European and American elites with events in France gave way to wariness as the revolution radicalized. After the abolition of the monarchy in 1792, the French Revolution entered a new and profoundly democratic phase.[14] The census system for elections to the National Assembly was abolished, and although the new system fell short of universal male suffrage (servants and anyone not on the tax rolls remained barred from voting), it was nevertheless far more democratic than the electoral system established in 1791. The new constitution was ratified through a plebiscite in which 1.8 million (out of perhaps 7 million potential voters) participated. Many women tried to vote, illustrating the zeal for popular participation.

However, the democratic experiment in France quickly went awry. As the new regime became embroiled in wars abroad and at home, the ruling body, the Jacobin-dominated Convention, suspended the new constitution and all elections. Authority was instead centralized in the Committee of Safety, which consisted of a mere twelve individuals. Free speech was abolished; religious liberty was likewise nullified as the Committee of Safety became engaged in an increasingly bitter struggle with the church. These events went hand in hand with considerable political violence. At the high point of the Terror, thousands of people were executed each week by specially created revolutionary tribunals. All in all, about 17,000 were condemned to death, of whom 2,600 were guillotined in Paris.

Widely publicized in the European and American press, the Terror sparked tremendous debate.[15] Many radicals continued to defend the French revolutionary regime. The Terror, they argued, was a necessary response to threats to the fledgling republic. (These threats were undoubtedly real: In the spring of 1793, Prussian-led troops invaded France to avenge the execution of Louis XVI; at the same time, a rebellion broke out against mass conscription in the Vendée, a region in the west of France, which soon turned into a full-fledged civil war.) Others argued that the revolutionary violence paled in comparison to the horrors of the ancien régime. The aging Königsberg philosopher Immanuel Kant, for instance, remained unrepentant in his support for the French Revolution. As one of his visitors reported, Kant believed that "all the horrors of France were unimportant compared with the chronic evil of despotism, from which France had suffered, and the Jacobins were probably right in all they were doing."[16]

Isaac Cruikshank, *The Democracy of France* (1794).

But to many other observers, the Terror showed that something was amiss with the revolutionary ideals. The violence showed that attempts to introduce a more democratic regime in large, populous nations such as France could end only in oppression and bloodshed. This message was visualized in an engraving by the Scottish caricaturist Isaac Cruikshank, published at the high point of the Terror in 1794. Cruikshank depicted the "Democracy of France" as a monster holding up the chopped-off heads of aristocrats while wearing a cap of liberty made of daggers. Cruikshank's message was clear: democracy could lead only to the Terror and the guillotine; its promise of freedom for all was a dangerous illusion.

This thesis seemed to be confirmed again in 1799, when attempts to restore political order in France ended in Napoleon Bonaparte's dictatorship. Even some of the revolution's most ardent supporters came to despair of the cause of liberty in France, and, by extension, Europe. Wordsworth, for instance, was devastated by Napoleon's rise to power, expressing his disillusionment in a 1802 poem addressed to the French: "Shame on you, feeble-heads, to Slavery prone!" Indeed, Wordsworth was so repulsed by the outcome of the French Revolution that eventually he became a staunch Tory and committed opponent of anything that smacked of democracy.[17]

The Terror led to a new outpouring of pamphlets attacking the revolutionary understanding of liberty. Some counterrevolutionaries were so shocked by the violence that they came to deny the value of freedom altogether—a view expressed most forcefully by the Catholic polemicist Joseph de Maistre. Maistre had grown up in Savoy, a French-speaking province of the kingdom of Piedmont, where he rose through the ranks to become a member of the *parlement,* the highest judicial body. He devoted much of his free time and resources to amassing one of the largest libraries in Piedmont. But his life was violently interrupted when the French revolutionary armies invaded in 1792, forcing the then thirty-nine-year-old Maistre into exile. Soon, he became one of the leading lights of the counterrevolution, turning against the opinions of his youth and denouncing the revolution as "satanic."[18]

Throughout his many writings, Maistre also engaged in a systematic critique of the revolutionary conception of freedom, which he particularly associated with the ideas of Jean-Jacques Rousseau. Maistre ridiculed Rousseau for believing that man was born free, claiming this "foolish assertion" was quite untrue. Man, if left to his own devices, was actually "too wicked to be free." Hence, Maistre claimed—much like Augustine had some 1,400 years earlier—that slavery, both in the sense of legal bondage and political subjection, was the natural and proper condition of mankind. Liberty in the sense of spiritual freedom was possible only under the guidance of Catholicism, and hence the pope should be given supreme authority not just over spiritual matters but also over the secular world.[19]

It is important to note, however, that Maistre's uncompromising rejection of freedom was exceptional. Most counterrevolutionaries, far from rejecting the value of freedom, tried to claim the mantle of liberty for themselves; they often did so by distinguishing, like Eberhard had done, between civil and political freedom. In the Netherlands, the Orangist Johan Meerman published a treatise titled *Civil Liberty Compared in its Beneficial Consequences with the Evil Consequences of Popular Liberty*. Written in 1793, it was meant to warn the Dutch against imitating the French example. As events in France illustrated, political freedom simply meant that power was given to demagogues. Hence, Patriot enthusiasm for the specious freedom of self-government threatened to destroy the civil liberty enjoyed by all Dutchmen. "Political freedom is by nature . . . the executioner, the destroyer, the murderer of civil," Meerman warned.[20]

Similarly, in France, the royalist Antoine Ferrand—member of a distinguished noble family—tried to counter the claim made by the "enemies of the monarchy" that this form of government had destroyed liberty. This claim, Ferrand argued, was based on a mistaken view of the nature of liberty. To have a share in legislation and therefore in sovereignty was to have "political liberty." But that kind of freedom should be distinguished from "civil liberty," the liberty to do whatever the laws did not prohibit. These two types of liberty were not just distinct from one another; they were often at odds. When carried to extremes, the enjoyment of political liberty could compromise the security of the citizens—and hence undermine their civil liberty.[21] Another staunch royalist, Auguste Creuzé de Lesser, agreed. In *On Liberty, or Summary of the History of Republics,* Creuzé de Lesser criticized the revolutionary identification between popular self-government and liberty. Liberty, he argued, was more easily preserved in nations that had no popular self-government, because democracy inevitably led to anarchy, and without order there could be no liberty. "I do not preach despotism, whatever one might say," Creuzé de Lesser concluded. "But order, order without which no liberty can exist."[22]

In Britain, similar ideas were propagated. Here, loyalists came to contrast the French democratic understanding of freedom with "British" liberty—which, they emphasized, meant something very different from popular self-government. Edmund Burke was the first of many conservative commentators to reject liberty "after the newest Paris fashion," while emphasizing that he was nevertheless very much in favor of the "manly, moral, regulated" liberty provided by the British constitution.[23] The English caricaturist Thomas Rowlandson gave visual expression to this idea in a popular engraving that contrasted French liberty—depicted as a medusa rampaging over decapitated bodies while holding a trident with an impaled head and decorated with caps of liberty—with British liberty. The latter is firmly associated with the rule of law, symbolized by a scroll marked "Magna Carta" in one of Liberty's hands and the scales of justice in the other. The image was reproduced on an earthenware mug for those loyalists who wished to be reminded on a daily basis of what freedom truly was.

Thomas Rowlandson, *The Contrast (1792): "British Liberty. French Liberty. Which Is Best?"*

An earthenware mug contrasting British and French liberty (1793).

Civil vs. Political Liberty

In short, in the decades after the outbreak of the Atlantic Revolutions, counterrevolutionary thinkers rejected the democratic theory of freedom again and again, arguing that freedom, or at least civil liberty, should be understood as the ability to peacefully enjoy one's life and possessions. It might be tempting to dismiss these arguments as self-serving and empty of meaning; and indeed, some counterrevolutionary publicists seemed to claim that *any* kind of government—as long as it was not democratic—was capable of guaranteeing liberty. But other counterrevolutionary thinkers developed more sophisticated arguments, reviving a number of claims already put forward by ancient critics of freedom while also developing new views. Some ideas developed by counterrevolutionary thinkers proved so powerful that they would continue to be echoed in the debate about freedom for decades to come.

These more thoughtful counterrevolutionaries pointed out—much like the Athenian oligarchs had over two millennia earlier—that the democratic theory of freedom was incoherent. According to the Atlantic revolutionaries, people could be free only if they governed themselves. But even in the most democratic states, their opponents argued, government was never exercised by common consent. Rather, in a democracy, the majority of the community ruled over everyone else. This meant that quite often, a sizable portion of the community—the minority—would have to submit to laws they had not consented to. The democratic definition of freedom was contradictory or even absurd; democracy did not lead to freedom for all but to the tyranny of the majority.[24]

Counterrevolutionary thinkers also argued—like Plato had—that democracy would lead to licentiousness rather than liberty. The idea that men ought to govern themselves implied that they could flaunt any law they disagreed with; hence a government based on popular sovereignty could end only in disorder and chaos—and thus in the destruction of liberty. John Wesley described Price's *On Liberty* as a "dangerous Tract," which, if put into practice, "would overturn all government, and bring in universal anarchy."[25] Another of Price's detractors, Adam Ferguson, likewise warned that "if any citizen were free to do what he pleased, this would be an extinction of liberty, for every one else would have the same freedom."[26]

These two claims—that democracy would lead to majoritarian tyranny and that it would result in anarchy—might seem contradictory. But in the view of thinkers like Wesley and Ferguson, that was not necessarily the case. They conjectured that democracy might lead, at first, to majoritarian tyranny and, in particular, to the tyranny of the poor over the rich. But this would ultimately lead to out-and-out anarchy as the destruction of property led to a war of all against all. According to one of Price's anonymous critics, the poor, if given the vote, would employ it to divest the rich of their possessions, and "property would become the most precarious and insecure thing in the world," resulting in chaos. The "blessings of civil liberty would be destroyed by what is most sophistically defined to be civil liberty."[27]

In short, during the great liberty debate of the late eighteenth century, arguments originally formulated by Greek critics of freedom were revived. However, eighteenth-century counterrevolutionaries also differed from their Greek predecessors in an important way. As we have seen, both the Greek oligarchs and Plato went on to claim that freedom had to be rejected as a political ideal. They argued that all politics was power politics or that political slavery to the "best man" was the most desirable political ideal. Eighteenth-century counterrevolutionaries, however, came to a different conclusion. They did not dismiss freedom; instead they argued that it should be redefined. But if freedom was not to be equated with popular self-government, and if civil liberty did not depend on political liberty, then how was freedom to be preserved? What were the institutional implications of the counterrevolutionary definition of liberty?

Counterrevolutionaries provided various answers to that question. Some of them argued that a free state was a state in which the government interfered as little as possible in citizens' lives. Eberhard suggested as much when he claimed that Prussians were freer than many republican citizens because they enjoyed greater religious freedom. Meerman made a similar argument. In order to support his case that the Dutch enjoyed civil liberty under their existing constitution and that, hence, democratic reforms were superfluous, he pointed out that Dutch laws allowed citizens to do more or less as they pleased. "The laws of this commonwealth," he remarked, interfered but little with a person's ability to act "as they see fit." Every inhabitant of the Netherlands was able to determine for themselves their choice of clothes, food, friends, and hobbies— indeed, their whole way of life. Adults were completely free to choose their spouses based solely on their romantic preferences. And the Dutch enjoyed freedom of speech, limited only by respect for civility and good manners.[28]

Yet other counterrevolutionaries, notably the Tory pamphleteer John Shebbeare, argued that civil freedom was best preserved through rule by a wise elite. The continued enjoyment of civil liberty—in the sense of personal security—Shebbeare argued, depended not on the limitation of power, but on the existence of a strong government, capable of enforcing the laws. If citizens could overstep the boundaries of the law with impunity, they were no longer free. This apparent paradox could be explained by the fact that other citizens—or even worse, public officials—would likewise have the same ability, and that therefore no one would be safe in the possession of their lives and goods.

The freedom afforded by the rule of law did not prevail under just any system of laws. One needed to distinguish, Shebbeare claimed, between freedom-enhancing and freedom-reducing systems of laws. A person could only be thought of as free when they were subjected to *just* laws—laws that were made in accordance with an objective standard of justice. But how to determine whether laws were just or not? Shebbeare's answer to that question was unequivocal: elites were better equipped to judge whether laws were just—whether they were protective of freedom—than ordinary citizens. A free government was not "the creature of the people." Instead, a free state was "created by the superior wisdom of a few." Happily, the English allowed themselves to be led by the intelligent few. This did not undermine their freedom, as the American revolutionaries claimed, but instead preserved it. The slavery they complained about was "nothing more than the subordination of folly to wisdom." By contrast, "civil liberty" was "the progeny of laws formed by the few . . . in consequence of this natural subordination of intellect in the number."[29]

Another popular theory, defended by Burke and others, was that freedom depended on the existence of checks and balances, which prevented authorities from acting arbitrarily. The notion of a balanced constitution had a long pedigree in British political thought and, over time, had served different polemical purposes. Burke and other British counterrevolutionaries turned it into an antidemocratic theory. Englishmen were free, they argued, not because they were able to exercise control over the way they were governed but because their constitution provided various checks against arbitrary government. Thus, as Burke explained, in the British constitution, "all its several parts are so constituted, as not alone to answer their own several ends, but also each to limit and control the others."[30] These checks and balances, moreover, had grown organically. They had not been dreamed up overnight by a philosopher in his ivory tower, but were the result of centuries of constitutional tinkering. Hence, the preservation of the balanced constitution—and therefore, of freedom—required rejecting drastic change.

Thus, counterrevolutionaries formulated very different answers in reply to the question of what a free state was supposed to look like. Some of them, like Meerman, implied that freedom depended on the *extent to which* one was governed—as long as one was able to more or less do what one wanted, one was free. Others, like Shebbeare, argued that a person could be counted as free depending on *how* they were governed—whether one was governed wisely or not. Yet others, like Burke, believed freedom to depend on checks and balances. From a theoretical point of view, these claims are, of course, quite distinct. But importantly, all these claims served the same purpose in counterrevolutionary discourse: they were used as alternatives to the democratic theory of freedom, which stipulated that a person was free or not depending on *who* governed. These alternative definitions of liberty also allowed counterrevolutionary thinkers to defend the existing regimes in England, the Netherlands, and France as being perfectly capable of preserving freedom—no matter how undemocratic they were.

The Atlantic revolutionaries did not take this barrage of criticism sitting down. Eberhard's essay, for instance, provoked an angry response by the Swiss republican thinker David Wyss, who, in his essay *On Civil and Political Liberty*, argued that the liberty enjoyed in Frederick the Great's Prussia was but "a house built on sand" because it was dependent on the arbitrary will of the ruler.[31] Similarly, Tom Paine described Burke's *Reflections* as "an outrageous abuse on the French Revolution, and the principles of liberty" and insisted that it was the British, not the French, who were in fact unfree. Paine claimed Britain's much-vaunted balanced constitution was simply a front for elite rule. "Is this freedom? Is this what M. Burke means by a constitution?" he asked rhetorically after listing all of the oligarchic features of the British constitution.[32]

A more philosophical response was formulated by Richard Price in his *Additional Observations on the Nature and Value of Civil Liberty*, which might be read as a reply to Shebbeare's definition of freedom as rule by a wise elite. Price started by tackling the objection that his conception of freedom encouraged licentiousness and anarchy. By saying that every man ought to be his own legislator, he explained, he had not wanted to imply that every individual should just do as they pleased without any restraint. Obviously, the restraint of law was necessary for the preservation of liberty. He wholeheartedly agreed with his opponents that the rule of law—and of just law, more specifically—was a necessary precondition for the preservation of liberty.

But Price went on to clarify how his view differed from his opponents': to him, laws could be freedom-preserving—or be just—only if the people collectively made them. As he put it, "A people will never oppress themselves, nor invade their own rights." By contrast, if they entrusted sovereign power to an individual or to a small elite, it was to be expected that the rulers would end up governing in an oppressive manner and that "the worst evils" would follow. Hence, Price concluded, freedom could exist only under popular self-government: "If a people would obtain security against oppression, they must seek it in themselves, and never part with the powers of government out of their own hands. It is only there they can be safe."[33]

Despite these efforts by Price, Paine, and other revolutionary thinkers, the counterrevolutionary campaign to redefine freedom had a considerable impact on public discourse. An early indication of this effect can be found in the venerable *Dictionary of the French Academy*. In its first edition of 1694, the dictionary, as we have seen, defined liberty "in relation to the State" as "a form of government in which the people has sovereign authority."[34] This definition remained more or less the same in all subsequent editions. But in the fifth edition of 1798, the first edition to be published after the outbreak of the French Revolution and the Terror, the French Academy adopted the counterrevolutionary distinction between political and civil liberty. It was now not "liberty" but "political liberty" that was defined as "a government in which the people participates in legislative power." By contrast, "civil liberty" was defined as "the power to do whatever is permitted by the laws" and was illustrated by the sample phrase "the laws are the guardians of liberty."[35]

Even more importantly, as we shall see, the counterrevolutionary critique of democratic freedom was picked up by new intellectual movements in the first decades of the nineteenth century, notably by European liberals and American Federalists. These movements resisted attempts to turn back the clock to the ancien régime, and, in that sense, their political agendas differed profoundly from those of Burke, Eberhard, and their ilk. At the same time, liberals and Federalists were no less wary of democracy than were the counterrevolutionaries.

The Invention of Modern Liberty in Restoration France

In 1815, revolution gave way to restoration on the European continent.[36] In June, Napoleon's armies were defeated at the Battle of Waterloo by a broad European coalition led by the duke of Wellington and the Prus-

sian general Count von Blücher. A few months later, in September, the
Holy Alliance was created. The brainchild of Tsar Alexander I, the alliance's main goal was to restore the prerevolutionary social and political
order—in particular, its religious and monarchical basis. Royals were
expected to lead their peoples and armies as "fathers of families." The
alliance was soon joined by all of Europe's kings, with the exception of
the pope and the British prince regent. Perhaps more importantly, the
Restoration was backed by the military might of the Austrian Empire; its
foreign minister Klaus von Metternich was determined to stave off any
threat to monarchical rule.

As a result, the first decades of the nineteenth century were characterized by the rise of neo-absolutism in Europe. All over the continent,
dethroned monarchs and ousted princelings were restored. Even the
Netherlands—which had been a republic since the 1590s—became a
monarchy: when William of Orange returned from exile in England, he
did so not as stadholder but as king of the newly created United Kingdom
of the Netherlands. Poland, now firmly under the Russians' thumb, was
likewise transformed from a republic into a constitutional monarchy. A
new constitution, sponsored by Alexander I, established a consultative
assembly with a relatively broad franchise. But the Poles lost their ability
to choose their king. The tsar was now to fulfill that role, appointing a
viceroy to rule in his name—this to the considerable dismay of the Polish
population, who waged two major insurrections against Russian rule during the course of the nineteenth century.

In some countries, such as France, a full-fledged return to the ancien
régime was avoided. Napoleon's victorious enemies, worried about the
unpopularity of the Bourbons in their home country, feared that a restoration of royal absolutism would reinflame revolutionary passions among
the French population. To avoid this, they insisted that Louis XVIII's
power be constrained by a written constitution, the Charter. Yet the
Charter was also a clear break with the revolutionary constitutional legacy.
While Louis XVIII was now expected to share legislative power with an
elected house of representatives, these representatives were chosen by a
tiny slice of the wealthiest part of the population: just 1 percent of adult
males had the right to vote. By way of comparison, the constitution of 1791,
written during the early, moderate phase of the French Revolution, had

given the vote to two thirds of adult males. Moreover, the Charter also created an aristocratic Chamber of Peers, modeled on the British example, thus making the French political system even more elitist.[37]

As hereditary rulers and traditional elites took back control, they set about suppressing ideas and movements that threatened a return to the revolutionary upheaval. In 1819, the murder of the reactionary thinker August Kotzebue by a student activist led to violent reprisals against suspected radicals in the German Confederation; in France, the assassination of the Duc de Berry, the heir to the French throne, led to a similar crackdown. But the reaction was also strong in states that were traditionally less repressive, such as Britain. A peaceful demonstration for parliamentary reform at St. Peter's Fields in Manchester was brutally dispersed by cavalry; about a dozen people died and hundreds more were wounded. Even though the "Peterloo massacre," as it was called, was widely decried in the press, British authorities were unrepentant. The massacre was followed by a clampdown on reformers all over Britain. Throughout Europe, radical democrats and would-be revolutionaries were driven underground.[38]

It is against this background that we must understand the emergence of the liberal political movement. The adjective "liberal" originally referred to individuals who gave generously. But in the early decades of the nineteenth century, it came to have political connotations. The term denoted politicians and political thinkers defending a third way, something in between royal absolutism and revolutionary democracy. Liberals opposed the Restoration's attempt to turn back the clock to the ancien régime. They had no nostalgia for absolute monarchy or for the feudal order that had been destroyed in 1789. They were often in favor of the revolutionary onslaught on the Catholic Church, which many of them saw as an obscurantist force. (They tended to be more sympathetic to Protestantism.) For all these reasons, they considered themselves the heirs of the French Revolution.[39]

At the same time, liberals vehemently rejected the democratic legacy of the revolutionary period. Tainted by its association with Jacobinism and Napoleonic despotism, democracy had come to be seen as an abhorrent political system by postrevolutionary elites and even by many erst-

while radicals. Hence, liberals' political programs, while very different
from those of the counterrevolutionaries, signified a remarkable retreat
from the relatively democratic regimes defended by the eighteenth-century
revolutionaries. Whereas revolutionaries such as Richard Price and Tom
Paine had rejected the British constitution for being oligarchic and unfree, nineteenth-century liberals tended to lionize the British model. They
were in favor of parliamentarism—the idea that legislative power should
be exercised by elected representatives, not by a king or queen. But liberals' support for parliaments or representative government was by no
means the same as support for democracy. As most liberals agreed, electoral power should remain limited to those deemed "capable"—a category
that, in the view of many liberal thinkers, included only a tiny slice of the
wealthiest part of the population.[40]

The counterrevolutionary conception of freedom as "civil" rather than
"political" liberty held obvious attractions for this new, liberal movement.
Liberals were the party of freedom—the opponents of royal despotism.
But, liberals were always careful to emphasize, the freedom they sought
to achieve was not the freedom provided by popular self-government—the
freedom that had led to Jacobinism and the Terror. Rather, it was the
freedom to peacefully enjoy one's life and goods. Thus, the antidemocratic theory of freedom became a central plank of the liberal platform in
many countries. At the same time, liberals were not content to just reit-
erate counterrevolutionary talking points. They also made a more original contribution to debate about freedom by reimagining civil liberty as
the quintessential "modern" liberty, which allowed them to argue that the
Atlantic revolutionaries' call for democratic freedom was not just wrong-
headed, but anachronistic.

In France, the liberal movement was particularly vibrant and intellec-
tually self-conscious. Wary of being tainted with the brush of Jacobinism, French liberals made a considerable effort to articulate how and
why their understanding of freedom differed from that of the revolutionary
generation. As a result, they produced several ideas that would have a
lasting influence on liberal thinking about freedom on both sides of the
Atlantic.[41] Notably, the Swiss-French thinker Benjamin Constant made a
hugely important contribution to liberal thinking about freedom. As a

young man, Constant had been so inspired by the revolutionary upheaval in France that, just days after the end of the Terror, he moved from his native Switzerland to Paris to be closer to the action. In letters from this period, he described himself as a "democrat" and defended the Terror as being necessary to defeat the enemies of liberty.[42] But over time, Constant became more critical of the excesses of the revolution and started describing himself as a defender of a third way between the counterrevolutionaries and the Jacobins. Eventually he became one of the most influential political theorists of the nineteenth century, read and revered by liberals from Latin America to Russia.[43]

In a series of published and unpublished writings produced between 1806 and 1819, Constant criticized the revolutionary identification of freedom with democratic self-government. He frequently invoked the counterrevolutionary distinction between civil and political liberty. Much like Eberhard and other counterrevolutionaries, Constant explained that civil liberty—the freedom to do whatever one liked within the boundaries of the law—was very different from political liberty—the freedom to participate in government. He also concurred with Eberhard that the former was far more important than the latter. This meant that attempts to enhance political freedom by sacrificing civil liberty were "absurd."[44]

But Constant also reformulated these ideas in a more original manner. He reframed the distinction between political and civil liberty as between "ancient" and "modern" liberty. Constant elaborated this contrast most famously in an 1819 speech to the Royal Atheneum in Paris, which was published as part of his four-volume *Lessons in Constitutional Politics*. When the ancients talked about liberty, Constant explained, they had meant something very different than what modern Europeans and Americans understood the word to mean. The liberty of the ancients, he said, consisted in "an active and constant participation in collective power." This "collective freedom" went hand in hand with "the complete subjection of the individual to the authority of the community." In the modern world, however, liberty had acquired a different meaning: it no longer denoted participation in political power or collective freedom, but individual liberty—"peaceful enjoyment and private independence."[45]

This dramatic change in the understanding of freedom had been triggered, Constant believed, by two major historical developments. First, the city-states of antiquity had given way to a world dominated by large, populous nations. In modern Europe, it was no longer possible for individuals to exercise sovereignty the way it had been exercised in the ancient world. In representative democracies, citizens were only tenuously involved in politics; their impact on political decision-making was negligibly small. Hence, the exercise of collective power had come to seem less like a desirable political ideal and more like a bothersome chore. Second, the advent of modernity had brought a transition from bellicose to commercial societies. Ancient city-states obtained their supplies mainly through warfare, not trade. But in the modern world, men's needs were supplied through commerce, without state intervention. Hence, modernity had fostered a new love of individual independence and a concomitant hatred of governmental interference.

The French revolutionaries, however, had mistakenly attempted to turn the clock back to antiquity. Misled by their enthusiasm for the ancients and by modern aficionados of antiquity, such as Jean-Jacques Rousseau and Gabriel Bonnot de Mably, the revolutionaries had failed to recognize the changes brought about by the passage of time. They tried to turn France into a modern Sparta, but the attempt had only made the French, as individuals, less free. When the French people resisted, the revolutionaries doubled down on their specious attempts to "liberate" the people. The Reign of Terror, that "inexplicable fever," was the terrible result of their efforts to introduce liberty *à l'ancienne* in the modern world.[46]

This was strong stuff. By redescribing civil liberty as the quintessential modern liberty, Constant introduced an important new argument against the democratic theory of freedom. He did not simply argue that it was *wrong* to identify liberty with popular self-government (which, after all, was hard to maintain in light of the fact that the democratic theory of freedom was so widespread); he also claimed that it was *anachronistic* to do so. The idea that one's ability to live a free life depended on the extent to which one was able to govern oneself might have been suitable for the ancients, for whom such self-government had been an actual reality. But it was simply unworkable—and hence undesirable—in the large, populous states of modern Europe.

If modern liberty was identical with civil liberty, and not with political liberty, then how was it to be secured? French liberals gave different answers to this question. Constant, sounding much like Meerman,
defended the idea that a state could offer freedom to its citizens only
when power was limited as much as possible. Rather than worrying
about who was to wield sovereign power, he wrote, the friends of liberty
should focus first and foremost on carefully circumscribing its extent:
"It is the degree of force, not its holders, which must be denounced."[47]
This was an idea Constant was to repeat over and over again in his
writings. He concluded his *Commentary on Filangieri,* generally considered his most mature political work, with the following admonition: "Let us therefore cross out the words repress, eradicate, and
even direct from the government's dictionary. For thought, for education, for industry, the motto of governments ought to be: *Laissez-faire et
laissez-passer.*"[48]

This embrace of minimal government also led Constant to a new appreciation of individual rights. Rights-talk had, of course, been widespread during the revolutions of the late eighteenth century, with political actors on both sides of the Atlantic issuing declarations or bills of
rights. But as we have seen, the Atlantic revolutionaries had thought of
individual rights as going hand in hand with popular self-government.
Pace James Madison, they had generally conceived of man's natural rights
as being threatened primarily by tyrannical and unaccountable governments. Hence, they had advocated the introduction of popular self-
government as the best way to secure natural rights. Indeed, the right to
self-government had featured quite prominently in the various declarations of rights issued in the final decades of the eighteenth century.[49]

Constant, however, espoused rights-talk for very different reasons. In
his view, rights should be thought of as demarcating a private sphere that
was to be free from government interference—including, or indeed especially, interference by democratic governments. He issued various model
constitutions, which typically included long lists of individual rights—
notably, individual freedom, freedom of expression, the right to property,
and the right to a fair trial. Conspicuously absent was the right to participate in government. Constant consistently emphasized that any infraction

of these rights was illegitimate, no matter how much democratic support the government might enjoy. "When legislation brings an interfering hand to bear on that part of human existence which is not within its sphere of responsibility," he wrote, "does it matter from what source it comes, does it matter whether it be the work of a single man or of a nation? If it came from the entire nation, except the citizen it torments, its acts would not be any more legal."[50]

Not all French liberals agreed with Constant's defense of minimal government as the best way to protect liberty. Some, such as Constant's friend and collaborator Germaine de Staël, attached more importance to checks and balances, so she argued for a bicameral system modeled on the British example.[51] "The first basis of all liberty is individual security," Staël wrote, "and nothing is finer than English legislation in this respect." She ended her *Considerations on the Principal Events of the French Revolution,* a memoir of the revolutionary years, with a long panegyric on the British Constitution and urged her compatriots to adopt this model, even if it required them to swallow their nationalistic pride. As she put it, "Truly, I do not see why the French or any other nation should reject the use of the compass because they were Italians who discovered it."[52]

Perhaps surprisingly, other liberals favored, as Shebbeare had, the paternal government of a wise elite as the best guarantee for freedom. These views were defended, in particular, by François Guizot. After being appointed as a history professor at the Sorbonne in 1812, Guizot became an influential liberal thinker and politician. Like Staël, he admired the British constitution, and he traced its genesis in his influential *History of Representative Government.* But unlike Staël, Guizot did not attach much importance to the checks and balances established by the British constitution. Instead, he believed the English were free because they were ruled by a wise elite. In his view, it was not the people, but "reason," that should be sovereign if despotism was to be avoided. In a free government, political power should be exercised by the most "capable" citizens. This principle had been recognized in Britain, where the electoral system was based on "capacity" rather than on "the sovereignty of the majority."[53]

In short, like the counterrevolutionaries, French liberals disagreed about the institutional implications of their theory of freedom, with some arguing that modern or civil liberty could best be preserved by limiting state power as much as possible, whereas others believed that British-style checks and balances or the rule of a wise elite would be most conducive to individual freedom. However, these theoretical differences notwithstanding, Constant, Staël, and Guizot agreed that democracy posed a threat to freedom. This underlying agreement is also reflected in the fact that all three thinkers believed that Britain, with its highly elitist political system, was the preeminent free state.

Yet there was another side to Restoration liberalism, which becomes clear when we turn once more to Constant's essay on "The Liberty of the Ancients Compared with that of the Moderns." The bulk of this essay, as we have seen, was devoted to a renunciation of political freedom as essentially anachronistic and therefore dangerous. But this was followed by a remarkable addendum, in which Constant seemed to retract much of what he had said earlier. In the final pages of his essay, he suddenly acknowledged that political or collective liberty was not just a potential threat to civil or individual liberty, but that it could also play a positive role in the preservation of the latter. It was necessary, he now argued, not to renounce political in favor of civil liberty but "to learn to combine the two together."[54]

This volte-face has puzzled many of Constant's readers. It can best be understood by taking into account the context in which Constant was writing. His ideas on liberty, and in particular his distinction between ancient and modern liberty, were first formulated in the wake of the Jacobin Terror. But by the time Constant gave his speech on the liberty of the ancients and moderns in 1819, the Jacobins were long defeated. At this stage, the major opposition facing Constant's liberals was the royalist faction, which aimed to reintroduce absolute monarchy—or so liberals suspected. In 1815, the royalists had obtained a major electoral victory, which raised liberal concerns that a return to the ancien régime might be imminent. By pointing to the value of political liberty, Constant was, in essence, calling on his fellow liberals to vote and use other forms of civic engagement to prevent the royalists from realizing their political agenda—thus reverting to a position close to that of the Atlantic revolutionaries.[55]

Yet we should be careful not make too much of such appeals to political liberty. When Constant's writings are taken as a whole, it is clear that he put much more emphasis on the idea that sovereignty should be limited and carefully circumscribed than on the idea that the people should exert vigorous control over the way they are governed. For Constant, the trauma of the Terror always loomed larger than that of the ancien régime. Hence, for Constant, as for other Restoration liberals, avoiding the excesses of political freedom tended to take priority over other political goals.[56]

That priority became clear again during the 1830 Revolution. In July, a revolt broke out in Paris against the authoritarian King Charles X. Since his accession to the throne in 1824, Charles had been quarreling with liberal deputies—the majority in the representative assembly—about various policies. Fed up with the liberal opposition, he dissolved the assembly on July 26 and tried to rule on his own. But this led to an outburst of popular violence in Paris. After a few days of fighting, the small royal garrison surrendered. On August 1, Charles, finally accepting that he could no longer maintain his crown, abdicated in favor of his grandson, the Duc de Bordeaux. But when it became clear that there was little support for a regency, Charles and the boy went into exile. The Bourbon dynasty, which had ruled France since Henri IV, was gone forever.[57]

For a few weeks, it seemed as if France was on the brink of a more democratic era. The French painter Eugène Delacroix celebrated the mood of democratic exuberance in his masterpiece *Liberty Leading the People*.[58] Delacroix depicted Liberty—personified as a young woman with bared breasts—leading a crowd over barricades. She holds a tricolor flag, the symbol of the French Revolution, in one hand and waves a musket with the other. Importantly, Liberty also sports the familiar red cap of liberty, thus visually linking the 1830 Revolution to its eighteenth-century predecessor.

Liberal elites, however, had no desire for a repeat of 1789. They quickly appointed Louis-Philippe of Orléans, who belonged to a junior

Eugène Delacroix, *Liberty Leading the People* (1830). Note the red cap of liberty worn as headgear by Liberty.

branch of the royal house, as king. In addition, they limited the suffrage to a tiny number of people: about 2 percent of adult males. The regime was liberalized, thus Roman Catholicism was degraded from the state religion to the religion "of the majority of Frenchmen." But it was not democratized.

Indeed, the liberal elites who took control of the 1830 Revolution made every effort to signal their ideological distance from their late-eighteenth-century predecessors. For instance the reconstituted National Guard received a new banner in place of its old one celebrating the defense of liberty and equality. Now its banner announced "liberty and public order," signaling, as one historian has put it, "the ideological limits of the new regime."[59] In another telling move, Delacroix's *Liberty Leading the People* was bought by the Ministry of the Interior and briefly exhibited in the Musée du Luxembourg. However, it quickly proved too radical for the tastes of France's new liberal government. It was removed on the orders of its director, Pierre-Paul Royer-Collard, who banished it to the reserves. As a contemporary later commented, it was "hidden in an attic for being too revolutionary."[60]

Throughout the 1840s, French liberals would continue to reject democracy as inherently illiberal. There were some exceptions, notably Alexis de Tocqueville. A member of an illustrious French noble family (his great-grandfather Malesherbes had defended Louis XVI during his trial), Tocqueville had grown up among staunch defenders of the monarchy. He might easily have become a conservative or even a reactionary, but after a months-long visit to the United States in the winter of 1830–1831, he was converted to democracy. In 1835, he published a book based on his travels, *Democracy in America,* in which he powerfully defended the idea that democracy was the regime of the future. The growth of social equality, he explained, would make political equality inevitable in the long run.

Tocqueville believed this development was to be hailed because only democracy allowed men to live free lives. Aristocratic regimes had become impossible. In the leveled societies of the modern world, the only alternative to democracy was dictatorship, where everyone would be equal— as slaves. Hence only democratic self-government could preserve freedom; or, as Tocqueville put it, "the gradual development of democratic institutions and mores should then be considered, not as the best, but as the sole means that remains for us to be free."[61]

Tocqueville's book was an unexpected bestseller in France and in the rest of Europe. Its reception, however, was quite uneven. His pro-democratic arguments were eagerly repeated by a renascent republican movement; French republican newspapers like *Le National* published rave reviews. But most liberal thinkers focused on the bits of his book that were critical of American democracy, such as the chapter that argued that American democracy was in danger of becoming a majoritarian tyranny. Competing works, such as Edouard Alletz's *The New Democracy,* argued that American-style democracy, far from being the wave of the future, represented an early, primitive kind of government. It was perfectly suitable, perhaps, for unsophisticated Americans. But in civilized Europe, elite government, not mass rule, was the future.[62]

Over time, Toqueville himself became more pessimistic about the compatibility of democracy and liberty. In his second volume published in 1840 (also titled, at the behest of his publisher, *Democracy in America,* even though it was, in many respects, very different from the 1835 volume), he put far more emphasis on the threats to freedom in a democratic society.[63] Democratization, Tocqueville now warned, might lead not to liberty but to a new kind of despotism, with a democratically elected government acting as a "paternal power" that sought to fix men "irrevocably in childhood."[64] Modern democratic citizens typically had very little leisure; they were preoccupied with making a living, which led them to focus on their own private affairs. This meant that they were only too happy when their governments took as many decisions as possible out of their hands. Hence, Tocqueville concluded, it was easier to establish an absolute and despotic government among a democratic people than among any other.

Tocqueville drew a rather paradoxical conclusion from this observation. The danger of democratic despotism, he argued in the 1840 volume, could best be combated with *more* democracy. The only reliable antidote against the tendency of democratic governments to establish themselves as "tutelary power" was a vibrant civic society. But many of his readers ignored those subtleties. Instead, they focused on Tocqueville's chilling vision of the coming democratic despotism. Throughout the nineteenth and twentieth centuries, Tocqueville's 1840 *Democracy in America* would be invoked again and again in defense of an antidemocratic agenda.

Liberal Freedom in Germany and Britain

In Germany, a liberal movement was slower to emerge than in France. This had much to do with the Germans' different revolutionary experience. In Prussia, there had been no revolution from below. Instead, after Prussia's humiliating defeat by Napoleon at the Battle of Jena in 1806, reforms were initiated from above. In an attempt to restore Prussia to its former glory, ministers such as Baron vom Stein and Karl August von Hardenberg liberalized the economy and public life. In 1812, for instance, Hardenberg gave Jews full equality in civil and political rights. This made Prussia one of the earliest countries to do so after France, which emancipated its Jews in 1791. (Britain was not to do so until 1858.) This put Prussian officials at war with bigoted local elites and others seeking to preserve particularistic privileges.

Reform-minded thinkers like Georg Wilhelm Friedrich Hegel, a philosophy professor at the University of Berlin, applauded such measures wholeheartedly.[65] Hegel's *Philosophy of Right* was, to a large extent, written to defend Hardenberg's reforms against critics such as the reactionary thinker Karl Ludwig von Haller who, in his *Restoration of Political Science*, defended the authority of Prussia's local elites as both natural and divine. When Hegel described the state as "the actualization of freedom," he was referring to the rational state being created by Hardenberg and other reformers.[66] Hegel's timing in making such claims, however, was rather unfortunate. In 1819, the murder of the conservative author Kotzebue provoked a sharp turn to the right throughout Germany. So when Hegel's *Philosophy of Right* was published, with its panegyric to the state as the best—nay, the only—guarantee of freedom, it seemed as if he was supporting a reactionary government.

As political reaction set in, a liberal movement fought back against idolization of the Prussian state and instead demanded the introduction of an English-style constitution, with the rule of law and representative institutions. Yet German liberals, like their French counterparts, were adamant that they did not support Jacobinism and full-fledged democracy.[67] Wilhelm Traugott Krug, a professor of philosophy at the University of Leipzig, was one of the earliest German thinkers to outline the political principles of liberalism in his 1823 *Historical Account of Liberalism,* which was also translated into Dutch. Liberals, Krug explained, were for free inquiry. They believed that political authorities should neither hold absolute sway over men nor infringe on the "external freedom" of their citizens. Hence, the power of the state should be limited accordingly, and educated citizens should be consulted via their representatives in the making of the law. But, Krug emphasized, that did not mean that liberals were for democracy. They abhorred "Jacobinusmus."[68]

Like their French counterparts, German liberals made clear that they were the party of freedom but not democracy. Hence, they readily adopted the counterrevolutionary distinction between civil and political freedom, as is illustrated by the writings of Carl von Rotteck, a professor of history and prolific liberal journalist. In the article "Freedom," published in 1838 in the influential *Staats-Lexikon,* Rotteck explained that freedom depended most on the limitation of state power and the recognition of individual rights. Rotteck also vaguely indicated that a modicum of "political liberty" might be beneficial at some future time but warned that it should be introduced only when the population was ready for it. If introduced without the necessary checks, popular power would lead to a "furious despotism." "Political freedom," Rotteck wrote, "devours or suppresses all particular rights of individuals." In addition, popular government tended to be highly unstable. Hence, republics, "intoxicated with dreams of freedom, all too often succumbed to absolutism and tyranny."[69]

Unlike French liberals, who were firmly in control of state power by 1830, German liberals failed to make much headway against the forces of reaction. Some German rulers, notably the grand duke of Baden, had issued liberal constitutions for their subjects and introduced representative bodies. But the experience had not been encouraging. After repeated conflicts with liberal representatives over the budget, the grand duke dissolved the assembly in 1823 and levied the taxes on his own authority. The regime started exercising far more control over elections, and a new law made the budget presentable only every three years. As a result, the constitution was moribund.

Faced with ascendant conservatism, some German liberals came to have doubts about their earlier renunciation of political freedom. In his *Self-Critique of Liberalism,* an essay published in 1843, Arnold Ruge, a professor at the University of Halle, denounced his fellow liberals for mistaking "the fantasy of freedom for a real one." The main demand of German liberals—the rule of law embodied in written constitutions—was not an adequate protection of freedom. To what extent could there be a rule of law, Ruge asked, when the laws continued to be made without citizens' consent? "The laws of free human beings must be their own product," he then concluded. If German liberals really wanted freedom, they should be prepared to fight for democracy and the "human rights of the revolution."[70]

Ruge took his own advice. During the 1848 revolutions, he organized the extreme left in the Frankfurt Parliament and, for some time, lived in Berlin, working as the editor of the journal *Reform*. He had to go into exile in London in 1849. There he formed the European Democratic Committee together with Giuseppe Mazzini and other exiled democrats. But that was not the path followed by most German liberals. Instead, as we shall see, the 1848 revolutions hardened most liberals in their conviction that democracy and freedom were different and even incompatible.[71]

In post-1815 Britain, debate about freedom evolved along broadly similar lines. The dramatic failure of the French Revolution had given a tremendous boost to Britons' esteem for their own constitution. In the wake of the Terror, even erstwhile radicals came to agree with Edmund Burke that democracy could only lead to anarchy or democratic despotism and that, hence, Britain's balanced constitution was the only true guarantee of freedom. The Scottish journalist James Mackintosh, who had been one of the most vocal advocates of the French Revolution in the early 1790s, became a committed defender of the doctrine of the balanced constitution.

In his 1791 *Vindiciae Gallica*, as we have seen, Mackintosh had defended the French Revolution for attempting to create a new and freer political system based on the rights of man. At the same time, he had vehemently denounced Burke's defense of the balanced English constitution as the palladium of liberty. Both the House of Lords and the Commons, Mackintosh pointed out, were under control of the upper classes, so the supposed checks and balances were largely "imaginary." The British constitution, far from instituting freedom for all, established elite despotism. Only democratic reforms could bring true freedom— understood as popular self-government—to the British people.[72]

But after the Terror, Mackintosh completely changed his tune. He came to adopt a position indistinguishable from Burke's. Liberty, he wrote in 1799, could best be defined as "security against wrong." A free government protected citizens both against each other and against oppression from the magistrate. This freedom did not require popular control over government; instead, it was achieved through the creation of checks and balances. "The best security which human wisdom can devise," Mackintosh reflected, "seems to be the distribution of political authority among different individuals and bodies, with separate interests, and separate characters, . . . each interested to guard their own order from oppression by the rest, each also interested to prevent any of the others from seizing on exclusive, and therefore despotic, power." Mackintosh also left no doubt that this kind of freedom was embodied in the British constitution, which he described as "this great work of liberty and wisdom."[73]

After 1815, such Burkean views continued to be widely embraced. Most British political thinkers and actors agreed that their constitution, with its checks and balances, was the only durable protection of freedom. Yet, as memories of the revolutionary era began to wane, it became increasingly possible to adopt a more critical attitude toward the political status quo. Whig thinkers and politicians, who now occasionally started describing themselves as "liberal" as well, began to argue that the suffrage (limited to about 10 percent of the adult male population) needed to be extended to include the middle classes. Such reforms were necessary, Whigs and liberals argued, to preserve British freedom.[74]

Yet their commitment to electoral reform did not imply that British Whigs and liberals believed that democratic self-government was a necessary precondition for freedom. Instead, they argued that reform was required to readjust the constitutional balance indispensable for the protection of liberty. Notably, reformers felt that, over time, the House of Commons had become too aristocratic and thus too similar to the House of Lords, which undermined the capacity of the Commons to act as a check on the Lords. An extension of the franchise would make the Commons less dependent on the Lords, thus restoring constitutional balance and ensuring that power would be checked by power. This did not imply a zeal for democracy as such; British liberals typically agreed that expansive democracy could only lead to the despotism of the poor over the rich.[75]

Some more radical political thinkers did argue for full-fledged democracy. Notably, the aging philosopher Jeremy Bentham emerged as a vocal defender of democracy in the early decades of the nineteenth century. Bentham, as we have seen, had been thoroughly repulsed by the Terror, and this had led him, like so many of his contemporaries, to reject popular government as an anarchical political system. But in the first decade of the nineteenth century, Bentham underwent a dramatic and rather unexpected conversion to democracy. His change of heart was largely provoked by a lack of interest among British political elites in his reform plans, notably his ill-fated Panopticon prison. This gradually convinced him that the British government was in thrall to "sinister interests." The monarchical and aristocratical elements, he now thought, simply worked for their own particular interests and thereby undermined the good of all. Bentham therefore pleaded for the introduction of a democratic republic with "virtually" universal suffrage—that is, manhood suffrage, excluding the illiterate.[76]

Yet Bentham refused to use the language of liberty to defend democracy. He continued to reject, much as he had in the 1790s, any appeal to emotive but in his view empty words such as "freedom" and "natural rights." "There are few words," Bentham wrote in his *Deontology*, "which, with its derivations, have been more mischievous than this word liberty. When it means anything beyond mere caprice and dogmatism, it means good government; and if good government had had the good fortune to occupy the same place in the public mind which has been occupied by the vague entity called liberty, the crimes and follies which have disgraced and retarded the progress of political improvement would hardly have been committed."[77] Instead, Bentham and his followers, the Philosophical Radicals, argued for democratic reform on the grounds of utility: preventing sinister interests from using political power for their own ends would bring good government—government that was truly in the interests of the majority.

Bentham's radical defense of democracy provoked no further debate about the relationship between freedom and democracy in Britain.[78] Most liberal and Whig reformers continued to argue for small, incremental reforms that were supposed to refine the constitutional balance rather than bring about popular self-government. After 1848, as we shall see, most British liberals continued to reject the democratic theory of freedom.

Debating Liberty in the Early American Republic

The new way of thinking about liberty, pioneered by counterrevolutionary thinkers, was adopted beyond post-1815 Europe, in the fledgling republic of the United States. American political movements rejected the revolutionary definition of freedom as democratic self-government, arguing instead that freedom was the preservation of personal security and the protection of individual rights—notably property rights.

That this happened at all is perhaps surprising. The American Revolution had introduced popular regimes on the state and federal levels without descending into anything like the Terror. That is not to say that the Americans experienced a velvet revolution—the death toll of the Revolutionary War in North America was, proportionately speaking, similar to that of the French Revolution. In addition, loyalist opponents of the new regime had been forced to emigrate in far greater numbers than in France, and many of them lost their properties. But unlike their French counterparts, American revolutionaries had never employed state terror against their enemies, and the American Revolution had never been reduced to the kind of internecine fighting that was characteristic of the Jacobin period.[79]

Nevertheless, after the revolutionary dust started to settle, some Americans came to harbor doubts about the desirability of popular government. Continued political violence in America—in particular, the outbreak of Shays' Rebellion in Massachusetts—helped foster a backlash against democracy. In the winter of 1786, a postwar economic downturn caused considerable hardship in Massachusetts. Farmers who could no longer pay their debts along with the heavy taxes imposed to pay for the war effort faced expropriation. Led by Daniel Shays, a veteran of the War of Independence, they armed themselves and tried to overthrow the state government. While Shays' Rebellion was easily suppressed by Massachusetts elites, it succeeded in rattling quite a few of them. They were particularly shocked that the Shaysites had invoked the revolutionary language of liberty to buttress their cause. Shaysites had said the Boston government resembled "British tyranny" and claimed that the backcountry farmers were being led "into slavery."[80]

In response, some members of the elite began to reject these revolutionary principles, claiming they led to anarchy and violence. During the conflict, the Shaysites were routinely condemned as a mob, which was motivated by violent and destructive passions and out to destroy the security of property and, hence, civil society. Occasionally, members of the Massachusetts elite took their invective further, condemning not just the behavior of the Shaysites but the whole political and social order created during the revolutionary years. Thus, Henry Knox, a Boston bookseller who had risen through the army and become secretary of war in 1789, came to question the wisdom of popular government itself. "The source of evil," he wrote, commenting on Shays' Rebellion, "is in the nature of the government, which is not constituted for the purposes of men possessing boisterous passions, and improper views."[81]

The backlash against democracy in the American republic was arguably boosted even further by the outbreak of the French Revolution and, in particular, the Terror. Initially, Americans had welcomed news of the French Revolution with general enthusiasm. Most Americans gratefully recalled how France had come to their aid during their revolutionary struggle with Great Britain; they were jubilant when, in 1792, the French overthrew their monarchy and created a republic much like the Americans had done ten years earlier. Some began wearing French tricolored cockades and singing French revolutionary songs. Victories of the French revolutionary armies were celebrated all over the United States. In Boston, in January 1793, a celebration of the victory against Prussia at Valmy involved thousands of citizens; it was the largest public celebration that had ever been held in North America.[82]

After the outbreak of the Terror, some Americans continued to express support for the French revolutionaries. Thomas Jefferson, a lifelong Francophile, was unfazed by the political violence unleashed in France. "The liberty of the whole earth was depending on the issue of the contest," he wrote to a friend in January 1793, "and . . . rather than it should have failed, I would have seen half the earth desolated. Were there but an Adam and an Eve left in every country, and left free, it would be better than as it is now." In May 1794, while the Terror was in high gear, Jefferson expressed the hope that France's eventual triumph against its foreign enemies would "bring at length kings, nobles and priests to the scaffolds which they have been so long deluging with human blood."[83] But other Americans, such as John Adams and Alexander Hamilton, came to view the French Revolution with horror. In their view, the Terror spelled the victory of licentiousness rather than of liberty. They worried that the same anarchical spirit was infecting America as well—that America's love of liberty was degenerating into a love of licentiousness.

As historian Lance Banning has argued, these differing interpretations of the French Revolution played a major role in the creation of the first American party system.[84] As we have seen, in 1787–1788, American revolutionaries had become divided between Federalists (those favoring a strong national government) and Antifederalists (those wanting to locate power mainly in the states). In the 1790s, however, under the impact of the French Revolution, the extent to which America should be democratized became the main bone of contention. The division between Federalists and Antifederalists now morphed into a division between Republicans, who saw themselves as fighting for the preservation and extension of popular self-government, and Federalists, who claimed to be the party of order, resisting a collapse into the anarchy and violence of France. (Federalists of the 1790s, it should be noted, can by no means be equated with Federalists of the 1780s; James Madison one of the federal constitution's main architects, became a prominent Republican.)

As political debate intensified, the more extreme Federalists became increasingly critical of the revolutionary settlement of 1788–1789. They proposed several constitutional changes designed to considerably lessen the influence of ordinary citizens on the political system. Some of the most hardline Federalists pleaded for radical constitutional changes, such as appointing senators for life to make them more independent from the popular vote. A few even argued the presidency should be a lifetime appointment, to bring the office closer to that of hereditary monarchy. But Federalists also proposed subtler changes to the political system. During the decades following the revolution, they consistently pushed for a judiciary as independent as possible from popular control, opposing Republican attempts to subject judges to popular election and to codify or abolish outright the (judge-made) common law.[85]

While they tried to steer the country away from a descent into Jacobinical democracy, Federalists frequently invoked the concept of liberty. (Their electioneering song was "Adams and Liberty," set to the tune of what would become the "Star-Spangled Banner."[86]) But they made it clear that the freedom they aimed to protect was not the freedom of people to govern themselves. Democratic freedom was not freedom at all, but licentiousness and anarchy. Rather, like British loyalists of the 1770s, they aimed to protect the freedom to peacefully enjoy one's life and goods under the rule of law. According to the Federalists, as historian Gordon Wood points out, "true liberty was reason and order, not licentiousness."[87] Restoring liberty therefore required curbing the exercise of popular power. In the 1770s and 1780s, too many Americans had allowed talk of freedom and equality to go to their heads; it was time to adopt a less populist politics.

Noah Webster played an important role in developing and advocating this new perspective on liberty.[88] Now mainly remembered as the author of the first American dictionary, Webster was closely involved in the struggle for independence. He was a contemporary and friend of John Adams, George Washington, and Alexander Hamilton. While he did not fight in the Revolutionary War, he was active as a propagandist for the American cause. But in the wake of Shays' Rebellion and especially after the outbreak of the Terror in France, Webster ended up renouncing his earlier enthusiasm for revolutionary ideals such as democracy. Instead, he promoted the British system, with its limited franchise, hereditary House of Lords, and monarch.

Webster's dramatic conversion from democratic republicanism to Anglophile elitism was also reflected in his thinking about freedom. As a young revolutionary, he had embraced the democratic conception of freedom propagated by Richard Price. In one of his earliest political pamphlets, the 1785 *Sketches of American Policy*—of which he sent a copy to Price, as a token of his admiration—Webster had recommended the introduction of a "representative democracy" in America and rejected the British constitution as a model for a free nation. Despite their frequent boasting, the British were in fact unfree, because their government was "independent of the people."[89]

But in the late 1780s and early 1790s, Webster started rethinking his understanding of freedom. The outbreak of the Terror in France played a crucial role in this development. Initially Webster, like most American revolutionaries, had welcomed the outbreak of revolution in France, which he saw as a revolution for liberty. "Fair Liberty, whose gentle sway First blest these shores, had cross'd the sea," he rejoiced in a poem.[90] But by 1794, his enthusiasm had dissipated. In the essay "Revolution in France," he expressed his concern about developments in the sister republic. In particular, Webster worried about Jacobin attempts to put political power directly into the hands of the people. Doing so could only result in anarchy and disorder. Human beings required "the corrective force of law" to prevent them from violating the rights of others. True freedom, therefore, required the restraint of a strong government—something that Jacobin democracy was unable to deliver. "To render every man free," Webster wrote, "there must be energy enough in the executive, to restrain any man and any body of men from injuring the person or property of any individual in the society."[91]

As time progressed, Webster only became more critical of the idea of democratic freedom; eventually, he came to reject not just Jacobinism but also American-style representative democracy as incompatible with true freedom. Americans wrongly believed, Webster wrote, that "democratic and republican governments" were, as a matter of course, "free government."[92] But in fact, there was just as much need to guard against the "uncontrolled power" of the people as against the tyranny of kings and nobles. The American founding fathers had ignored this truth; they had failed to introduce sufficient safeguards against popular power. Hence, America had frequently been plagued by anarchy and licentiousness ever since its founding: "the people, or portions of them, rising in multitudes, above all law, and violating the rights of property, and personal safety."[93]

To solve this problem, Webster proposed restricting the power of ordinary people over government. Specifically, he argued that the Senate should be elected by the wealthy, to protect their rights against the numerical power of the poor. The judiciary and executive offices should likewise be made more independent from the popular element, by giving all judges and the most important officials tenure for life. This program alone, Webster concluded, would ensure the preservation of liberty in the United States. "If men will not have a king, they must have laws and magistrates, armed with power to bring them all into obedience. If this is not the fact, there is no free government."[94]

Webster was not alone in his views, which were shared by many other Federalists. Rufus King, a prominent Federalist leader, wrote an essay on "words with wrong meaning," and his first example was "liberty," a word he thought his contemporaries abused by identifying it with democracy.[95] John Jay, another Federalist luminary, emphasized civil liberty, the right of all citizens to do, "in peace, security, and without molestation," whatever the laws allowed them to do.[96]

In short, the call for a new understanding of liberty became a central plank of the Federalist Party's platform.[97] However, the Federalist attempt to redefine liberty in an antidemocratic manner continued to be contested and resisted in the American republic, much more so than in Europe. Whereas in postrevolutionary Europe, republicans and democrats had been muzzled and driven underground by censorship and repression, in America, revolutionary ideals continued to be vigorously defended by the Federalists' opponents, the Republicans.[98] As Jefferson explained in his inaugural presidential address, Republicans stood for "a jealous care of the right of election by the people" as well as "absolute acquiescence in the decisions of the majority." Those were the principles upon which the United States had been founded, and they should continue to be "the creed of our political faith, the text of civic instruction, the touchstone by which to try the services of those we trust."[99]

James Madison also rejected the Federalist understanding of freedom, articulating his position in a series of articles written for the *National Gazette* in 1792. "Who are the best keepers of the people's liberties?" Madison asked. American politicians, he explained, gave two very different answers to that question. The "Anti-republicans" were convinced that "the people are stupid, suspicious, licentious." Hence, they believed that the people should "think of nothing but obedience, leaving the care of their liberties to their wiser rulers." By contrast, the Republicans, Madison continued, believed that "the people themselves" were the most reliable keepers of their own liberty, because "the sacred trust can be no where so safe as in the hands most interested in preserving it."[100]

In this struggle, the Republicans ended up victorious. Unsurprisingly, the high-minded elitism of many Federalists did not endear the party to the mass of voters created by the ever-more democratic suffrage systems of the early republic. Even though Federalist John Adams was elected as president in 1796, he was defeated in 1800 by the Republican leader Thomas Jefferson. In 1804, Jefferson went on to defeat the Federalist candidate Charles Cotesworth Pinckney of South Carolina even more resoundingly; the Federalist Party subsequently imploded and stopped running candidates for office. Indeed, the Federalists had revealed themselves to be so out of touch with the rest of the country that many of them disengaged completely from public life. A remarkable number withdrew not merely from politics but from society as well.[101]

Their defeat made the Federalists gravely pessimistic about the prospects of liberty in America; they became convinced that the republic would soon give away to Caesarism as it had in France. In 1803, Fisher Ames penned a postmortem of the Federalist program, ominously titled "The Dangers of American Liberty." Until recently, he wrote, Americans had believed that "our publick tranquility" as well as "our liberty" were safely and firmly established. But this was now revealed to have been false: "We have all the time floated . . . down the stream of events, till we are now visibly drawn within the revolutionary suction of the Niagara, and everything that is liberty will be dashed to pieces in the descent."[102]

In particular, the American republic was imperiled by the "democratick licentiousness" peddled by Virginian politicians like Jefferson and Madison, who aimed to throw all power into the hands of "democratick zealots or Jacobin knaves." Attempts by the Federalists to warn their compatriots of impending doom had been ignored and ridiculed. Instead, most Americans would "persist in thinking our liberty cannot be in danger, till it is irretrievably lost." Indeed, Ames remarked despairingly, "it is even the boast of multitudes, that our system of government is a pure democracy."[103] But as both Roman history and the more recent experience of the French Republic taught, the descent of democracy into Caesarism was unavoidable:

> A democracy cannot last. Its nature ordains, that its next change shall be into a military despotism, of all known governments, per-

haps, the most prone to shift its head, and the slower to mend its vices. The reason is, that the tyranny of what is called the people, and that by the sword, both operate alike to debase and corrupt, till there are neither men left with the spirit to desire liberty, nor morals with the power to sustain justice. Like the burning pestilence that destroys the human body, nothing can subsist by its dissolution but vermin.[104]

Ames was willing to concede that American democracy might not descend into military despotism as quickly as French democracy had. America did not have cities as large as London or Paris, making its government less subject to the passions of urban mobs. It also had a much smaller army, which made the establishment of a military despotism harder than in ancient Rome or France. But there was no doubt that liberty would eventually succumb. As Ames concluded, "Brissot will fall by the hand of Danton, and *he* will be supplanted by Robespierre. The revolution will proceed in exactly the same way, but not with so rapid a pace, as that of France."[105]

Such dire warnings about the future of American liberty, as Ames himself despondently admitted, largely fell on deaf ears. Between 1800 and 1830, American politics further democratized, as most state conventions eliminated all voter restrictions for white males. By the 1830s, men like Ames and Webster had come to appear as "political relics," as one historian has put it.[106] (The picture looked very different for free black men and for women: to the extent that they had voting rights, these were now increasingly taken away. In 1802, Ohio was the first state to disenfranchise free blacks; others followed suit. In 1828 no more than eight states still officially allowed voting by free blacks. Women were even more radically excluded: the only state where women enjoyed the franchise, New Jersey, reversed this in 1807.[107])

Nevertheless, the Federalist campaign to redefine freedom had more of an impact on the political culture of the early republic than it might have seemed at first. One vector of Federalist influence was America's first and most famous lexicon, Webster's *American Dictionary of the English Language*. Webster had started working on his dictionary in 1800, long after he had exchanged his youthful enthusiasm for democracy for a commitment to elitist government. Unsurprisingly, he carefully refrained from linking liberty to democracy, defining liberty instead as "an exemption from the arbitrary will of others, which exemption is secured by established laws, which restrain every man from injuring or controlling another." The rule of law was, in other words, essential to freedom: "Hence the restraints of law are essential to civil liberty," Webster emphasized. "The liberty of one depends not so much on the removal of all restraint from him, as on the due restraint upon the liberty of others."[108]

Even more importantly, the Federalist conception of freedom was picked up again in the 1830s by a new political movement, the Whigs.[109] After the implosion of the Federalist Party had left the field to the Republicans (who had started calling themselves the Democratic Republicans), ideological strife declined markedly; the subsequent years of one-party rule are usually described as the Era of Good Feelings. But with the election of the brashly populist general Andrew Jackson in 1828, new political fault lines emerged. While Jackson referred to his followers as "Democrats," an opposition took shape that started calling itself "Whig." For the next twenty years, Whigs and Democrats would constitute the two major parties of what historians describe as the second party system. Whigs and Democrats differed over many issues, including economic and fiscal matters, foreign policy, and slavery—although both parties had members committed to the preservation of slavery, the Democrats had an official commitment to the preservation of slavery in the South, whereas the Whigs did not.

The parties also disagreed about the meaning and nature of liberty. Jacksonian Democrats, like Jeffersonian Republicans, identified freedom with majority rule and popular government, albeit limited to white males. The Whig view was more complex. On the one hand, Whigs were deeply troubled by Jackson's autocratic behavior. A former military man, Jackson was used to command, and he frequently made it clear that he would brook no opposition. As president, he vetoed more congressional bills than all of his predecessors combined. Many Whigs began to think of Jackson as a bully and a tyrant who was dangerous to the liberties of the republic. Hence, his opponents started calling him "King Andrew" and started calling themselves "Whigs," in honor of the Whigs of 1776 who had opposed America's previous monarch, George III.[110]

Andrew Jackson as "King Andrew the First." Cartoon from anonymous artist c. 1832, used in Whig campaigns.

But many Whigs were critical not just of Jackson's personal power; they became equally skeptical of popular sovereignty as a foundation for freedom.[111] This was perhaps unsurprising considering that Jackson's policies were supported by a majority of the white male electorate, leaving him in power for eight years, followed by another four years served by his handpicked successor Martin van Buren. In this context, the Federalist conception of freedom, with its emphasis on law and order rather than on popular power as the basis of freedom, came to seem relevant again. For instance Horace Greeley, the founder and editor of the influential Whig newspaper the *New York Tribune,* wrote that the essence of freedom lay in the supremacy of law over will, "whether the will, or wills, of the one, the few, or the many." Greeley went on to explain that "if the ruler—whether a monarchy or a majority—be above the Law, then the Government is a despotism; but if the ruler and the ruled are alike governed [by] well settled, clearly defined law, then that State is essentially a Free one."[112]

What all this meant remained rather vague. Unlike Federalist thinkers such as Webster and Ames, American Whigs wisely refrained from arguing for lifetime Senate appointments and other unpopular measures. Instead, they talked about the constitution as a bulwark against unrestrained popular power. (The Whig motto during the 1840 presidential campaign was "Harrison, Tyler and Constitutional Liberty."[113]) Mainly, they put their hopes in the Supreme Court and in the independence of the judiciary more generally as a check on popular power.[114] Long after the demise of the Whig Party, as we shall see, the cardinal importance of an independent judiciary would continue to be a central article of faith among American opponents of the democratic theory of freedom.

CHAPTER 6

The Triumph of Modern Liberty

I N 1853, a tome entitled *On Civil Liberty and Self-Government* came out in Philadelphia. Its author, Francis Lieber, had started out as a Prussian soldier. Despite his valiant defense of the homeland against French invaders (he was severely wounded at the battle of Waterloo), Lieber fell afoul of the Prussian authorities for his support of the unification of Germany. He emigrated to the United States and became, in rapid succession, the head of a gymnastics school in Boston, a journalist and encyclopedia editor, and a professor of politics and history at South Carolina College. (Somewhere along the way, he managed to earn a PhD, albeit in mathematics). In *On Civil Liberty,* dedicated to his students, Lieber hoped to answer once and for all the thorny questions of what freedom was and how it could be best established in a political community. His book ran to over 500 pages, showing he did not find this an easy task. But his contemporaries must have thought that he had done something right, because Lieber's book became a bestseller. It was reprinted eight times, the last time in 1911, forty years after his death. The book was assigned to generations of Yale students as part of the undergraduate curriculum.[1]

So what was freedom? Instead of answering this question directly, Lieber, as befitted a professional academic, started with a long digression on the history of freedom. In particular, he set out to make clear that the definition of freedom had changed substantially since antiquity. "That which the ancients understood by liberty," he wrote, "differed essentially from what we moderns call civil liberty." To the ancients, liberty consisted "in the degree of participation in government." As a result, they thought of freedom as something that could be achieved only in and through the state. By contrast, moderns understood liberty very differently—indeed, in a manner that was almost the exactly opposite of the ancient way of thinking. Modern people had come to identify freedom with "the protection of the individual, and the undisturbed action of society in its minor and larger circles." Unlike the ancients, the moderns therefore believed that freedom could be realized not through the state but by keeping the state out of individuals' lives.[2]

Lieber's definition of freedom was clearly inspired by Constant's distinction between ancient and modern liberty, even though the German-American thinker added flourishes of his own.[3] Constant had attributed the transition from ancient to modern liberty to social changes and, in particular, to the rise of commercial society, with its concomitant individualist outlook. Lieber pointed instead to a cultural transformation: the rise of Christianity. By attributing a "priceless individual value" to each human, Christian doctrine had dealt a major blow to the tendency of the ancients to privilege the state above the individual. After the downfall of the Roman Empire, German tribes who flooded the European continent with their "Teutonic spirit of personal independence" also helped to develop "the idea of individual rights."[4]

But in other respects, Lieber stuck closely to the script established by Constant a few decades earlier. Lieber drew attention to the differences between ancient and modern liberty not simply for historical interest but also, like his French predecessor, because he was firmly convinced that the political ideals of the ancients exercised a pernicious influence in the modern world. Beginning with the French Revolution, which had been motivated not just by "Rousseauism" but by "Plutarchism" as well, all attempts to reintroduce ancient liberty had ended in despotism.[5] Any attempt to revive ancient freedom—to identify liberty with democracy—must therefore be resisted, and liberty must be redefined. Individuals could be free only when they were interfered with as little as possible. This meant that, in a political society, one was free to the extent that one enjoyed the largest amount of "untrammeled action."[6]

As *On Civil Liberty* illustrates, throughout the nineteenth century, political thinkers continued to propagate the idea that freedom in the proper, modern sense of the word was the protection of personal security and individual rights, not democracy. The reason for this is not hard to find. In the course of the nineteenth century, distrust of democracy, sparked by the failure of the French Revolution, was kept alive by subsequent political developments. In Europe, the revolutions of 1848 played a key role. The first Europe-wide attempt to reintroduce democracy after the Atlantic Revolutions, the 1848 revolutions, ended in another episode of violence, followed by the introduction of a Bonapartist dictatorship. In the United States, later developments, notably the backlash against democracy provoked by black enfranchisement and mass migration in the final decades of the nineteenth century, similarly inspired political elites to reject the democratic theory of freedom with increasing insistence.

As a result, the nineteenth century produced a flurry of books on both sides of the Atlantic, which emphasized the opposition between freedom and democracy and redefined freedom as the limitation of state power. These attempts to redefine freedom, however, by no means went unchallenged. Radical democrats continued to defend the revolutionary conception of freedom. In addition, around the turn of the century, the liberal understanding of freedom was challenged by new political movements, notably women's rights campaigners, socialists, populists, and progressives. As a result, the liberal understanding of freedom increasingly came to be seen as a thinly veiled defense of elite interests rather than as an appealing political ideal. Yet, after World War II, such critical voices were largely drowned out. In the context of the Cold War, the understanding of freedom as personal security and individual rights, which had originally been pioneered by the counterrevolutionaries, was reimagined as the key value of Western civilization.

After 1848: Modern Liberty in France

In 1848, revolutions erupted all over Europe. Unrest began in Sicily, where, in January, a small band of rebels took to the streets of Palermo to protest high taxes and call for a written constitution. The king of the Two Sicilies gave in almost immediately, promising political reforms. A month later, in February, similar protests erupted in Paris, leading to the abdication of King Louis-Philippe. A provisional government was then created, promising to make France a republic and to introduce manhood suffrage. Within two weeks, crowds inspired by these victories appeared on the streets of Munich, Vienna, Pest, Krakow, Venice, and many other European cities. These, too, garnered results: throughout central and eastern Europe, national assemblies were called to draft new and more democratic constitutions. Never before—and never thereafter—was the European continent struck by revolutionary upheaval on such a broad scale. The end of the Restoration seemed nigh.[7]

As it had been more than half a century earlier, the struggle for democracy in 1848 was articulated as a fight for freedom. Underlining this continuity with the past, the red cap of liberty appeared again. In Paris revolutionaries took once more to wearing the cap on the streets, and it appeared on the walls of public buildings. Eugène Delacroix's *Liberty Leading the People*—with its prominent representation of the red cap of liberty—was dug up from the hiding place to which it had been consigned during the July Monarchy and exhibited in the Luxembourg gallery. The renewed importance of this antique symbol of liberty is also illustrated by Honoré Daumier's famous caricature *Last Council of the Ex-Ministers,* published in the journal *Charivari* on March 9, 1848. Daumier's sketch showed a female figure with a liberty bonnet, throwing open the doors to the darkened chambers of the July Monarchy's government and letting in the dazzling light of the new order. As Liberty enters with confident stride, the former ministers scramble over one another in a panic to exit via the nearest window.[8]

As it turned out, the 1848 revolutions resembled their 1789 predecessor in another important way: they failed. In France, the Second Republic was replaced, just like the first one, by a Bonapartist dictatorship. Louis Napoleon, Napoleon's nephew, obtained a surprise victory in the elections

Honoré Daumier, "The Last Meeting of the Ex-Ministers," *Le Charivari*, March 9, 1848.

of December 1848, becoming president of the Second Republic. In 1851, he dissolved the National Assembly, thus committing a coup d'état. A year later, he established the Second Empire. In the German-speaking world, reaction took a more traditional shape. Refusing to cooperate with the revolutionary Frankfurt parliament, the Prussian king Friedrich Wilhelm IV used his control over the army, as well as internal divisions within the reform movement, to defeat the insurgents. The Austrian emperor had more difficulty restoring order, but eventually, helped by Russian troops, he succeeded in putting down all uprisings in his lands.

The reasons for failure were complex. In France, popular veneration of Napoleon I, carefully cultivated by his heirs throughout the 1830s and 1840s, played an important role in his nephew's election victory. (Louis Napoleon's name was simply the only one many first-time electors even knew.) In Central and Eastern Europe, the prestige of hereditary monarchy played a similar role, although, just as importantly, traditional authorities also continued to enjoy the support of the army, led by an aristocratic officer corps that had no love for revolution. Finally, and perhaps most crucially, the revolutions were hampered by dissensions between the bourgeois, moderate revolutionaries, and more radical democrats. While the former were perhaps dissatisfied with royal absolutism, they were also mortally afraid of a resurgence of Jacobinism. These dissensions were further exacerbated when, in June 1848, Parisian workers rebelled against the new republican regime because it reneged on earlier promises to address the unemployment problem. The June Days, as this revolt came to be known, struck terror in propertied classes all over Europe and led many moderate revolutionaries to throw in their lot with the defenders of the Restoration.[9]

In the view of liberal thinkers, 1848 confirmed what they had known all along: democracy could bring only despotism. Hence in the second half of the nineteenth century, they preached with renewed emphasis that the ancient, democratic definition of liberty be relinquished for a more modern understanding. Revolutionary attempts to set men free by democratizing the political system always had the very opposite effect, they argued. As demonstrated anew by the failure of 1848, unfettered democracy could lead only to anarchy—as it had during the June Days—or tyranny, as illustrated by the return of Bonapartism. True liberty was something very different—it consisted of personal security and the protection of individual rights—and freedom, in this sense of the word, had nothing to do with manhood suffrage.

These claims were put forward most forcefully in France, where the 1848 revolution led to a new flowering of liberal thought. In the immediate aftermath of Louis Napoleon's power grab, public debate was stilted by press censorship. But after 1860, the Second Empire took a more liberal turn. The regime's control over the press and electoral system was relaxed. (Under the Second Empire, a representative body continued to exist, elected by manhood suffrage, but the regime habitually manipulated the elections). Liberal thinkers used these new opportunities to reflect extensively on what had gone wrong in 1848. Like Benjamin Constant a half century earlier, they quickly concluded that mistaken ideas about liberty had played a major role in the failure of the Second Republic.

Édouard de Laboulaye, a politician and enthusiastic admirer of Constant, was liberalism's most influential voice in France. As a law professor at the prestigious Collège de France, Laboulaye originally was interested in the history of antiquity and the Middle Ages. But the revolution of 1848, which occurred when he was thirty-seven, was a major turning point in his intellectual career. The events of 1848, he explained twenty-five years later, "made me a political writer."[10] In particular, Laboulaye became convinced that the 1848 revolution had gone awry at least in part because his compatriots had started from the wrong political ideas—and notably from the wrong conception of liberty. The downfall of the "noble institutions" of the July Monarchy was, as he put it, due to a lack of "liberal ideas" in France. "What has condemned us," he reflected, "is as always the false notion of the state. We have confused electoral and parliamentary sovereignty with liberty."[11]

Laboulaye embarked on an intensive one-man propaganda campaign to change the hearts and minds of the French. In 1861, he reissued Constant's *Lessons in Constitutional Politics,* which included the famous 1819 essay on ancient and modern liberty. In 1863 Laboulaye published *The State and Its Limits,* in which he formulated his own version of these ideas. In the titular essay, as well as in the essay "Antique Liberty and Modern Liberty," he set out to trace what he described as the "genealogy" of the idea of freedom, reiterating Constant's distinction between ancient and modern liberty. Like Constant, Laboulaye explained at length that France's revolutionary leaders, as they remained beholden to outdated "ancient" conceptions of liberty, had set France on the course to despotism rather than freedom.[12]

At the same time, Laboulaye's writings highlight an important difference between 1860s liberals and their predecessors from the Restoration period. Constant and other Restoration liberals had all explicitly rejected democracy as a political regime; they had looked instead at Britain as their main model. Laboulaye's generation, by contrast, had been convinced by Alexis de Tocqueville that the advent of democracy was unavoidable in an age of growing social equality. Perhaps more importantly, after 1848, it had become politically unacceptable in France to talk about limiting the suffrage. The Second Empire was founded on the principle of popular sovereignty, and there were regular elections on the basis of manhood suffrage, albeit heavily manipulated by the regime. Hence, during the 1860s, French liberals tended to accept democracy as a fait accompli.

This had a considerable impact on liberal political thought. Whereas earlier liberals, such as Germaine de Staël and François Guizot, had argued that liberty was best protected by introducing a mixed constitution with a strong aristocratic element, or by handing over the reins of government to a wise elite, such explicitly paternalistic claims largely fell by the wayside in the second half of the nineteenth century. Instead liberals came to argue, as Constant had, that freedom depended, first and foremost, on the limitation of state power. This allowed them to claim that they were in favor of democracy—or, at least, that they were not against it—as long as government power was limited enough that the newly enfranchised masses would remain unable to wield their electoral power to impose democratic despotism.

Laboulaye was careful to emphasize that he did not oppose democracy as such. He supported universal suffrage, as he made clear in "The Liberal Party," an election manifesto published simultaneously with *The State and Its Limits.* But he felt the dangerous tendencies of democracy had to be checked—not by taking political power away from the people but by making sure that state power was hedged in. A large part of Laboulaye's election manifesto was therefore devoted to a discussion of the "liberties" and "natural rights" that all states were to protect—a list that included property rights, religious liberty, and liberty of education and association. More generally, he argued, government had to be organized along the lines of *"laissez-faire, laissez-passer"* which was the "maxim of modern society." After all, had not the revolutions of 1688, 1776, and 1789 all been waged to "give back sovereignty" to the individual?[13]

Laboulaye also brought this point home in a different fashion. Like his older contemporary Tocqueville, Laboulaye was a committed Americanophile. But unlike Tocqueville, who, in 1835, depicted Americans as free because they lived under a democracy, Laboulaye was convinced that

Americans were free because they lived under minimal government. He invested considerable energy in propagating American-style small government as a political model for France. This was the thrust of his course on American history at the Collège de France in 1850, the content of which became a successful book.[14] Laboulaye's most influential contribution to American idolatry was *Paris in America,* a short novel published in 1863 that was translated into English, German, and Greek. It remained in print until the early twentieth century and was described by reviewers as "one of the most original and entertaining books of the day."[15]

Paris in America told the story of a Parisian doctor, René Lefèbvre, who, along with his family, was magically transported one night from Paris to a little village in the United States. While his family members remembered nothing of their Parisian existence, the good doctor did, and at first he did nothing but complain about his new surroundings. Lefèbvre was baffled by the presence of a bathroom in his house, which had hot and cold running water. (In Paris, he had been used to communal baths.) He was also scandalized to discover that his American son-in-law was a grocer rather than a bureaucrat. But above all, Lefèbvre was scared of the lawlessness that America represented to him: "It was done! I was in America, unknown, alone, in a country without government, without laws, without an army, without police, in the midst of a savage, violent and greedy people. I was lost!"[16]

But after a while, American life began to grow on this French everyman. In particular, he began to appreciate that America was not so much lawless as free. In the United States, he discovered to his astonishment, all people—even women—were free to do what they wanted. For the benefit of slow readers, Lefèbvre's American guide spelled out the contrast between France and America. In France, he explained, legislators had never even entertained the idea that society—that is, "the free action of individuals united"—could play a role in the political life of a nation. But in the United States, society was given the broadest role possible. The United States was "a collection of families who did everything for themselves." There was nothing comparable to that in France. On the contrary, in France there was but one thing: the government, an "immense polyp, that pushed its tentacles everywhere, that caught hold of everything, took everything, suffocated everything."[17]

By the end of the novel, Lefèbvre completely converted to the American way of life—that is, to the idea that government should be kept as far as possible from the affairs of citizens and that citizens should do everything "for themselves." Waking up again in his own home in Paris, he tried to convince his family and friends—as well as a doctor called in to tend to him—of the superior freedom enjoyed in the United States:

> "Is there a government in America?" asked [his friend,] the lawyer, "or have you at least found traces of it, by any chance?"
>
> "Sir," I answered, "they enjoy the most beautiful of all governments: the one that administers the least, that leaves its citizens the most freedom to govern themselves."
>
> "Effect of opium!" said [Doctor] Olybrius. "Everyone knows that America is pure anarchy!"[18]

As Laboulaye's writings illustrate, even when they came around to democracy as such, many nineteenth-century liberals continued to argue that democratization itself was not the key to preserving liberty—that liberty should not be confused with democracy. Auguste Nefftzer—author of the article "Liberalism" in the *General Dictionary of Politics,* published in the 1860s—voiced this idea even more forcefully. In his article, Nefftzer distinguished between "the liberal spirit" and "the democratic spirit." Democrats, he explained, sought a specific form of government. Liberalism, by contrast, was focused on preserving liberty. These pursuits were not necessarily contradictory, but they were also by no means identical. In other words, it was perfectly possible to have democracy without liberty—or to have liberty without democracy. Thus, the French Revolution, apart from a brief initial phase in 1789, had been "democratic to excess," but it had been "in no way liberal."[19]

This insight—that democracy and liberty, even though perhaps compatible, were not the same—also led to a new concept: liberal democracy. This term, which would become extremely popular in the final decades of the twentieth century, was introduced by the French liberal Charles de Montalembert in the 1860s.[20] In a speech to Belgian Catholics in Malines in 1863, Montalembert tried to make clear why he believed that the inevitable triumph of democracy would be good for Catholics—as long as it was the right kind of democracy. He distinguished between "liberal democracy" and "democracy purely egalitarian" and explained that the great challenge of the future would be to reconcile democracy with liberty. This would not be an easy task, Montalembert explained, since history had proven that "the natural affinity" of democracy was with despotism and revolution. In order to liberalize democracy, it was therefore of paramount importance to recognize individual rights—such as the right to religious freedom—as inviolable and sacred.[21]

After 1848: Liberal Freedom in Britain and Central Europe

In 1848, Britain was largely unaffected by revolutionary upheaval. Hence, the revolution here inspired less soul-searching among educated elites than it had in France. Nevertheless, many British Whigs—who now increasingly described themselves as liberals—saw 1848 as a cautionary tale about the illiberal effects of democracy. Thomas Macaulay, for instance, a Whig politician and historian, reacted with horror when the 1848 revolutions broke out. Even though he had little sympathy for the sclerotic Habsburg Empire, he regarded the attempt by Hungarian nationalists to create their own liberal state as an unacceptable threat to the European balance of power. But above all, Macaulay was dismayed by the overthrow of the liberal July Monarchy in France. His disgust at the February Revolution was only intensified in the wake of the June Days, and the brutal crushing of the workers' revolt delighted him. When Louis Napoleon overthrew the Second Republic and established a dictatorship, Macaulay's main reaction was relief.[22]

In the wake of the 1848 revolutions, Macaulay became more persuaded than ever that democracy, by provoking class warfare, could lead only to the demise of liberty. "I have long been convinced," he wrote to an American acquaintance in 1857, "that institutions purely democratic must, sooner or later, destroy liberty or civilization, or both." The "pure democracy" established in France in 1848 illustrated as much. "During a short time," he wrote, "there was reason to expect a general spoliation, a national bankruptcy, a new partition of the soil, a maximum of prices, a ruinous load of taxation laid on the rich for the purpose of supporting the poor in idleness." Happily, the danger was averted thanks to Louis Napoleon's coup d'état. As Macaulay put it, "Liberty is gone, but civilization has been saved." Macaulay had "not the smallest doubt" that the introduction of a democratic government would have exactly the same effects in Britain. "Either the poor would plunder the rich, and civilization would perish, or order and prosperity would be saved by a strong military government, and liberty would perish."[23]

Not all British liberals, however, were frightened by 1848 into a crude dismissal of democracy as the tyranny of the poor over the rich. A subtler view was expressed by Walter Bagehot, one of the most influential journalists of the mid-Victorian period. Bagehot offhandedly rejected the notion that democracy would cause "massacre and confiscation," as "unthinking people" believed. While such dangers were indeed suggested by the "*instantia terrifica* of the original French Revolution," more recent experience pointed to a different danger. The Second Empire, after all, was based on universal suffrage, but that government had not turned into a red republic. Instead, Louis Napoleon's rule was based on "the fear and ignorance of innumerable rural proprietors." Democracy, in short, might not lead to the annihilation of society, but it would lead to the reign of the ignorant and hence the "enslavement" of more intelligent voters.[24]

To stave off these dangers, British Whigs and liberals like Macaulay and Bagehot continued to insist on elite rule. Unlike their French counterparts, they did not believe in constraining or compromising with democracy. Macaulay preached a rigid adherence to the settlement of 1832, which had given the vote to about 20 percent of adult males. Indeed, the purpose of his massive—and massively popular—*History of England,* the first two volumes of which came out in 1849, was to celebrate the Reform Bill of 1832 as the fulfillment of the Glorious Revolution. Bagehot was more open to reform than Macaulay, but he believed the vote should be extended only to the "intellectual class of artisans." Democracy should, at all costs, be avoided. The masses were "infinitely too ignorant" to participate in government.[25]

There were important exceptions to the antidemocratic trend among the British intelligentsia. The most notable was John Stuart Mill, who, like Laboulaye, ended up defending a constrained kind of democracy. As Jeremy Bentham's godson, Mill grew up a committed radical. (An acquaintance described the young Mill as the "apostle of the Benthamites."[26]) It should therefore come as no surprise that Mill was a lifelong defender of democracy. Indeed, Mill was, in certain respects, more radical than Bentham and his father James Mill, because, unlike them, he supported female suffrage. (James Mill had argued that women did not need to vote, since their interests would be automatically represented by their fathers or husbands.[27])

Yet Mill's mature views of freedom and democracy were much closer to those of French liberals like Laboulaye than to Bentham's and his father's. In the 1830s and 1840s, he grew increasingly disenchanted with Bentham's and James Mill's uncompromising defense of majoritarian democracy, evolving away from what he described as "pure democracy" toward a "modified form." This development, as Mill explained in his *Autobiography,* had much to do with his reading of French authors, notably Alexis de Tocqueville. (Coincidentally, it was also around this time that Mill started identifying as a liberal rather than a radical.)[28]

Mill first expressed his liberal stance in a lengthy review of Tocqueville's *Democracy in America,* published in 1840 in the *Edinburgh Review.* Reading Tocqueville convinced Mill that democracy had indeed become inevitable in modern societies. But Tocqueville's arguments also persuaded Mill that liberty in these new democratic societies would be constantly threatened by the tyranny of the majority. Moreover, democratic majorities might not be inclined only to abuse their power to enact oppressive legislation; as Tocqueville noted, and Mill wholeheartedly agreed, democracy might also lead to majoritarian tyranny over the public mind, making the oppressive tendencies of democracy all the more difficult to check. Thus, Mill noted, when anti-Catholic arsonists burned down an Ursuline convent in Massachusetts, no jury had been willing to convict them.[29]

These ideas also found expression in Mill's most famous and influential reflection on the meaning of freedom—his 1859 essay *On Liberty.*

Mill prefaced this essay with a long introduction in which he traced the genealogy of the concept of liberty. He explained that liberty had initially been understood as popular self-government by the revolutionaries of the late eighteenth century. Growing experience with democracy, however, had revealed that "abuse of power," notably by the majority, was just as likely under this type of government as under any other. It therefore became clear that freedom primarily required "the limitation . . . of the power of government over individuals."[30] The question, then, was where to draw the line. Mill, who remained Bentham's faithful disciple in this regard, did not talk about natural rights as demarcating the sphere of private independence. Instead, he introduced his famous harm principle: a government should prohibit only those actions that are potentially harmful to others.

In making the case for limited government power, Mill was not concerned with popular attacks on the rights of property. Rather, like Bagehot, he worried about the "small minority" of the "persons of genius," who were necessarily "more individual" than other people and therefore in danger of being oppressed by the "collective mediocrity."[31] This was to remain a key issue for Mill, who addressed the topic again in his *Considerations on Representative Government,* published two years after *On Liberty.* In *Considerations,* he again worried that democracy would "place the principal power in the hands of classes more and more below the highest level of instruction in the community."[32]

By arguing for a constrained democracy, Mill was able to reconcile his youthful radicalism with his later concerns about the oppression of "persons of genius." At the same time, Mill's French-inspired focus on the tyranny of the majority deflected his attention away from a problem foregrounded by Bentham and James Mill: that of minoritarian tyranny—notably, the tyranny of the oligarchic elite that used its control over the British political system to further its own interests. With the benefit of hindsight, this concern might seem more apposite than Mill's worries about "collective mediocrity." Perhaps it would be unfair to describe the mid-Victorian state as "a government for the few, to the injury of the many," but that description does seem more apt than that of a majoritarian tyranny. After all, when *On Liberty* was published, about 20 percent of adult men in England could vote, and any extension of the franchise was strenuously opposed by the ruling elite.

Among liberals in Central and Eastern Europe, the 1848 revolutions initially provoked much the same response as in France and Britain. The Hungarian politician József Eötvös made this clear in *The Dominant Ideas of the Nineteenth Century and Their Impact on the State*. Eötvös, who had made a name as a defender of such traditional liberal causes as Jewish emancipation, had supported the early, liberal phase of the Hungarian Revolution of 1848. But he became disillusioned when the revolution took a more radical course. In 1853, he published *Dominant Ideas*, an attempt to investigate what had gone wrong not just in Pest but all over Europe.[33] Just as Constant had done in the wake of the Terror, Eötvös argued that the concept of liberty had been misunderstood by the revolutionaries and by Europeans at large. More specifically, under the influence of Rousseau and the French revolutionary tradition, liberty had come to be confused throughout Europe with "the principle of the people's supremacy." But such confusion could only lead to democratic despotism. Eötvös, therefore, ended his book with a call for a different definition of liberty—as respect for "well-earned rights."[34]

Eötvös's worries about democracy's illiberal tendencies were widely shared among liberals in Central and Eastern Europe. Generally speaking, the experience of the 1848 revolutions drove a wedge between moderate liberal reformers and more radical democrats throughout the region. In the Habsburg Empire, the 1848 revolutions were followed by severe repression and the return of absolutism. As a result, many liberals, including Eötvös, withdrew from the public sphere and returned to political discussion only in the late 1850s, when the neo-absolutist regime started to disintegrate. After the Prussians defeated the Habsburg Empire in the Seven Weeks' War of 1866, the Habsburg regime was liberalized but by no means democratized: the suffrage for the new assemblies created in Austria and Hungary remained extremely limited. Yet for many liberals, particularly those on the Hungarian side, the constitutional changes of 1867 seemed to bring a successful close to the struggle for liberty.[35]

In Germany, 1848 likewise caused a lasting divide between moderate liberals and democrats, and liberals of different persuasions continued to regard the introduction of universal suffrage in 1848 as a youthful mistake.[36] Liberals were soon confronted with the resurgence of strong, authoritarian government, however, when in 1862, Wilhelm I appointed Otto von Bismarck as his minister. Bismarck set out to unite the various German lands under Prussian leadership, thus realizing a long-held liberal dream. But his various foreign policy victories made his authority unassailable. As a result, in the 1860s and 1870s, German liberals became increasingly worried about the threat posed to freedom by neo-absolutism rather than by democracy.

Johann Kaspar Bluntschli, a professor of politics at Heidelberg, was particularly vocal about royal absolutism's threat to liberal values. Bluntschli was a cosmopolitan thinker, plugged into international liberal networks—he was a friend of Édouard de Laboulaye and Francis Lieber— and he espoused many recognizably liberal ideas.[37] In *The Theory of the State,* a treatise on constitutional law published in the mid-1870s, he sharply distinguished, as Benjamin Constant had, between modern and ancient attitudes toward state power. The "ancient state," he explained, possessed "too much power." The citizen was "nothing, except as a member of the state." By contrast, in the modern world, men were not "absorbed in the state" but rather developed themselves independently. They exercised their rights not according to the will of the sovereign state but according to "their own lights."[38]

From Bluntschli's perspective, however, democracy formed no immediate threat to this modern, liberal order. In his view, the resurgence of authoritarianism was far more dangerous. Monarchy was stronger than ever. It had obtained "a most decisive predominance in Western Europe." Bluntschli therefore admonished the "ruling dynasties" of Europe to lay aside "their medieval prejudices" and make more room for the input of "the demos."[39] This view, of course, was very different from that expressed by Laboulaye and Macaulay. Nevertheless, this should not lead us to think of Bluntschli or other German liberals as democrats. Though he argued for greater public control over legislation, Bluntschli flatly denied that what he described as the "proletariate" had any role to play in politics—they were not part of the demos. Instead, his preferred political model, like Macaulay's or Bagehot's, was a highly elitist representative system.[40]

Liberalism vs. Collectivism in Fin de Siècle Europe

After 1848, in short, liberals all over Europe asserted anew that freedom could best be understood as individual rights and not as democratic self-government. But debate about the nature and meaning of liberty did not end there. The next phase came in the final decades of the nineteenth century, as a renewed push for democracy in Europe, most notably in France and Britain, reignited liberal concerns about majoritarian tyranny. In France, the turn to democracy happened abruptly and chaotically. After a humiliating defeat against Prussia in 1870, the Second Empire was overthrown, and the country was again plunged into chaos. Revolt broke out in Paris, where workers created their own regime, the Commune, which was promptly and bloodily suppressed. Desperate for order and stability, the French seemed ready to countenance a restoration of their traditional monarchy. But when the Comte de Chambord, the pretender to the throne, insisted on the white flag—the traditional color of the Bourbons—France's establishment, including its military, refused to budge. They would fight only under the tricolor. With monarchy ruled out, France's elites created the Third Republic in 1875—a democratic republic based on manhood suffrage. To everyone's surprise—including, and perhaps especially, the French themselves—the new regime proved remarkably durable.[41]

In Britain, the advent of democracy, at least at first sight, happened more gradually. In 1867, a Tory government introduced the Second Reform Act, which extended the vote to about 30 percent of the adult male population. As revealed by parliamentary debates, the expansion of the franchise was enacted upon the principle of the balanced constitution. The 1867 Act was therefore not supposed to be a milestone on the road to democracy. In response to conservative criticism of the reform, Benjamin Disraeli, the conservative leader responsible for steering the Second Reform Act through Parliament, noted dryly that excluding two-thirds of all adult males was "not quite the form which an overpowering democracy assumes."[42]

Seventeen years later, in 1884, the Third Reform Act enfranchised about 60 percent of the adult male population. From a twenty-first-century perspective, the most striking thing about the 1884 reform is how many people it continued to exclude from political participation: a sizeable portion of the adult male electorate and all women. But contemporaries believed the law had brought full-blown democracy to Britain, an impression strengthened by the arguments made by its main sponsor, liberal leader William Gladstone. Gladstone, who was extremely popular with the working classes, had grown convinced that working men were just as fit to exercise power as were the upper classes. He therefore no longer used the language of balance. Instead, he claimed that every man, in principle, had a right to vote—thus making clear that the end-goal of reform should be genuine manhood suffrage.[43]

The sudden advent of democracy in France and Britain reawakened liberal fears about democracy, and all the more so because democracy seemed to go hand in hand with the rise of what many called "collectivism." In the 1880s, governments in various European countries started introducing legislation to protect laborers, lessen the risk of financial crisis, and insure citizens in sickness and old age. The motivations behind the emergence of these embryonic welfare states were diverse. European governments were becoming concerned about the ill health of their male populations, which made them less battle-ready. Religious concerns also played a role, as did worries about wildcat strikes and other forms of working-class revolt. But to liberal opponents, the rise of collectivism seemed, first and foremost, a byproduct of the growing influence of the masses in politics.[44]

Liberal thinkers in France and Britain responded to these developments with their now-familiar incantations of the dangers of democracy. But liberal discourse also subtly changed in the 1880s and 1890s. From Constant onward, liberals were concerned about democratic attacks on property rights. "Arbitrary power over property," Constant warned, "is soon followed by arbitrary power over people."[45] But this was one concern among many. Constant was equally worried about freedom of religion and press freedom. His plea for laissez-faire was never an exclusively economic doctrine; it was a general admonition to governments not to interfere with their citizens' lives.

But in the 1880s, as governments all over Europe became more interventionist, liberals became increasingly focused on threats to the existing distribution of property and the free market. This shift went hand in hand with the growing prominence of laissez-faire economists in the debate about freedom. While James Mackintosh, Édouard de Laboulaye, and Thomas Macaulay had all been lawyers, the liberal thinkers who came to dominate public debate in the 1880s and 1890s were often trained as classical economists. They saw interventionist policies such as an eight-hour workday and mandatory insurance against sickness as dangerous deviations from orthodox economic ideas. Liberal economists left their ivory towers and tried to convince their contemporaries that such policies posed a mortal threat not just to economic growth but to liberty.

In France, liberal concerns about collectivism were expressed most forcefully by Paul Leroy-Beaulieu. A scion of the liberal *haute bourgeoisie* and a professor of economics at the prestigious Collège de France, Leroy-Beaulieu had initially welcomed the creation of the Third Republic, which, during the first years of its existence, was dominated by liberal politicians. He applauded France's new leaders for restoring order and putting down the Commune. But after a few years, Leroy-Beaulieu became concerned about what he considered the profligacy of the new regime. In 1877, he issued a sharp criticism of the government's new budget. His point was simple: the state was spending too much.[46]

Leroy-Beaulieu wrote a series of essays and books, in which he tried to combat these nefarious developments. His efforts culminated in *The Modern State,* a book based on a series of lectures at the Collège de France, published in 1890. Leroy-Beaulieu immediately struck a highly alarmist note. "Western civilization," he warned in the preface, was under the threat of a "new serfdom" that followed from the idolization of state power. This, he said, was a direct consequence of introducing democracy. Modern states had made it impossible for the general interest to be defended, because majoritarian democracies necessarily ruled in the interests of the working classes. Hence, the "liberal commercial regime" was under threat in all modern states, even though this was objectively the best economic system.[47]

This was not to say that Leroy-Beaulieu was in favor of abolishing democracy. He expressly rejected the idea that a "bureaucratic" state such as Prussia would be a better model. But he did emphasize that the modern state needed to be constrained. All the state needed to do was to protect preexisting "natural rights." The bulk of his book was devoted to a detailed analysis of which functions the state should exercise and, especially, which ones it should not. If his warnings were not heeded, he concluded, the expanding power of the modern state would lead to "collectivism," the end of all liberty, and even the "destruction of Western civilization."[48]

In Britain, the liberal thinker Herbert Spencer propagated equally gloomy views about the future of freedom. The son of a teacher, Spencer got his start working for the new industry of railroads. But during a career break, he started writing about political and economic matters. A self-trained scholar—Spencer never attended university—he went on to write a wide range of influential works, mostly arguing against what he called "over-legislation." Upon Spencer's death, the *Manchester Guardian* ranked him "among the two or three most influential writers of the last half-century."[49]

At the outset of his intellectual career, Spencer was optimistic about the compatibility between democracy and freedom. The working classes, he felt, understood that small government was in their favor; hence the extension of the suffrage would not threaten individual liberty. In the 1860s, however, as franchise reform became ever more likely, Spencer changed his tune. In the 1863 article "Parliamentary Reform: the Dangers and the Safeguards," Spencer reflected on the danger that a proposed expansion of the franchise posed to freedom. He was particularly worried about the increased influence of trade unions. The very existence of trade unions, he argued, showed that working men held "erroneous" views about "fundamental social relations." Their opposition to freedom of contract showed that they "ill understand the nature of freedom." Such men, in other words, "would almost appear to be incapacitated for the guardianship of their own freedom and that of their fellow-citizens."[50]

By the 1880s, Spencer's concern about the tyrannical tendencies of working men had evolved into a full-fledged fear of democratically imposed socialism. In his most well-known and polemical work, *The Man versus the State* (1884), Spencer memorably described "socialism" (by which he meant reformist schemes such as progressive taxation) as a system inevitably leading to "slavery," since it forced men to hand over the fruits of their labor to the government. "All socialism involves slavery," Spencer wrote. "What is essential to the idea of a slave? . . . That which fundamentally distinguishes the slave is that he labours under coercion to satisfy another's desires. . . . It matters not whether his master is a single person or a society."[51]

According to Spencer, state coercion was no less oppressive if introduced with popular consent. Thus, he opened *The Man versus the State* with a long complaint about various social reforms recently introduced in Britain. It did not matter, he emphasized, that these new regulations had been imposed by a government responsible to the people. "The authority of a popularly-chosen body," he wrote, echoing Constant, "is no more to be regarded as an unlimited authority than the authority of a monarch; and . . . as true Liberalism in the past disputed the assumption of a monarch's unlimited authority, so true Liberalism in the present will dispute the assumption of unlimited parliamentary authority."[52]

Leroy-Beaulieu's and Spencer's views were shared by many fin de siècle liberals. One of Spencer's main supporters was Lord Elcho, a politician best known for his strenuous opposition to parliamentary reform in the 1860s. By the early 1880s, Elcho concluded that his worst fears about class legislation had come true. This spurred him to found the Liberty and Property Defence League, a pressure group that aimed to defeat "collectivist" legislation and to produce propaganda to combat socialist influence among all classes. The league sent "liberty missionaries" to the London parks, and it organized "liberty-limelight entertainments" and antisocialist lantern shows.[53] In France, Paul Leroy-Beaulieu's brother Anatole created the Committee for the Defense of Social Progress to counteract the influence of socialism. The committee was consciously modeled on Elcho's Defence League.[54]

In short, by 1900, British and French liberals were more worried than ever that freedom was being threatened by democracy, which was now seen as inevitably leading to collectivism. In Germany, liberals were less concerned about the threat of democracy to liberty—mainly because that threat continued to seem so much more remote than in France or Britain. The creation of the German Reich by Otto von Bismarck in 1871 had only strengthened royal authority, and German officials continued to be largely unaccountable to the general public. Under these circumstances, German liberals such as Max Weber saw bureaucracy, rather than democracy, as the gravest threat to modern freedom.[55] But across the Atlantic, Leroy-Beaulieu's and Spencer's fears found a more receptive audience.

Modern Liberty in the United States, 1848–1914

In 1848, North America was spared revolutionary upheaval. But, as in Europe, events precipitated renewed reflection on the nature and meaning of liberty.[56] The two major American political parties—the Whigs and the Democrats—diverged in their reaction to the European revolutions, particularly the February Revolution in France. Democrats responded enthusiastically to the overthrow of monarchy in France. The Democrats' party platform, adopted in May 1848, tendered "fraternal congratulations" to the newly established Republic of France for acting upon "the grand political truth" of "the sovereignty of the people." Indeed, the Democrats were so taken with the new French Republic that they adopted its official slogan as their own. Lewis Cass and William Butler, the Democratic candidates for president and vice president, ran on a platform of "Liberty, Equality and Fraternity, the Cardinal Principles of True Democracy."[57]

The Whig Party regarded the February Revolution with more ambivalence. On the one hand, humanitarian reformers, a sizeable contingent within the party, naturally sympathized with their counterparts in Europe; they rejoiced, in particular, when the new French Republic abolished slavery in its colonies. On the other hand, many Whigs were apprehensive about what they perceived to be the French propensity to licentiousness rather than freedom. They feared that the February Revolution would prove to be another unfortunate experiment in mob rule—a fear that seemed confirmed by the violence of the June Days. Senator Daniel Webster, one of the Whig's most important spokesmen, despaired that "regulated, restrained, constitutional liberty" would ever govern the French. Only "a fierce democracy" seemed to their taste.[58]

Whig concerns about the 1848 revolutions were most clearly articulated by the German-born intellectual Francis Lieber. Lieber was described by his European friends as "a Liberal both as man and as scholar."[59] But in the context of the United States, he can better be labeled a Whig. After migrating to the United States in his late twenties, he befriended prominent Whigs such as Joseph Story, a Supreme Court justice famous for his strong defense of property rights. Lieber also became close to the up-and-coming Whig politician Charles Sumner, one of the leading abolitionists of his age, although Lieber himself was opposed to radical abolitionism. (His preferred solution for ending slavery was to replace it with serfdom, whereby slaves would be given the opportunity to earn money, so that the intelligent and diligent would be able to buy their own freedom.)[60]

In June 1849, a year after the outbreak of the February Revolution, Lieber published an essay titled "Anglican and Gallican Liberty," in which he articulated many of the same concerns as Daniel Webster. But Lieber did not just heap invective on the French; he also set out to clarify why they had taken a wrong turn. And in his view, false ideas about the nature and meaning of liberty went a long way to explain the French predicament. "The French," he wrote, "look for the highest degree of political civilization in *organization,* that is, in the highest degree of interference by public power. The question whether this interference be despotism or liberty is decided solely by the fact who interferes, and for the benefit of which class the interference takes place." It was only by this logic that they could mistake their "present dictatorship" for freedom.[61]

Lieber contrasted this pernicious "Gallican" conception of liberty with the "Anglican" one shared by England and the United States. In England and America, he explained, liberty was not confused with democracy. Instead, the Anglicans understood freedom to mean that "all that can be done by private enterprise ought to be left to it, and that the people ought to enjoy the fruits of competition in the highest possible degree."[62] Lieber ended his analysis by calling on European countries to follow the Anglican example rather than the Gallican. "However dazzling the effects of democratic absolutism occasionally may be," he concluded, "it is still not freedom, which, like dew, nourishes every blade in its own individuality, and thus produces the great combined phenomenon of living nature."[63]

A few years later, Lieber further developed these ideas in *On Civil Liberty,* his most ambitious and wide-ranging contribution to the debate about freedom. He now began his analysis by distinguishing, in a Constantian vein, between ancient and modern conceptions of freedom. But Lieber also reiterated his earlier point that this distinction could be usefully construed as a difference between Gallican and Anglican liberty. Because of their Protestant and Teutonic heritage, the English and their colonial offspring, the Americans, had been led to adopt modern ways of thinking about freedom, whereas the French had remained stuck in the ancient conception.[64]

On this theory, the identification of freedom with democracy was not just anachronistic; it was also un-American. This was, of course, a rather surprising claim in light of the fact that, in 1853, the United States was far more democratic than Europe, where autocracies and oligarchies continued to set the tone. Lieber therefore devoted much time to explaining that the American political system was based not on the principle of popular sovereignty but on "institutional" self-government. What this concept precisely meant remained tantalizingly vague, even though Lieber devoted pages and pages to explaining it. Mainly, it seemed to imply that, in America, power was restricted and balanced by division among many different government agencies and by the power of the independent, unelected judiciary to review the constitutionality of the laws. But Lieber was crystal clear about one thing: institutional self-government was something very different from pure democracy. Lieber admitted that American experience suggested "no liberty can be imagined without a democratic element," but that was not the impetus of his argument. Instead, he emphasized that "equality and democracy of themselves are far from constituting liberty." Or, put differently, "Arbitrary power does not become less arbitrary because it is the united power of many."[65]

Conservative Whigs like Lieber did not have much influence outside of narrowly elite circles. Lieber's ideas about freedom were resoundingly rejected by the Democrats; and even among Whigs, his attempt to distinguish between freedom and popular government might not have been widely shared. Throughout the 1840s, Whig pundits and politicians were more likely to depict executive overreach, rather than majority rule, as a threat to freedom.[66]

That changed in the wake of the Civil War, which not only was the death knell of slavery but also, at least initially, brought about the biggest expansion of American democracy since the introduction of white manhood suffrage in the 1820s. In addition, the 1870s and 1880s saw an enormous influx of working-class migrants to the United States, migrants who swelled the ranks of the American proletariat. Both these developments made American elites far more receptive to the anxieties about democracy that had long been harbored by European liberals. Indeed, as we shall see, it is at this time that the term "liberal" was first imported into American political debate.

The Civil War was caused by increasingly bitter disputes between the Northern and Southern states about the expansion of slavery.[67] From 1845 to 1848, the annexation of Texas and the Mexican War had brought enormous new territories into the Union, raising the question of whether slavery should be allowed in the new states. The issue was all the more important because the expansion of slavery into new territories would strengthen the hand of slaveholders in Congress, making the peaceful abolition of slavery even more unlikely than it already was. Quarrels over free soil led to the breakup of the Whig Party, which split between "Conscience" and "Cotton" Whigs. In the 1850s a new, exclusively Northern party emerged, the Republican Party, which was devoted to resisting the expansion of slavery to new territories, particularly Kansas. Northern Democrats increasingly abandoned their party for the Republican Party, further polarizing the country between an anti-slave North and the slaveholding South. In 1860, the Republican nominee, Abraham Lincoln, won the presidential election. In response, eleven Southern states seceded from the Union and established a separate Confederate government in February 1861. Lincoln saw the secession as illegal and believed he had no other option than to reconquer the South. In 1863, when Lincoln issued his famous Emancipation Proclamation, the complete eradication of slavery became an object of the war.

By the end of the war, some came to argue that emancipation, in and of itself, did not suffice to set African Americans free. In the antebellum period, free blacks had been relegated to the status of second-class citizens, as they became largely disenfranchised in both the South and North. True liberty, black abolitionists emphasized in the wake of the Civil War, was about more than juridical status; it required political rights as well. As the former slave and abolitionist orator Frederick Douglass put it, soon after the South's surrender in 1865, "Slavery is not abolished until the black man has the ballot." Newly freed blacks in the South wholeheartedly agreed. After the war, freedmen started organizing local and state conventions and petitioned Congress for the franchise. Appropriating the revolutionary legacy for their own purposes, they drew up declarations claiming their inalienable rights, including the right to vote.[68]

White southerners reacted furiously. They tried to preserve their dominance by introducing the black codes, which denied blacks political rights. But the Republican-dominated Congress responded. The Civil Rights Act of 1866 and the Fourteenth Amendment to the Constitution both proclaimed birthright citizenship and equal rights for all Americans. In 1870, the Fifteenth Amendment barred states from making race a requirement for voting. "[This] must be done," insisted Senator William Stewart of Nevada, the amendment's sponsor. "It is the only measure that will really abolish slavery. It is the only guarantee . . . that each man shall have a right to protect his own liberty."[69]

The Civil War, as historian Eric Foner has reminded us, generated a new, effervescent enthusiasm for freedom understood as popular self-government. Just as it had during the Revolution of 1776, the expansion of American democracy, this time to black men, inspired new claims for inclusion, notably by women. Elizabeth Cady Stanton, a prominent abolitionist, proclaimed that women, no less than blacks, had arrived at a "transition period, from slavery to freedom." In particular, Stanton and other feminist leaders held high hopes that, after the war, Republicans would extend the suffrage to women and black men. (These hopes were quickly disappointed. Votes for women were never even seriously considered. The Fourteenth Amendment, while prohibiting disenfranchisement of adult males, implicitly endorsed the exclusion of women from the vote.)[70]

But the radicalism of the Reconstruction period also provoked a backlash against democracy and democratic freedom. The expansion of American democracy to black men came under attack almost as soon as it had been proclaimed. When, in 1877, Republicans agreed to withdraw the remaining federal troops from the South, Southern whites wasted no time in undoing the results of the Reconstruction period. Over the next three decades, states legislatures enacted a series of rules that disenfranchised blacks by various means, including grandfather clauses (laws limiting suffrage to people whose ancestors had voted before the Civil War), poll taxes (fees charged for voting), white primaries (laws dictating that only Democrats could vote and that only whites could be Democrats), and literacy tests. Whites also turned to violence, terrorizing blacks who might otherwise exercise their rights. The issue of black suffrage disappeared from the national agenda for nearly a century, revived only by the Civil Rights movement in the 1950s.[71]

But the backlash against democracy soon extended to poor white males as well, as American elites became increasingly worried about mass migration from Europe. By 1890, 9 million Americans, out of a total of 63 million, were foreign-born. There had been sudden influxes of the migrants before, but the new wave was larger than any of its predecessors and provoked that much more anxiety as a result. In addition, the postwar migrants flocked predominantly to cities instead of the countryside, as their predecessors had. The explosive population growth in cities such as New York and Chicago had an important impact on the political system. Party machines were created, where "bosses" delivered votes and other political favors in exchange for money and kickbacks.[72]

Not only did many of the new arrivals appear to have been corrupted by the promises of political grifters, it seemed that some were imbued with socialist and anarchist ideas. A series of violent clashes in the 1880s and 1890s between employers and largely migrant workforces made it appear that all too many immigrants were committed to the overthrow of the political and economic status quo. On May 4, 1886, for instance, a peaceful rally at Haymarket Square in Chicago, in support of an eight-hour workday, turned violent when an unknown person threw dynamite at the police. The bomb blast and ensuing gunfire resulted in the deaths of seven police officers and at least four civilians; dozens of others were wounded. In the aftermath of the explosion, eight anarchists—most of them German-born migrants—were convicted, though there was no evidence that any of them had been responsible for the bombing.[73]

Many political observers—including several Republicans—began to worry that democracy would bring about the demise of America liberty.

Francis Parkman, scion of a wealthy Boston family and a celebrated historian, complained in 1878 about the "monstrosities of negro rule in South Carolina." But he was equally scandalized by the "populous cities" filled with "masses of imported ignorance and hereditary ineptitude," which led to the "municipal corruption of New York." These examples of democracy run amok threatened to undermine liberty: "Liberty was the watchword of our fathers, and so it is of ourselves. But, in their hearts, the masses of the nation cherish desires not only different from it, but inconsistent with it. They want equality more than they want liberty."[74]

To express these concerns, Gilded Age critics of American democracy drew on the indigenous traditions of Federalist and Whig political thought. But Gilded Age thinkers were also inspired by European liberals, especially by British thinkers such as Herbert Spencer. Hence they started calling themselves "liberal" as well; in 1872, they even founded a Liberal-Republican Party. Echoing Spencer, they argued that, to preserve liberty, government power needed to be restricted as much as possible.[75]

The most influential advocate of the new, liberal way of thinking was William Graham Sumner.[76] The son of an English immigrant laborer, Sumner managed to become a highly popular professor of political and social science at Yale College. Appointed in 1873, he continued for four decades in that chair. He made a name in academic circles as a pioneering sociologist and social Darwinist, but he was also an influential political and legal thinker, responsible for introducing many of Spencer's ideas to the United States. Moreover, Sumner was a prolific contributor to popular magazines and newspapers, which gave him a much larger influence than his work as an educator alone might have.

Sumner rehearsed many of the ideas developed in the 1790s by hardline Federalists such as Fisher Ames. Like Ames, he believed that liberty could survive only if popular power was checked by strong countermajoritarian institutions. Indeed, he explicitly rejected democratic government, arguing in favor of "republics" instead. By making this distinction, Sumner gave an entirely new meaning to the word "republican." During the American Revolution and its immediate aftermath, "republic" had been more or less synonymous with popular government; hence the Jeffersonians, the most prodemocratic faction of the early United States, had called themselves Republicans. In Sumner's view, however, a republic was very different from a democracy because it did not rely on majority rule. Instead, it created safeguards to protect the individual against the "numerical majority."[77] In Sumner's view, the veto of the president, the power of the Senate, and, above all, an independent judiciary were "important institutional checks on democracy."[78]

Sumner made a considerable effort to convince his readers that this skeptical attitude toward democracy had been shared by the founders themselves; indeed, as he explained, a rejection of democracy was the bedrock of the American political system. "The public men of the Revolutionary period," he wrote, "were not democrats—they feared democracy. . . . They therefore established by the Constitution a set of institutions which are restrictions of democracy."[79] But the "constitutional republic" crafted by the founders had been transformed by the next generation into a "democratic republic." In this hybrid, the "element of democracy" was "the aggressive element . . . all the time trying to subjugate the institutions of the constitutional republic" and thereby "establish democratic absolutism." What had protected America all along was its "constitutionalist legacy."[80]

Under the influence of Spencer, Sumner also put considerable emphasis on another idea: that freedom was best protected against democratic despotism by limiting the sphere of the state as much as possible. In the essay "State Interference," the Yale professor explained that, in the olden days, the dogma of the divine right of kings was used to legitimate any extension of state power. The "new democracy," having inherited state power, showed "every disposition to use that power as ruthlessly as any other governing organ has ever used it."[81] But the coming democratic despotism, Sumner warned, would be far worse than the tyranny of even the worst of the Roman emperors. He sketched a nightmarish vision of a future "when a man's neighbors are his masters; when the 'ethical power of public opinion' bears down upon him at all hours and as to all matters; when his place is assigned to him and he is held in it, not by an emperor or his satellites, who cannot be everywhere all the time, but by the other members of the 'village community' who can."[82]

The danger of democratic despotism, Sumner argued, could best be avoided by restricting the sphere of government as much as possible. State regulation, even regulation to do good, was anathema to liberty. It was, of course, true that the "Prussian bureaucracy" was capable of providing various services to its citizens that were lacking in the United States. But, Sumner warned, if Americans wanted "to be taken care of as Prussians and Frenchmen are," to achieve this would mean "sacrificing some of their personal liberty."[83] Adult men, in a free state, must be left to make their own contracts and defend themselves. Sumner concluded that "laissez faire"—"mind your own business"—was "nothing but the doctrine of liberty."[84]

Gilded Age liberals like Sumner were far more effective in reshaping American politics than their Federalist or Whig predecessors. However, that might not be apparent at first sight. The newfangled liberalism, after all, was not terribly successful in terms of electoral politics. Like the Federalists of old, Gilded Age liberals found it difficult to convince people to vote for their antidemocratic programs. The Liberal-Republican Party was a short-lived affair. They ran one presidential candidate, Horace Greeley, in 1872. The election was a disaster for the new party: Republicans regained two-thirds majorities in both houses of Congress. Greeley did not carry a single electoral vote north of the Mason-Dixon line. The liberals would never again attempt to form a separate party. Hence, historians have described them as "leaders without followers."[85]

Yet their political influence should not be underestimated. America's legal elites proved highly receptive to their arguments. At the end of the nineteenth century, the Supreme Court and other judiciaries issued several decisions invalidating federal and state statutes that sought to regulate working conditions. Legal elites were motivated not so much by a crude desire to protect the business community or by an embrace of laissez-faire economic doctrine. Instead they wanted to protect freedom, which they thought was being threatened by the tyranny of the majority—that is, the working classes. For instance, John F. Dillon, a federal judge and American Bar Association president, described the income tax as "class legislation of the most pronounced and vicious type" and manifestly "violative of the constitutional rights of the property owner."[86]

Even more strikingly, the Gilded Age was characterized by a widespread push to make voting harder not just for blacks but also for poor whites and immigrants in the crowded cities of the North. An increasing number of states in the North and West introduced literacy requirements. In addition, residency requirements were made more onerous, and paupers who had received public aid were excluded from voting. All this resulted in what one historian has described as a "sustained, nationwide contraction of suffrage rights" in the decades before World War I. While such measures were often presented as necessary to combat voter fraud, there is little doubt that the antidemocratic arguments developed by Gilded Age liberals also played an important role.[87]

This development did not go unnoticed in Europe. Indeed, some European liberals now began to praise the political system of the United States—which had so long been seen as a beacon of democracy—for its ability to put a check on the popular will.[88] In 1885, Henry Maine, an influential British legal historian, published a series of essays titled *Popular Government*. As these essays illustrated, Maine was disenchanted with the politics of a democratizing Britain. (His book was published one year after the passage of the Third Reform Bill, which extended the franchise to about 60 percent of the adult male population.) He feared that the rise of democracy posed a major threat to the security of property and, thereby, to liberal progress as well. In his view, full-blown democracy could best be compared to "a mutinous crew, feasting on a ship's provisions, gorging themselves on the meat and intoxicating themselves with the liquors, but refusing to navigate the vessel to port."[89]

Maine was far less pessimistic, however, about the future of American democracy—precisely because, in his view, America was less democratic than Britain was in danger of becoming. Like Sumner, Maine believed the American founders had aimed to create a republic, not a democracy. That is why, in 1787, the suffrage was deliberately made to be "extremely limited in many of the States."[90] In addition, the Senate and Supreme Court, as well as the extensive powers of the presidency, had all been designed to keep popular power in check. The ideas behind these measures, Maine noted, were all "of British origin." The US constitution was, in reality, a version of the British constitution as it existed at the end of the eighteenth century. But unforeseen developments were eradicating all the existing safety valves in Britain by concentrating real power in the increasingly democratic House of Commons. In the United States, by contrast, the founders' checks on democracy had proven more durable.

Thus, Maine positively contrasted the US constitution, with its many checks and balances on popular power, with "all the infirmities of our [British] constitution in its decay." American individualism was protected, in particular, by freedom of contract, which Maine considered to be the primary constitutional bulwark against "democratic impatience and socialistic fantasy." (Maine conveniently forgot to mention that the Supreme Court had only begun to assert a constitutional right to freedom of contract in the final decades of the nineteenth century.)[91] Whereas earlier generations had admired (or vilified) America as the archetypical democracy, Maine's book revealed that, by the late nineteenth century, European liberals had come to see the American political system as a bulwark of freedom because its institutions were less responsive to popular pressure for redistribution than were those of European parliamentary democracies.

This new understanding of the nature of American freedom received symbolic expression in Frédéric Auguste Bartholdi's iconic statue *Liberty Enlightening the World*. Sculpted in the 1870s and 1880s, the Statue of Liberty was a brainchild of the French Americanophile Édouard de Laboulaye, who conceived of it as a gift from the French people to the Americans. (It was paid for by public subscription.) Today, it has become the best known American symbol of liberty and has been featured in endless movies, TV series, and cartoons. Because of its position near Ellis Island, it is often associated with openness toward migration, a connotation strengthened by the addition to the statue, nearly twenty years after its erection, of a bronze plaque featuring Emma Lazarus's poem welcoming the tired, the poor, and "huddled masses yearning to breathe free."

But the statue's original message was quite different: it was meant to propagate the antidemocratic understanding of freedom held by nineteenth-century liberals. Laboulaye and other supporters of the project wanted the statue to encourage an association among liberty, order, and personal security. That is why they deliberately rejected the traditional symbol of freedom: the cap of liberty. "This is not liberty

Frédéric Auguste Bartholdi's iconic statue *Liberty Enlightening the World* (1886).
Note the "tablets of the law" in Lady Liberty's hand.

with a red bonnet on her head," Labouleye emphasized, "and a pike in her hand who runs over fallen bodies." (He was referring, in all likelihood, to Delacroix's painting.) Because the statue was meant to foster respect for orderly liberty, Bartholdi agreed that the cap of liberty should be replaced and found another symbol: a crown of stars. He also gave Liberty what Laboulaye described as "tablets of the law," reflecting the idea that freedom was best guaranteed by the rule of law—rather than by popular self-government.[92]

Around the turn of the century, in short, the counterrevolutionary conception of liberty had become more widely accepted in the United States than ever before. While, for most of the nineteenth century, this way of thinking had been defended in public debate by relatively few, most of whom were disgruntled members of the elite, this changed in the wake of a backlash against democracy provoked by the Civil War and mass migration. Doubts about the political abilities of blacks and new migrants led Gilded Age liberals to claim that liberty needed protection from democracy. That protection was secured by limiting state power, instituting countermajoritarian institutions, and restricting the suffrage.

Contesting Modern Liberty in Europe, 1880–1945

In the 1880s and 1890s, liberal concerns about the dangers of democracy reached fevered levels on both sides of the Atlantic. But at the same time, vocal challenges to these liberal ideas about freedom emerged. In Europe, the Atlantic revolutionaries' call for democratic freedom was revived, first and foremost, by a burgeoning women's rights movement. Ever since Olympe de Gouges had questioned male domination in 1791, feminists had challenged the exclusion of women from the political sphere in the name of freedom. By the end of the nineteenth century, these efforts had spawned a mass movement. In Britain, suffragists led by Emmeline Pankhurst mounted a militant campaign for the women's vote, staging mass rallies and pioneering new forms of civil disobedience such as hunger strikes.[93]

Pankhurst and her allies explicitly modeled the fight for female suffrage on the ideals of the Atlantic revolutionaries. Thus, on a trip to the United States, Pankhurst reminded her audience of the sacrifices made for

American freedom. Echoing Patrick Henry's famous words, she declared that the suffragists, too, were prepared to choose death over slavery. "We won't do it ourselves," Pankhurst explained, "but we will put the enemy in the position where they will have to choose between giving us freedom or giving us death."[94] Other feminists likewise invoked the example of these earlier freedom fighters. In 1884, Hubertine Auclert, a French feminist, appealed rather dramatically to her American counterparts, May Wright Sewall and Susan B. Anthony, for help in the struggle against male domination: "We call upon you to come to our aid, as your countrymen, a century ago, besought France to help them escape the subjection of England. Will you not come to our help as Lafayette and his legion flew to yours?"[95]

Evidently, French feminists and British suffragists did not agree with liberals such as Herbert Spencer and Paul Leroy-Beaulieu that the best way to stave off serfdom was simply to limit state activity as much as possible. The best way was democracy. The membership card of the Women's Social and Political Union, founded by Pankkhurst, declared that the right to vote was the "basis of all liberty."

Suffragists were not the only ones claiming the mantle of the Atlantic revolutionaries. In the final decades of the nineteenth century, a worldwide economic slump, the Long Depression, sparked political discontent on both sides of the Atlantic.[96] In Europe and the United States, new political movements took shape under various names: radicalism, socialism, populism, and progressivism. Activists held diverse views, but they all rejected the liberal conception of freedom as a narrow defense of class interests—a false freedom. True freedom, they argued, required establishing democratic control over both the political and economic sphere. Their arguments, as we shall see, would have considerable effect, eventually persuading even many self-professed liberals to adopt a broader conception of freedom.

Radicals, socialists, populists, and progressives were in favor of democratic reforms; they often fought alongside suffragists for women's rights, and they tended to defend other measures designed to enhance popular control over government. But they were even more focused on extending democracy to the economic sphere. As social reformers agreed, a person could not be called truly free if they lacked control over their working

Membership card of the Women's Social and Political Union, designed by Sylvia Pankhurst (1906).

lives. Hence, liberty required more than giving all people the vote. It also required changes in the economic system to make workers less dependent on factory owners and financial elites.[97]

In making such claims, radicals, socialists, populists, and progressives extended and radicalized the Atlantic revolutionaries' way of thinking about freedom. To be sure, the revolutionaries of the late eighteenth century had recognized that political freedom depended on economic equality. Yet to the Atlantic revolutionaries, the relationship between economic equality and political freedom had been an indirect one: economic equality was needed to avoid oligarchy. Economic equality was a necessary precondition for political liberty, not a form of liberty in its own right. Their nineteenth-century successors disagreed. To them, the freedom to govern oneself should not just be limited to the political sphere; it should also be part and parcel of the economic sphere. Doing away with economic domination was a goal in and of itself.

Nineteenth-century reformers were also far more radical in their critique of the existing economic order. Apart from a tiny fringe, the Atlantic revolutionaries—including the Jacobins—had never questioned the sanctity of property rights or free market economy, even if they wanted to distribute property to as many individuals as possible. Nineteenth-century social reformers agreed that this no longer sufficed. In industrialized nations, they argued, the dream of a property-holding democracy— essentially, of a nation of small farmers—had become unrealistic. They argued for alternative economic arrangements that, they hoped, would give workers control over their labor. The more radical among them argued for abolishing private property and nationalizing the means of production, although this could mean various things. (It might imply a demand for higher taxes on certain national resources such as land, rather than a call for the state to take over the management of these resources.) Many also argued that the state had a responsibility to actively intervene in the economy to level the playing field, which was now skewed in favor of the rich and powerful.

In France, these arguments were put forward primarily by the radicals or radical-socialists (they used these names interchangeably). The Radical Party appeared for the first time in the French Assembly in 1876. It united deputies who wanted to defend the further democratization of the

French political system, notably the Senate, which was elected indirectly rather than directly. Some radicals also favored other democratizing reforms, such as referenda on the Swiss model. But soon, their main focus became social reform; in particular, they defended social insurance schemes, a progressive income tax, labor protections, and cheap credit for farmers. Until 1936, they were the largest party on the left, although they received increasing competition from Marxist parties after 1900.[98]

French radicals presented their struggle for social reform as an extension and revitalization of the Atlantic revolutionaries' struggle for self-government. This was made clear in a treatise outlining the official party doctrine, titled *Radical Politics,* crafted by historian and journalist Ferdinand Buisson, a deputy for the party. It was now generally accepted, Buisson wrote, that the people needed to be sovereign "so that all men can be free, so that all men can be equal in rights." But could a person be called truly free—even politically speaking—if they depended for their daily bread on the "goodwill" of others? Surely, such a person possessed only a "nominal and derisory freedom." Social reforms were therefore necessary to complete the revolution that had begun in 1789. The principle of popular self-government, which the French Revolution had introduced into the political order, now needed to be extended to the economic order.[99]

Similar views were expressed by French socialists, the Radical Party's main rivals on the left. The Socialist Party had little electoral success until 1900, but its share of the vote steadily increased in the years leading up to World War I, reaching 17 percent in 1914. The party was an amalgam of orthodox Marxists and more independent-minded socialists; the influence of the latter increased as the party became more successful. In many respects, the socialists' political program was indistinguishable from that of their radical competitors; however, unlike the radicals, socialists were at least in theory committed to the abolition of private property.[100]

Like their radical counterparts, French socialists emphasized that they were the party of freedom. Jean Jaurès, a philosophy professor who became the leader of the Socialist Party in 1902, emphasized as much throughout various writings. For men to become truly autonomous, truly free, Jaurès explained, they needed the means to act, to be free. This meant that all should be given an equal part in political power, so that no man would have to stand in another's shadow. But this also meant that each individual should have an equal stake in controlling the means of production, so that "no man would have to depend for his livelihood on another, so that no man would be obligated to alienate even a part of his labour or his liberty to those who held control over the productive forces." In short, the key doctrine of socialism was "*ni roi, ni capitaliste*" (neither king nor capitalist).[101]

Like Buisson, Jaurès declared socialism the heir of the French Revolution's emancipatory agenda. His four-volume *Socialist History of the French Revolution* proudly declared, "We are the party of democracy and the Revolution." The French Revolution, Jaurès explained, had "affirmed the idea of democracy to its fullest extent," establishing rights and liberties for all. "Socialism," he continued, "proclaims and rests on these new rights. It is a democratic party to the highest degree since it wants to organize the sovereignty of all in both the economic and political spheres."[102]

By describing their goal as the extension of democratic sovereignty from the political to the economic sphere, French radicals and socialists were offering a very different view of freedom from that defended by laissez-faire liberals such as Paul Leroy-Beaulieu, who had argued that the only way to preserve freedom was to limit state activity as much as possible. When confronted with a choice between these two conceptions, the French electorate overwhelmingly preferred that of Buisson and Jaurès. In 1871, at the beginning of the Third Republic, liberals had formed a large group in the assembly, and men such as Albert de Broglie, the grandson of Germaine de Staël, had held key leadership positions. But in subsequent years, voters deserted the party in droves, and liberal deputies dwindled to a tiny minority. By contrast, radicals and socialists saw their share of the popular vote grow to nearly 40 percent in 1914.[103]

In Britain, a nascent socialist movement likewise defended its agenda as a revitalization and extension of the democratic conception of freedom. Sidney and Beatrice Webb, the founders of the influential Fabian Society, a research body affiliated with the embryonic Labour Party, saw the goal of socialism as the extension of democracy from the political to the economic sphere. In their widely read book, *Industrial Democracy*, the

Webbs chided the American and French revolutionaries for not realizing that the "personal power" they drove from "throne" and "altar" should also be driven from "the farm, the factory and the mine." Industrial democracy—the goal of Fabian socialism—was to complete political democracy and establish freedom in the full sense of the word. By contrast, principles such as "freedom of contract" or "freedom of enterprise" had nothing to do with freedom at all. Instead, these notions were usually invoked by the possessing classes "to compel other less powerful people to accept their terms." Hence this sort of freedom was "not distinguishable from compulsion."[104]

These socialist critiques spurred a number of British liberals, who were eager to avoid the fate of their French counterparts, to radically rethink their ideological commitments. In 1909, the British economist and social reformer John Hobson argued in *The Crisis of Liberalism* that liberalism had "failed" in most European countries, because it had started from a set of "narrow intellectual principles." Historically, Hobson explained, liberals had tended to identify liberty with an "absence of restraint." But now it was becoming clear that a "more constructive" idea of liberty was needed to rejuvenate the liberal movement. Notably, liberals needed to embrace the idea that state interference could enhance rather than harm freedom, as long as the power of the state was used to level the economic playing field.[105] Many British liberals agreed. The idea that freedom had to be thought of as something "positive" rather than as something "negative" became widespread between 1900 and 1914.[106]

The most important spokesman for the new liberalism was Leonard Hobhouse. Trained at Oxford, Hobhouse worked as a journalist and as the secretary of a labor union before becoming a professor of sociology at the University of London. He wrote several influential books, most notably *Democracy and Reaction* and *Liberalism,* in which he aimed to steer liberals away from rigid adherence to the laissez-faire conception of freedom defended by Herbert Spencer and Paul Leroy-Beaulieu.[107]

"The nineteenth century might be called the age of Liberalism," Hobhouse wrote, "yet its close saw the fortunes of that great movement brought to their lowest ebb." Both at home and abroad, those who represented liberal ideas had suffered "crushing defeats." But this was the least of the causes for anxiety, Hobhouse emphasized. Something much worse than electoral defeat had befallen liberalism: "Its faith in itself was waxing cold. It seemed to have done its work. It had the air of a creed that is becoming fossilized as an extinct form."[108] In particular, rigid adherence to laissez-faire had gotten liberalism in trouble.

The old liberalism, Hobhouse explained, had been mainly negative. It had sought to break down barriers that hampered human development. And before the advent of democracy, such an essentially destructive project made sense. "The earlier liberalism," Hobhouse wrote, "had to deal with authoritarian government in church and state. It had to vindicate the elements of personal, civil, and economic freedom; and in so doing it took its stand on the rights of man." Hence liberalism had become wedded to the idea that the function of government was limited and definable. Liberals had become convinced that governments should retain the natural right of man as accurately as the conditions of society allowed, and "to do naught beside."[109]

But in the conditions of modern society, Hobhouse went on to argue, this kind of liberalism had become inadequate. In the economic sphere, laissez-faire brought not liberty for all but rather the oppression of the weak by the strong. Just as important, a rigid insistence on laissez-faire was no longer appropriate now that the state was under the control of the people. As the government had become "the organ of the community as a whole," even if imperfectly so, measures to ameliorate the lot of the working classes were not paternalistic; they were expressions of self-rule. In modern democracies, government was the "servant" of the people and the acts of government could therefore be considered acts of the people themselves.[110]

British liberals, in short, made a conscious effort to rethink their ideological commitments in the face of socialist critiques. This strategy seemed to work: in Britain, the Liberal Party did not decline as it had in France. Of course, British liberals' continued electoral success might also be attributed to various other, nonideological causes. The legacy of Gladstone, whose personal popularity had made the British Liberal Party much more broad-based than French liberalism had ever been, was important. The restriction of the suffrage—which remained at 60 percent of the adult male

population until 1914—might have also played a role. But the greater electoral success of the British Liberal Party, whatever its causes, enhanced
the prestige of the new liberalism.[111]

In Germany, the call for a new freedom took on a different and more
utopian character. This had much to do with the influence of Karl Marx
on German socialism. In 1867, Marx, previously a largely unknown
journalist and political activist, had become famous overnight with the
publication of his masterpiece *Capital*, a trenchant critique of traditional
political economy. Marx's views were subsequently adopted by the Social Democratic Party of Germany (SPD), founded in the 1870s to represent the interests of workers. Although Bismarck banned the party in
1878, it became legal again in 1890. During the next elections, the SPD
obtained 20 percent of the vote, and by World War I it was the largest
party in Germany. The SPD was a powerful amplifier of Marxist ideas,
but the autocratic nature of the Reich limited its influence on policy.[112]

A rejection of the liberal theory of freedom was at the heart of Marxist
political thought. In one of his earliest writings, the *Communist Manifesto,* Marx and coauthor Friedrich Engels developed a scathing attack
on the idea that freedom had anything to do with the protection of property rights. "Property," they wrote, "is alleged to be the groundwork of
all personal freedom, activity and independence." But in reality, the existence of private property allowed only "the exploitation of the many by
the few." This was not freedom, but "bourgeois freedom"—the freedom
of a single class. (When first published in 1848, the *Manifesto* was read by
only a handful of people, but it gained a much broader readership when
it was republished in 1872.)[113]

But Marxist doctrine was less clear in terms of its own, alternative conception of freedom. Marx and his orthodox followers refrained from
talking about freedom as something that could be realized in the here and
now. In Marx's view, the whole of human history since the invention of
agriculture had been characterized by class struggle and oppression. At
any given period, one class had dominated all the others due to its economic strength. And seemingly emancipatory events, such as the French
Revolution, had in fact been nothing of the kind: 1789 had simply trans-
ferred power from the nobility to the bourgeoisie. Only the coming proletarian revolution, Marx taught, would truly bring freedom for all, by

abolishing private property and thereby ending centuries of class strife. In this new society, Marx predicted, "the free development of each" person would be "the condition for the free development of all."[114]

But because the proletarian revolution would initiate a radical rupture with preceding history, the contours of the new, communist society that would emerge in its wake were essentially unknowable. The science of political economy could predict the downfall of the capitalist system, but it could not predict what lay on the other side of the abyss. "Never yet in the history of mankind has it happened that a revolutionary party was able to foresee, let alone determine, the forms of the new social order which it strove to usher in," Karl Kautsky, the SDP's main theorist, remarked in 1891. It was therefore "childish," he continued irritably, to demand of the socialist that he draw "a picture of the commonwealth which he strives for."[115]

Marxists did, on occasion, speculate about the future form of society. In his enormously influential exposition of Marxist theory, the *Anti-Dühring* of 1878, Engels suggested that in the communist society, the state, as an apparatus of oppression, "dies out" because nothing remains to be repressed. Marx himself similarly suggested that the free society might take a rather anarchist form. In the *Civil War in France,* Marx lauded the brief-lived Paris Commune—the workers' government that had taken over Paris in 1871—for smashing the existing state power. If it had succeeded, Marx noted, the Commune would have "restored to the social body all the forces hitherto absorbed by the state parasite feeding upon, and clogging the free movement of, society."[116] But these suggestions were never fully worked out by either theorist.

Marxist theory, in short, left unanswered many questions about what a free state would look like. Hence it injected a decidedly utopian strand into socialist thinking, despite Marx's explicit rejection of utopianism.[117] But in terms of practical politics, Marxists were by no means wild-eyed revolutionaries. The SPD's program was very similar to that of the French radical-socialists or even the new liberals. Hobhouse, for instance, saw much to like in the Erfurt Program, the SPD's 1891 election manifesto.[118] The first demand of the Erfurt Program was universal suffrage—including for women—and its second demand was "self-determination and self-government of the people." The program also sought various social reforms such as free medical care and a graduated income tax. More generally, Marx and his followers consistently argued that the path to communism went through democracy: the growing numbers of the proletariat, they argued, would necessarily lead the SPD to electoral victory, allowing it to peacefully abolish capitalism.[119]

Thus, by 1914, the call for democratic freedom had been revived with a vengeance in Europe—but it had also been profoundly transformed. In France and Britain, new radical and socialist movements argued that real freedom required an end to both political and economic domination—and, hence, that democracy needed to be extended from the political to the economic sphere. In Germany, Marxist thinkers developed a more utopian alternative to the liberal conception of freedom. All of these movements dismissed liberal freedom as a narrow defense of class interests—a false freedom rather than a compelling political ideal. Everywhere, the "old" liberalism seemed to be on the defensive. Indeed, the only kind of liberalism that seemed to still be thriving was Britain's new liberalism, which rejected the negative conception of liberty as laissez-faire in favor of a broader, more positive understanding of the term.

In the wake of World War I, debate about freedom in Europe was further complicated by a series of dramatic political developments. In March 1917, the tsarist regime in Russia collapsed and a democratic republic was established. But a few months later, during the October Revolution, the fledgling republic was overthrown in turn by the Bolsheviks, a Marxist group. The prolonged civil war that followed was eventually won by the Bolsheviks who established the Union of Soviet Socialist Republics in 1922. Events in Russia sparked a broader communist-revolutionary wave in Europe that lasted until 1923. Yet no other Marxist movement at the time succeeded in keeping power, even while the Bolshevik regime endured.[120]

Vladimir Lenin and other Bolshevik ideologues described their new regime as a "proletarian dictatorship." They borrowed this concept from Marx and Engels, who had used it to describe the political condition following the proletarian revolution. But the Bolsheviks gave a decidedly new twist to this concept. Marx and Engels, who had agitated for democracy and universal suffrage for most of their lives, claimed that this dictatorship was to be established peacefully, via elections, not via a coup engineered by a small vanguard such as the Bolsheviks. Marx and Engels had also maintained that the proletarian dictatorship would be a relatively brief transitory phase; it would allow the proletarians to seize control over the means of production and to establish the new communist society, which would then automatically end the class struggle as well as the need for a proletarian dictatorship. Hence, the concept of proletarian dictatorship had played a negligible role in Marxist theory before 1917.[121]

In Bolshevik political doctrine, however, the notion came to have a much more central place. In his "Theses and Report on Bourgeois Democracy and the Dictatorship of the Proletariat," Lenin presented proletarian dictatorship as the main alternative to "bourgeois democracy." In capitalist countries, Lenin explained, "all that exists is bourgeois democracy." It was therefore necessary to establish a dictatorship of the oppressed class (the proletariat) over its oppressors and exploiters (the bourgeoisie), in order to overcome the exploiters in their fight to maintain domination. Freedom of the press and freedom of assembly, Lenin continued, were nothing more than the freedom of the rich to tell lies and to subvert the efforts of the proletarians. Abolishing those false freedoms was therefore prerequisite to the creation of the new communist society, which would bring true liberty for all.[122]

The Bolshevik Revolution provoked vigorous debate within the socialist movement about the relationship between political and economic freedom. A number of prominent Marxist thinkers roundly rejected the idea that a dictatorship—even if it was of the proletarian variety—could be a basis for human freedom. In a 1918 pamphlet, *Dictatorship of the Proletariat,* Karl Kautsky vehemently rejected the idea that socialism was compatible with dictatorship or with anything that even smacked of "paternalism." The goal of socialist parties, he wrote, was not simply the abolition of private property but "the abolition of every kind of exploitation and oppression, be it directed against a class, a party, a sex, or a race." This required a "proletarian class struggle," but not at any cost—for, as Kautsky put it, "socialism without democracy is unthinkable." Kautsky would continue to defend these views for the rest of his life. After 1917, most of his intellectual energies were devoted to criticizing Bolshevism. (Bolsheviks returned the favor; Lenin denounced Kautsky as a "renegade" and wrote several violent polemics against the German thinker.[123])

At the same time, the success of the Bolsheviks convinced quite a number of European Marxists—who started calling themselves "communists"— that a Soviet-style proletarian dictatorship was the best path to social revolution and, ultimately, freedom. In 1919, this group formed the Third International, which officially committed communist parties to the principle of the dictatorship of the proletariat. As the *Manifesto of the Communist International* explained, "Only the proletarian dictatorship" could solve "the present crisis." Parliamentary democracy was not real democracy at all, because in reality all important decisions were taken by the "finance-oligarchy." Existing democracies just made "formal declarations of rights and liberties" that were unattainable for the proletariat. Soviet-style government would give the workers the "means" to enjoy their "rights and liberties." This was not a destruction of democracy but the creation of a "higher working-class democracy."[124]

The October Revolution also had an important effect on debate about freedom outside of the socialist movement. The Bolshevik threat led to a minor resurgence in the call for negative liberty in Europe. Ludwig von Mises, an Austrian economist and hardline defender of the night-watchman state, for instance, published a book-length defense in 1927 of laissez-faire liberalism. True liberalism, Mises asserted, propagated freedom in the sense of minimal government. All the state should do was protect private ownership of the means of production. As Mises put it, "As the liberal sees it, the task of the state consists solely and exclusively in guaranteeing the protection of life, health, liberty, and private property against violent attacks. Everything that goes beyond this is an evil."[125] But this kind of liberalism, Mises acknowledged, was under threat. In continental Europe, liberalism had all but disappeared as a political force. Only in Britain were liberals still a viable political movement, but in Mises's view, they were actually nothing but "moderate socialists."[126]

In Mises's analysis, the demise of "true" liberalism had much to do with the increasing competition from communists, who made all kinds of false promises to the gullible masses. A revitalization of liberalism was therefore necessary. There was no need of "popular slogans" to win "the favor of the masses." Liberalism, Mises concluded, "has no party flower and no party color, no party song and no party idols, no symbols and no slogans. It has the substance and the arguments. These must lead it to victory."[127]

But this was not in fact a winning strategy in interwar Europe, as Mises himself seemed to realize: "If men cannot be enlightened, if they persist in error, then nothing can be done to prevent catastrophe," he wrote.[128] Even before 1914, liberal parties had been in decline in many parts of Europe. But after the expansion of the suffrage that followed World War I, they went into freefall. Even in Britain the Liberal Party faltered, hampered by a disastrous split in 1916 over the conduct of the war. The outbreak of the Great Depression in 1929 made laissez-faire liberalism even less attractive, as the crisis fatally undermined the intellectual authority of liberal economics, which had already been considerably damaged in the wake of the Long Depression of the 1870s to 1890s.[129]

Not laissez-faire liberalism, but fascism—an avowedly authoritarian movement—was the main beneficiary of the red scare. The Bolshevik Revolution encouraged the rise of new right-wing movements, exemplified by Benito Mussolini's Fascist Party (created in 1919) and Adolph Hitler's National Socialist German Workers' Party (founded in 1920). Throughout Europe, these movements managed to overthrow democracy, as ruling elites in many countries showed themselves to be "anti-communists first, democrats second." As a result, political debate in Europe was profoundly transformed. By the mid-1930s, Mark Mazower notes, "liberalism looked tired, the organized Left had been smashed and the sole struggles over ideology and governance were taking place within the Right—among authoritarians, traditional conservatives, technocrats and radical right-wing extremists."[130] Debate about freedom would not revive until 1945.

Contesting Gilded Age Liberalism in the United States

As in Europe, new political movements emerged in the 1880s and 1890s in the United States that challenged Gilded Age liberalism and its identification of freedom as laissez-faire. The first of these movements, populism, emerged among American farmers, who had been hit hard by falling prices for agricultural goods. But populism also attracted coal miners, railroad workers, and other laborers. They were convinced that their misery was largely caused by political abuses. Those who had corporate and financial power, populists believed, used their control over government to rig the economic system in their own favor. The populist reaction was to demand that the government be made to respond to the concerns of ordinary people; hence they defended various measures such as referenda, the secret ballot, and the direct election of senators and the president. But they also propagated state intervention to directly alleviate the suffering of the poor, level the economic playing field, and give every worker due rewards for their labor. Populists attempted to put this program into practice by founding the People's Party, which fielded candidates for the presidential elections of 1892 and 1896.[131]

Around 1900, the populist movement fizzled out as farmers' fortunes increased with the world economy. But the struggle for political and social reform was now taken up by the so-called progressives. Progressives, who were generally middle-class, espoused a markedly different style of political activism. As one historian put it, "Populists raised hell; Progressives read pamphlets."[132] But they co-opted and popularized many of the populists' political and social demands, such as the adoption of the secret ballot and the direct election of senators, along with various interventionist measures, such as the demand for a progressive income tax. They did not found a new party—although there was a short-lived Progressive Party, this was mainly a vehicle for the personal ambitions of Theodore Roosevelt—but by 1900, both Democrats and Republicans had progressive wings. After 1914, many progressives, who closely followed intellectual developments in Britain, also came to describe themselves as "new" liberals, to underscore their kinship with British social liberals such as Hobson and Hobhouse.[133]

Just like radicals and socialists in Europe, populists and progressives developed a thoroughgoing critique of Gilded Age liberals' conception of freedom, a critique articulated most extensively by Woodrow Wilson. The son of a wealthy Southern family, Wilson was an unlikely progressive standard bearer. Originally a conservative Democrat, he had objected to the influence of populists such as William Jennings Bryan on

Democratic politics. (In 1896, Bryan was selected as the candidate for president by both the People's Party and the Democrats). But over time, Wilson changed his mind, and when he sought the Democratic presidential nomination in 1912, he did so as a progressive. Indeed, he actively sought the support of Bryan, which he duly received.[134]

During his campaign, Wilson promised to bring a "new freedom" to America. (In 1913, his campaign speeches were published as a book with that title.)[135] To do so, he explained, required political reforms that would restore power to the people; Wilson therefore promised to introduce presidential primaries, limits on campaign spending for corporations, and the direct election of US senators. The "masters of the government of the United States," Wilson explained, were the "capitalists and manufacturers." But the control they exercised over government had brought "thralldom instead of freedom." Americans needed to be given the opportunity to take back control. Wilson's aim was, therefore, to "bring the government back to the people."[136]

The political reforms required, Wilson argued, were not an attack on the "republican institutions" of the country (as, for instance, Sumner had claimed); such a charge was "absurd." The idea that the people should rule was the "ground principle" of the American republic, a point he illustrated by quoting the Virginia Declaration of Rights. Enhancing popular control over government, then, would simply bring the United States back to its original principles. "No man who understands the principles upon which this Republic was founded has the slightest dread of the gentle—though very effective—measure by which the people are again resuming control over their own affairs."[137]

But such democratic reforms, Wilson continued, did not suffice to give Americans back their liberty; economic reforms were necessary as well. Thus he proposed a graduated income tax, a central bank under the control of the federal government, and antitrust policies. Economic reforms were just as necessary for freedom as purely political reforms, he argued, because Americans were not free under the current economic conditions. "Why? Because the laws of this country do not prevent the strong from crushing the weak," Wilson thundered. "That is the reason, and because the strong have crushed the weak the strong dominate the industry and the economic life of this country."[138]

From this perspective, the liberty defended by Sumner and laissez-faire liberals was a false liberty, a point Wilson did not hesitate to make explicit. Under modern economic conditions, he explained, there could be no fair play between individuals and corporate interests. Hence the "watchful interference, the resolute interference, of the government" was necessary to redress the balance in favor of those without economic power. "Freedom to-day," had to be "something more than being let alone." The program of a "government of freedom," he concluded, "must in these days be positive, not negative merely."[139]

Unsurprisingly, America's Gilded Age liberals rejected these claims. Among these liberals was Wilson's opponent for the presidency in 1912, the Republican William Howard Taft. An Ohioan from a well-to-do family, Taft had studied at Yale, where William Graham Sumner was among his professors. Later in life, Taft singled out Sumner as an important intellectual influence.[140] After his defeat by Wilson, Taft, a legal scholar by training, became a professor at Yale, where he lectured on modern government. Taft's course lectures were published in 1913 as *Popular Government: Its essence, its Permanence and its Perils.* While an academic work, it was also an explicit indictment of Wilson's progressive conception of freedom.[141]

Liberty, Taft argued, had nothing to do with majority rule. Instead, a free government was a government in which individual rights, notably the right to property, were secure. Any government that refused to recognize the sanctity of individual rights, Taft wrote, and any government that held "the lives, the liberty and the property of its citizens subject at all times to the absolute disposition and unlimited control of even the most democratic depository of power," could be described only as a despotism. "It is true it is a despotism of the many, of the majority, if you choose to call it so, but it is none the less a despotism."[142]

From this perspective, democracy was not the key to liberty. Taft was in favor of popular government, he explained, but it should not be made into a "fetish." "We are in favor of a rule by as many of the people in a democracy as will secure a good government," he wrote, "and no more."[143] By contrast, Taft considered the federal judiciary to be the "bulwark of the liberty of the individual." Continental countries also had "abstract declarations" of the right to liberty and property, Taft noted, but these were dead letters, because they lacked the specific protection the English and American judicial systems provided: that individuals could appeal to the courts to protect their rights against "the aggression of a majority of the electorate."[144]

In short, by 1914, American political debate had come to revolve around two very different conceptions of liberty. On the one hand, Gilded Age liberals such as Taft maintained that freedom was all about the protection of individual rights—above all, the right to property. Democracy had to be curtailed to the extent that it threatened these rights. On the other hand, populists and progressives such as Wilson argued that true freedom could be brought about only by revitalizing American democracy. This was to happen through the creation of new instruments for popular rule, such as referenda; through the direct election of senators; and through legislation designed to give Americans greater control over their economic lives, making them less dependent on the vagaries of the market.

World War I had one particularly important effect on this debate: it upended age-old notions about the gendered nature of democratic freedom. Since the 1890s, women's rights activists had been campaigning for female suffrage. This campaign culminated in 1917, when women's rights activists started picketing the White House, carrying banners asking, "Mr. President, how long must women wait for liberty?" At the same time, American entry into the global conflict gave suffragists the opportunity to contribute to the war effort and, in so doing, to highlight their fitness for the vote. The suffragists' adroit handling of the war crisis, coupled with continuing political pressure on Congress and the president, was rewarded in January 1918, when the president announced his support of a federal suffrage amendment "as a war measure."[145]

In other respects, the war had only a small impact on the debate in the United States, where, unlike Europe, the Marxist movement had always been weak. But that did not prevent a brief red scare in the summer of 1919. After a string of anarchist bombings, thousands of anarchists and socialists were arrested and deported, many of them to Russia. The arrests and subsequent executions of Nicola Sacco and Bartolomeo Vanzetti, two Italian anarchists and immigrants, on trumped-up charges of murder, left little doubt about the hostility of certain sections of the political and judicial elites to left-wing political actors. But compared to

Europe, where fear of Bolshevism sparked the rise of fascism and Nazism, along with the violent suppression of all forms of leftism, response to the communist threat in America was far less extreme.[146]

But if communism did not inspire a far-right backlash in the United States, it probably played a role in reviving Gilded Age liberalism. In the 1920s, the most important spokesman of this kind of liberalism was Herbert Hoover, an engineer, businessman, and Republican politician. In the final speech of his victorious 1928 presidential campaign, Hoover criticized the idea that the state could and should intervene in the economy. "Every step of bureaucratizing of the business of our country poisons the very roots of liberalism—that is, political equality, free speech, free assembly, free press, and equality of opportunity," he warned. "It is the road not to more liberty, but to less liberty. Liberalism should be found not striving to spread bureaucracy but striving to set bounds to it." Hoover claimed this liberalism—the liberalism of limited government—as the quintessential American creed: "For a hundred and fifty years liberalism has found its true spirit in the American system, not in the European systems."[147]

But the ascendancy of Gilded Age liberalism was not to last. In 1929, the Wall Street stock market crashed, and America was hit by the Great Depression. Americans had experienced slumps before, but nothing like this. Between 1929 and 1932, the economy seemed to be in freefall. As the monetary system tottered in the wake of the crisis, the unemployment rate climbed from 9 percent in 1930 to 16 percent in 1931 to 23 percent in 1932. In an age without a social safety net, unemployment spelled disaster for many families. One in four Americans suffered from want of food, even though food prices had collapsed. Indeed, prices were so low that it did not pay to bring harvests to market. Wheat was left to rot in the fields while city dwellers went hungry. Shantytowns sprang up around the great cities.[148]

It quickly became clear to American voters that Hoover had no answer to the Depression. In 1932, he was soundly beaten by Franklin Delano Roosevelt, who went on to implement the New Deal, an ambitious package of reforms. In what has been described as an "orgy of law-making," Roosevelt and his cabinet tackled the unemployment crisis. But they also transformed the social contract in a more fundamental way by creating a safety net for Americans down on their luck. Roosevelt and his allies came to the rescue of foreclosed farmers, established unemployment benefits, and invested in public projects that put idle workers back on the job. The National Labor Relations Act of 1935 allowed workers to more freely organize themselves and negotiate better deals with their employers.[149]

Like Hoover, Roosevelt called himself a liberal, but he made it abundantly clear that he took liberalism to mean something very different from the anti-statist liberalism represented by his defeated opponent. Following instead the lead of British new liberals such as Leonard Hobhouse, Roosevelt believed in a broader conception of liberty. During one of his many fireside chats, he told the American people that he rejected "a return to that definition of liberty under which for many years a free people were being gradually regimented into the service of the privileged few." He added, "I prefer and I am sure you prefer that broader definition of liberty under which we are moving forward to a greater freedom, a greater security for the average man than he has ever known in the history of America."[150]

Roosevelt's 1932 election victory can therefore be seen as a victory of a new and more social liberalism over the old Gilded Age liberalism. This was also made explicit by John Dewey, a Columbia University professor and an ardent supporter of the New Deal. Dewey was a prolific and influential public intellectual, contributing on a regular basis to the *New Republic* and other outlets. Like Hobhouse, with whom he was friendly, Dewey argued that the "earlier liberalism," which had identified liberty "as a matter in which individual and government are opposed parties" had made sense in a time of "despotism." But now that the government had become "popular," the old idea was degenerating into the "pseudo-liberalism" of Herbert Hoover, which was blatantly elitist. In the modern world, "it was absurd to conceive liberty as that of the business entrepreneur and ignore the immense regimentation to which workers are subjected."[151]

Roosevelt emphasized that his way of thinking about liberty had deep roots in the American past; that it was an extension and radicalization of the promise of the American Revolution. During his acceptance speech at the Democratic National Convention in 1936, the president appealed to the example of that earlier fight for liberty. The American people had defeated the political tyranny of George III in the War of Independence. Now it was time to destroy economic tyranny, for the political equality won in 1776 had become meaningless in the face of growing economic inequality. Hence the time had come "to pledge ourselves to restore to the people a wider freedom; to give to 1936 as the founders gave to 1776."[152]

Not everyone agreed. After Roosevelt's election, business interests created the Liberty League, which argued for "constitutional liberty" and tried to portray Roosevelt's broader conception of freedom as un-American. In 1936, Al Smith—a former progressive Democrat who, to the dismay of many of his erstwhile supporters, had joined the Liberty League—insisted that there was no middle ground between old-fashioned American liberty and the new evil of communist dictatorship. "There can be only the clear pure fresh air of free America or the foul breath of Communistic Russia," he declared in a speech delivered at the Washington Mayflower hotel. Despite the efforts of the Liberty League, Roosevelt won reelection in a landslide.[153]

Roosevelt's 1936 reelection briefly brought to a close the half-century of debate about the nature and meaning of freedom that had begun with the rise of Gilded Age liberalism. Under his leadership, Americans seemed to have made their choice for the new freedom, which would extend the promise of the American Revolution—to give ordinary citizens control over the way they were governed—from politics to the economic sphere. But in the postwar period, Gilded Age liberalism and its concomitant identification of liberty with laissez-faire politics made a remarkable comeback. In order to understand how that happened, we need to take account of how the Cold War affected political debate in both the United States and Europe.

Freedom in the Wake of the Cold War

In the first few years after the Allied victory in 1945, it was taken for granted that the war had been fought for the kind of freedom defended by FDR in 1936. Such views were expressed most explicitly in the United States. When Roosevelt was reelected once more in 1944, he talked about the necessity of a second Bill of Rights, guaranteeing economic security.

The founders, he explained during his State of the Union address, had given citizens inalienable political rights. But more recently Americans had come to agree that "true individual freedom cannot exist without economic security and independence." "Necessitous men are not free men," Roosevelt explained. "People who are hungry and out of a job are the stuff of which dictatorships are made." Hence, Congress should strengthen Americans' economic protections by introducing rights to a living wage, a decent home, and health care.[154] Many agreed. For instance, the *New Republic,* in September 1945, lauded the "participation of democratic government in the economic process." Such involvement "extended the sphere of freedom" rather than endangering it. In the modern world, government was liberty's "protector," and full employment "a milestone on the road to freedom."[155]

Across the Atlantic, a similar bell was sounded. In the United Kingdom, the Labour Party was proud to "stand for freedom" in the general election of 1945, which it won by a landslide.[156] Similarly, in France, the Popular Republican Movement, which came out of the noncommunist resistance, declared in its first manifesto in 1944 that it supported a "revolution" to create a state "liberated from the power of those who possess wealth."[157] This desire for revolution was not shared by all Europeans though. In Germany, there was less of an appetite for the invocation of grandiose principles in the immediate aftermath of the war. Unsurprisingly, the overriding interest was a return to normalcy and stability. The German Christian Democrats, for instance, successfully campaigned on the slogan *"Sicher ist sicher"*—safe is safe.[158]

Yet, the debate about freedom soon took a dramatic new turn. In the late 1940s and 1950s, the laissez-faire conception of freedom defended by Paul Leroy-Beaulieu, Herbert Spencer, and William Graham Sumner—a conception of freedom that in preceding decades had been widely dismissed as overly "negative"—was revived. A transatlantic coalition of intellectuals, most of whom described themselves as liberals, came to argue with increasing insistence that freedom should be understood solely as the absence of state interference. Any state intervention was necessarily an infringement on individual liberty, even when implemented by a democratic government. Indeed, liberty in this limited, negative sense of the word was now reimagined as the key value of Western civilization.

In order to understand the remarkable resurgence of laissez-faire liberty after 1945, we need to turn to a new development in the postwar period: the advent of the Cold War. By 1946, it was becoming increasingly clear that the defeat of Nazism and fascism had not resulted in universal peace. Instead, new fault lines came into place, now between former allies: the United States and the Soviet Union. The conflict was partly driven by concerns about national security. But mutual distrust was undoubtedly exacerbated by differences in ideological outlook. In the wake of the total defeat of Nazism and fascism, many in the United States perceived Russian communism as the greatest threat to the American way of life, and vice versa. Soon, the international system was divided between the self-described "free world" of the West and the communist East.[159]

The Cold War had a major impact on intellectual life in the United States and Europe. With astonishing speed, communism took the place of Nazism as the main ideology to be combated both at home and abroad. The United States was gripped by a second red scare, which was far more intense than that of 1918–1919. The Communist Party was outlawed, and measures were taken to combat the spread of communism in labor unions. In addition, an anticommunist crusade was launched to combat the supposed infiltration of the US government and Hollywood film industry, which culminated in Joseph McCarthy's infamous witch hunt for Communist Party members and fellow travelers. In continental Europe, communist parties were likewise outlawed in some countries, notably in West Germany and Greece. Elsewhere they were tolerated but their members harassed.

In addition to these heavy-handed tactics, policymakers and intellectuals turned to the power of ideology. If the West was to win the Cold War, it had to come up with an attractive alternative to communism. This was all the more urgent because communism had proven appealing to many in the West. In some parts of Western Europe, communist parties, boosted by their prominent role in the resistance against Nazism, obtained significant electoral successes in the immediate aftermath of the war: in France, the communist PCF obtained 28 percent of the vote in 1946, while Italian communists obtained 19 percent of the vote in the same year.[160]

In response to these developments, a coalition of transatlantic intellectuals took shape. They created a new ideology—Cold War liberalism—that was expressly anti-Marxist. Cold War liberals were not necessarily against state intervention or the push for economic security. But they believed that state power should only be wielded with the greatest circumspection, as a necessary evil. At no time could the state—not even a democratic state—be thought of as an emancipatory agent. Hence, they embraced the limited conception of freedom defended by Gilded Age liberals that others had rejected as overly "narrow" and "negative."[161]

An early and highly influential attempt to spell out these ideas was Friedrich Hayek's *The Road to Serfdom*. An Austrian economist, Hayek had moved to the United Kingdom in 1931 to take a position at the London School of Economics. In this new context, Hayek soon emerged as a leading defender of free markets. He was particularly disturbed by the success of the Beveridge Report, which proposed the creation of a social safety net in Britain. The report sold over a million copies when it was published in 1942, demonstrating the appetite in Britain for economic reform. In reply, Hayek wrote *The Road to Serfdom,* which appeared in 1944 in England and the United States. In 1945 *Reader's Digest* published an abridged version that reached yet more Americans.[162]

Hayek's main objection against "socialism" or "planning" (he used these words interchangeably) was political rather than economic: planning led to serfdom and totalitarianism. Planning meant that one had to decide on a social goal or a common purpose around which to organize a society. "The making of an economic plan involves the choice between conflicting or competing ends—different needs of different people," he explained. But which needs would be met and which would not would be known only to the experts, so they would end up making all the most important decisions. The distrust this necessarily created would erode democracy itself. Hence democracy worked only when it was "restricted to fields where agreement among a majority could be achieved by free discussion"—which, in Hayek's view, excluded all major economic issues.[163]

To Hayek, Nazi Germany and the Soviet state were the starkest examples of the illiberal tendencies of socialist planning. But he stressed that planning also undermined freedom within democratic societies. Therefore constant vigilance was necessary, lest all democracies in the West traveled the road to serfdom. Hayek drove this point home in the chapter "Totalitarians in our Midst." "Democratic socialism," he wrote, "the great utopia of the last few generations, is not only unachievable, but . . . to strive for it produces something utterly different—the very destruction of freedom itself."[164]

More generally, Hayek warned against making "a fetish of democracy." His contemporaries, he explained, talked too much of democracy and too little of the values it served. Democracy was "essentially a means, a utilitarian device for safeguarding internal peace and individual freedom." As such, it was by no means infallible. Indeed, it was "at least conceivable" that democratic majorities might be as oppressive as the worst dictatorships. At the same time, history taught there might be "much more cultural and spiritual freedom under an autocratic rule than under some democracies."[165]

Hayek argued that by focusing on the totalitarian threat to democracy, many had come to adopt the "misleading and unfounded belief" that, "so long as the ultimate source of power is the will of the majority, the power cannot be arbitrary." But this was patently untrue. "It is not the source but the limitation of power which prevents it from being arbitrary. Democratic control may prevent power from becoming arbitrary, but it does not do so by its mere existence. If democracy resolves on a task which necessarily involves the use of power which cannot be guided by fixed rules, it must become arbitrary power."[166]

The Road to Serfdom was met with fierce criticism from left-leaning journalists and intellectuals, who, with good reason, saw Hayek's book as an attack not just on Nazism and communism but on democratic socialism and New Deal liberalism as well. But the reception of *The Road to Serfdom* also demonstrates how the advent of the Cold War gave new credibility to the idea that any kind of state intervention—no matter how much democratic support it enjoyed—should be seen as an infraction on liberty. The condensed version of Hayek's book distributed by *Reader's Digest* in 1945 sold over a million copies. By the time Hayek arrived in the United States later that year for a five-week lecture tour, he had become a phenomenon. A lecture sponsored by the Town Hall Club in New York drew an overflow crowd of more than 3,000 listeners and was broadcast over the radio.[167]

But the laissez-faire conception of liberty was not just revived by hard-line free marketeers such as Hayek. Similar ideas also came to be defended by political thinkers who had no economic objections to state intervention, such as the British philosopher Isaiah Berlin.[168] Berlin was by no means a dogmatic defender of free markets; indeed, he had little interest in economic debates. But Berlin was a lifelong and staunch anti-Marxist, and this led him to view strong states with suspicion. The state, he argued, might have a legitimate role to play in providing economic security and thus making people less receptive to the lure of extremist ideologies. But the expansion of state power was also dangerous—it undermined human freedom. Hence, state intervention should always be undertaken with circumspection.[169]

Berlin made this explicit in his 1950 paper "Political Ideas in the Twentieth Century," in which he reflected on the growing influence of what he described as "totalitarian" attitudes even in the free West. The understandable human desire for security—and, above all, economic security—he argued, had encouraged acquiescence to an ever-bigger state. But this "great transformation," with its genuine material gains, had necessarily been accompanied by a loss of individual liberty.[170] In the West, no less than in the Soviet Union, "growing numbers of human beings are prepared to purchase this sense of security even at the cost of allowing vast tracts of life to be controlled by persons who, whether consciously or not, act systematically to narrow the horizon of human activity to manageable proportions, to train human beings into more easily combinable parts—interchangeable, almost prefabricated, of a total pattern."[171]

This trend was less pronounced in the United States, where Berlin approvingly observed that "the nineteenth century survives far more powerfully than anywhere else."[172] But in Western Europe, the "paternalistic state" had severely curtailed the individual's liberties "in the interest (the very real interest) of his welfare or of his sanity, his health, his security, his freedom from want and fear." As a result, the individual's "area of choice" had "grown smaller," in order to create "a simpler and better regulated life," guaranteed by "an efficiently working order, untroubled by agonizing moral conflict."[173]

Unlike Hayek, however, Berlin did not conclude his essay by pleading for a restraint of state power. He recognized that planning was necessary to preserve an acceptable quality of life and that "we cannot sacrifice either freedom or a minimum standard of welfare." Instead, he argued for an "ambiguous compromise." Planning had become a necessary instrument in modern societies, and it should therefore not be abandoned. But neither should it be enthusiastically embraced. Berlin maintained that citizens should be encouraged to regard the state and its scientific planners with a healthy amount of distrust: "We must not submit to authority because it is infallible but only for strictly and openly utilitarian reasons, as a necessary evil."[174]

These views also informed Berlin's thinking on freedom. Between 1950 and 1958, Berlin worked on a series of books, essays, and public talks on liberty, culminating in his seminal essay *Two Concepts of Liberty*. In his lectures and talks, Berlin defended the key idea that freedom as noninterference—what he called "negative" liberty—was the only kind of freedom worth having, and that any other, more "positive" definition of the concept was an obfuscation or a lie.[175] Freedom was in its "primary sense" a "negative concept," he wrote in *Political Ideas in the Romantic Age*. "To demand freedom is to demand the absence of human activities which cross my own." By contrast, "the notion of positive liberty" was "founded on a confusion, and a confusion which has cost a great many human lives."[176]

Berlin, it should be noted, used the term "positive liberty" to describe a number of quite different conceptions of freedom, including the Stoic idea that a person could only be truly free if they mastered their own passions. But he made it quite clear that in rejecting positive liberty, he was also rejecting the democratic theory of freedom. Invoking the authority of Benjamin Constant, he wrote that democracies could, without ceasing to be democratic, oppress freedom. Liberty was therefore "principally concerned with the area of control, not with its source." Or, as Berlin put it as well: "Freedom in this [negative] sense is not, at least not logically, connected with democracy or self-government." Freedom, in other words, was "not incompatible" with some kinds of autocracy, or at any rate with the absence of self-government.[177]

Berlin's position was starkly different, indeed, exactly the opposite from that of new liberals such as Hobhouse and Dewey. In Berlin's view, the only truly "liberal" definition of freedom was purely negative: freedom from state interference. Berlin restored the moral high ground to this form of freedom, which social reformers had rejected as nonsensical or egoistic. He described it (again, much as Constant had done), as a way of thinking about freedom most appropriate to the modern world. In *Two Concepts of Liberty*, he argued that negative liberty was "liberty as it has been conceived by liberals in the modern world from the days of Erasmus (some would say of Occam) to our own."[178]

But Berlin also introduced a new idea: that negative liberty was the very essence of Western civilization—as opposed to "Eastern," positive liberty. In his BBC lecture series on "Freedom and Its Betrayal," for instance, he talked about negative liberty as "the Anglo-French notion of freedom," as opposed to the "German" concept of freedom elaborated in the writings of Johann Gottlieb Fichte.[179] And in *Two Concepts of Liberty*, the homeland of negative liberty was even more narrowly defined: it was not an Anglo-French notion, but freedom as it had been defined by "the classical English political philosophers."[180] Berlin also praised negative liberty as a "mark of high civilization on part of both individuals and communities." Its decline "would mark the death of a civilization, of an entire moral outlook."[181]

Not everyone was convinced by Berlin's arguments. Marshall Cohen, an American philosophy professor, dismissed the publication of Berlin's *Two Concepts* as "less an event in philosophy than in the cold war." Cohen claimed that, by identifying the liberal tradition with negative liberty, Berlin had ignored "the great historical demands of liberals for popular sovereignty and for governmental intervention in economic affairs."[182] Overall, however, Berlin's contribution to the debate about liberty was received enthusiastically. His lectures and papers on freedom were widely discussed in the popular press. In a glowing review published in the *Times Literary Supplement*, *Two Concepts* was described as an important and timely restatement of John Stuart Mill's *On Liberty*.[183]

Some Cold War liberals took a more nuanced position. Raymond Aron, a French philosopher and influential anti-Marxist, rejected both liberal and social-democratic "extremism," arguing that there was not just "one exclusive definition of liberty."[184] He explained as much in a series of 1963 lectures, which were published as *An Essay on Liberties*. Aron started out by agreeing with Hayek (whom he quoted repeatedly) that democracy and liberalism were, at least in principle, very different things. "Liberalism is a way of conceiving the goal and limits of state power," he said, whereas "democracy is a way of conceiving the designation of those who exercise power."[185] Certain instances of state intervention, even when democratically legitimate, were detrimental to freedom. By way of example, Aron invoked the elevated taxation rates of his time—the highest income bracket was taxed at 90 percent. These rates were hard to justify, he believed: they did not bring in that much revenue, were easily evaded, and, above all, originated in the erroneous belief that it was up to the state to determine how wealth was distributed in society.

At the same time, Aron made clear that he rejected "the dogmatism of liberalism," as much as the "dogmatism of democracy."[186] Even though some forms of state intervention could, indeed, be seen as harming freedom, it was untrue that any kind of interventionism *always* infringed upon individual liberty. In short, it was wrong to think of the state as necessarily a liberator or an oppressor; rather, the state could be either, depending on the circumstances. To determine whether a society was free, different kinds of criteria must be taken into account. If one failed to recognize that the concept of freedom could legitimately be defined in different ways, one was in danger of being forced to argue that a form of oppression was legitimate simply because it was democratic. Similarly, one might claim that a particular act of state interference was oppressive, even though the liberties lost through such interference paled in comparison to the liberties gained.

As Aron's work illustrates, some postwar liberals continued to reject an unequivocal embrace of freedom as noninterference.[187] Nevertheless, even Aron defended the idea that there was a fundamental difference between liberty and democracy. He concluded *An Essay on Liberties* by arguing that the liberties most under threat in his own day were those advocated by thinkers like Hayek—these liberties, therefore, were most in need of defense.[188]

Cold War liberals did not just revive nineteenth-century ideas about liberty, they also brought back the concept of liberal democracy originally introduced by French liberals in the 1860s. In *Liberal Democracy: Its Merits and Prospects,* J. Roland Pennock developed the idea that democracy was worth defending only when it was committed to the general tenets of traditional liberalism. This meant, Pennock explained, that there should be restrictions on the rights of democratic majorities to have their way, lest they harm "true freedom." The best way to prevent democracy from descending into nonliberal or "plebiscitary" democracy was to establish judicial guardianship over legislative power.[189] Upon its publication in 1950, Pennock's book was criticized by some as "conservative." But many others saw it as "timely"; as one reviewer remarked, while it represented "a return to the philosophical enterprise of the eighteenth and nineteenth centuries," this was "a revival we might all very well attend."[190]

Of course, Cold War liberalism was contested as well. Outside of the liberal camp, intellectuals kept arguing for a different, more democratic understanding of freedom, as illustrated by the writings of Hannah Arendt. A philosophy professor at the University of Chicago and the New School, Arendt was one of Cold War liberalism's most influential critics. In *On the Human Condition* and in the essay "What is Freedom?" Arendt developed an impassioned outcry against what she described as the arid and empty understanding of freedom propagated by liberal thinkers such as Berlin. Arguing against what she described as the "liberal credo, 'The less politics the more freedom,'" she pleaded instead for a more genuinely political conception of freedom; freedom to be achieved through political participation.[191]

At the same time, Arendt's writings illustrate the sway that Cold War liberalism had over the postwar mind. For even though Arendt defended a very different way of thinking about liberty, she subscribed to the Berlinian view about the genealogy of freedom. Like Berlin, she believed that a more political understanding of freedom held a marginal position in the history of Western political thought. The idea that freedom was "freedom *from* politics," she wrote, had been central to "the entire modern age." It arose out of "the early Christians' suspicion of and hostility against the public realm." "Our philosophical tradition," she concluded, "is almost unanimous in holding that freedom begins where men have left the realm of political life inhabited by the many."[192]

After 1945, in sum, the idea that freedom was coterminous with the absence of state interference, not with democracy, was again revived—with a vengeance. In the brave new world of the Cold War, the broader understanding of freedom defended by radicals, socialists, and progressives came to seem positively dangerous. Instead, in their quest to combat the despotic enemy—which included both the Soviet Union and the "totalitarians" within Western societies themselves—postwar liberals like Hayek and Berlin rejected the claim that state coercion, even when undertaken by a democratic government, could enhance freedom. It now became customary again to talk about freedom as something that could be realized only through the limitation of state power. Thus, the counterrevolutionary conception of freedom invented in the 1790s was reimagined as the very essence of Western civilization.

Epilogue

Freedom in the Twenty-First Century

W HAT DOES IT MEAN to be free in a society or as a society? The history of freedom narrated in this book yields, broadly speaking, two very different answers to this question. In earlier times, political thinkers and movements in what is commonly described as the West identified freedom with popular self-government—with a people's ability to exercise control over the way they are ruled. Freedom with this definition was a fighting concept. Throughout the centuries, men and women— including Athenian democrats, Roman plebeians, Florentine humanists, and Atlantic revolutionaries—contested existing power structures and demanded greater control over them in the name of liberty. Often these self-proclaimed freedom fighters ended up replacing old power structures with new hierarchies. But the language of freedom they used was open-ended. They talked about freedom as depending on "democracy," "self-rule," and "popular government," but not on, for instance, "androcracy." For this reason freedom remained available for appropriation by groups that continued to be excluded from politics.

During the course of the nineteenth and twentieth centuries, however, the democratic conception of freedom became increasingly contested. This had much to do with the backlash against the Atlantic Revolutions of the late eighteenth century. In the decades after 1776, revolutionaries from Boston to Warsaw initiated a fundamental challenge to the political status quo, arguing for, and in some cases achieving, a dramatic increase in popular control over government—and doing so in the name of freedom. Their commitment to freedom also led the Atlantic revolutionaries to push for a legal framework that would make their societies more egalitarian, as many were convinced that a more or less equal distribution of property was no less necessary for the preservation of liberty that was popular self-government.

But this radical challenge to the status quo generated a powerful backlash against democracy—and against the democratic theory of freedom. Opponents of democracy claimed that true liberty—civil or modern liberty—was not secured by popular self-government but by protecting personal security and individual rights. Far from a bulwark of liberty, democracy put its survival at risk. In the decades following the outbreak of the Atlantic Revolutions, this view was propagated first and foremost by counterrevolutionaries. But in due course, it also came to be adopted by continental liberals, Federalists, and Whigs, all of whom argued that unbridled democracy posed a threat to liberty.

These groups were inspired by various concerns. When emphasizing that democracy might be harmful to liberty, counterrevolutionary, liberal, Federalist, and Whig thinkers were sometimes motivated by fears of mob rule and anarchy, which they believed to be the inevitable end point of democracy. Others worried, as John Stuart Mill did, about the oppression of vulnerable minorities such as freethinkers. But most often, concerns about the illiberal nature of democracy were sparked by fears about its redistributive effects. Economic equality came to be seen not as an important mainstay for liberty but as its worst enemy. The push for equality, it was argued, harmed freedom directly, by infringing on individual property rights, and indirectly, by inducing people to hand over power to a paternalistic state or a Caesarist dictator.

The turn to this "modern" understanding of freedom did not go unchallenged. It was fiercely contested by thinkers who continued to embrace the revolutionary conception of liberty, arguing for the extension of suffrage to blacks, women, and the poor. From the 1880s onward, moreover, radicals, socialists, populists, and progressives set out to revitalize the legacy of the Atlantic revolutionaries by arguing for a broader conception of freedom—a view that ended up persuading even many self-described liberals. But after 1945, the counterrevolutionary conception of liberty got a new lease on life. In the increasingly polarized context of the Cold War, the notion that any kind of state intervention was an infringement on liberty, even when such intervention was democratically sanctioned, again became widely accepted. Indeed, this particular understanding of liberty was reimagined as the core ideal of the West.

Of course, the Cold War is since long over. Even so, we continue to be beholden to the conception of freedom originally invented by the opponents of the Atlantic Revolutions and revived by Cold War liberals. Today, the West's most ardent freedom fighters (who are now more likely to call themselves conservative than liberal) remain more concerned with limiting state power than with enhancing popular control over government. In political debate, this concept of freedom is often invoked to point out the threat posed by democratic socialism, or by democracy more generally, to individual liberty. Freedom today is a battering ram against democracy rather than an ideal that favors extending popular control over government.

In the United States, those on the right of the political spectrum wholeheartedly embrace such Cold War (or, if you will, nineteenth-century) ideas about liberty. Friedrich Hayek's original *Road to Serfdom* remains in print. But American conservatives can also turn to the *New Road to Serfdom*, published in 2010 by the British Tory politician and pundit Daniel Hannan, to warn the American people against the "specter of social democracy."[1] Or they might pick up *Liberty and Tyranny*, which spent twelve weeks as a number-one *New York Times* bestseller. In a direct echo of Herbert Spencer, author Mark Levin, a conservative radio host, asserts that "private property and liberty are inseparable" and that, hence, "the illegitimate denial or diminution of his private property enslaves him to another and denies him his liberty."[2] Similar arguments can be found in a host of other books, including Walter E. Williams's *Liberty versus the Tyranny of Socialism* and Ron Paul's *Liberty Defined.*[3]

Right-wing pundits and politicians have done more than adopt freedom as their watchword. They have also continued to propagate other tropes invented by nineteenth-century Whigs and Gilded Age liberals. Thus, the idea invented by thinkers such as William Graham Sumner—that the United States is a republic and not a democracy, and that there is a crucial difference between the two—remains popular among the right. It is a concept often invoked to legitimate institutional constraints on the popular will, such as in judicial review. These restraints are identified as part of the United States's "republican" (read: undemocratic) legacy. As in the nineteenth century, such constraints are typically defended as instrumental to preserving liberty against majoritarian tyranny.[4]

But if we want to understand how completely the nineteenth-century conception of freedom has displaced its democratic rival, we need to look beyond conservative thought. What is perhaps most striking about current debate is that even among self-professed centrist or liberal intellectuals, there is a tendency to think of democracy as primarily a threat to liberty. This view has been defended influentially by the CNN host and liberal pundit Fareed Zakaria. In his bestselling book *The Future of Freedom,* Zakaria argues that the only kind of democracy worth preserving is *liberal* democracy—the kind of democracy that places severe constraints on the expression of the popular will in order to preserve freedom. In Zakaria's view, liberal democracy is under pressure primarily outside the West; his main motivation in writing is to argue for a change in America's foreign policy, away from unthinking support for what Zakaria describes as "plebiscitary democracy." But Zakaria also warns that liberal democracy is being undermined in the United States; he identifies the growing influence of "public pressures" on Congress and the "dominance of primaries and polls" as worrisome signs of the erosion of liberal democracy. His book is therefore intended as "a call for self-control, for a restoration of balance between democracy and liberty. It is not an argument against democracy. But it is a claim that there can be such a thing as too much democracy—too much of an emphatically good thing."[5]

This view has wide currency among liberals in the United States. To give but one further example, in a recent much-discussed book, *The People vs. Democracy: Why Our Freedom Is in Danger and How to Save It,* Yascha Mounk, a German-American intellectual, maintains that "the two core components of liberal democracy—individual rights and the popular will—are increasingly at war with each other." Unlike Zakaria, Mounk posits that this conflict is at least partially caused by the increasingly unresponsive nature of current political systems in the West, driven, in turn, by the undemocratic preferences of elites. But like Zakaria, Mounk claims that "our freedom" is threatened by the "illiberal" views of "the people." As a result, "liberal democracy, the unique mix of individual rights and popular rule that has long characterized most governments in North America and Western Europe," Mounk concludes, "is coming apart at its seams."[6]

In virtually every American political camp, the idea that freedom should be identified with personal security and individual rights predominates. But perhaps we would do well to remember that there is another side to the story of freedom. After all, for centuries freedom was seen as a compelling ideal because it called for the establishment of greater popular control over government, including the use of state power to enhance the collective well-being. In particular, we might do well to remember that, for the founders of our modern democracies, freedom, democracy, and equality were not in tension but were inherently intertwined.

Notes

Introduction: An Elusive Concept

1. Algernon Sidney, *Discourses Concerning Government,* ed. Thomas G. West (Indianapolis: Liberty Fund, 1996), 17. In highlighting the persistence of antique conceptions of freedom throughout time, this book draws on Quentin Skinner's and Philip Pettit's work. See Skinner's *Liberty before Liberalism* (Cambridge: Cambridge University Press, 1998) and Pettit's *Republicanism: A Theory of Freedom and Government* (Oxford: Oxford University Press, 1997). Note, however, that I prefer to talk about "democratic" rather than "republican" freedom (Skinner's and Pettit's preferred term). I do so because, first, in my view, this way of thinking about freedom had its roots in ancient Greece as much as it did in Rome, and second, "democratic" better captures the essence of this way of thinking about freedom: that is, freedom required democratic self-government.

2. Continental Congress, "Declaration and Resolves", in Jack Rakove, ed., *Declaring Rights: A Brief History with Documents* (Boston: Bedford Books, 1998), 65.

3. Quoted in Wyger Velema, *Republicans: Essays on Eighteenth-Century Dutch Political Thought* (Leiden: Brill, 2007), 152.

4. Yvonne Korshak, "The Liberty Cap as a Revolutionary Symbol in America and France," *Smithsonian Studies in American Art,* 1 (1987): 52–69.

5. Johann August Eberhard, "Ueber die Freyheit des Bürgers und die Principien der Regierungsformen," in *Vermischte Schriften. Erster Theil* (Halle: Johann Jacob Gebauer, 1784), 1–28.

6. The idea that modern freedom emerged in the West due to long-term developments such as the rise of religious tolerance and the emergence of a market economy is, for instance, a key idea informing the thirteen-volume series *The Making of Modern*

347

Freedom. It must be noted, however, that the individual volumes in this series do not necessarily start from the same assumption. See R. W. Davis, series ed., *The Making of Modern Freedom*, 13 vols. (Stanford: Stanford University Press, 1992–2003).

7. Eberhard, "Ueber die Freyheit des Bürgers," 1.

8. Paul Leroy-Beaulieu, *L'État moderne et ses fonctions* (Paris: Guillaumin, 1900), x, 460; my translation.

9. William Graham Sumner, *What Social Classes Owe to Each Other* (New York: Harper and Brothers, 1911), 120.

10. Mary Beard, *SPQR: A History of Ancient Rome* (New York: W. W. Norton, 2015), 341–342.

11. Kurt Raaflaub, "Freedom in the Ancient World," in the *Oxford Classical Dictionary*, ed. S. Hornblower and A. Spawforth, rev. 3rd ed. (Oxford: Oxford University Press, 2003). On the importance of slavery in the early history of freedom, see also Orlando Patterson's *Freedom*, vol. 1, *Freedom in the Making of Western Culture* (New York: Basic Books, 1991).

12. Peter Garnsey, *Ideas of Slavery from Aristotle to Augustine* (Cambridge: Cambridge University Press, 1996), 107–127.

13. For the Stoics, see Suzanne Bobzien, *Determinism and Freedom in Stoic Philosophy* (Oxford: Clarendon Press, 1998). For early modern debates, see James A. Harris, *Of Liberty and Necessity: The Free Will Debate in Eighteenth-Century British Philosophy* (Oxford: Oxford University Press, 2005).

14. Those curious about the development of antislavery ideas may wish to consult David Brion Davies's classic study *The Problem of Slavery in Western Culture*, repr. ed. (Oxford: Oxford University Press, 1988); as well as, for a more recent overview, Joseph Miller, *The Problem of Slavery as History: A Global Approach* (New Haven: Yale University Press, 2012). For the intellectual history of free will, see, for instance, Michael Frede, *A Free Will: Origins of the Notion in Ancient Thought*, ed. A. A. Long (Berkeley: University of California Press, 2011).

15. Anthony Reid, "Merdeka: The Concept of Freedom in Indonesia," in *Asian Freedoms: The Idea of Freedom in East and Southeast Asia*, ed. David Kelly and Anthony Reid (Cambridge: Cambridge University Press), 146–149.

16. Wael Abu-Uksa, *Freedom in the Arab World: Concepts and Ideologies in Arabic Thought in the Nineteenth Century* (Cambridge: Cambridge University Press, 2016). For the Japanese case, see Douglas R. Howland, *Translating the West: Language and Political Reason in Nineteenth-Century Japan* (Honolulu: University of Hawaii Press, 2002) and Daniel V. Botsman, "Freedom without Slavery? 'Coolies,' Prostitutes, and Outcastes in Meiji Japan's 'Emancipation Moment,'" *American Historical Review* 116, no. 5 (2011): 1323–1347.

17. Kostas Vlassopoulos, *Unthinking the Greek Polis: Ancient Greek History beyond Eurocentrism* (Cambridge: Cambridge University Press, 2007), 1.

18. Benjamin Constant, *Political Writings,* ed. Biancamaria Fontana (Cambridge: Cambridge University Press, 1988), 308–328.

19. Francis Lieber, *On Civil Liberty and Self-Government* (London: Richard Bentley, 1853). Historians have also shown that the emergence of the term "the West" itself was highly polemical. For a good overview of this literature, see Georgios Varouxakis, "The

Godfather of 'Occidentality': Auguste Comte and the Idea of 'the West,'" *Modern Intellectual History*, 16, no. 2 (2019): 411–441.

20. See Siep Stuurman, "The Canon of the History of Political Thought: Its Critique and a Proposed Alternative," *History and Theory* 39, no. 2 (2000): 147–166.

21. Quentin Skinner, *Visions of Politics*, vol. 1: Regarding Method (Cambridge: Cambridge University Press, 2002), 59.

22. David Armitage, "What's the Big Idea? Intellectual History and the *Longue Durée*," *History of European Ideas* 38, no. 1 (2012): 493–507; Peter Gordon, "Contextualism and Criticism in the History of Ideas," in *Rethinking Modern European Intellectual History*, ed. Darrin McMahon and Samuel Moyn (Oxford: Oxford University Press, 2014), 32–55; Darrin McMahon, "The Return of the History of Ideas?," in McMahon and Moyn, *Rethinking*, 13–31.

For recent examples of "big" intellectual history, see Darrin McMahon, *Happiness: A History* (New York: Atlantic Monthly Press, 2006); Lynn Hunt, *Inventing Human Rights: A History* (New York : W.W. Norton, 2007); Samuel Moyn, *The Last Utopia* (Cambridge, MA: Harvard University Press, 2010); Sophia Rosenfeld, *Common Sense: A Political History* (Cambridge, MA: Harvard University Press, 2014); James Kloppenberg, *Toward Democracy: The Struggle for Self-Rule in European and American Thought* (Oxford: Oxford University Press, 2016); Siep Stuurman, *The Invention of Humanity: Equality and Cultural Difference in World History* (Cambridge, MA: Harvard University Press, 2017); David Armitage, *Civil Wars: A History in Ideas* (New York: Alfred A. Knopf, 2017); Helena Rosenblatt, *The Lost History of Liberalism: From Ancient Rome to the Twenty-First Century* (Princeton: Princeton University Press, 2018).

1. Slaves to No Man: Freedom in Ancient Greece

1. For the story of Sperthias and Bulis, see Herodotus, *The Histories*, trans. Robin Waterfield, ed. Carolyn Dewald (Oxford: Oxford University Press, 1998), 7.135–136. Unless otherwise indicated, I have used the English translations of ancient Greek texts made available in the Loeb Classical Library. References are to either lines or to books and paragraphs, as is customary, rather than to page numbers.

2. Aristotle, *Politics*, trans. C. D. C. Reeve (Indianapolis: Hackett, 1998), 1327b25–30.

3. For this argument, see Martin Ostwald, "Freedom and the Greeks," in *The Origins of Modern Freedom in the West*, ed. R. W. Davis (Stanford: Stanford University Press, 1995), 35–63; Orlando Patterson, *Freedom*, vol. 1, *Freedom in the Making of Western Culture* (New York: Basic Books, 1991), 7; and Kurt Raaflaub, "Freedom in the Ancient World," in *Oxford Classical Dictionary*, ed. Simon Hornblower and Antony Spawforth, 3rd ed. (Oxford: Oxford University Press, 1996). On the importance of "slavery" as a metaphor in Greek thought more generally, see P. Hunt, "Slaves in Greek Literary Culture," in *The Cambridge World History of Slavery*, vol. 1, *The Ancient Mediterranean World*, ed. K. Bradley and P. Cartledge (Cambridge: Cambridge University Press, 2011), 22–47.

Note that not all historians agree with this view. For a contrary argument—that freedom originated in, respectively, the Ancient Near East and Hebrew culture—

compare Daniel C. Snell, *Flight and Freedom in the Ancient Near East* (Leiden: Brill, 2001); Matthew Martin III and Daniel C. Snell, "Democracy and Freedom," in *A Companion to the Ancient Near East,* ed. Daniel C. Snell (Oxford: Wiley-Blackwell, 2004), 397–407; Eva von Dassow, "Liberty, Bondage and Liberation in the Late Bronze Age," *History of European Ideas* 44, no. 6 (2018): 658–684; Michael Walzer, *Exodus and Revolution* (New York: Basic Books, 1985); and Remi Brague, "God and Freedom: Biblical Roots of the Western Idea of Liberty," in *Christianity and Freedom,* ed. T. S. Shah and A. D. Hertzke (Cambridge: Cambridge University Press, 2016), 391–402.

4. Quoted in S. N. Kramer, *The Sumerians: Their History, Culture and Character* (Chicago: Chicago University Press, 1963), 317. For a more general discussion of the meaning of *andurarum* and *amargi,* see Manfried Dietrich, "Die Frage nach der personlichen Freiheit im Alten Orient," in *Mesopotamica—Ugaritica—Biblica: Festschrift für Kurt Bergerhof zur Vollendung seines 70. Lebensjahres am 7. Mai 1992,* ed. Manfried Dietrich and Oswald Lorenz (Kevelaer: Butzon & Berker; Neukirchen-Vluyn: Neukirchener Verlag, 1993), 45–58.

5. Exod. 2:24, 20:2 (King James Version).

6. Jonathan Stökl, "'Proclaim Liberty throughout All the Land unto All the Inhabitants Thereof!' Reading Leviticus 25:10 through the Centuries," *History of European Ideas* 44, no. 6 (2018): 685–701.

7. For the Greek identification of freedom with democracy, see Kurt Raaflaub, *The Discovery of Freedom in Ancient Greece,* trans. Renate Franciscono (Chicago: Chicago University Press, 2004), 203–249.

8. See Raaflaub, *Freedom in Ancient Greece,* 23–57.

9. Hesiod, *Works and Days,* 202.

10. Homer, *Iliad,* 6.414.

11. Ibid., 2.204. On Homeric political thought, see Kurt Raaflaub, "Poets, Lawgivers, and the Beginnings of Political Reflection in Archaic Greece," in *The Cambridge History of Greek and Roman Political Thought,* ed. C. Rowe and M. Schofield (Cambridge: Cambridge University Press, 2000), 23–59. Note that Raaflaub argues that the Homeric epics depict a society that is already well on its way to being a society of equals.

12. For an overview of Greek politics in the Archaic period, see Jonathan Hall, *A History of the Archaic Greek World: Ca. 1200–479 BC* (Oxford: Wiley-Blackwell, 2007).

13. Martin Ostwald, "The Reform of the Athenian State by Cleisthenes," in *The Cambridge Ancient History,* vol. 4, *Persia, Greece and the Western Mediterranean, c.525 to 479 BC,* ed. John Boardman et al. (Cambridge: Cambridge University Press, 1988), 303–346; It should be noted that the earliest attested use of the word "demokratia" occurred in Herodotus, ca. 430; however, the word was probably in use much earlier. For this point, see Eric Robinson, *The First Democracies: Early Popular Government Outside Athens* (Stuttgart: Steiner, 1997), 45.

14. Aristotle, *Politics,* 4.1297b.

15. Kurt Raaflaub, "Soldiers, Citizens and the Evolution of the Early Greek Polis," in *The Development of the Polis in Archaic Greece,* ed. Lynette G. Mitchell and P. J. Rhodes (London: Routledge, 1997), 24–38; Ian Morris, "The Strong Principle of Equality," in *Demokratia: A Conversation on Democracies, Ancient and Modern,* ed. Josiah Ober and Charles W. Hedrick (Princeton: Princeton University Press, 1996), 19–48; Christian

Meier, *A Culture of Freedom: Ancient Greece and the Origins of Europe* (Oxford: Oxford University Press, 2011). For an overview of the debate about the origins of democracy in Athens, see Kurt Raaflaub, Josiah Ober, and Robert Wallace, *Origins of Democracy in Ancient Greece* (Berkeley: University of California Press, 2007).

16. Solon, *Elegy and Iambus,* 1.5.2.

17. Herodotus, *Histories,* 5.55. Note, however, that the earliest reference linking the defeat of tyranny in Athens to the establishment of freedom is Herodotus. The only earlier source we have—drinking songs celebrating Harmodius and Aristogeiton's deed— linked their overthrow of tyranny to the establishment of political equality ("isonomia") rather freedom. See Ostwald, "Freedom and the Greeks." For the oral tradition about the overthrow of tyranny in Athens, see Rosalind Thomas, *Oral Tradition and Written Record in Classical Athens* (Cambridge: Cambridge University Press, 1989), 257–261.

18. Aristotle, *Athenian Constitution,* 18.

19. Kurt Raaflaub, "Stick and Glue: The Function of Tyranny in Fifth-Century Athenian Democracy," in *Popular Tyranny: Sovereignty and Its Discontents in Ancient Greece,* ed. Kathryn Morgan (Austin: University of Texas Press, 2013), 59–93.

20. Ostwald, "Freedom and the Greeks." But compare Raaflaub, who argues that the cult was a historical fiction invented either by Herodotus or his Samian informants. Raaflaub, *The Discovery of Freedom,* 110–111.

21. See Raaflaub, *The Discovery of Freedom,* 29–45; Ostwald, "Freedom and the Greeks." For the impact of the Persian wars on Greek national consciousness more generally, see Edith Hall, *Inventing the Barbarian: Greek Self-Definition through Tragedy* (Oxford: Oxford University Press, 1989). For an account of the Greco-Persian wars, see Lisa Kallet, "The Fifth Century: Political and Military Narrative," in *Classical Greece, 500–323 BC,* ed. Robin Osborne (Oxford: Oxford University Press, 2000), 170–196.

22. Aeschylus, *The Persians,* 232. I have modified the translation for readability.

23. Ibid., 176.

24. See Ostwald, "Freedom and the Greeks," 43–44.

25. Simon Hornblower, "Herodotus' Influence in Antiquity," in *The Cambridge Companion to Herodotus,* ed. Carolyn Dewald and John Marincola (Cambridge: Cambridge University Press, 2006), 306–318.

26. Kurt Raaflaub, "Philosophy, Science and Politics: Herodotus and the Intellectual Trends of His Time," in *Brill's Companion to Herodotus,* ed. Egbert Bakker et al. (Leiden: Brill, 2002), 149–186; Sara Forsdyke, "Herodotus, Political History and Political Thought," in Dewald and Marincola, *Herodotus,* 224–241.

27. Herodotus, *Histories,* 8.143.

28. Ibid., 6.11.

29. Ibid., 6.109.

30. Carolyn Dewald, "Form and Content: The Question of Tyranny in Herodotus," in Morgan, *Popular Tyranny,* 25–58.

31. Herodotus, *Histories,* 3.80.

32. Ibid.

33. Ibid., 5.78.

34. For this point, see Dewald, "The Question of Tyranny in Herodotus"; Michael Flower, "Herodotus and Persia," in Dewald and Marincola, *Herodotus,* 274–289.

35. Herodotus, *Histories,* 3: 30–35.

36. Ibid., 5:25.

37. Ibid., 4.84.

38. Ibid., 7.45–46.

39. Ibid., 7.39.

40. Ibid., 8.118.

41. Ibid., 8.119.

42. Ibid., 5.20.

43. Jessica Priestley, *Herodotus and Hellenistic Culture: Literary Studies in the Reception of the Histories* (Oxford: Oxford University Press, 2014), 19–50.

44. Euripides, *Suppliant Women,* 441–453.

45. Thucydides, *The Peloponnesian War,* trans. Martin Hammond, intro. P. J. Rhodes (Oxford: Oxford University Press, 2009), 2.37.2.

46. According to Rosalind Thomas, for instance, "'Freedom' [in ancient Greece] was active, political freedom for a community to run itself, rather than the freedom of individuals to act as they wished in private life"; see Thomas, "The Classical City," in Osborne, *Classical Greece,* 70. For a similar view, see also Max Pohlenz, *Freedom in Greek Life and Thought: The History of an Ideal,* trans. Carl Lofmark (Dordrecht: Reidel, 1966).

47. See Mogens H. Hansen, "The Ancient Athenian and the Modern Liberal View of Liberty," in Ober and Hedrick, *Demokratia,* 91–104; Robert W. Wallace, "Law, Freedom and the Concept of Citizens' Rights in Democratic Athens," in Ober and Hedrick, *Demokratia,* 105–119; P. Cartledge and M. Edge, "'Rights,' Individuals, and Communities in Ancient Greece," in *A Companion to Greek Political Thought,* ed. R. K. Balot (Oxford: Oxford University Press, 2009), 149–163.

48. Josef Wiesehöfer, *Ancient Persia from 550 BC to 650 AD,* trans. Azizeh Azodi (London: I. B. Tauris, 2001), 31. For an account of the political structure of the Persian Empire, see also Pierre Briant, *From Cyrus to Alexander: A History of the Persian Empire,* trans. Peter Daniels (Winona Lake: Eisenbrauns, 2002). But compare Kostas Vlassopoulos, *Unthinking the Greek Polis: Ancient Greek History beyond Eurocentrism* (Cambridge: Cambridge University Press, 2007), 101–121. Vlassopoulos points out that, on the local level, many Near Eastern cities enjoyed a form of self-government very much like that of the Greek poleis.

49. Inscription on Darius's tomb, quoted in Briant, *From Cyrus to Alexander,* 178.

50. Josef Wiesehöfer, "The Achaemenid Empire," in *The Dynamics of Ancient Empires: State Power from Assyria to Byzantium,* ed. Ian Morris and Walter Scheidel (Oxford: Oxford University Press, 2009), 77.

51. Briant, *From Cyrus to Alexander,* 302–354.

52. Martin Ostwald, "The Reform of the Athenian State by Cleisthenes," in Boardman et al., *Cambridge Ancient History,* vol. 4, 303–346.

53. Paul Cartledge, *Spartan Reflections* (London: Gerald Duckworth, 2001). Unlike Athens, however, not all Spartan citizens were automatically eligible to participate in

the popular assembly; only those able to pay for the communal dining halls, where Spartan citizens had their meals, were allowed to do so.

54. Mogens H. Hansen, *The Athenian Democracy in the Age of Demosthenes: Structure, Principles, Ideology*, trans. J. A. Cook (London: Blackwell, 1991). For the number of slaves in Athens, see T. E. Rihll, "Classical Athens," in *The Cambridge World History of Slavery*, ed. K. Bradley and P. Cartledge (Cambridge: Cambridge University Press, 2011) 48–73.

55. Thucydides, *History of the Peloponnesian War*, 2.45.2. For the position of women in ancient Athens, see Roger Just, *Women in Athenian Law and Life* (London: Routledge, 1989); Robin Waterfield, *Athens: A History. From Ancient Ideal to Modern City* (London: Macmillan, 2004), 182–200.

56. E. Fantham et al., *Women in the Classical World* (Oxford: Oxford University Press, 1994), 68–127.

57. Rihll, "Classical Athens," 60.

58. Aristophanes, *Assemblywomen*, in *Three Plays by Aristophanes: Staging Women*, ed. and trans. Jeffrey Henderson (London: Routledge, 1996), 1000–1027.

59. For an analysis of Aristophanes's play that emphasizes its favorable portrayal of female rule, see Josiah Ober, *Political Dissent in Democratic Athens: Intellectual Critics of Popular Rule* (Princeton: Princeton University Press, 2001), 122–155. But compare Paul Cartledge, *Aristophanes and His Theatre of the Absurd* (Bristol: Bristol Classical Press, 1990), 32–42. Cartledge reads Aristophanes's play as a critique of the idea of female leadership.

60. Aristotle, *Politics*, 1.1254b.

61. For a general discussion of the similarities and differences between ancient and modern democracies, see Ober and Hedrick, *Demokratia*.

62. See A. Shapur Shahbazi, "The Achaemenid Persian Empire (550–330 BC)," in *Oxford Handbook of Iranian History*, ed. Touraj Daryaee (Oxford: Oxford University Press, 2012), 120–141.

63. Paul Cartledge, "The Helots: A Contemporary Review," in Bradley and Cartledge, *World History of Slavery*, 74–90.

64. Rihll, "Classical Athens," 48–73.

65. Robin Waterfield, *Athens: A History, from Ancient Ideal to Modern City* (New York: Basic Books, 2004), 187. But compare Josine Blok, *Citizenship in Classical Athens* (Cambridge: Cambridge University Press, 2017). Blok shows that, while women were excluded from political participation, they had an important role in the public sphere through their participation in religious rites.

66. Numa Denis Fustel de Coulanges, *La cité antique: étude sur le culte, le droit, les institutions de la Grèce et de Rome* (Paris: Hachette, 1867), 262–267. My translation.

67. Hansen, *Athenian Democracy in the Age of Demosthenes*, 74–81.

68. Robert Wallace, "The Legal Regulation of Private Conduct at Athens: Two Controversies on Freedom," *Ethics & Politics* 9, no. 1 (2007): 158. See also David Cohen, *Law, Sexuality and Society:. The Enforcement of Morals in Classical Athens* (Cambridge: Cambridge University Press, 1991). But compare Oswyn Murray, "Cities of Reason," in *The Greek City from Homer to Alexander*, ed. Oswyn Murray and Simon Price (Oxford: Clarendon Press, 1990), 1–28, for a view closer to Fustel de Coulange's.

69. For a general overview of these constitutional changes, see Josiah Ober, *Mass and Elite in Democratic Athens: Rhetoric, Ideology and the Power of the People* (Princeton: Princeton University Press, 1989).

70. For this estimate, see M. I. Finley, *Politics in the Ancient World* (Cambridge: Cambridge University Press, 1983), 74.

71. For this estimate, see Hansen, *Athenian Democracy in the Age of Demosthenes,* 132.

72. For a description of the relief sculpture, see Homer A. Thompson, "Excavations in the Athenian Agora: 1952," *Hesperia: The Journal of the American School of Classical Studies at Athens* 22, no. 1 (1953): 25–56.

73. Funeral oration reported in Plato, *Menexenus,* 238e–239a in *Complete Works,* ed. John M. Cooper (Indianapolis: Hackett, 1997).

74. For a general analysis of this text and its import, see Ober, *Political Dissent,* 14–27. However, I disagree with Ober's judgment that the Old Oligarch "has no very obvious generic successors in surviving classical literature." Ober, *Political Dissent,* 27.

75. Old Oligarch, *Constitution of the Athenians,* 1.

76. Ibid., 2.

77. Ibid., 1.

78. Ibid., 2.

79. On Thucydides's life and career, see L. Canfora, "Biographical Obscurities and Problems of Composition," in *Brill's Companion to Thucydides,* ed. Antonis Tsakmakis and Antonios Rengakos (Leiden: Brill, 2006), 3–32.

80. See Lawrence Tritle, "Thucydides and Power Politics," in Tsakmakis and Rengakos, *Thucydides,* 469–494. But compare Mary Nichols, *Thucydides and the Pursuit of Freedom* (Ithaca: Cornell University Press, 2015), who understands Thucydides as a theorist of freedom.

81. Thucydides, *The Peloponnesian War,* 3.81 .

82. Ibid., 3.82.

83. For the sophist movement, see Jacqueline de Romilly, *The Great Sophists in Periclean Athens* (Oxford: Clarendon Press, 1998).

84. For a comprehensive overview of (what little we know of) the sophists' political views, see W. Guthrie, *The Sophists* (Cambridge: Cambridge University Press, 1971), 135–163.

85. Plato, *The Republic,* 1.338e, in Cooper, *Complete Works.*

86. Xenophon, *Memorabilia,* 1.2.46.

87. Xenophon, *Hellenica,* 2.3.

88. Ibid., 2.4.22.

89. Isocrates, *Areopagiticus,* 7.62.

90. The literature on Plato's political thought has by now grown to enormous proportions. For a good overview of the most important scholarly assessments of Plato's politics, see Ober, *Political Dissent,* 156–247. On Plato specifically as a critic of democratic freedom, see Mogens H. Hansen, "Democratic Freedom and the Concept of Freedom in Plato and Aristotle," *Greek, Roman, and Byzantine Studies* 50 (2010): 1–27; Melissa Lane, "Placing Plato in the History of Liberty," *History of European Ideas* 44 (2018): 702–718.

91. Malcolm Schofield, "Plato in His Time and Place," in *The Oxford Handbook of Plato,* ed. Gail Fine (Oxford: Oxford University Press, 2008), 41–68.

92. On the authenticity of the *Seventh Letter*, see M. Schofield, "Plato and Practical Politics," in Rowe and Schofield, *Greek and Roman Political Thought*, 293–302.

93. Plato, *Seventh Letter*, 7.324d, in Cooper, *Complete Works*.

94. Gregory Vlastos, "The Historical Socrates and Athenian Democracy," *Political Theory* 11, (1983): 495–516; Ellen Meiksins Wood and Neal Wood, "Socrates and Democracy: A Reply to Gregory Vlastos," *Political Theory* 14 (1986): 55–82; Melissa Lane, "Socrates and Plato: an Introduction," in Rowe and Schofield, *Greek and Roman Political Thought*, 155–163.

95. Plato, *The Republic*, 8.562c.

96. Ibid., 8.557b.

97. Ibid., 8.563c.

98. Ibid., 8.557c.

99. Ibid., 8.562d.

100. See Jakub Filonik, "'Living as One Wishes' in Athens: The (Anti-)Democratic Polemics," *Classical Philology* 114(2019): 1–24.

101. Plato, *The Republic*, 6.488d.

102. Ibid., 9.590d.

103. Plato, *Clitophon*, 408, in Cooper, *Complete Works*.

104. A. Laks, "The Laws," in Rowe and Schofield, *Greek and Roman Political Thought*, 258–292.

105. Plato, *Laws*, 3.691c, in Cooper, *Complete Works*.

106. Ibid., 7.328c.

107. Ibid., 3.698b.

108. For Isocrates's life and intellectual career, see Ober, *Political Dissent*, 249–290. Note that Isocrates defended monarchy, as well, in some of his other texts. See F. W. Walbank, "Monarchies and Monarchic Ideas," in *The Cambridge Ancient History*, vol. 7.1, *The Hellenistic World*, ed. F. W. Walbank et al. (Cambridge: Cambridge University Press, 1984), 62–100.

109. Isocrates, *Areopagiticus*, 28.

110. David Teegarden, *Death to Tyrants! Ancient Greek Democracy and the Struggle against Tyranny* (Princeton: Princeton University Press, 2014), appendix.

111. The following paragraphs are based on Robin Osborne, "The Fourth Century: Political and Military Narrative," in Osborne, *Classical Greece*, 197–222; and Robin Waterfield, *Creators, Conquerors, and Citizens: A History of Ancient Greece* (Oxford: Oxford University Press, 2018), 351–468.

112. Demosthenes, *Philippic*, 2.6.25.

113. Andrew Bayliss, *After Demosthenes: The Politics of Early Hellenistic Athens* (London: Continuum, 2011), 94.

114. See Susanne Carlsson, *Hellenistic Democracies: Freedom, Independence and Political Procedure in Some East Greek City-States* (Stuttgart: Steiner, 2010).

115. Malcolm Schofield, "Social and Political Thought," in *The Cambridge History of Hellenistic Philosophy*, ed. Keimpe Algra et al. (Cambridge: Cambridge University Press, 1999), 739–770.

116. For a general overview of Aristotle's *Politics*, see F. D. Miller, *Nature, Justice and Rights in Aristotle's Politics* (Oxford: Oxford University Press, 1997). For Aristotle's

lack of engagement with the new political realities of his time, see Malcolm Schofield, "Aristotle: An Introduction," in Rowe and Schofield, *Greek and Roman Political Thought*, 310–320. However, note that Aristotle also produced a treatise titled
On Kingship. Its contents are unfortunately unknown, but this treatise might con-
ceivably have been more pro-monarchical. See Walbank, "Monarchies and Monarchic Ideas."

117. See Hansen, "Democratic Freedom and the Concept of Freedom in Plato and Aristotle." Hansen also provides a useful discussion of alternative interpretations of Aristotle's conception of freedom. For a more general discussion of Aristotle's critique of
Athenian democracy, see Andrew Lintott, "Aristotle and Democracy," *Classical Quarterly* 42 (1992): 114–128.

118. Aristotle, *Politics*, 1317b0–15.

119. Ibid., 1310a30–35.

120. Ibid., 1318a25.

121. Ibid., 1318b30–35. Note that Aristotle's enthusiasm for even a more moderate form of
democracy was lukewarm at best: he presented it as a "good enough" constitution. As
he explained in books seven and eight of *Politics*, the best constitution would ideally
be more similar to that of the Spartan regime, with an extremely narrowly defined citizen body able to live in leisure, thanks to the labor of Helot-like agricultural slaves.
However in these later chapters, he never mentioned the word "freedom" nor its antonym "slavery"; rather, he presented this as the constitution most likely to allow people
to achieve "happiness."

122. G. J. D. Aalders, *Political Thought in Hellenistic Times* (Amsterdam: Hakkert, 1975);
Walbank, "Monarchies and Monarchic Ideas"; D. Hahm, "Kings and Constitutions:
Hellenistic Theories," in Rowe and Schofield, *Greek and Roman Political Thought*,
457–476.

123. For the turn to inner freedom in the Hellenistic period, see Patterson, *Freedom*, 165–
199. For the continued defense of democratic freedom by Hellenistic Greeks, see
Carlsson, *Hellenistic Democracies*. But compare this with Benjamin Gray's argument
that, in the Hellenistic period, Greeks began to put more emphasis on "individual
choice and diversity within the citizen-body" as the key characteristics of freedom; Benjamin Gray, "Freedom, Ethical Choice and the Hellenistic Polis," *History of European Ideas* 44 (2018): 719–742, 739.

124. Hunt, "Slaves in Greek Literary Culture."

125. Euripides, *Hecuba*, 864.

126. Xenophon, *Economics*, 1.22–23.

127. Xenophon, *Memorabilia*, trans. Amy Bonnett, introd. Christopher Bruell (Ithaca and
London: Cornell University Press, 1994), 1.2.6.

128. Diogenes Laertius, *Lives of Eminent Philosophers*, ed. and trans. R. D. Hicks (London:
William Heinemann, 1925), 7.2.37.

129. See, for instance, Diogenes Laertius, *Lives of Eminent Philosophers*, 7:121–123.

130. On Philo's life and career, see Erwin Goodenough, *The Politics of Philo Judaeus: Practice and Theory* (New Haven: Yale University Press, 1938), 1–20.

131. Philo Judaeus, *Every Good Man is Free*, 43–47.

132. Ibid., 40–43.

133. Ibid., 59–61.

134. Ibid., 124–127.

135. Ibid., 95–96.

136. Ibid., 107–111.

137. The following paragraphs are based on Goodenough, *The Politics of Philo Judaeus*, 1–20.

138. Quoted in ibid., 18–19.

2. The Rise and Fall of Roman Liberty

1. Livy, *The History of Rome*, 1.49–56. Unless otherwise indicated, I have used the English translations of ancient Roman texts made available in the Loeb Classical Library. References are to either lines or to books and paragraphs, as is customary, rather than to page numbers.

2. Cicero, *On the Commonwealth*, 1.39a in *On the Commonwealth and On the Laws*, ed. and trans. James Zetzel (Cambridge: Cambridge University Press, 1999). On the meaning of the term "res publica" in the Roman world, see Werner Suerbaum, *Vom antiken zum frühmittelalterlichen Staatsbegriff: Über Verwendung und Bedeutung von res publica, regnum, imperium und status von Cicero bis Jordanis*, 3rd ed. (Münster: Aschendorff, 1977). For the ancient historians' perception of the republic and principate as different historical periods, see Karin Sion-Jenkis, *Von der Republik zum Principat: Ursachen für den Verfassungswechsel in Rom im historischen Denken der Antike* (Stuttgart: Steiner, 2000), 19–53. But compare James Hankins's argument that the term "res publica" was never used by Roman historians or thinkers to denote a regime different from and more popular than monarchy; Hankins, "Exclusivist Republicanism and the Nonmonarchical Republic," *Political Theory* 38, no. 4 (2010): 452–482.

3. Dionysius of Halicarnassus, *Roman Antiquities*, 5.8.

4. Plutarch, *Brutus*, 1.1.

5. Livy, *History of Rome*, 4.5.

6. The following paragraphs are based on Mary Beard, *SPQR: A History of Ancient Rome* (New York: W. W. Norton, 2015), 131–168.

7. Livy, *History of Rome*, 6.37.

8. See Valentina Arena, *Libertas and the Practice of Politics in the Late Roman Republic* (Cambridge: Cambridge University Press, 2012), 78; P. A. Brunt, "Libertas in the Republic," in *The Fall of the Roman Republic and Related Essays*, ed. P. A. Brunt (Oxford: Clarendon Press, 1988), 282–350; Joy Connolly, *The Life of Roman Republicanism* (Princeton, NJ: Princeton University Press, 2014), 16. It is worth emphasizing this point, because it is often (wrongly) argued that the Romans had a very different and more elitist conception of freedom from the Greeks. See, for instance, Kurt Raaflaub, "Freiheit in Athen und Rom: Ein Beispiel divergierender politischer Begriffsentwicklung in der Antike Author," *Historische Zeitschrift* 238, no. 3 (1984): 529–567. More recently, Benjamin Straumann has argued along similar lines that Roman political thought was characterized by a "deep proto-liberal concern with Constantian themes such as the limits of legislation and popular sovereignty"; Straumann, *Crisis and Constitutionalism:*

Roman Political Thought from the Fall of the Republic to the Age of Revolution (Oxford: Oxford University Press, 2016), 6.

9. For an overview of this discussion, see Beard, *SPQR*, 150–153; Kurt A. Raaflaub, ed., *Social Struggles in Archaic Rome: New Perspectives on the Conflict of the Orders* (Oxford: Blackwell, 2005).

10. Arena, *Libertas and the Practice of Politics*, 40.

11. For Greek influence on Roman intellectual development, see Elizabeth Rawson, *Intellectual Life in the Late Roman Republic* (London: Duckworth, 1985); A. Momigliano, "The Origins of Rome," in *The Cambridge Ancient History*, vol. 7.2, *The Rise of Rome to 220 BC*, ed. F. W. Walbank et al., assisted by A. Drummond (Cambridge: Cambridge University Press, 1990), 52–112.

12. Andrew Lintott, *The Constitution of the Roman Republic* (Oxford: Oxford University Press, 1999), 51–52.

13. Beard, *SPQR*, 303–313.

14. Livy, *History of Rome*, 34.1. About this episode in Livy, see E. Fantham et al., *Women in the Classical World* (Oxford: Oxford University Press, 1994), 263–264.

15. Livy, *History of Rome*, 34.3.

16. Ibid., 34.7.

17. Ibid.

18. The overview of the Roman political system of the early republic in the following paragraphs is based on Beard, *SPQR*, 184–192; Lintott, *Constitution of the Roman Republic*, esp. 191–213; Claude Nicolet, *The World of the Citizen in Republican Rome*, trans. P. S. Falla (Berkeley: University of California Press, 1980), esp. 207–316.

19. For this estimate, see A. Lintott, "Political History, 146–95 BC," in *The Cambridge Ancient History*, vol. 9, *The Last Age of the Roman Republic, 146–43 BC*, ed. J. Crook, A. Lintott, and E. Rawson (Cambridge: Cambridge University Press, 1994), 46–47.

20. In much of the older historiography on Rome's early political history, the Roman Republic is presented as a thoroughly elitist, oligarchic regime. This traditional view was pioneered by Matthias Gelzer and given its most influential expression by Ronald Syme. See Gelzer, *Die Nobilität der römischen Republik* (1912; repr., Stuttgart: Teubner, 1983); Syme, *The Roman Revolution* (1939; repr., Oxford: Oxford University Press, 2002). However, since the 1980s this view has been revised, most notably by Fergus Millar, *The Crowd in Rome in the Late Republic* (Ann Arbor: University of Michigan Press, 1998). Historians of the Roman Republic now put more emphasis on the popular elements in the Roman constitution that existed alongside elitist institutions. For an overview of this debate, see J. A. North, "Democratic Politics in Republican Rome," *Past & Present* 126, no. 1 (1990): 3–21. For more recent contributions to the debate, see Alexander Yakobson, "Popular Power in the Roman Republic," in *A Companion to the Roman Republic*, ed. Nathan Rosenstein and Robert Morstein-Marx (Malden, MA: Blackwell, 2006), 383–400. Yakobson concludes that the "actual content of Roman public life was shaped by a complicated interplay between these powerful forces [of democracy and aristocracy]." Yakobson, "Popular Power in the Roman Republic," 389.

21. Valerius Maximus, *Memorable Deeds and Sayings: One Thousand Tales from Ancient Rome*, trans. Henry John Walker (Indianapolis: Hackett, 2004), 7.5.2.

22. Quoted in Lintott, *Constitution of the Roman Republic,* 203.

23. For this anecdote, see Beard, *SPQR,* 190.

24. Ibid., 239–240.

25. On Polybius's life and career, see F. W. Walbank, *Polybius* (Berkeley: University of California Press, 1972).

26. Polybius, *Histories,* 6.16.

27. The following paragraphs are based on Beard, *SPQR,* 209–252; T. P. Wiseman, *Remembering the Roman People: Essays on Late-Republican Politics and Literature* (Oxford: Oxford University Press, 2008).

28. On the debate between the *populares* and *optimates* and their respective usage of the concept of freedom, see Arena, *Libertas and the Practice of Politics,* 73–168.

29. Sallust, *Fragments of the Histories,* 3.34; Sallust, *The War with Jugurtha,* 31.11.

30. See Arena, *Libertas and the Practice of Politics,* 40.

31. Cicero, *On the Commonwealth,* 1.47–49.

32. Sallust, *The War With Jugurtha,* 31.11.

33. Plutarch, *Tiberius Gracchus,* 20.

34. See Jed W. Atkins, "Non-Domination and the *Libera Res Publica* in Cicero's Republicanism," *History of European Ideas* 44, no. 6 (2018): 756–773. But compare Neal Wood's depiction of Cicero as a reactionary spokesman for the optimates for whom "libertas means essentially their own freedom to rule the masses without impediment and to accumulate riches without hindrance." Neal Wood, *Cicero's Social and Political Thought* (Berkeley: University of California Press, 1991), 150. In *Crisis and Constitutionalism,* 149–190, Benjamin Straumann similarly presents Cicero as a protoliberal intent on defending property rights against state interference.

35. Cicero, *On the Commonwealth,* 1.43.

36. Cicero, *On the Laws,* 3.25, in *On the Commonwealth and On the Laws,* ed. and trans. James Zetzel (Cambridge: Cambridge University Press, 1999).

37. Ibid., 3.38.

38. See Arena, *Libertas and the Practice of Politics,* 73–168.

39. For a recent overview of the debate about the causes of the downfall of the republic, see Robert Morstein-Marx and Nathan Rosenstein, "The Transformation of the Republic," in *A Companion to Roman Republic,* ed. Robert Morstein-Marx and Nathan Rosenstein (Malden, MA: Blackwell, 2010), 625–637. A classic contribution is Mary Beard and Michael Crawford, *Rome in the Late Republic: Problems and Interpretations* (London: Duckworth, 1985).

40. Quoted in Beard, *SPQR,* 243.

41. For this evocative detail, see Plutarch, *Sulla,* 36.

42. See Wiseman, *Remembering the Roman People,* 188–221.

43. For a discussion of Caesar's ultimate ambitions, see Adrian Goldsworthy, *Caesar: The Life of a Colossus* (New Haven: Yale University Press, 2006), 493–500.

44. Quoted in ibid., 158.

45. Ibid., 500.

46. Plutarch, *Brutus,* 9.

47. On Caesar's death and its aftermath, see Wiseman, *Remembering the Roman People,* 211–234.

48. On Cicero's role in the crisis of the late republic, see Thomas Mitchell, *Cicero: The Senior Statesman* (New Haven: Yale University Press, 1991).

49. Cicero, *Philippics*, 3.14, 2.44, in *The Orations of Marcus Tullius Cicero*, trans. C. D. Yonge (London: George Bell and Sons, 1903), vol. 4.

50. Beard, *SPQR*, 341–342.

51. For Augustus's attempts to depict his regime as a restoration of the republic, see Karl Galinsky, *Augustus: Introduction to the Life of an Emperor* (Cambridge: Cambridge University Press, 2012), 61–83.

52. Fergus Millar, *Rome, the Greek World, and the East,* vol. 1, *The Roman Republic and the Augustan Revolution,* ed. Hannah M. Cotton and Guy M. Rogers (Chapel Hill: University of North Carolina Press, 2002), 264.

53. Augustus, "Res Gestae," in *The Roman Empire: Augustus to Hadrian*, ed. and trans. R. K. Sherk (Cambridge: Cambridge University Press, 1988), 42.

54. Chaim Wirszubski, *Libertas as a Political Idea at Rome during the Late Republic and Early Principate* (Cambridge: Cambridge University Press, 1960), 159; Lothar Wickert, "Der Prinzipat und die Freiheit," in *Symbola Coloniensia Josepho Kroll sexagenario A.D. VI. Id. Nov. a. MCMIL oblata* (Cologne: B. Pick, 1949), 113–141, provides abundant evidence for the Roman emperors' claims to support "libertas."

55. See Millar, *Rome, the Greek World, and the East,* vol. 1, 260–270. But compare Chaim Wirszubski's argument that after the fall of the republic, "libertas" came to mean "order, security, and confidence" and was thus held to be compatible with one-man rule. Wirszubski, *Libertas as a Political Idea,* 156.

56. Appian, *Roman History,* preface 1.6. This process was completed by the late second and early third centuries, when, as Millar argues, the emperor emerged from what remained of the senatorial context and could be seen as a wholly independent monarch. Fergus Millar, *The Emperor in the Roman World, 31 B.C.-AD 337* (London: Duckworth, 1977), 350.

57. Dio Cassius, *Roman History,* 47.39.

58. As Millar points out, the Roman emperors also drew actively on the precedents created by Hellenistic kings. See Millar, *Emperor in the Roman World,* 198.

59. For the role of women in the Roman Empire, see Fantham et al., *Women in the Classical World,* esp. chap. 11 and 13. For the quotes, see Tacitus, *Annals,* 12.37, 12.7. Note that some women also gained greater opportunities to exercise power on the lower rungs of society, as Emily Hemelrijk reminds us. Hemelrijk, "Public Roles for Women in the Cities of the Latin West," in *A Companion to Women in the Ancient World,* ed. S. L. James and S. Dillon (Chichester: Wiley-Blackwell, 2012), 478–490.

60. Quoted in Fergus Millar, *Rome, the Greek World, and the East,* vol. 2, *Government, Society, and Culture in the Roman Empire,* ed. Hannah M. Cotton and Guy M. Rogers (Chapel Hill: University of North Carolina Press, 2004), 111.

61. For the imperial historians' retreat into nostalgia, see Joy Connolly, "Virtue and Violence: The Historians on Politics," in *The Cambridge Companion to the Roman Historians,* ed. Andrew Feldherr (Cambridge: Cambridge University Press, 2009), 181–194. For the ideological opposition against the empire more generally, see Sam Wilkinson, *Republicanism during the Early Roman Empire* (London, New York: Continuum,

2012). Wilkinson's study convincingly corrects the commonly accepted view that there was no opposition to the Empire or that that opposition was solely motivated by personal ambition. For that older view, see Ramsay MacMullen, *Enemies of the Roman Order: Treason, Unrest, and Alienation in the Empire* (Cambridge, MA: Harvard University Press, 1966).

62. On Livy's glorification of the republic, see P. Martin, "Livy's Narrative of the Regal Period: Structure and Ideology," in *A Companion to Livy,* ed. B. Mineo (Chichester: Wiley-Blackwell, 2015), 259–273. Note, however, that other scholars understand Livy as an out-and-out apologist of the Augustan regime, or, alternatively, as a historian more interested in the decline of moral virtue than in constitutional change. For these positions, see, respectively, Bernard Mineo, "Livy's Political and Moral Values and the Principate," in Mineo, *Companion to Livy,* 139–154; Thomas Wiedemann, "Reflections of Roman Political Thought in Latin Historical Writing," in *The Cambridge History of Greek and Roman Political Thought,* ed. Christopher Rowe and Malcolm Schofield (Cambridge: Cambridge University Press, 2000), 517–531.

63. For an overview of Livy's life and career, see Ronald Syme, "Livy and Augustus," *Harvard Studies in Classical Philology,* no. 64 (1959): 27–87.

64. Livy, *History of Rome,* prologue to bk. 1.

65. Thus Livy, at one point, commented that "such is the nature of the populace; they are either cringing slaves or haughty tyrants. They know not how with moderation to spurn or to enjoy that liberty which holds the middle place." Livy, *History of Rome,* 24.25.

66. Ibid., 1.56.

67. Plutarch, *Brutus,* 1.1.

68. For the continued veneration for republican heroes during the early imperial period, see Wilkinson, *Republicanism,* 40–44, 126.

69. Seneca, *De Constantia Sapientis,* 2.2. For Seneca's views on the fall of the republic, see Miriam Griffin, *Seneca: A Philosopher in Politics* (Oxford: Clarendon Press, 1992). Note that Seneca was by no means a consistent defender of the republic. In *On Mercy* he tried to promote loyalty to Nero, not the republic, by showing Nero's innocence and mercy. See Wilkinson, *Republicanism,* 131.

70. For an overview of Plutarch's life and work, see M. Beck, "Introduction," in *A Companion to Plutarch,* ed. M. Beck (Chicester: Wiley-Blackwell, 2014), 1–12.

71. For the argument that Plutarch's *Parallel Lives* must be read as a defense of the republic, see P. A. Stadter, "Plutarch and Rome," in Beck, *Companion to Plutarch,* 13–31. However, Plutarch was by no means a consistent defender of republicanism. In his more abstract political writings, he advocated the Platonic ideal of the philosopher-king. See, for instance, C. Pelling, "Political Philosophy," in Beck, *Companion to Plutarch,* 149–162.

72. Plutarch, *Cato the Younger.*

73. Ibid., 70.

74. Plutarch, *Brutus,* 3.4.

75. Plutarch, *Cicero.*

76. Since the early modern period, there has been a lively debate about how to interpret the political message of Tacitus's writings. Tacitus has been alternatively interpreted as a defender of liberty and the republic—the "red" Tacitus. But he has also frequently been read as a proponent of power politics and a strong monarchy—the "black" Tacitus. About these different interpretations of Tacitus's writings, see D. Kapust, "Tacitus and Political Thought," in *A Companion to Tacitus*, ed. V. E. Pagán (Chichester: Wiley-Blackwell, 2011), 504–528. Needless to say, this author agrees with the "red" interpretation of Tacitus.

77. For Tacitus's life and career, see A. R. Birley, "The Life and Death of Cornelius Tacitus," *Historia* 49, no. 2 (2000): 230–247.

78. Herbert W. Benario, "The Annals," in *Companion to Tacitus*, ed. Pagán, 101–121.

79. Tacitus, *The Annals: The Reigns of Tiberius, Claudius, and Nero*, trans. J. C. Yardley (Oxford: Oxford University Press, 2008), 1.1.

80. Tacitus, *Annals*, 5.9.

81. Ibid., 6.40.

82. Ibid., 15.35, 13.25, 16.17.

83. Ibid., 15.44.

84. For Tacitus's claim that after Augustus elections had become a charade, see, for instance, Tacitus, *Annals*, 1.81 and 11.22.

85. For this point, see S. Oakley, "*Res olim dissociabiles*: Emperors, Senators and Liberty," in *The Cambridge Companion to Tacitus*, ed. A. Woodman (Cambridge: Cambridge University Press, 2009), 184–194.

86. Tacitus, *Annals*, 2.32, 3.70, 3.65.

87. On Nero's rule, see ibid., 13–16.

88. Ibid., 16.36.

89. Tacitus, *The Life of Cnæus Julius Agricola*, 3.1–8.

90. But compare Chaim Wirszubski, who argues that Tacitus "conceived *libertas* less as a constitutional right than as the individual will and courage to be free." Wirszubski, *Libertas as a Political Idea*, 165. Mark Morford similarly argues that, to Tacitus, "liberty" was something that existed in all well-ordered states, including the empire. Morford, "How Tacitus Defined Liberty," *ANRW*, 11.33.4 (1991): 3420–3449.

91. Tacitus, *Annals*, 15.49.

92. For these events, see Wilkinson, *Republicanism*, 35–58.

93. Beard, *SPQR*, 394.

94. Syme, "Livy and Augustus"; Birley, "The Life and Death of Cornelius Tacitus"; Plutarch, *Caesar*.

95. On Dio's life and career, see C. P. Jones, *The Roman World of Dio Chrysostom* (Cambridge, MA: Harvard University Press, 1978). On his political philosophy, see C. Gill, "Stoic Writers of the Imperial Era," in Rowe and Schofield, *Greek and Roman Political Thought*, 597–615.

96. Dio Chrysostom, *The Third Discourse on Kingship*, 78–79.

97. Dio Chrysostom, *The Second Discourse on Kingship*, 6.

98. Francis Dvornik, *Early Christian and Byzantine Political Philosophy: Origins and Backgrounds*, vol. 1 (Washington, DC: Dumbarton Oaks Center for Byzantine Studies, 1966).

99. See Carlos F. Noreña, *Imperial Ideals in the Roman West: Representation, Circulation, Power* (Cambridge: Cambridge University Press, 2011), 284–297.

100. The following paragraphs are based on W. H. C. Frend, "Persecutions: Genesis and Legacy," in *The Cambridge History of Christianity,* ed. M. M. Mitchell and F. M. Young (Cambridge: Cambridge University Press, 2006), 501–523; A. Cameron, "Constantine and the 'Peace of the Church,'" in Mitchell and Young, *History of Christianity,* 538–551.

101. See Frances Young, "Christianity," in Rowe and Schofield, *Greek and Roman Political Thought,* 635–660; H. Drake, "The Church, Society and Political Power," in *The Cambridge History of Christianity,* vol. 2, *Constantine to c. 600,* ed. A. Casiday and F. Norris (Cambridge: Cambridge University Press, 2007), 403–428; A. Ritter, "Church and State up to c.300 CE," in *The Cambridge History of Christianity,* vol. 1, *Origins to Constantine,* ed. Margaret M. Mitchell and Frances M. Young, (Cambridge: Cambridge University Press, 2006), 524–537.

102. Rom. 13 (New Revised Standard Version).

103. Quoted in Young, "Christianity," 649.

104. Eusebius, *Church History: Life of Constantine the Great: Oration in Praise of Constantine,* trans. Ernest Cushing Richardson (Buffalo, NY: Christian Literature, 1890), 1110–1175. For Eusebius's Platonism, see N. H. Baynes, "Eusebius and the Christian Empire," in *Byzantine Studies and Other Essays,* ed. N. H. Baynes (London: Athlone Press, 1955), 168–172. For the influence of Eusebius on Byzantine political philosophy, see Dvornik, *Early Christian and Byzantine Political Philosophy,* vol. 2, 611–622; J.-M. Sansterre, "Eusèbe de Césarée et la naissance de la théorie 'césaropapiste,'" *Byzantion,* no. 42 (1972): 131–195, 532–594.

105. Eusebius, *Church History,* 1118.

106. Dvornik, *Early Christian and Byzantine Political Philosophy,* vol. 2, 725–726. As Dvornik shows, many other Christian thinkers came independently to the same conclusion.

107. On Augustine's political philosophy, see R. W. Dyson, *St. Augustine of Hippo and the Christian Transformation of Political Philosophy* (London: Continuum Press, 2005), esp. 48–88. On Augustine's life and career, see J. O'Donnell, "Augustine," in *The Cambridge Companion to Augustine,* ed. E. Stump and N. Kretzmann (Cambridge: Cambridge University Press, 2001), 8–25.

108. Augustine, *The City of God,* trans. William Babcock, annot. by Boniface Ramsey (Hyde Park, NY: New City Press, 2013), 2.19.6.

109. Ibid., 2.19.15.

110. For a discussion of the concept of freedom in both the Old and the New Testament, see R. Brague, "God and Freedom: Biblical Roots of the Western Idea of Liberty," in *Christianity and Freedom,* ed. T. Shah and A. Hertzke (Cambridge: Cambridge University Press, 2016), 391–402. Early Christian thinkers also talked a great deal about "slavery"—in the sense of submission to God—as a positive value. For that point, see Dale B. Martin, *Slavery as Salvation: The Metaphor of Slavery in Pauline Christianity* (New Haven: Yale University Press, 1990).

111. Gal. 3:28–4:11 (NRSV).

112. 1 Cor. 7:21–24 (NRSV).

113. This is by no means the only possible interpretation of 1 Cor. 7:21–24. For an overview of the debate about the meaning of this controversial passage, see Martin, *Slavery as Salvation*, 63.

114. For this point, see Peter Garnsey, *Ideas of Slavery from Aristotle to Augustine* (Cambridge: Cambridge University Press, 1996), 191–243. For Ambrose's life and career, see R. Markus, "The Latin Fathers," in *The Cambridge History of Medieval Political Thought c.350–c.1450*, ed. J. Burns (Cambridge: Cambridge University Press, 1988), 92–122.

115. Ambrose, *Letters*, trans. Mary Melchior Beyenka (New York: Fathers of the Church, 1954), 287.

116. Ibid., 292.

117. Ibid., 288.

118. Ibid., 296.

119. Ibid., 299.

120. See Dvornik, *Early Christian and Byzantine Political Philosophy*, vol. 2, 113. But compare with Anthony Kaldellis, "Political Freedom in Byzantium: The Rhetoric of Liberty and the Periodization of Roman History," *History of European Ideas* 44, no. 6 (2018): 795–811. Kaldellis argues that the cult of freedom survived into the Byzantine period.

121. Quoted in D. M. Nicol, "Byzantine Political Thought," in Burns, *History of Medieval Political Thought*, 55.

122. Anthony Kaldellis, "Republican Theory and Political Dissidence in Ioannes Lydos," *Byzantine and Modern Greek Studies* 29, no. 1 (2005): 9. For Byzantine debate about republicanism in later ages, see V. Syros, "Between Chimera and Charybdis: Byzantine and Post-Byzantine Views on the Political Organization of the Italian City-States," *Journal of Early Modern History*, no. 14 (2010): 451–504.

123. Nicol, "Byzantine Political Thought," 53.

124. Chris Wickham, *The Inheritance of Rome: Illuminating the Dark Ages 400–1000* (New York: Penguin, 2009), 111–254.

125. For this point, see Rosamond McKitterick, "Politics," in *The Early Middle Ages: Europe 400–1000*, ed. Rosamond McKitterick (Oxford: Oxford University Press, 2001); Bjorn Weiler, "Political Structures," in *The Central Middle Ages*, ed. Daniel Power (Oxford: Oxford University Press, 2006), ch. 3.

126. See J. Nelson, "Kingship and Empire," in Burns, *History of Medieval Political Thought*, 211–251; P. King, "The Barbarian Kingdoms," in Burns, *History of Medieval Political Thought*, 123–154.

127. On Isidore, see King, "The Barbarian Kingdoms," 141. Similarly, Gregory the Great, deeply influenced by Augustine, argued that bad rulers should be accepted as a punishment by God. See Markus, "The Latin Fathers," 92–122. For Hincmar of Rheims, see Nelson, "Kingship and Empire."

128. For this point, see Mario Turchetti, *Tyrannie et tyrannicide de l'Antiquité à nos jours* (Paris: Classiques Garnier, 2013), 205–290.

129. A good example of this view can be found in Thomas Aquinas's *On Kingship*. There were, of course, some exceptions to this commonly accepted view; notably, John of Salisbury in his *Policraticus* defined the difference between "king" and "tyrant" as

revolving around whether a ruler obeyed the law. To some thinkers, in short, adherence to the law—not moral virtue—was the hallmark of true kingship. See Antony Black, *Political Thought in Europe, 1250–1450* (Cambridge: Cambridge University Press, 1992), 152–155.

130. On the popularity of this medieval genre, see Roberto Lambertini, "Mirrors for Princes," in *Encyclopedia of Medieval Philosophy,* ed. Henrik Lagerlund (Dordrecht: Springer, 2011), 791–797. For an overview of the genre, see Lester Born, "The Perfect Prince: A Study in Thirteenth- and Fourteenth-Century Ideals," *Speculum: A Journal of Mediaeval Studies* 3, no. 4 (1928): 470–504.

131. On the investiture controversy, see Black, *Political Thought in Europe, 1250–1450*, 42–84.

132. For a classic overview of the usage of "libertas" as a slogan during the investiture controversy, see Gerd Tellenbach, *Libertas: Kirche und Weltordnung im Zeitalter des Investiturstreites* (Stuttgart: W. Kohlhammer, 1936). For a more recent study, see Brigitte Szabó-Bechstein, *Libertas ecclesiae: Ein Schlüsselbegriff des Investiturstreits und seine Vorgeschichte, 4.-11. Jahrhundert* (Rome: Libreria Ateneo Salesiano, 1985).

133. For this point, see John C. Barnes, "Historical and Political Writing," in *Dante in Context,* ed. Zygmunt G. Barański and Lino Pertile (Cambridge: Cambridge University Press, 2015), 354–370.

134. See Quentin Skinner, *The Foundations of Modern Political Thought,* vol. 1, *The Renaissance* (Cambridge: Cambridge University Press, 1978), 3–65.

135. Quoted in Serena Ferente, "The Liberty of Italian City-States," in *Freedom and the Construction of Europe,* vol. 1, *Religious Freedom and Civil Liberty,* ed. Quentin Skinner and Martin van Gelderen (Cambridge: Cambridge University Press, 2013), 157–175.

136. Ptolemy of Lucca, with portions attributed to Thomas Aquinas, *On the Government of Rulers: De Regimine Principum,* trans. and ed. James M. Blythe (Philadelphia: University of Pennsylvania Press, 1997), 238.

137. On the internal divisions within Italian city-states, see Daniel Philip Waley and Trevor Dean, *The Italian City-Republics* (London: Routledge, 2013), chap. 7.

138. There has been a good deal of dispute over the authorship and authenticity of *On Kingship*. Some modern scholars believe that it was written by one of Thomas's disciples rather than by the famous theologian himself. But the prevailing view is that Thomas wrote the first two books of the treatise. After the death of its dedicatee in December 1267, he abandoned it, but it was nevertheless circulated either on its own or with a continuation by Aquinas's disciple Ptolemy of Lucca. See R. W. Dyson, Introduction in *Aquinas: Political Writings,* ed. R. W. Dyson (Cambridge: Cambridge University Press, 2002), xvii–xxxvi.

139. Ptolemy of Lucca, with portions attributed to Thomas Aquinas, *On the Government of Rulers,* 66. But compare Samuel K. Cohn, *Lust for Liberty: The Politics of Social Revolt in Medieval Europe, 1200–1425* (Cambridge, MA: Harvard University Press, 2008). Kohn argues that a freedom-centric ideology was prevalent in the later Middle Ages.

140. On the demise of the Italian city-republics, see Waley and Dean, *Italian City Republics,* chap. 8.

3. The Renaissance of Freedom

1. Dante Alighieri, *The Divine Comedy of Dante Alighieri*, vol. 1, *Inferno*, trans. and ed. by Robert M. Durling, (New York: Oxford University Press, 1996), canto 10, 20, 34.19–34.67.

2. For the convergence between the political views of Dante's *Divine Comedy* and his *Monarchy*, see Joan M. Ferrante, *The Political Vision of the "Divine Comedy"* (Princeton, NJ: Princeton University Press, 1984), 3–43.

3. Dante Alighieri, *Monarchy*, trans. and ed. Prue Shaw (Cambridge: Cambridge University Press, 1996), 86.

4. Ibid., 21.

5. For Dante's political views in their historical context, see Charles Till Davis, "Dante and the Empire," in *The Cambridge Companion to Dante*, ed. Rachel Jacoff (Cambridge: Cambridge University Press, 2007), 257–269.

6. For Bruni's life and career, see James Hankins and Gordin Griffiths, "General Introduction," in *The Humanism of Leonardo Bruni: Selected Texts*, by Leonardo Bruni, trans. and introd. Gordon Griffiths, James Hankins and David Thompson (Binghamton, NY: Medieval & Renaissance Texts & Studies in conjunction with the Renaissance Society of America, 1987), 1–37.

7. Leonardo Bruni, "A Dialogue Dedicated to Pier Paolo Vergerio," in *The Three Crowns of Florence: Humanist Assessments of Dante, Petrarca and Boccaccio*, ed. and trans. David Thompson and Alan F. Nagel (New York: Harper & Row, 1972), 48.

8. Jacob Burkhardt, *The Civilization of the Renaissance in Italy*, trans. S. G. C. Middlemore, intro. Peter Burke (London: Penguin Books, 1990), 98.

9. See, for instance, Jerry Brotton, *The Renaissance: A Very Short Introduction* (Oxford: Oxford University Press, 2006), 9.

10. For this critique of Burckhardt, see, for instance, Peter Burke, *The Renaissance* (London: Macmillan, 1987), 1.

11. Hans Baron first pointed to the Renaissance's crucial importance to the history of freedom in his seminal work *The Crisis of the Early Italian Renaissance Civic Humanism and Republican Liberty in an Age of Classicism and Tyranny*, 2 vols. (Princeton, NJ: Princeton University Press, 1955). Note, however, that according to Baron, specific political circumstances, notably the crisis provoked by the Florentine-Milanese War of 1402, played as important a role in increasing freedom-talk in Italy as the rediscovery of ancient texts and sources. This view, however, has been criticized by historians who have shown that the revival of the ancient cult of freedom predated the crisis of 1402, suggesting a more independent role for the Renaissance. Most notably, Quentin Skinner made this argument in *The Foundations of Modern Political Thought*, vol. 1, *The Renaissance* (Cambridge: Cambridge University Press, 1978) and then did so more explicitly in *Visions of Politics*, vol. 2, *Renaissance Virtues* (Cambridge: Cambridge University Press, 2002), 1–9.

The Baron-Skinner interpretation of the political impact of the Renaissance, it should be noted, strongly diverges from an older historiographical tradition that argued that the Renaissance rediscovery of ancient texts, rather than fostering a cult of freedom, provided intellectual support for the growth of princely power in Italy and the rest of Europe. The rediscovery of antiquity, the reasoning goes, diminished the prestige of traditional Christian morality and gave fifteenth- and sixteenth-century intellectuals access to a world with a very different value system, one that valued ruthlessness and ambition more than Christian humility and forbearance. This was translated into a new political code that celebrated the pragmatic imperatives of "reason of state" over and above traditional morality. This view of the Renaissance's impact on the history of political thought, mainly based on a superficial reading of Machiavelli's *The Prince,* is now generally rejected by historians. See James Hankins, "Humanism and the Origins of Modern Political Thought," in *The Cambridge Companion to Renaissance Humanism,* ed. J. Kraye (Cambridge: Cambridge University Press, 1996), 118–141.

12. The literature on the humanist movement is vast. The essays collected in *Renaissance Humanism: Foundations, Forms, and Legacy,* 3 vols., ed. A. Rabil (Philadelphia: University of Pennsylvania Press, 1988–1991) and in Kraye, *Cambridge Companion to Renaissance Humanism* give a good overview of the Anglophone scholarship on humanism. For a more recent single-author overview, see Charles Nauert, *Humanism and the Culture of Renaissance Europe,* rev. ed. (1996; Cambridge: Cambridge University Press, 2006).

13. See Peter Burke, *The Renaissance Sense of the Past* (London: Edward Arnold, 1969). Note, however, that some medievalists dispute this account. See Janet Coleman, *Ancient and Medieval Memories: Studies in the Reconstruction of the Past* (Cambridge: Cambridge University Press, 1992).

14. Petrarch is often described as the "father of humanism." Recent scholarship has challenged this view by pointing to important precursors and the medieval features of his intellectual and artistic outlook. See, for instance, Ronald Witt, *In the Footsteps of the Ancients: The Origins of Humanism from Lovato to Bruni* (Leiden: Brill, 2003). Despite such qualifications, Petrarch's importance to the humanistic Renaissance is undeniable. See the essays on Petrarch in Rabil, *Renaissance Humanism,* vol. 1.

15. Petrarch, *Africa,* trans. and annot. Thomas G. Bergin and Alice S. Wilson (Newhaven, CT: Yale University Press, 1977), bk. 9, 638–641. On Petrarch's innovativeness in describing his own age as one of light, compared to the preceding Dark Ages, see Theodore E. Mommsen, "Petrarch's Conception of the 'Dark Ages,'" *Speculum* 17, no. 2 (April 1942): 226–242.

16. Petrarch, *Africa,* bk. 9, 638–641.

17. For this characterization of Salutati, see *Ciceronian Controversies,* ed. and trans. JoAnn Della Neva and Brian Duvick (Cambridge, MA: Harvard University Press, 2007), 237. For the rediscovery of ancient texts, see Leighton Durham Reynolds and Nigel Guy Wilson, *Scribes and Scholars: A Guide to the Transmission of Greek and Latin Literature* (Oxford: Oxford University Press, 1991), 121–163.

18. For the emergence of this definition of the term "republic" in the Italian Renaissance, see James Hankins, "Exclusivist Republicanism and the Non-Monarchical Republic," *Political Theory* 38, no. 4 (2010): 452–482.

19. See, for instance, Alison Brown, "The Humanist Portrait of Cosimo de' Medici, Pater Patriae," *Journal of the Warburg and Courtauld Institutes* 24, no. 3/4 (1961): 186–221.

20. See Hans Baron, *From Petrarch to Leonardo Bruni: Studies in Humanistic and Political Literature* (Chicago, London: University of Chicago Press, for the Newberry Library, 1968), 7–50. Remarkably, however, Baron does not refer to Petrarch's public letters to Cola di Rienzo, which provide the clearest evidence of his role in reviving the cult of ancient freedom. Note that Baron's reading of Petrarch as a defender of ancient freedom has been contested. For an overview of the debate, see Craig Kallendorf, "The Historical Petrarch," *The American Historical Review* 101, no. 1 (February 1996): 130–141.

21. Petrarch, *The Revolution of Cola di Rienzo,* ed. Mario Cosenza (New York: Italica Press, 1986), 15–20.

22. Ibid., 166.

23. The key role of Florentine humanists in the revival of the ancient cult of freedom in Renaissance Italy was first highlighted by Hans Baron in his *Crisis of the Early Italian Renaissance.* Baron's thesis has generated considerable controversy, however. For an overview, see James Hankins, "The 'Baron Thesis' after Forty Years and Some Recent Studies of Leonardo Bruni," *Journal of the History of Ideas* 56, no. 2 (1995): 309–338; James Hankins, ed., *Renaissance Humanism: Reappraisals and Reflections* (Cambridge: Cambridge University Press, 2000).

24. On Florentine politics, see John Najemy, *A History of Florence 1200–1575* (Oxford: Wiley-Blackwell, 2006); Lorenzo Tanzini, "Tuscan States: Florence and Siena," in *The Italian Renaissance States,* ed. Andrea Gamberini and Isabella Lazzarini (Cambridge: Cambridge University Press, 2012), 90–111.

25. Quoted in Najemy, *History of Florence,* 298. For the rise of the Medici more generally, see Arthur Field, *The Intellectual Struggle for Florence: Humanists and the Beginnings of the Medici Regime, 1420–1440* (Cambridge: Cambridge University Press, 2017).

26. Some humanists, it should be noted, also supported the Medici and their attempts to turn Florence into a principality by praising Cosimo as a model Platonic philosopher-ruler or a latter-day Augustus. See Brown, "The Humanist Portrait."

27. Alamanno Rinuccini, "Liberty," in *Humanism and Liberty: Writings on Freedom from Fifteenth-Century Florence,* ed. and trans. Renée Neu Watkins (Columbia: University of South Carolina Press), 186–224. For more details about Rinuccini's life, see the introduction by Watkins.

28. Machiavelli's importance to the revival of the ancient cult of freedom in Renaissance Italy has been highlighted by Quentin Skinner in a series of landmark studies, beginning with his discussion of the Florentine thinker in *Foundations of Modern Political Thought,* vol. 1, continued in G. Bock, Q. Skinner, and M. Viroli, eds., *Machiavelli and Republicanism* (Cambridge: Cambridge University Press, 1990) and the essay on Machiavelli in Skinner, *Visions of Politics,* vol. 2. For an important alternative interpretation of Machiavelli as a theorist of "classical virtue" rather than of ancient liberty, see J. G. A. Pocock, *The Machiavellian Moment: Florentine Political Thought and the Atlantic Republican Tradition* (Princeton, NJ: Princeton University Press, 1975). By contrast, Paul Rahe, *Against Throne and Altar: Machiavelli and Political Theory Under the English Republic* (Cambridge: Cambridge University Press, 2008), depicts Machiavelli as a theorist who radically broke with ancient political thought (see especially chap. 1).

29. For details about Machiavelli's upbringing and early life, see Roberto Ridolfi, *The Life of Niccolò Machiavelli*, trans. Cecil Grayson (London: Routledge, 1963), 133–154.

30. Niccolò Machiavelli, *Discourses on Livy,* trans. and ed. Julia Conway Bondanella and Peter Bondanella (Oxford: Oxford University Press, 1997), 156–161.

31. Ibid., 27. For an analysis of Machiavelli as a defender of popular government, see John McCormick, *Machiavellian Democracy* (Cambridge: Cambridge University Press, 2011). Note that this reading ruptures with the more traditional understanding of Machiavelli as a defender of the more elitist mixed constitution. For this reading, see Quentin Skinner, *Machiavelli: A Very Short Introduction* (Oxford: Oxford University Press, 1981), 72–76.

32. Machiavelli, *Discourses on Livy,* 100, 134.

33. Erwin Panofsky, *Renaissance and Renascences in Western Art* (Boulder: Westview Press, 1972); Anthony Grafton, Glenn W. Most, and Salvatore Settis, eds., *The Classical Tradition* (Cambridge, MA: Harvard University Press, 2013), 196.

34. Nauert, *Humanism,* 60–101.

35. R. R. Bolgar, *The Classical Heritage and its Beneficiaries* (Cambridge: Cambridge University Press, 1954), 280.

36. Peter Burke, "A Survey of the Popularity of Ancient Historians," *History and Theory* 5, no. 2 (1966): 135–152.

37. Nauert, *Humanism,* 60–101. There is lively dispute about the nature of humanism's impact on the Renaissance Italian educational curriculum. Robert Black, *Humanism and Education in Medieval and Renaissance Italy: Tradition and Innovation in Latin Schools from the Twelfth to the Fifteenth Century* (Cambridge: Cambridge University Press, 2001) argues for continuity and conservatism, not innovation, in medieval and Renaissance teaching. Black's analysis is disputed by Paul Grendler, *Schooling in Renaissance Italy: Literacy and Learning, 1300–1600* (Baltimore: Johns Hopkins University Press, 1989), who provides abundant evidence that there were substantial curricular changes.

38. For an analysis of the revival of the ancient cult of freedom in Renaissance visual and dramatic arts, see Peter Bondanella, *The Eternal City: Roman Images in the Modern World* (Chapel Hill: University of North Carolina Press, 1987).

39. For an extensive description and analysis of these frescoes, see Edna Southard, *The Frescoes in Siena's Palazzo Pubblico 1289–1539: Studies in Imagery and Relations to Other Communal Palaces in Tuscany* (New York: Garland Publishing, 1979), 354–371. See also Nicolai Rubinstein, "Political Ideas in Sienese Art: The Frescoes by Ambrogio Lorenzetti and Taddeo di Bartolo in the Palazzo Pubblico," *Journal of the Warburg and Courtauld Institutes* 21, no. 3/4 (1958): 179–207.

40. Quoted in Southard, *The Frescoes in Siena's Palazzo Pubblico,* 362.

41. Ibid., 363.

42. Rubinstein, "Political Ideas in Sienese Art."

43. Bondanella, *Eternal City,* 59. See also D. J. Gordon, "Gianotti, Michelangelo and the Cult of Brutus," in *The Renaissance Imagination,* ed. Stephen Orgel (Berkeley: University of California Press, 1975), 233–246.

44. Quoted in Gordon, "The Cult of Brutus," 235.

45. See Manfredi Piccolomini, *The Brutus Revival: Parricide and Tyrannicide during the Renaissance* (Carbondale: Southern Illinois University Press, 1991), 35–94.

46. Quoted in Najemy, *History of Florence,* 356.

47. Rinuccini, "Liberty," 196.

48. Quoted in Gordon, "The Cult of Brutus," 235.

49. Quoted in ibid., 236.

50. Gene Brucker, "The Italian Renaissance," in *A Companion to the Worlds of the Renaissance,* ed. Guido Ruggiero (Oxford: Blackwell, 2002), 23–38.

51. On the transformation of Italian political thought during the sixteenth century, see Maurizio Viroli, *From Politics to Reason of State: The Acquisition and Transformation of the Language of Politics, 1250–1600* (Cambridge: Cambridge University Press, 1992); Vittor Ivo Comparato, "From the Crisis of Civil Culture to the Neapolitan Republic of 1647: Republicanism in Italy between the Sixteenth and Seventeenth Centuries," in *Republicanism: A Shared European Heritage,* vol. 1, *Republicanism and Constitutionalism in Early Modern Europe,* ed. Quentin Skinner and Martin van Gelderen (Cambridge: Cambridge University Press, 2002), 169–194.

   Note that this transformation did not happen overnight: as Nicolas Scot Baker argues in *The Fruit of Liberty: Political Culture in the Florentine Renaissance, 1480–1550* (Cambridge, MA: Harvard University Press, 2013), there was continuity in Florence between the older, republican political culture and the new princely political culture; notably, the concept of freedom was still important under the Medici. Alison Brown also points out how the Medici initially appropriated liberty-talk before it eventually faded away, in "De-masking Renaissance Republicanism," in *Renaissance Civic Humanism: Reappraisals and Reflections,* ed. J. Hankins (Cambridge: Cambridge University Press, 2000), 179–199.

52. Randolph Starn, *Contrary Commonwealth: The Theme of Exile in Medieval and Renaissance Italy* (Berkeley: University of California Press, 1982), 148–160.

53. See Bondanella, *Eternal City,* 135. But for a different reading of the libretto, see Wendy Heller, "Tacitus Incognito: Opera as History in '*L'incoronazione di Poppea,*'" *Journal of the American Musicological Society* 52, no. 1 (1999): 39–96.

54. Claudio Monteverdi and G. F. Busenello, *L'incoronazione di Poppea (The Coronation of Poppea): An Opera in a Prologue and Three Acts,* ed. Alan Curtis, trans. Arthur Jacobs (London: Novello, 1990), 256–260.

55. See William Bouwsma, *Venice and the Defense of Republican Liberty: Renaissance Values in the Age of the Counter Reformation* (Berkeley: University of California Press, 1968).

56. With regard to the terminology used to describe these ancient political models, note that most—but by no means all—northern humanists explicitly rejected the idea that they were democrats—a term that was associated with anarchy and mob rule. See Russell Hanson, "Democracy," in *Political Innovation,* ed. Terence Ball, James Farr, and Russell L. Hanson (Cambridge: Cambridge University Press, 1989), 68–89. Instead, they frequently used the term "popular government," as well as "republic" or "commonwealth," to describe their preferred form of government. The latter two terms applied to a broad range of kingless governments: it could just as easily mean an Athenian-style democracy as a highly restrictive regime in which

power was monopolized by the few. For early modern meanings of the term "republic," see Mager, "Republik." For the French usage, see Raymonde Monnier, "République, Républicanisme, Républicain," in *Handbuch politisch-sozialer Grundbegriffe in Frankreich 1680–1820,* ed. Hans Jürgen Lüsebrink and Jörn Leonhard (De Gruyter: Oldenbourg, 2016), vol. 21. In addition, many humanists also expressed—much like the Roman *optimates* had—a preference for "mixed government," in which the "democratic" element was restrained by an "aristocratic" and "monarchical" element. However, preference for a mixed constitution was not as ubiquitous in humanist thought as is sometimes claimed. For this argument, in reference to English humanism in particular, see Jonathan Scott, *Commonwealth Principles: Republican Writing of the English Revolution* (Cambridge: Cambridge University Press, 2004), 131–150.

57. Peter Burke, *The European Renaissance: Centers and Peripheries* (Oxford: Wiley, 1998); Peter Burke, "The Historical Geography of the Renaissance," in *A Companion to the Worlds of the Renaissance,* ed. Guido Ruggiero (Oxford: Blackwell, 2002), 88–104; Nauert, *Humanism,* 102–131; Bolgar, *The Classical Heritage,* 302–379.

58. For these numbers, see, respectively, Burke, "Survey," 136 and Andrew Pettegree, *Reformation and the Culture of Persuasion* (Cambridge: Cambridge University Press, 2005), 191.

59. For an analysis of prevailing political systems in early modern Europe, see Mark Greengrass, "Politics and Warfare," in *The Sixteenth Century,* ed. Euan Cameron (Oxford: Oxford University Press, 2009), 58–88; Richard Bonney, *The European Dynastic States, 1494–1660* (Oxford: Oxford University Press, 1991); Neithart Bulst, "Rulers, Representative Institutions and Their Members as Power Elites: Rivals or Partners?," in *Power Elites and State Building,* ed. Wolfgang Reinhard (Oxford: Clarendon Press, 1996), 41–58.

60. W. P. Blockmans, "Alternatives to Monarchical Centralisation: The Great Tradition of Revolt in Flanders and Brabant," in Koeningsberger, *Republiken und Republikanismus,* 145–154.

61. Andreas Würgler, "The League of Discordant Members or How the Old Swiss Confederation Operated and How it Managed to Survive for So Long," in *The Republican Alternative: The Netherlands and Switzerland Compared,* ed. André Holenstein, Thomas Maissen, and Maarten Prak (Amsterdam: Amsterdam University Press, 2008), 29–50.

62. Jan Waszink, introduction to Justus Lipsius, *Politica: Six Books of Politics or Political Introduction,* ed. and trans. Jan Waszink (Assen: Van Gorcum, 2004), 3–204. On Lipsius's *Admiranda,* see Marc Laureys, "The Grandeur That was Rome: Scholarly Analysis and Pious Awe in Lipsius's *Admiranda,*" in *Recreating Ancient History. Episodes from the Greek and Roman Past in the Arts and Literature of the Early Modern Period,* ed. Karl Enenkel, Jan de Jong, and Jeanine de Landtsheer (Leiden-Boston: Brill, 2001).

63. For a similar argument, with a particular focus on the French tradition, see Jean-Fabien Spitz, *La liberté politique: essai de généalogie conceptuelle* (Paris: Presses Universitaires de France, 1995). An overview of the dissemination of republican arguments in early modern Europe is offered in *Republicanism : A Shared European Heritage,* ed.

Skinner and van Gelderen (2 vols.). Note, however, that most essays focus on the eighteenth century.

64. For an overview, see the essays in Mack Holt, ed., *Renaissance and Reformation France 1500–1648* (Oxford: Oxford University Press, 2002), notably Philip Benedict's "The Wars of Religion, 1562–1598."

65. Étienne de la Boétie, *On Voluntary Servitude*, trans. David Schaefer, in *Freedom over Servitude: Montaigne, La Boétie and On Voluntary Servitude,* ed. David Schaefer (Westport, CT: Greenwood Press, 1998), 189–222. On La Boétie's education and early life, see Simone Goyard-Fabre, introduction to the Flammarion edition of *Discours de la servitude volontaire,* by Étienne de la Boétie (Paris: GF Flammarion, 1983).

66. On the dissemination of La Boétie's text, see Simone Goyard-Fabre, "Le Contr'un de La Boétie. Étude d'une œuvre," *L'École des Lettres* LXXIV, 7, 1er janvier 1983, 37–43; 8, 15 janvier 1983, 41–51; François Moureau, "Boétie à l'épreuve de la Révolution française: éditions et travestissements du Contr'Un," in *Étienne de La Boétie, sage révolutionnaire et poète périgourdin, Actes du colloques international de Duke University (26–28 mars 1999),* ed. Marcel Tétel (Paris: Champion, 2004), 293–306.

67. La Boétie, *On Voluntary Servitude,* 191.

68. Ibid., 194.

69. Ibid., 221–222.

70. On Hotman's life and the historical context in which he wrote *Francogallia,* see the introduction to François Hotman, *Francogallia,* ed. and trans. Ralph Giesey and J. H. M. Salmon (Cambridge: Cambridge University Press, 1972).

71. Hotman, *Francogallia,* 299–300.

72. Ibid., 297–299.

73. Ibid., 292–293.

74. Jacques Bénigne Bossuet, *Politics Drawn from the Very Words of Holy Scripture,* ed. and trans. Patrick Riley (Cambridge: Cambridge University Press, 1991).

75. Almut Bues, "The Formation of the Polish-Lithuanian Monarchy in the Sixteenth Century," in *The Polish-Lithuanian Monarchy in Context, c. 1500–1795,* ed. Richard Butterwick (Basingstoke: Palgrave, 2001).

76. Anna Grześkowiak-Krwawicz, "Anti-Monarchism in Polish Republicanism in the Seventeenth and Eighteenth Centuries," in Skinner and Van Gelderen, *Republicanism,* vol. 1, 43–60, quote on 45. See also Anna Grześkowiak-Krwawicz, *Queen Liberty: The Concept of Freedom in the Polish-Lithuanian Commonwealth* (Leiden: Brill, 2012).

77. For an overview of the Dutch Revolt and the political debate it provoked, see Martin van Gelderen, *The Political Thought of the Dutch Revolt 1555–1590* (Cambridge: Cambridge University Press, 2002).

78. See the essays on the sixteenth and seventeenth centuries in E. O. G. Haitsma Mulier and Wyger Velema, eds., *Vrijheid: een geschiedenis van de vijftiende tot de twintigste eeuw* (Amsterdam: Amsterdam University Press, 1999).

79. Hugo Grotius, *The Antiquity of the Batavian Republic,* ed. and trans. Jan Waszink et al. (Assen: Van Gorcum, 2000), 95.

80. Rabo Herm. Scheels, *Vertoog van de gemeene vryheid, waarbij nog komt Theoph. Hogers Redevoering, betoogende dat J. Caesar een Tiran is geweest, uyt het Latyn verrtaalt*

door Otho Hendrik Ruperti, met eene voorrede behelzende eene korte schets va het leven des schryvers ('s Gravenhage: Kornelis Boucquet, 1742).

81. See Ann Hughes, *The Causes of the English Civil War* (Basingstoke: Macmillan, 1991).

82. See Skinner, *Liberty before Liberalism,* as well as the essays on the English Revolution in Skinner, *Visions of Politics,* vol. 2. Note that this reading ruptures with an older interpretation of the English Revolution, which understood it as a revolution for religious liberty that turned into a revolution for political liberty; as argued, for instance, in William Haller, *Liberty and Reformation in the Puritan Revolution* (New York: Columbia University Press, 1955). It breaks, as well, with a historiographical tradition portraying the English Revolution as inspired by common law arguments. For this latter claim, see J. G. A. Pocock, *The Ancient Constitution and the Feudal Law: A Reissue with a Retrospect* (Cambridge: Cambridge University Press, 1987); Glenn Burgess, *The Politics of the Ancient Constitution: An Introduction to English Political Thought, 1603–1642* (London: Macmillan, 1992). Note also that there is considerable debate in the literature about the question of when exactly the ancient cult of freedom was introduced in England, with some historians arguing that it was revived only after the execution of Charles I, and not before. For this argument, see Blair Worden, "Republicanism, Regicide and Republic: The English Experience," in Skinner and Van Gelderen, *Republicanism,* vol. 2, 307–327; Blair Worden, *The English Civil Wars 1640–1660* (London: Weidenfeld & Nicolson, 2009).

83. "A Declaration of the Parliament of England, Expressing the Grounds of Their Late Proceedings, and of Setling the Present Government in the Way of a Free State," in *The Struggle for Sovereignty: Seventeenth-Century English Political Tracts,* ed. Joyce Lee Malcom (Indianapolis: Liberty Fund, 1999), vol. 1, 381–384. For the political culture of the English Republic more generally, see S. Kelsey, *Inventing a Republic: The Political Culture of the English Commonwealth, 1649–1653* (Manchester: Manchester University Press, 1997).

84. According to Blair Worden, the term "republican" did not become common in English political debate until the 1680s. Cf. Worden, "Liberty for Export: 'Republicanism in England, 1500–1800,'" in *European Contexts for English Republicanism,* ed. Gaby Mahlberg and Dirk Wiemann (Farnham: Ashgate, 2013), 13–32.

85. Quoted in Scott, *Commonwealth Principles,* 152.

86. Marchamont Nedham, *The Excellencie of a Free-State; Or, The Right Constitution of a Commonwealth,* ed. Blair Worden (Indianapolis: Liberty Fund, 2011), 10.

87. Algernon Sidney, *Discourses Concerning Government,* ed. Thomas G. West (Indianapolis: Liberty Fund, 1996), 17.

88. Rachel Hammersley, "James Harrington's *The Commonwealth of Oceana* and the Republican Tradition," in *The Oxford Handbook of Literature and the English Revolution,* ed. Laura Lunger Knoppers (Oxford: Oxford University Press, 2012); Blair Worden, "James Harrington and the Commonwealth of Oceana, 1656," in *Republicanism, Liberty, and Commercial Society, 1649–1776,* ed. D. Wootton (Stanford, CA: Stanford University Press, 1994), 82–110; Blair Worden, "Harrington's Oceana: Origins and Aftermath, 1651–1660," in Wootton, *Republicanism,* 111–138.

89. For Harrington's use of the term "democracy," see Rachel Hammersley, "Rethinking the Political Thought of James Harrington: Royalism, Republicanism and Democracy," *History of European Ideas* 39, no. 3 (2013): 354–370.

90. Harrington, *The Oceana and Other Works,* 142–143.

91. Ibid., 93.

92. Ibid., 51.

93. Ibid., 67.

94. Ibid., 66.

95. Ibid., 51.

96. Ibid., 57.

97. Ibid., 51.

98. For Harrington's reference to Machiavelli as a precursor in thinking about economic equality as necessary for liberty, see ibid., 39. Harrington's proposed "agrarian law" was also inspired by ancient precedents, notably Tiberius and Gaius Gracchus's laws redistributing conquered land among Rome's poor. But it is important to note that none of Harrington's ancient sources presented the Gracchi's agrarian laws as designed to buttress Roman freedom or the Roman political system more generally. Instead, Plutarch and other ancient authors made clear that the Gracchi introduced these laws purely for socioeconomic reasons; namely, to alleviate the misery of poor, landless Roman citizens. See Plutarch, *Tiberius Gracchus,* 8.1–7.

99. For the debate about agrarian laws in early modern political thought, with an extensive discussion of Harrington's contribution, see Eric Nelson, *The Greek Tradition in Republican Thought* (Cambridge: Cambridge University Press, 2004), 49–126. Note, however, that Nelson understands Harrington's proposals for redistribution very differently from the author of this book. According to Nelson, Harrington believed that the state should be ruled by the best men; hence extremes in wealth, which warp character and banish virtue, should be avoided. In Nelson's account, in short, Harrington defended redistribution of wealth because it allowed domination by the best men and not because it made possible freedom in the sense of nondomination. See Nelson, *Greek Tradition,* 124.

100. For the Polish political system, see Butterwick, *The Polish-Lithuanian Monarchy in Context*; for the Dutch Republic, see Maarten Prak, "Verfassungsnorm under Verfassungsrealitat in den niederlandischen Stadten des spaten 17. und 18. Jahrhunderts: Die Oligarchie in Amsterdam, Rotterdam, Deventer und Zutphen, 1672/75–1795," in *Verwaltung und Politik in Stadten Mitteleuropas: Beitrage zu Verfassungsnorm und Verfassungswirklichkeit in altstandischer Zeit,* ed. W. Ehbrecht (Cologne-Vienna: Böhlau, 1994), 55–83.

101. Grześkowiak-Krwawicz, *Queen Liberty,* 41.

102. Scheels, *Vertoog van de gemeene Vryheid.*

103. John Milton, *The Ready and Easy Way to Establish a Free Commonwealth,* ed. Evert Mordecai Clark (New Haven, CT: Yale University Press, 1915), vol. 2, 183.

104. Andreas Wolanus, *De libertate politica sive civile: libellus lecti non indignus* (Cracow: M. Wirzbięta, 1572), chap. 6 (no pagination); my translation.

105. For an overview of the de la Courts' oeuvre and the context in which it was written, see Arthur Weststeijn, *Commercial Republicanism in the Dutch Golden Age: The Political Thought of Johan & Pieter de la Court* (Leiden: Brill, 2012), 25–68.

106. Johan and Pieter de la Court, *Consideratieën van Staat ofte Politieke Weegschaal, waar in met veelen reedenen, omstandigheden, exempelen, en fabulen wert overwogen; welke forme der regeeringe, in speculatie gebout op de practijk, onder de menschen de beste zy. Beschreven door V.H.,* 3rd ed. (Ysselmonde: Querinus Overal, 1662). For the enthusiastic description of the Athenian model, see de la Court, *Consideratieën van Staat,* 578–615.

107. Scott, *Commonwealth Principles,* 135–139; Samuel Glover, "The Putney Debates: Popular vs. Élitist Republicanism," *Past & Present,* no. 164 (August 1999): 47–80.

108. Quoted in Scott, *Commonwealth Principles,* 158.

109. Quoted in ibid., 138.

110. De la Court, *Consideratieën van Staat,* 519–520.

111. Thomas Hobbes, *Leviathan: Revised Student Edition,* ed. Richard Tuck (Cambridge: Cambridge University Press, 1996), 149–150.

112. This interpretation was classically formulated by nineteenth-century Protestant historians such as T. B. Macaulay and John Lothrop Motley. For a more recent iteration of this view, see, for example, James Young, *Reconsidering American Liberalism: The Troubled Odyssey of the Liberal Idea* (Boulder: Westview Press, 1996).

113. For this argument, see Chapter 1.

114. Ernst Troeltsch, *Protestantism and Progress: A Historical Study of the Relation of Protestantism to the Modern World,* trans. W. Montgomery (London: Williams and Norgate, 1912). For a more recent restatement of this revisionist view, see G. Burgess, "Political Obedience," in *The Oxford Handbook of the Protestant Reformations,* ed. Ulinka Rublack (Oxford: Oxford University Press, 2016).

115. Martin Luther, "On Christian Freedom," in *Luther's Works,* ed. Helmut T. Lehmann (Philadelphia: Muhlenberg Press, 1962). See also Perez Zagorin, *How the Idea of Religious Toleration Came to the West* (Princeton, NJ: Princeton University Press, 2003), 46–92; Benjamin Kaplan, *Divided by Faith: Religious Conflict and the Practice of Toleration in Early Modern Europe* (Cambridge, MA: Harvard University Press, 2007), 22–28.

116. Quoted in Kaplan, *Divided by Faith,* 24.

117. Ibid.

118. Quoted in Zagorin, *Religious Toleration,* 76. For Luther's evolving views on the role of secular authority in the punishment of heresy, see James Estes, "Luther on the Role of Secular Authority in the Reformation," *Lutheran Quarterly* 17, no. 2 (2003): 199–225.

119. John Calvin, "Christian Freedom," in *Institutes of the Christian Religion,* ed. and trans. John McNeill and F. L. Battles (Philadelphia: Westminster Press, 1960), 1: 836. See also Zagorin, *How the Idea of Religious Toleration Came to the West,* 46–92.

120. G. H. Williams, *The Radical Reformation* (Philadelphia: Westminster Press, 1962). For the impact of the radical Reformation on political thought, see Michael Baylor, ed., *The Radical Reformation* (Cambridge: Cambridge University Press, 1991); Michael Baylor, "Political Thought in the Age of the Reformation," in *The Oxford Handbook of the History of Political Philosophy,* ed. George Klosko (Oxford: Oxford University Press, 2011).

121. Zagorin, *How Religious Toleration Came to the West,* 9–13.

122. John Dunn, "The Claim to Freedom of Conscience: Freedom of Speech, Freedom of Thought, Freedom of Worship?," in *From Persecution to Toleration: The Glorious Revolution and Religion in England,* ed. Ole Peter Grell, Jonathan I. Israel, and Nicholas Tyacke (Oxford: Oxford University Press, 1991), 181. See also John Dunn, *The Political Thought of John Locke* (Cambridge: Cambridge University Press, 1969), 264.

123. A classic exposition of this view is in C. B. MacPherson, *The Political Theory of Possessive Individualism* (Oxford: Clarendon Press, 1962). For a more recent example, see Ellen Meiksins Wood, *Liberty and Property: A Social History of Western Political Thought from Renaissance to Enlightenment* (London: Verso, 2012), esp. 17–26.

124. Brian Tierney's work has been particularly influential in this regard; see, for instance, Brian Tierney, *Religion, Law, and the Growth of Constitutional Thought, 1150–1650* (New York: Cambridge University Press, 1982). For an accessible summary, see Brian Tierney, "Freedom and the Medieval Church," in *The Origins of Modern Freedom in the West,* ed. R. W. Davis (Stanford, CA: Stanford University Press, 1995). Also important is Annabel Brett, *Liberty, Right and Nature: Individual Rights in Later Scholastic Thought* (Cambridge: Cambridge University Press, 1997).

125. Quentin Skinner, *The Foundations of Modern Political Thought,* vol. 2, *The Age of Reformation* (Cambridge: Cambridge University Press, 1978); Knud Haakonssen, *Natural Law and Moral Philosophy from Grotius to the Scottish Enlightenment* (Cambridge: Cambridge University Press, 1996). Note that a similar thesis has also been put forward by Richard Tuck, "The 'Modern' Theory of Natural Law," in *The Languages of Political Theory in Early-Modern Europe,* ed. Anthony Pagden (Cambridge: Cambridge University Press, 1987), 99–119. However, Tuck depicts the rise of modern natural law as the result of a reaction against humanist skepticism rather than the Reformation.

126. Richard Tuck has aptly described the natural rights tradition as "Janus-faced" in his *Natural Rights Theories: Their Origin and Development* (Cambridge: Cambridge University Press, 1979). For the divergent and even contradictory political implications of natural rights doctrine, see also Dan Edelstein, *On the Spirit of Rights* (Chicago: University of Chicago Press, 2018).

127. On Grotius's life, see Richard Tuck's introduction to *The Rights of War and Peace: Book 1.*

128. Hugo Grotius, *The Rights of War and Peace: Book 1,* ed. Richard Tuck (Indianapolis: Liberty Fund, 2005), 260–272, quote on 1143. See Tuck, *Natural Rights Theories,* 58–81. For a very different reading of Grotius's views on liberty, see Daniel Lee, "Popular Liberty, Princely Government, and the Roman Law in Hugo Grotius's *De Jure Belli ac Pacis,*" *Journal of the History of Ideas* 72, no. 3 (2011), 371–392.

129. Samuel Pufendorf, *The Political Writings of Samuel Pufendorf,* ed. and trans. Craig Carr and Michael Seidler (Oxford: Oxford University Press, 1994), 204.

130. Spinoza, *Complete Works,* 531.

131. Jean-Jacques Rousseau, *The Social Contract and Other Later Political Writings,* ed. and trans. Victor Gourevitch (Cambridge: Cambridge University Press, 1997), 50.

132. For Locke's theory of freedom as essentially "republican," see James Tully, *An Approach to Political Philosophy: Locke in Contexts* (Cambridge: Cambridge University Press, 1993), 301. More generally, for Locke as a radical, republican, and even democratic

thinker, see Richard Ashcraft, *Locke's Two Treatises of Government* (London: Unwin Hyman, 1987); Ian Shapiro, "John Locke's Democratic Theory," in *Two Treatises of Government and A Letter Concerning Toleration,* ed. Ian Shapiro (New Haven: Yale University Press, 2003), 309–340. This interpretation of Locke is controversial. For a very different reading, see John Marshall, *John Locke: Resistance, Religion and Responsibility* (Cambridge: Cambridge University Press, 1994), 216–218.

For the argument that Locke's view on political liberty was, in many ways, closer to Rousseau's than has been recognized, see Christopher Brooke, "'*Locke en particulier les a traitées exactement dans les mêmes principes que moi*': Revisiting the Relationship between Locke and Rousseau," in *Locke's Political Liberty: Readings and Misreadings,* ed. Christopher Miqueu and Mason Chamie (Oxford: Voltaire Foundation, 2009), 69–82. Dan Edelstein points to the similarities between Locke's and Spinoza's theories of natural rights in his *Spirit of Rights,* 46–56.

133. John Locke, *Two Treatises of Government,* ed. Peter Laslett (Cambridge: Cambridge University Press, 1960), 328.

134. Ibid., 284.

135. Ibid., 356, 363.

136. Thomas Hobbes, *Leviathan,* ed. Richard Tuck (Cambridge: Cambridge University Press, 1996), 148.

137. Ibid., 149. See Quentin Skinner, *Hobbes and Republican Liberty* (Cambridge: Cambridge University Press, 2008).

138. Jon Parkin, *Taming the Leviathan: The Reception of the Political and Religious Ideas of Thomas Hobbes in England 1640–1700* (Cambridge: Cambridge University Press, 2007), 364.

139. Robert Filmer, *Patriarcha and Other Political Works,* ed. Peter Laslett (Oxford: Blackwell, 1949), 49.

140. On this new genre and on the *Dictionary of the French Academy* more specifically, see John Considine, *Academy Dictionaries, 1600–1800* (Cambridge: Cambridge University Press, 2014).

141. "Liberté," in *Le Dictionnaire de l'Académie française,* 1st ed. (1694), vol. 1. Accessed through ARTFL.

142. "Liberté," in *Dictionnaire universel, contenant généralement tous les mots français tant vieux que modernes et les termes de toutes les sciences et des arts,* vol. 2: F-O, ed. Antoine Furetière (The Hague and Rotterdam: A. et R. Leers, 1690), 453. On this dictionary, see Considine, *Academy Dictionaries,* 45–50.

143. "Free," in *Cyclopædia, or, An Universal Dictionary of Arts and Sciences,* ed. Ephraim Chambers, 1st ed. (1728), vol. 1. Accessed through ARTFL. On this dictionary, see Considine, *Academy Dictionaries,* 106–108.

144. For a discussion of this image and of the importance of emblem books to the history of freedom more generally, see Skinner, *Hobbes and Republican Liberty,* 70–71.

145. Cesara Ripa, *Iconologia* (Venice: Cristoforo Tomasini, 1645), 375.

146. Quoted in Grześkowiak-Krwawicz, *Queen Liberty,* 53.

147. Lieven de Beaufort, *Verhandeling van de Vryheit in den Burgerstaet* (Leiden: Samuel Luchtmans, 1737), 53. For de Beaufort, see Wyger Velema, *Republicans: Essays on Eighteenth-Century Dutch Political Thought* (Leiden: Brill, 2007), 56–64.

148. "English Bill of Rights 1689," an electronic publication of *The Avalon Project at the Yale Law School: Documents in Law, History and Diplomacy* (New Haven: The Avalon Project, 1996), https://avalon.law.yale.edu/17th_century/england.asp.

149. *English Historical Documents,* vol. 8, *1660–1714,* ed. Andrew Browning (London: Eyre & Spottiswoode, 1953), 129–134.

150. See Caroline Robbins, *The Eighteenth-Century Commonwealthman: Studies in the Transmission, Development and Circumstance of English Liberal Thought from the Restoration of Charles II until the War with the Thirteen Colonies* (Cambridge, MA: Harvard University Press, 1959).

4. Freedom in the Atlantic Revolutions

1. Patrick Henry, "Give Me Liberty or Give Me Death," speech delivered at St. John's Church, Richmond, Virginia, March 23, 1775, https://avalon.law.yale.edu/18th_century/patrick.asp.

2. Jacob Axelrad, *Patrick Henry: The Voice of Freedom* (New York: Random House, 1947), 105–111.

3. The classic overview of the Atlantic Revolutions remains R. R. Palmer's *Age of the Democratic Revolution: A Political History of Europe and America, 1760–1800,* rev. ed. (1959–1964; Princeton, NJ: Princeton University Press, 2014). For more recent overviews that continue the story of the Atlantic Revolutions up until the 1840s, see Manuela Albertone and Antonino de Francesco, eds., *Rethinking the Atlantic World: Europe and America in the Age of Democratic Revolutions* (Basingstoke: Palgrave Macmillan, 2009); David Armitage and Sanjay Subrahmanyam, eds., *The Age of Revolutions in Global Context, c. 1760–1840* (Basingstoke: Palgrave Macmillan, 2009); Janet Polasky, *Revolutions without Borders: The Call to Liberty in the Atlantic World* (New Haven, CT: Yale University Press, 2016); Wim Klooster, *Revolutions in the Atlantic World: A Comparative History* (New York: New York University Press, 2009).

4. For the causes of the Atlantic Revolutions, see Jack Goldstone, *Revolution and Rebellion in the Early Modern World* (Berkeley: University of California Press, 1991); Klooster, *Revolutions in the Atlantic World;* Keith Michael Baker and Dan Edelstein, introduction to *Scripting Revolution: A Historical Approach to the Comparative Study of Revolutions* (Stanford: Stanford University Press, 2015).

5. Katherine Harper, "Cato, Roman Stoicism, and the American 'Revolution'" (PhD diss., University of Sydney, 2014), 167.

6. David Hackett Fisher, *Liberty and Freedom: A Visual History of America's Founding Ideas* (Oxford: Oxford University Press, 2003), 49, 69.

7. About the circulation of revolutionary ideas and slogans more generally in the Atlantic world, see Polasky, *Revolutions without Borders.*

8. Quoted in Sophie Wahnich, *In Defence of the Terror: Liberty or Death in the French Revolution* (London: Verso, 2012), 24.

9. Frans Grijzenhout, "De verbeelding van de vrijheid in de Nederlandse kunst, 1570–1870," in *Vrijheid: Een geschiedenis van de vijftiende tot de twintigste eeuw,* ed. E. O. G. Haitsma Mulier and W. R. E. Velema (Amsterdam: Amsterdam University Press, 1999), 253–286.

10. Anna Grześkowiak-Krwawicz, *Queen Liberty: The Concept of Freedom in the Polish-Lithuanian Commonwealth* (Leiden: Brill, 2012), 112.

11. Jean-Jacques Dessalines, "The Haitian Declaration of Independence," in *Slave Revolution in the Caribbean, 1789–1804: A Brief History with Documents,* trans. and ed. Laurent Dubois and John D. Garrigus (Boston: Bedford: St. Martin's, 2006), 124.

12. Andreas Stolzenburg, "Freiheit oder Tod—ein missverstandenes Werk Jean Baptiste Regnaults?" *Wallraf-Richartz Jahrbuch* 48 / 49 (1987–1988): 463–472.

13. On the enthusiastic reception of Price's treatise, see Carl Cone, *Torchbearer of Freedom: the Influence of Richard Price on Eighteenth Century Thought* (Lexington: University of Kentucky Press, 1952), 69–73.

14. Richard Price, *Political Writings,* ed. D. O. Thomas (Cambridge: Cambridge University Press, 1991), 46.

15. Ibid., 21–23.

16. Ibid., 26.

17. Ibid., 37.

18. Ibid., 26.

19. For a similar reading of the American revolutionaries' conception of freedom, see Eric Foner, *The Story of American Freedom* (New York: W. W. Norton & Company, 1998), 12–28. But compare Yiftah Elazar, "The Liberty Debate: Richard Price and His Critics on Civil Liberty, Free Government, and Democratic Participation" (PhD diss., Princeton University, 2012). Elazar argues that Price's definition of freedom was "unusually democratic for its time"; Elazar, "The Liberty Debate," 5. The interpretation here presented also differs from John P. Reid's, who argues that the colonial Americans had different and more legalistic understandings of freedom as rule of law; Reid, *The Concept of Liberty in the Age of American Revolution* (Chicago: Chicago University Press, 1988).

Surprisingly, there is no book-length study of the French revolutionaries' conception of freedom. Shorter treatments are Gerd van den Heuvel, "Liberté," in *Handbuch politisch-sozialer Grundbegriffe in Frankreich 1680–1820,* ed. Rolf Reichardt and Hans-Jurgen Lusebrink (Munich: Oldenbourg, 1996), 16: 85–121; Mona Ozouf, "Liberty," in *A Critical Dictionary of the French Revolution,* ed. François Furet and Mona Ozouf, trans. Artur Goldhammer (Cambridge, MA: Harvard University Press, 1989), 716–727.

For the Dutch Patriots' conception of freedom, see Wyger Velema, *Republicans: Essays on Eighteenth-Century Dutch Political Thought* (Leiden: Brill, 2007), esp. 139–159. For the revolutionary Poles' conception of freedom, see Grześkowiak-Krwawicz, *Queen Liberty,* chap. 6.

20. Thomas Jefferson, "A Summary View of the Rights of British America (July 1774)," in *Political Writings,* ed. Joyce Appleby and Terence Ball (Cambridge: Cambridge University Press, 2004), 70–71.

21. Quoted in Velema, *Republicans,* 152.

22. Gabriel Bonnot de Mably, *Des droits et des devoirs du citoyen,* ed. Jean-Louis Lecercle (Paris: M. Didier, 1972), 48; my translation. For a discussion of the dissemination of Mably's text in 1789, see Lecercle's introduction to the critical edition.

23. Grześkowiak-Krwawicz, *Queen Liberty,* 113.

24. Price, *Political Writings,* 26.

25. Seth Cotlar, "Languages of Democracy in America from the Revolution to the Election of 1800," in *Re-imagining Democracy in the Age of Revolutions: America, France, Britain, Ireland 1750–1850,* ed. Joanna Innes and Mark Philp (Oxford: Oxford University Press, 2013), 14. For the democratic nature of the American Revolution generally speaking, see Gordon Wood, *The Radicalism of the American Revolution* (New York: Knopf, 1992), 229–304. For the democratic aspirations behind the federal Constitution in particular, see Larry Kramer, *The People Themselves: Popular Constitutionalism and Judicial Review* (Oxford: Oxford University Press, 2004). Note that this view is contested. For the argument that the Federal Constitution attempted to enshrine elite rule, see, for instance, Michael Klarman, *The Framers' Coup: The Making of the United States Constitution* (Oxford: Oxford University Press, 2016).

26. Quoted in Cotlar, "Languages of Democracy," 23.

27. Alexander Hamilton, James Madison, and John Jay, *The Federalist Papers,* ed. Lawrence Goldman (Oxford: Oxford University Press, 2008), 52. See, for a similar definition of "republic," *The Federalist Papers,* 188.

28. Palmer, *Age of Democratic Revolution,* 252.

29. Grześkowiak-Krwawicz, *Queen Liberty,* 102–103.

30. Emmanuel Joseph Sieyès, "The Debate between Sieyès and Tom Paine," in *Political Writings: Including the Debate between Sieyès and Tom Paine in 1791,* ed. Michael Sonenscher (Indianapolis: Hackett, 2003), 163–173.

31. Pierre Rosanvallon, "The History of the Word 'Democracy' in France," *Journal of Democracy* 6, no. 4 (1995): 140–154; Ruth Scurr, "Varieties of Democracy in the French Revolution," in Innes and Philp, *Re-imagining Democracy,* 57–68.

32. Palmer, *The Age of the Democratic Revolution.*

33. There is lively debate about the extent to which the American revolutionaries can be characterized as Harringtonians in the sense that, like Harrington, they defended redistributive measures. According to Gordon Wood, the American revolutionaries made some nods toward Harringtonianism but almost completely abandoned it after 1776. Wood, *The Creation of the American Republic, 1776–1787* (Chapel Hill: University of North Carolina Press, 1998), 89. By contrast, Eric Nelson shows that Harringtonianism had a much longer influence. Nelson, *The Greek Tradition in Republican Thought* (Cambridge: Cambridge University Press, 2006), 195–233. However, Nelson maintains that the American founding fathers propagated redistributive measures "only in the service of explicitly hierarchical ends." As he argues, they "advocated the redistribution of wealth so that they could institute and preserve a particular structure of rulership: a structure in which a few elect, virtuous men rule, and all the rest are ruled." By contrast, this author agrees with Stanley N. Katz, who argues that the revolutionary revision of the inheritance laws was propelled by egalitarian republicanism. See Katz, "Republicanism and the Law of Inheritance in the American Revolutionary Era," *Michigan Law Review* 76, no. 1 (1977): 1–29.

34. Noah Webster, *Sketches of American Policy* (Hartford: Hudson and Goodwin, 1785), 18.

35. Carole Shammas et al., *Inheritance in America: From Colonial Times to the Present* (New Brunswick, NJ: Rutgers University Press, 1987), Table 1.1.

36. Quoted in Katz, "Republicanism and the Law of Inheritance," 15.

37. Shammas, *Inheritance in America,* Table 3.1.

38. Quoted in Katz, "Republicanism and the Law of Inheritance," 14.

39. Quoted in ibid., 14.

40. Johnson Kent Wright, *A Classical Republican in Eighteenth-Century France: The Political Thought of Mably* (Stanford: Stanford University Press, 1997), 94–109. For the point that Mably's inspiration for these ideas was Harringtonian, see Michael Sonenscher, "Republicanism, State Finances and the Emergence of Commercial Society in Eighteenth-Century France—or from Royal to Ancient Republicanism and Back," in *Republicanism: A Shared European Heritage,* vol. 2, *The Values of Republicanism in Early Modern Europe,* ed. Quentin Skinner and Martin van Gelderen (Cambridge: Cambridge University Press, 2002), 278.

41. Quoted in M. Darrow, *Revolution in the House: Family, Class, and Inheritance in Southern France, 1775–1825* (Princeton: Princeton University Press, 2014), 6–7.

42. Quoted in Katz, "Republicanism and the Law of Inheritance," 22–23.

43. Darrow, *Revolution in the House,* 3–19. For a discussion of Jacobin inheritance laws, see also J. Gross, *Fair Shares for All: Jacobin Egalitarianism in Practice* (Cambridge: Cambridge University Press, 1996), chap. 4.

44. Rose, "The 'Red Scare' of the 1790s," 113.

45. S. Peabody, "Slavery, Freedom, and the Law in the Atlantic World, 1420–1807," in *The Cambridge World History of Slavery,* vol. 3, *AD 1420–AD 1804,* ed. D. Eltis and S. Engerman (Cambridge: Cambridge University Press, 2011), 594–630; E. Melton, "Manorialism and Rural Subjection in East Central Europe, 1500–1800," in Eltis and Engerman, *World History of Slavery,* 3: 297–322.

46. Samuel Johnson, *Taxation no Tyranny; an Answer to the Resolutions and Address of the American Congress* (London: T. Cadell1775), 89.

47. Quoted in Helena Rosenblatt, *The Lost History of Liberalism* (Princeton, NJ: Princeton University Press, 2018), 37–38.

48. But compare Edmund Morgan, who argues that many white Americans' daily experience with slavery reinforced their attachment to their own freedom: "Slavery may not have turned Virginians into republicans, but they may have had a special appreciation of freedom dear to republicans, because they saw every day what life could be without it." Morgan, *American Slavery, American Freedom* (New York and London: W. W. Norton, 1975), 376.

49. Quoted in Foner, *Story of American Freedom,* 32.

50. Quoted in Rosenblatt, *Liberalism,* 38.

51. Wood, *Radicalism of the American Revolution,* 186.

52. Foner, *Story of American Freedom,* 35.

53. James T. Kloppenberg, *Toward Democracy: The Struggle for Self-Rule in European and American Thought* (Oxford: Oxford University Press, 2016), 360.

54. Jean-Daniel Piquet, *L'émancipation des noirs dans la Révolution française (1789–1795)* (Paris: Karthala, 2002); Jeremy Popkin, *You Are All Free: The Haitian Revolution and the Abolition of Slavery* (Cambridge: Cambridge University Press, 2010).

55. Foner, *Story of American Freedom,* 37.

56. Quoted in ibid., 35.

57. Klooster, *Revolutions in the Atlantic World,* 84–116; Kwame Nimako and Glenn Willemsen, *The Dutch Atlantic: Slavery, Abolition and Emancipation* (London: Pluto Press; 2011), chap. 4.

58. For these numbers, see Melvin Edelstein, *The French Revolution and the Birth of Electoral Democracy* (Farnham: Ashgate, 2014), 67–73; Donald Ratcliffe, "The Right to Vote and the Rise of Democracy, 1787–1828," *Journal of the Early Republic* 33, no. 2 (2013): 230.

59. Quoted in Mart Rutjes, *Door gelijkheid gegrepen: democratie, burgerschap en staat in Nederland, 1795–1801* (PhD diss., University of Amsterdam, 2012), 172; my translation.

60. Edelstein, *Birth of Electoral Democracy,* 43–74.

61. Ralph Ketcham, *The Anti-Federalist Papers and the Constitutional Convention Debates* (Harmondsworth, UK: Penguin, 2003), 146.

62. Olympe de Gouges, *Les droits de la femme. À la Reine* (Paris, 1791). I have used the translation in *The French Revolution and Human Rights: A Brief Documentary History,* trans. and ed. Lynn Hunt (Boston: Bedford Books of St. Martin's Press, 1996), 124–129.

63. Eveline Koolhaas-Grosfeld, "Voor man en maatschappij: Over vrouwen in de Bataafse Tijd," in *Het Bataafse experiment: Politiek en cultuur rond 1800,*" ed. Frans Grijzenhout, Wyger Velema, and Niek van Sas (Nijmegen: Uitgeverij Vantilt, 2015), 100.

64. Edelstein, *Birth of Electoral Democracy,* 48.

65. Ketcham, *Constitutional Convention Debates,* 154

66. Edelstein, *Birth of Electoral Democracy,* 58–64.

67. Wood, *The Radicalism of the American Revolution.*

68. For the classical inspiration of the American revolutionaries, see John Pocock, *The Machiavellian Moment: Florentine Political Thought and the Atlantic Republican Tradition* (Princeton, NJ: Princeton University Press, 1975), 506–552. Note that Pocock argues that the American Revolution took a different and anticlassical turn in the 1780s. More recent literature, however, has abundantly documented the continuing impact of classical ideas and examples on American political actors until well into the early nineteenth century. See, in particular, Carl J. Richard, *The Founders and the Classics: Greece, Rome, and the American Enlightenment* (Cambridge, MA: Harvard University Press, 1994). See also Meyer Reinhold, *Classica Americana: The Greek and Roman Heritage in the United States* (Detroit: Wayne State University Press, 1984); Margaret Malamud, *Ancient Rome and Modern America* (Malden, MA: Wiley-Blackwell, 2009); M. N. S. Sellers, *American Republicanism: Roman Ideology in the United States Constitution* (New York: New York University Press, 1994); David J. Bederman, *The Classical Foundations of the American Constitution: Prevailing Wisdom* (Cambridge: Cambridge University Press, 2008); Gordon Wood, *The Idea of America: Reflections on the Birth of the United States* (New York: Penguin Books, 2011), 57–79; Eran Shalev, *Rome Reborn on Western Shores: Historical Imagination and the Creation of the American Republic* (Charlottesville: University of Virginia Press, 2009).

For the influence of antiquity in the Dutch Patriot Revolution, see Wyger Velema, "Conversations with the Classics: Ancient Political Virtue and Two Modern Revolutions," *Early American Studies: An Interdisciplinary Journal* 10, no. 2 (2012): 415–438; S. R. E. Klein, *Patriots Republikanisme. Politieke cultuur in Nederland (1766–1787)*

(Amsterdam: Amsterdam University Press, 1995); N. C. F. van Sas, *De metamorfose van Nederland. Van oude orde naar moderniteit, 1750–1900* (Amsterdam: Amsterdam University Press, 2004), 129–143; Wyger Velema, *Omstreden Oudheid. De Nederlandse achttiende eeuw en de klassieke politiek* (Amsterdam: Amsterdam University Press, 2010).

For the influence of the classics on the French Revolution, the standard work remains Harold T. Parker's *The Cult of Antiquity and the French Revolutionaries: A Study in the Development of the Revolutionary Spirit* (New York: Octagon Books, 1965). More recent works include Jacques Bouineau, *Les toges du pouvoir, ou la Révolution de droit antique* (Toulouse: Association des Publications de l'Université de Toulouse-le Mirail et Editions Eché, 1986); Claude Mossé, *L'Antiquité dans la Révolution française* (Paris: Albin Michel, 1989); and Chantal Grell, *Le dix-huitième siècle et l'antiquité en France: 1680–1789* (Oxford: Voltaire Foundation, 1995). Grell ends her exhaustive study, somewhat surprisingly, before the outbreak of the Revolution.

Note that some scholars, despite the overwhelming evidence of classical influence on the Atlantic Revolutions, continue to describe these exclusively as "Enlightenment" Revolutions. See, for instance, J. Israel, *The Expanding Blaze: How the American Revolution Ignited the World, 1775–1848* (Princeton, NJ: Princeton University Press, 2017).

69. Carl J. Richard, *The Founders and the Classics: Greece, Rome, and the American Enlightenment* (Cambridge, MA: Harvard University Press, 1994), 232. For the classical education of the Atlantic revolutionaries, see Philip Ayres, *Classical Culture and the Idea of Rome in Eighteenth-Century England* (Cambridge: Cambridge University Press, 1997); Caroline Winterer, *The Culture of Classicism: Ancient Greece and Rome in American Intellectual Life, 1780–1910* (Baltimore: Johns Hopkins University Press, 2002); and Harold Parker, *The Cult of Antiquity and the French Revolutionaries: A Study in the Development of the Revolutionary Spirit* (New York: Octagon Books, 1965), chap. 1.

70. Hackett Fisher, *Liberty and Freedom,* 37–46. About the appearance of the liberty cap in revolutionary America, see Yvonne Korshak, "The Liberty Cap as a Revolutionary Symbol in America and France," *Smithsonian Studies in American Art* 1, no. 2 (1987): 52–69.

71. Maurice Agulhon, *Marianne au combat. L'imagerie et la symbolique républicaines de 1789 à 1880* (Paris: Flammarion, 1979), 28; Parker, *Cult of Antiquity,* 140; Richard Wrigley, "Transformations of a Revolutionary Emblem: The Liberty Cap in the French Revolution," *French History* 11, no. 2 (1997): 131–169; and Annie Jourdan, "L'allégorie révolutionnaire de la liberté à la république," *Dix-huitième siècle,* no. 27 (1995): 503–532.

72. Malamud, *Ancient Rome and Modern America,* 10. For the reception of Addison's play in America, see Albert Furtwangler, "Cato at Valley Forge," *Modern Language Quarterly* 41, no. 1 (1980): 38–53; Frederic M. Litto, "Addison's *Cato* in the Colonies," *William and Mary Quarterly* 23, no. 3 (1966): 431–449; and Harper, "Cato, Roman Stoicism, and the American 'Revolution.'"

73. Litto, "Addison's *Cato.*"

74. Quoted in Richard, *Founders and the Classics,* 74.

75. Ibid., 108.

76. About the political impact of Voltaire's *Brutus,* see Robert L. Herbert, *David, Voltaire, "Brutus," and the French Revolution: An Essay in Art and Politics* (London: Allen Lane, 1972); Denise Baxter, "Two Brutuses: Violence, Virtue, and Politics in the Visual Culture of the French Revolution," *Eighteenth-Century Life* 30, no. 3 (2006): 51–77.

77. Quoted in Herbert, *David, Voltaire, "Brutus," and the French Revolution,* 13.

78. Ibid., 15.

79. Ibid., 88.

80. Ibid., 74.

81. Quoted in Baxter, "Two Brutuses," 63.

82. Quoted in W. Percival, "Greek and Roman History in the French Revolution," *Classical Review* (1963): 157.

83. John Adams, *Thoughts on Government: Applicable to the Present State of the American Colonies. In a Letter from a Gentleman to his Friend* (Philadelphia: John Dunlap, 1776).

84. Shalev, *Rome Reborn,* 151–187.

85. Richard, *Founders and the Classics,* 232–233. But compare Wilfred Nippel's argument that American revolutionaries, in fact, made a clear break with ancient models in both practical and theoretical constitutional matters. Nippel, *Ancient and Modern Democracy: Two Concepts of Liberty?,* trans. K. Tribe (Cambridge: Cambridge University Press, 2016), 144.

86. Parker, *Cult of Antiquity,* 84.

87. Ibid., 147.

88. But compare Nippel, *Ancient and Modern Democracy,* 148–203. According to Nippel, "there was really no serious attempt in France to further the introduction of ancient models"; by contrast, "there was far more emphasis upon an identification with ancient role models of civic virtue than with any effort to replicate institutions." Quoted on 148 and 178.

89. Quoted in Velema, "Conversations with the Classics," 197.

90. Friedrich Schlegel, "Essay on the Concept of Republicanism Occasioned by the Kantian Tract 'Perpetual Peace,'" in *The Early Political Writings of the German Romantics,* ed. Frederick Beiser (Cambridge: Cambridge University Press, 1996), 103–104.

91. Quoted in Reinhold, *Classica Americana,* 25.

92. Quoted in Nippel, *Ancient and Modern Democracy,* 162.

93. Hamilton, Madison, and Jay, *The Federalist Papers,* 44–45.

94. For the Battle of the Books, see Larry Norman, *The Shock of the Ancient: Literature and History in Early Modern France* (Chicago: University of Chicago Press, 2011). For the impact of this debate on political thought, see Annelien de Dijn, "Political and Social Thought: Montesquieu, Voltaire, Diderot, Rousseau, Raynal," in *The Cambridge History of French Thought, Part I: To 1789,* ed. Jeremy Jennings and Michael Moriarty, (Cambridge: Cambridge University Press, 2019), 241–248.

95. Jean-Jacques Rousseau, *The Social Contract and Other Later Political Writings,* ed. and trans. Victor Gourevitch (Cambridge: Cambridge University Press, 1997), 114–115.

96. Price, *Political Writings,* 24.

97. Ibid., 25.

98. Hamilton, Madison, and Jay, *The Federalist Papers,* 68.

99. Ibid., 53.

100. Ibid.

101. Ibid., 176.

102. Nicolas de Condorcet, *Political Writings,* ed. Steven Lukes and Nadia Urbinati (Cambridge: Cambridge University Press, 2012), 36, 166. For Condorcet's vision of representative democracy, see Nadia Urbinati, *Representative Democracy: Principles and Genealogy* (Chicago: University of Chicago Press, 2006), 176–222.

103. J. G. A. Pocock, *Virtue, Commerce, and History: Essays on Political Thought and History, Chiefly in the Eighteenth Century* (Cambridge: Cambridge University Press, 1976), 20.

104. Agulhon, *Marianne au combat.*

105. For a classic elaboration of this view, see Louis Hartz, *The Liberal Tradition in America: An Interpretation of American Political Thought Since the Revolution* (New York: Harcourt, Brace and World, 1955). For more recent restatements, see Isaac Kramnick, *Republicanism and Bourgeois Radicalism: Political Ideology in Late Eighteenth-Century England and America* (Ithaca, London: Cornell University Press, 1990); Joyce Appleby, *Liberalism and Republicanism in the Historical Imagination* (Cambridge, MA: Harvard University Press, 1992); and James P. Young, *Reconsidering American Liberalism: The Troubled Odyssey of the Liberal Idea* (Boulder: Westview Press, 1996). The "Lockean" interpretation of the American Revolution has been contested by scholars arguing that American revolutionaries were, in fact, more influenced by the early modern republican tradition. The most influential statements of this view are by Gordon S. Wood, *The Creation of the American Republic, 1776–1787* (Chapel Hill: University of North Carolina Press, 1969) and J. G. A. Pocock, *The Machiavellian Moment: Florentine Political Thought and the Atlantic Republican Tradition* (Princeton, NJ: Princeton University Press, 1975). Today, most historians of the American founding argue that the revolutionaries were influenced by both traditions simultaneously. For the forging of this new consensus, see Alan Gibson, "Ancients, Moderns and Americans: The Republicanism-Liberalism Debate Revisited," *History of Political Thought* 21, no. 2 (2000): 261–307.

106. For this argument, see, in particular, Appleby's and Kramnick's work, as well as Eric MacGilvray, *The Invention of Market Freedom* (Cambridge: Cambridge University Press, 2011).

107. See Chapter 3.

108. Price, *Political Writings,* 20. But compare Dan Edelstein, *On the Spirit of Rights* (Chicago: Chicago University Press, 2019), chap. 6. Edelstein acknowledges that Locke's view on rights was close to Rousseau's, but he argues that the American revolutionaries ruptured with Locke and adopted a more libertarian understanding of rights.

109. Josiah Tucker, *A Treatise Concerning Civil Government in Three Parts* (London: T. Cadell, 1781), 39.

110. Quoted in James Moore, "Natural Rights in the Scottish Enlightenment," in *The Cambridge History of Eighteenth-Century Political Thought,* ed. Mark Goldie and Robert Wokler (Cambridge: Cambridge University Press, 2006), 315.

111. Jack Rakove, ed., *Declaring Rights: A Brief History with Documents* (Boston: Bedford Books, 1998), 65. Many of the newly founded American states also drew up declarations

of rights; those of Virginia, Pennsylvania, and Massachusetts all proclaimed the right of the people to govern themselves.

112. Wood, *Creation of the American Republic,* 609. For a more recent restatement of this view, see Jack Rakove, "Parchment Barriers and the Bill of Rights," in *A Culture of Rights: The Bill of Rights in Philosophy, Politics and Law—1791 and 1991,* ed. Michael Lacey and Knud Haakonssen (Cambridge: Cambridge University Press, 1991), 102.

113. Quoted in Paul Finkelman, "James Madison and the Bill of Rights: A Reluctant Paternity," *The Supreme Court Review* 9, no. 301 (1990): 312.

114. Hamilton, Madison, and Jay, *The Federalist Papers,* 420.

115. Ketcham, *Constitutional Convention Debates,* 245.

116. Rakove, *Declaring Rights,* 143. It should be noted that not all Antifederalists were democrats; thus George Mason and Elbridge Gerry, two of the earliest and most prominent Antifederalists, had expressed their deep mistrust about popular involvement prior to and during the Constitutional Convention. They and other Antifederalists were opposed to the federal constitution precisely because it would undercut the prominence of local or state elites and compromise their own authority. However, overall the Antifederalists couched their opposition to the federal constitution in democratic terms. See Kloppenberg, *Toward Democracy,* 414.

117. Quoted in Rakove, *Declaring Rights,* 161.

118. Quoted in ibid., 176–177.

119. Quoted in ibid., 175. For Madison's lack of enthusiasm for a bill of rights, see Finkelman, "James Madison and the Bill of Rights,"301–347.

120. Hamilton, Madison, and Jay, *The Federalist Papers,* 54. See Greg Weiner, "James Madison and the Legitimacy of Majority Factions," *American Political Thought* 2, no. 2 (2013): 198–216. For Madison's commitment to republican liberty more generally, see Lance Banning, *The Sacred Fire of Liberty: James Madison and the Founding of the Federal Republic* (Ithaca: Cornell University Press, 1998), 216. For the debate about the tyranny of the majority during the American Revolution more generally, see Annelien de Dijn, "Republicanism and Democracy: The Tyranny of the Majority in 18th-century Political Debate," in *Republicanism and the Future of Democracy,* ed. Yiftah Elazar and Geneviève Rousselière (Cambridge: Cambridge University Press, 2019) 59–74.

121. See Michael Zuckert, *The Natural Rights Republic: Studies in the Foundation of the American Political Tradition* (Notre Dame, IN: University of Notre Dame Press, 1996).

122. On the framing of the 1789 Declaration, see Stephane Rials, *La déclaration des droits de l'homme et du citoyen* (Paris: Hachette, 1988), 115–320.

123. *Archives Parlementaires,* ed. J. Mavidal, E. Laurent, and E. Clavel, 82 vols. (Paris, 1872–1913), vol. 8, 438–439.

124. Ibid., 439; my translation.

125. Ibid.; my translation.

126. For the view that the Declaration was an essentially Rousseauvian document, see François Furet, *The French Revolution 1770–1814,* trans. Antonia Nevill (Oxford, Malden, MA: Blackwell, 1992), 74. Note, however, that according to Furet, this Rousseauvian character of the French Declaration served to distinguish it from the American rights declarations that were supposedly more libertarian, a view with which this author disagrees. It should also be noted that most scholars see the Declaration as more ambig-

uous, combining both a libertarian defense of individual rights and more Rousseau-vian elements. See, for instance, Rials, *La déclaration,* 321–474; Philippe Raynaud, "La déclaration des droits de l'homme et du citoyen," in *The French Revolution and the cre-ation of Modern Political Culture,* vol. 2, *The Political Culture of the French Revolu-tion,* ed. Keith M. Baker and Colin Lucas (Oxford: Pergamon Press, 1988), 139–149. Note that this debate is complicated by the question of the relation between the Dec-laration's Rousseauvianism and the Terror. According to Furet and other revisionist historians such as Keith Baker, the embrace of Rousseauvian concepts, such as the gen-eral will, was at least partly responsible for the revolution's descent into violence from 1793 to 1794. See Baker, *Inventing the French Revolution: Essays on French Political Culture in the Eighteenth Century* (Cambridge: Cambridge University Press, 1990), 305. This view, however, has been rejected in more recent accounts of the Terror. For an overview of this debate, see Jack Censer, "Historians Revisit the Terror—Again," *Journal of Social History* 48, no. 2 (2014): 383–403.

127. Edmund Burke, *Select Works of Edmund Burke,* vol. 2, *Reflections on the Revolution in France* (Indianapolis: Liberty Fund, 1999), 150–151.

128. Gregory Claeys, *Thomas Paine: Social and Political Thought* (Boston: Unwin Hyman, 1989), 112.

129. Thomas Paine, *Collected Writings,* ed. Eric Foner (New York: The Library of Amer-ica, 1995), 538.

130. James Mackintosh, *Vindiciae Gallicae and Other Writings on the French Revolution,* ed. Donald Winch (Indianapolis: Liberty Fund, 2006), 98.

131. Ibid., 94.

132. Jeremy Bentham, *The Works of Jeremy Bentham,* ed. John Bowring (Edinburgh: Wil-liam Tait, 1843), 2: 501, 522. For date of the treatise, see J. H. Burns, *Bentham and the French Revolution* (London: Royal Historical Society, 1966), 16: 111, n. 2.

133. De Gouges, *Les droits de la femme,* 5; my translation.

134. Quoted in Karen Offen, *European Feminisms, 1700–1950: A Political History,* 65.

135. For this debate, see Lynn Hunt, *Inventing Human Rights: A History* (New York: W. W. Norton, 2007), 146–175 and Samuel Moyn, "On the Nonglobalization of Ideas," in *Global Intellectual History,* ed. Samuel Moyn and Andrew Sartori (New York: Co-lumbia University Press, 2013).

5. Inventing Modern Liberty

1. Johann August Eberhard, "Ueber die Freyheit des Bürgers und die Principien der Regierungsformen," in *Vermischte Schriften. Erster Theil* (Halle: Johann Jacob Ge-bauer, 1784), 1–28. On Eberhard's essay and its reception, see Simone Zurbuchen, "Theorizing Enlightened Absolutism: The Swiss Republican Origins of Prussian Monarchism," in *Monarchisms in the Age of Enlightenment: Liberty, Patriotism, and the Common Good,* ed. Hans W. Blom, John Christian Laursen, Luisa Simonutti (To-ronto: University of Toronto Press, 2007), 240–266.

2. Horst Dippel, *Germany and the American Revolution, 1770–1800: A Sociohistorical In-vestigation of Late Eighteenth-Century Political Thinking,* trans. Bernhard A. Uhlen-dorf (Wiesbaden: Steiner, 1978), 90–91, quote on 311.

3. See Chapter 3.

4. Eberhard, "Ueber die Freyheit des Bürgers," 7.

5. Ibid., 26.

6. William Wordsworth, *Poems of William Wordsworth,* vol. 2, *Collected Reading Texts from the Cornell Wordsworth,* ed. Jared Curtis (Penrith: Humanities-Ebooks, LLP, 2009), 204, 174.

7. On British responses to the American Revolution, see Eliga H. Gould, *The Persistence of Empire: British Political Culture in the Age of the American Revolution* (Chapel Hill: University of North Carolina Press, 2000), 148–180. For the French counterrevolution: Jacques Godechot, *La Contre-Révolution. Doctrine et action. 1789–1804* (Paris: Presses Universitaires de France, 1984). For the Dutch Orangists, see Wyger Velema, *Republicans: Essays on Eighteenth-Century Dutch Political Thought* (Brill: Leiden, 2007), 159–178.

8. Bee Wilson, "Counter-Revolutionary Thought," in *The Cambridge History of Nineteenth-Century Political Thought,* ed. Gareth Stedman Jones and Gregory Claeys (Cambridge: Cambridge University Press, 2011), 30.

9. Quoted in Marc. A. Goldstein, *The People in French Counter-Revolutionary Thought* (New York: Peter Lang, 1988), 89.

10. See Yiftah Elazar, "The Liberty Debate: Richard Price and His Critics on Civil Liberty, Free Government, and Democratic Participation" (PhD diss., Princeton University, 2012).

11. John Wesley, *Some Observations on Liberty: Occasioned by a Late Tract* (Edinburgh, 1776), 4–5.

12. Adam Ferguson, *Remarks on a Pamphlet Lately Published by Dr. Price* (London: T. Cadell, 1776), 8, 13.

13. Quoted in Velema, *Republicans,* 156.

14. See Isser Woloch, "The Contraction and Expansion of Democratic Space During the Period of the Terror," in *The French Revolution and the Creation of Modern Political Culture,* vol. 4, *The Terror,* ed. K. M. Baker (Oxford: Pergamon, 1994), 309–325; Marisa Linton, "Terror and Politics," in *The Oxford Handbook of the French Revolution,* ed. David Andress (Oxford: Oxford University Press, 2015), 471–486.

15. Historians still debate the exact causes of the derailment of the French Revolution into the Terror. An influential interpretation, elaborated by Marxist historians such as Albert Mathiez, attributes the Terror to circumstances: war and civil strife forced the Jacobins to defend the revolutionary gains against its enemies and they used (justified) violence to do so, as a necessary evil. In the 1980s, a new school emerged, of whom François Furet is the most notable proponent, explaining the Terror as the result of the democratizing tendencies of the revolution. In the most recent work on the Terror, however, this revisionist (and, as some have argued, counterrevolutionary) interpretation has been rejected; instead, historians such as Sophie Wahnich in her *In Defence of the Terror: Liberty or Death in the French Revolution* (London: Verso, 2012) have depicted the Terror as neither the necessary outcome of the French Revolution nor a policy of arbitrary violence and intimidation. Rather, it was a conscious attempt to defend the revolution and contain and control outbursts of popular violence. For an overview of the literature, see Jack

Censer, "Historians Revisit the Terror—Again," *Journal of Social History* 48, no. 2 (2014): 383–403.

16. Quoted in G. P. Gooch, *Germany and the French Revolution* (London: Longmans, Green, 1920), 269.

17. Wordsworth, *Poems of William Wordsworth*, 640. For the influence of the Terror on Wordsworth, see Emma Mason, "Life," in *The Cambridge Introduction to William Wordsworth* (Leiden: Cambridge University Press, 2010), 16–19. For the effect of the Terror on British political debate more generally, see Mark Philp, *Reforming Ideas in Britain: Politics and Language in the Shadow of the French Revolution, 1789–1815* (Cambridge: Cambridge University Press, 2013), 40–70.

18. Jean-Louis Darcel, "The Roads of Exile, 1792–1817," in *Joseph de Maistre's Life, Thought, and Influence: Selected Studies,* ed. Richard A. Lebrun (Montreal: McGill-Queen's University Press, 2001), 15–31.

19. Joseph de Maistre, *The Pope, Considered in His Relations with the Church: Temporal Sovereignties, Separated Churches, and the Cause of Civilization,* trans. Aeneas Dawson (London: C. Dolman, 1850), 237–245.

20. Johan Meerman, *De burgerlyke vryheid in haare heilzaame, de volks-vryheid in haare schadelyke gevolgen voorgesteld* (Leiden: Luchtmans, 1793), 42; my translation. On Meerman's treatise in the context of 1780s Dutch debate about freedom, see Velema, *Republicans*, 42.

21. Antoine de Ferrand, *Théorie des révolutions, rapprochée des principaux événemens qui en ont été l'origine, le développement ou la suite; avec une table générale et analytique,* 4 vols. (Paris: Michaud, 1817), 2: 206–230.

22. A. Creuzé de Lesser, *De la liberté* (Paris : L.G. Michaud, 1832), 126; my translation.

23. Edmund Burke, *Reflections on the Revolution in France and on the Proceedings in Certain Societies in London Relative to That Event* (Cambridge: Cambridge University Press, 2014), 7, 36.

24. For example, *Civil Liberty Asserted, and the Rights of the Subject Defended, against the Anarchical Principles of the Reverend Dr. Price* (London: J. Wilkie, 1776).

25. Quoted in Elazar, "The Liberty Debate," 89.

26. Ferguson, *Remarks on a Pamphlet,* 4.

27. *Civil Liberty Asserted,* 20–21.

28. Meerman, *De burgerlyke vryheid,* 16.

29. John Shebbeare, *An Essay on the Origin, Progress and Establishment of National Society, in Which the Principles of Government, the Definitions of Physical, Moral, Civil, and Religious Liberty Contained in Dr. Price's Observations, are Fairly Examined and Fully Refuted* (London: J. Bew, 1776), 32.

30. Edmund Burke, *Further Reflections on the Revolution in France,* ed. Daniel E. Ritchie (Indianapolis: Liberty Fund, 1992), 195.

31. Quoted in Zurbuchen, "Theorizing Enlightened Absolutism," 254–258.

32. Thomas Paine, *Collected Writings* (New York: Library of America, 1995), 434, 471.

33. Richard Price, *Political Writings,* ed. D. O. Thomas (Cambridge: Cambridge University Press, 1991), 83–84.

34. "Liberté," in *Le Dictionnaire de l'Académie française,* 1st ed. (1694), vol. 1. Accessed through ARTFL.

35. "Liberté," in *Le Dictionnaire de l'Académie française*, 5th ed. (1798). Accessed through ARTFL.

36. For the politics of the Restoration, see Robin Winks and Joan Neuberger, *Europe and the Making of Modernity, 1815–1914* (New York: Oxford University Press, 2005), 11–40.

37. Malcolm Crook, "Elections and Democracy in France, 1789–1848", in *Re-imagining Democracy in the Age of Revolutions: America, France, Britain, Ireland 1750–1850*, ed. Joanna Innes and Mark Philp (Oxford: Oxford University Press, 2013), 83–100.

38. For the wholesale suppression of revolutionary movements and ideas in this period, see Adam Zamoyski, *Phantom Terror: Political Paranoia and the Creation of the Modern State, 1789–1848* (New York: Basic Books, 2015).

39. On the changing meanings of "liberal" and "liberalism," see Helena Rosenblatt, *The Lost History of Liberalism* (Princeton, NJ: Princeton University Press, 2018). For the characterization of nineteenth-century liberals as defenders of a "third way" between Jacobinism and Restoration, see Alan Kahan, *Liberalism in Nineteenth-Century Europe: The Political Culture of Limited Suffrage* (Basingstoke: Palgrave Macmillan, 2003), 3.

40. Ibid.

41. For an extensive analysis of the debate about freedom in post-revolutionary France, see Annelien de Dijn, *French Political Thought from Montesquieu to Tocqueville: Liberty in a Levelled Society* (Cambridge: Cambridge University Press, 2008).

42. K. Steven Vincent, *Benjamin Constant and the Birth of French Liberalism* (New York: Palgrave Macmillan, 2011), 33.

43. For the reception of Constant's thought: Helena Rosenblatt, "Eclipses and Revivals: Constant's Reception in France and America 1830–2007," in *The Cambridge Companion to Constant,* ed. Helena Rosenblatt (Cambridge: Cambridge University Press, 2009), 351–378.

44. Benjamin Constant, *Principles of Politics Applicable to All Governments,* ed. Etienne Hofmann, trans. Dennis O'Keeffe, introd. Nicholas Capaldi (Indianapolis: Liberty Fund, 2003), 386. For 1806 as a turning point in Constant's intellectual career, see Etienne Hofmann, *Les "Principes de politique" de Benjamin Constant,* vol. 1, *La genèse d'une oeuvre et l'évolution de la pensée de leur auteur (1789–1806)* (Geneva: Droz, 1980), 93, 100, 119, 161; Helena Rosenblatt, *Liberal Values; Benjamin Constant and the Politics of Religion* (Cambridge: Cambridge University Press, 2008). But compare Vincent, *Constant,* who puts more emphasis on the continuity in Constant's intellectual trajectory.

45. Benjamin Constant, *Political Writings,* ed. Biancamaria Fontana (Cambridge: Cambridge University Press, 1988), 316. For Constant's defense of modern liberty, see Jeremy Jennings, "Constant's Idea of Modern Liberty," in Rosenblatt, *Cambridge Companion to Constant,* 69–91.

46. Ibid., 113.

47. Ibid., 176.

48. Benjamin Constant, *Commentary on Filangieri's Work,* trans. and ed. Alan S. Kahan (Indianapolis: Liberty Fund, 2015), 261.

49. See Chapter 4.

50. Ibid., 32. Note that Constant did recognize the principle of the sovereignty of the people, but this simply meant, in his view, that governments were always based, to some

extent, on popular consent—and that was true of all governments not based exclusively on force. "Theocracy, royalty, aristocracy, whenever they rule men's minds, are simply the general will," he wrote. "When, on the other hand, they fail to rule them, they are nothing but force." Constant, *Political Writings*, 175.

51. Germaine de Staël, *Considerations on the Principal Events of the French Revolution, Newly Revised Translation of the 1818 English Edition*, ed., annot., and introd. Aurelian Craiutu (Indianapolis: Liberty Fund, 2008), 343.

52. Staël, *Considerations*, 659, 725.

53. François Guizot, *The History of the Origins of Representative Government in Europe*, trans. Andrew R. Scoble, introd. Aurelian Craiutu (Indianapolis: Liberty Fund, 2002), 334. On Guizot's elitist liberalism, see Aurelian Craiutu, *Liberalism under Siege: The Political Thought of the French Doctrinaires* (Lanham: Lexington Books, 2003), 123–147.

54. Constant, *Political Writings*, 327.

55. For the changing political context in which Constant wrote, see Stephen Holmes, *Benjamin Constant and the Making of Modern Liberalism* (New Haven, CT: Yale University Press, 1984).

56. But compare Bryan Garsten, "Liberalism and the Rhetorical Vision of Politics," *Journal of the History of Ideas* 73, no. 1 (2012): 83–93. Garsten argues that Benjamin Constant was the intellectual heir of early modern republicanism, not its critic. For the argument that the liberal movement, more generally, must be seen as the heir of early modern republicanism, see Andreas Kalyvas and Ira Katznelson, *Liberal Beginnings: Making a Republic for the Moderns* (Cambridge: Cambridge University Press, 2008); Andrew Jainchill, *Reimagining Politics after the Terror: The Republican Origins of French Liberalism* (Ithaca: Cornell University Press, 2008).

57. J. P. T. Bury, *France: 1814–1940*, intro. Robert Tombs (London: Routledge, 2003), 31–33.

58. Albert Boime, *Art in an Age of Counterrevolution (1815–1848)* (Chicago: University of Chicago Press, 2004), 237–263.

59. Ibid., 252.

60. Albert Boime, *Art in an Age of Civil Struggle, 1848–1871* (Chicago: University of Chicago Press, 2007), 16.

61. Alexis de Tocqueville, *Democracy in America: Historical-Critical Edition of De La démocratie en Amérique*, 4 vols., ed. Eduardo Nolla, trans. James T. Schleifer (Indianapolis: Liberty Fund, 2010), 2: 512.

62. Françoise Mélonio, *Tocqueville and the French*, trans. Beth Raps (Charlottesville and London: University Press of Virginia, 1998), 33–36.

63. For the differences between the first and the second volume of the *Democracy*, see Seymour Drescher, "Tocqueville's Two *Démocraties*," *Journal of the History of Ideas* 25, no. 2 (1964): 201–216.

64. Tocqueville, *Democracy in America*, 4: 1250–1251.

65. Terry Pinkard, *Hegel: A Biography* (Cambridge: Cambridge University Press, 2000), 418–494.

66. G. W. F. Hegel, *Elements of the Philosophy of Right*, ed. Allen Wood, trans. H. B. Nisbet (Cambridge: Cambridge University Press, 1991), 282.

67. Rosenblatt, *Lost History of Liberalism,* 69–71.

68. W. T. Krug, *Geschiedkundig tafereel van het Liberalismus van ouden en lateren tijd* (Amsterdam, 1823), 79–81; my translation.

69. Carl von Rotteck, "Freiheit," in *Staats-Lexikon oder Encyklopädie der Staatswissenschaften In Verbindung mit vielen der angesehensten Publicisten Deutschlands,* vol. 6, ed. Carl von Rotteck and Carl Welcker (Altona: Johann Friedrich Hammerich, 1838), 71; my translation.

70. Arnold Ruge, " Eine Selbstkritik des Liberalismus," in *Vormärz und Revolution, 1840–1849: Quellen zum Politischen Denken der Deutschen im 18. Jahrhundert,* ed. Hans Fenske (Darmstadt: Wissenschaftliche Buchgesellschaft, 1976), 80.

71. See Stephan Walter, *Demokratisches Denken zwischen Hegel und Marx. Die politische Philosophie Arnold Ruges. Eine Studie zur Geschichte der Demokratie in Deutschland* (Düsseldorf: Droste, 1995).

72. James Mackintosh, *Vindiciae Gallicae and Other Writings on the French Revolution,* ed. Donald Winch (Indianapolis: Liberty Fund, 2006), 116.

73. Ibid.. 233–238.

74. For the influence of Edmund Burke on post-1815 Whigs, see Abraham Kriegel, "Liberty and Whiggery in Early Nineteenth-Century England," *The Journal of Modern History* 52 (1980): 253–278. For the introduction of the term "liberal" into British political debate, see Jörn Leonhard, "From European Liberalism to the Languages of Liberalisms: The Semantics of 'Liberalism' in European Comparison," *Redescriptions: Yearbook of Political Thought and Conceptual History* 8 (2004), 29.

75. Corinne Comstock Weston, *English Constitutional Theory and the House of Lords, 1556–1832* (London: Routledge, 1965), 217–258.

76. See Philip Schofield, *Utility and Democracy: The Political Thought of Jeremy Bentham* (Oxford: Oxford University Press, 2006), 137–170.

77. Jeremy Bentham, *Deontology; or, the Science of Morality: In Which the Harmony and Co-Incidence of Duty and Self-Interest, Virtue and Felicity, Prudence and Benevolence, Are Explained and Exemplified,* vol. 2, *Practice Of The Social Science* (London: Longman, Rees, Orme, Browne, Green & Longman, 1834), 60.

78. For a very different account of Bentham's views on liberty, see Quentin Skinner, *Liberty Before Liberalism* (Cambridge: Cambridge University Press, 1998) 96–98; and Philip Pettit, *Republicanism: A Theory of Freedom and Government* (Oxford: Oxford University Press, 1997), 41–50. Skinner and Pettit argue that Bentham and his followers were responsible for the displacement of the democratic theory of freedom by a new, liberal conception of freedom. But it is more accurate to say that Bentham was trying to get rid of vague, emotive appeals to liberty in general, rather than that he opposed the democratic theory of freedom. For a similar argument, see Yiftah Elazar, "Liberty as a Caricature: Bentham's Antidote to Republicanism," *Journal of the History of Ideas,* 76 (2015) 417–439.

79. For a comparative perspective on the political violence in the American and French Revolutions, see Dan Edelstein, "What Was the Terror?," in Andress, *French Revolution,* 453–470.

80. Quoted in Michal Jan Rozbicki, *Culture and Liberty in the Age of the American Revolution* (Charlottesville: University of Virginia Press, 2011), 166.

81. Ibid., 171.

82. Gordon Wood, *Empire of Liberty: A History of the Early Republic, 1789–1815* (Oxford: Oxford University Press, 2010), 175.

83. Quoted in ibid., 181.

84. Lance Banning *Founding Visions: The Ideas, Individuals, and Intersections That Created America,* ed. and introd. Todd Estes (Lexington: The University Press of Kentucky, 2014), 322.

85. For the Federalist political program, see David Hackett Fischer, *The Revolution of American Conservatism: The Federalist Party in the Era of Jeffersonian Democracy* (New York: Harper and Row, 1965). For the Federalist view on the judiciary, see Wood, *Empire of Liberty,* 400–432. Note that the most prominent Federalists, such as John Adams and Hamilton, denied that they were out to reverse the settlement of 1791.

86. Quoted in David Hackett Fischer, *Liberty and Freedom: A Visual History of America's Founding Ideas* (New York: Oxford University Press, 2005), 172.

87. Wood, *Empire of Liberty,* 105.

88. For Webster's life and work, see Richard M. Rollins, *The Long Journey of Noah Webster* (Philadelphia: University of Pennsylvania Press, 1980).

89. Noah Webster, *Sketches of American Policy* (Hartford: Hudson and Goodwin, 1785), 20.

90. Quoted in Rollins, *Noah Webster,* 65.

91. Noah Webster, *A Collection of Papers on Political, Literary, and Moral Subjects* (New York: Webster and Clark, 1843), 40.

92. Ibid., 272.

93. Ibid.

94. Ibid., 285.

95. Rufus King, *The Life and Correspondence of Rufus King; Comprising His Letters, Private and Official, His Public Documents, and His Speeches,* vol. 5, *1807–1816,* ed. Charles R. King (New York: G. P. Putnam's Sons, 1898), 96.

96. Quoted in Hackett Fischer, *The Revolutions of American Conservatism,* 7.

97. Hackett Fischer, *Liberty and Freedom,* 204. For a different view, see Michal Rozbicki, who argues that American elites—including the Federalists—continued to use a more democratic idiom. Rozbicki, *Culture and Liberty in the Age of the American Revolution,* 163–222.

98. But compare Seth Cotlar, who argues that the reaction against the Terror provoked a "reining in of democratic possibilities" in the United States, like in Europe. Cotlar, *Tom Paine's America: The Rise and Fall of Transatlantic Radicalism in the Early Republic* (Charlottesville: University of Virginia Press, 2011), 4.

99. Quoted in Lance Banning, ed., *Liberty and Order: The First American Party Struggle* (Indianapolis: Liberty Fund, 2004), 264.

100. James Madison, "Who are the Best Keepers of the People's Liberties?," in *The Mind of James Madison: The Legacy of Classical Republicanism,* ed. Colleen Sheehan (Cambridge: Cambridge University Press, 2017), 269.

101. Hackett Fischer, *Revolution of American Conservatism,* 26.

102. Fisher Ames, *Works of Fisher Ames Compiled by a Number of His Friends* (Boston: T. B. Wait, 1809), 380.

103. Ibid., 390.

104. Ibid., 419.

105. Ibid., 437.

106. Sean Wilentz, *The Rise of American Democracy*, (New York: W. W. Norton, 2005), 4.

107. Donald Ratcliffe, "The Right to Vote and the Rise of Democracy, 1787–1828," *Journal of the Early Republic* 33, no. 2 (2013): 246.

108. "Liberty," in Noah Webster, *An American Dictionary of the English Language* (New York: S. Converse, 1828), vol. 2, 48.

109. For the emergence of the Whig Party and the creation of the Second Party System, see Daniel Walker Howe, *What Hath God Wrought: The Transformation of America, 1815–1848* (Oxford: Oxford University Press, 2007), 276.

110. Hackett Fischer, *Liberty and Freedom,* 209.

111. For accounts of Whig ideology, stressing their suspicion of demagogues and majority rule, see Lawrence Kohl, *The Politics of Individualism: Parties and the American Character in the Jacksonian Era* (Oxford: Oxford University Press, 1989), 177–185; Harry L. Watson, *Liberty and Power: The Politics of Jacksonian America* (New York: Hill and Wang, 2006), esp. 231–254.

112. Quoted in Kohl, *Politics of Individualism,* 181.

113. Hackett Fischer, *Freedom and Liberty,* 211.

114. For this point, see Kohl, *Politics of Individualism,* 177–185.

6. The Triumph of Modern Liberty

1. For Lieber's life and career, see Frank Freidel, *Francis Lieber: Nineteenth-Century Liberal* (Baton Rouge: Louisiana State University Press. 1948).

2. Francis Lieber, *On Civil Liberty and Self-Government* (London: Richard Bentley, 1853), 28–31.

3. Lieber did not refer to Benjamin Constant's writings in *On Civil Liberty,* but as a friend and correspondent of Édouard de Laboulaye and other French liberals, he likely would have known about Constant's distinction between ancient and modern liberty.

4. Lieber, *On Civil Liberty,* 34.

5. Ibid., 333–334.

6. Francis Lieber, "Anglican and Gallican Liberty," in *The Miscellaneous Writings of Francis Lieber,* vol. 2, *Contributions to Political Science,* ed. Francis Lieber (Philadelphia: J.B. Lippincott, 1881), 378.

7. See Jonathan Sperber, *The European Revolutions, 1848–1851* (Cambridge: Cambridge University Press, 2005).

8. Albert Boime, *Art in an Age of Civil Struggle, 1848–1871* (Chicago: University of Chicago Press, 2008), 16, 47.

9. For an analysis of 1848's failure, see Sperber, *The European Revolutions*, notably chap. 5. For the Napoleonic myth and its contribution to the establishment of the Second Empire, see Sudhir Hazareesingh, *The Legend of Napoleon* (London: Granta Books, 2014), esp. chap. 7.

10. Quoted in Walter Dennis Gray, *Interpreting American Democracy in France: The Career of Édouard Laboulaye* (Newark: University of Delaware Press, 1994), 36.

11. Édouard de Laboulaye, *L'État et ses limites suivi d'essais politiques sur Alexis de Toc- queville, l'instruction publique, les finances, le droit de petition* (Paris: Charpentier, 1863), 43–45; my translation.

12. Ibid., 4–137.

13. Édouard de Laboulaye, *Le parti libéral: son programme et son avenir* (Paris: Charpen- tier, 1863), 120; my translation. On the antidemocratic nature of Orleanist liberalism, see Mark Hulliung, *Citizens and Citoyens: Republicans and Liberals in America and France* (Cambridge, MA: Harvard University Press, 2002), 65–66.

14. Gray, *Interpreting American Democracy in France*, 38.

15. Quoted in ibid., 67.

16. Édouard de Laboulaye, *Paris en Amérique* (Paris: Charpentier, 1863), 16; my translation.

17. Ibid., 336; my translation.

18. Ibid., 421; my translation.

19. Auguste Nefftzer, "Libéralisme," in *Dictionnaire général de la politique*, ed. Maurice Block (Nancy: Berger-Levrault, 1873), 188–194; my translation.

20. For this point, see Helena Rosenblatt, *The Lost History of Liberalism* (Princeton, NJ: Princeton University Press), 163.

21. Charles de Montalembert, *L'église libre dans l'état libre: Discours prononcés au Con- grès catholique de Malines, par le comte de Montalembert* (Paris: C. Douniol, 1863), 17; my translation.

22. Robert E. Sullivan, *Macaulay: The Tragedy of Power* (Cambridge, MA: Harvard Uni- versity Press, 2009), 323.

23. Quoted in Charles A. Betts, "Macaulay's Criticism of Democracy and Garfield's Reply," *Open Court*, XXXII (1918), 273–279.

24. Walter Bagehot, *The English Constitution*, ed. Paul Smith (Cambridge: Cambridge University Press, 2001), 190.

25. Sullivan, *Macaulay*, 323; Bagehot, *The English Constitution*, 191, 186. For the effect of the 1848 Revolutions on the debate about reform in Britain more generally, see Margot Finn, *After Chartism: Class and Nation in English Radical Politics 1848–1874* (Cam- bridge: Cambridge University Press, 1993), chap. 2.

26. Quoted in Richard Reeves, *John Stuart Mill: Victorian Firebrand* (London: Atlantic Books, 2007), 324.

27. James Mill, *Political Writings*, ed. Terence Ball (Cambridge: Cambridge University Press, 1992), 27.

28. Vincent Guillin, "The French Influence," in *A Companion to Mill*, ed. Christopher Macleod and Dale E. Miller (Hoboken: John Wiley & Sons, 2016), 133. For the develop- ment of Mill's views on democracy, see J. H. Burns, "J. S. Mill and Democracy, 1829–61," in *Mill: A Collection of Critical Essays*, ed. J. B. Schneewind (London: Macmillan, 1968), 280–328 and Georgios Varouxakis, "Mill on Democracy Revisited," in Macleod and Miller, *A Companion to Mill*, 454–471. For Mill's identification as liberal rather than rad- ical, see his essay "Tories, Whigs, and Radicals," *Westminster Review*, xxv (1836): 293.

29. John Stuart Mill, "De Tocqueville on Democracy II," in *The Collected Works of John Stuart Mill*, vol. 18, *Essays on Politics and Society Part I*, ed. John M. Robson, intro- duction by Alexander Brady (Toronto: University of Toronto Press, 1977), 176–177.

30. John Stuart Mill, *On Liberty and Other Writings* (Cambridge: Cambridge University Press, 2011), 5–8.

31. Ibid., 112, 120.

32. John Stuart Mill, *The Collected Works of John Stuart Mill,* vol. 19, *Essays on Politics and Society Part II,* ed. John M. Robson, introduction by Alexander Brady (Toronto: University of Toronto Press, 1977), 457.

33. For Eötvös's life and work, see D. Mervyn Jones's introduction to *The Dominant Ideas of the Nineteenth Century and Their Impact on the State,* vol. 1, *Diagnosis,* by József Eötvös, trans., ed., and annot. D. Mervyn Jones (New York: Columbia University Press, 1996), 13–56. For the response to 1848 in Central Europe more generally, see Balázs Trencsényi, Maciej Janowski, et al., *A History of Modern Political Thought in East Central Europe,* vol. 1, *Negotiating Modernity in the 'Long Nineteenth Century'* (Oxford: Oxford University Press, 2016), chap. 6.

34. Eötvös, *The Dominant Ideas of the Nineteenth Century,* 178.

35. Trencsényi, Janowski, et al., *History of Modern Political Thought in East Central Europe,* 273.

36. See Dieter Langewiesche, *Liberalism in Germany,* trans. Christiane Banerji (Princeton: Princeton University Press, 2000), 61.

37. On J. K. Bluntschli's liberalism, see Robert Adcock, *Liberalism and the Emergence of American Political Science: A Transatlantic Tale* (Oxford: Oxford University Press, 2014), 53–58.

38. J. K. Bluntschli, *The Theory of the Modern State* (Oxford: Clarendon Press, 1895), 58–59. Note that Bluntschli's work was originally published in German in 1875–1876.

39. Bluntschli, *Theory of the Modern State,* 423, 425.

40. Ibid., 194.

41. J. P. T. Bury, *France, 1814–1940* (London: Routledge, 2003), chap. 9.

42. Quoted in Robert Saunders, "Democracy," in *Languages of Politics in Nineteenth-Century Britain,* ed. David Craig and James Thompson (Basingstoke: Palgrave Macmillan, 2013), 153.

43. Quoted in ibid., 156. On Gladstone's role in bringing about the Third Reform Act, see D. A. Hamer, *Liberal Politics in the Age of Gladstone and Rosebery: A Study in Leadership and Policy* (Oxford: Clarendon Press, 1972), 76–77.

44. Stein Kuhnle and Anne Sander, "The Emergence of the Western Welfare State," in *The Oxford Handbook of the Welfare State,* ed. Herbert Obinger et al. (Oxford: Oxford University Press, 2010), 61–80.

45. Benjamin Constant, *Political Writings,* ed. Biancamaria Fontana (Cambridge: Cambridge University Press, 1988), 263.

46. For Paul Leroy-Beaulieu's life and intellectual career, see Dan Warshaw, *Paul Leroy-Beaulieu and Established Liberalism in France* (DeKalb: Northern Illinois University Press, 1991).

47. Paul Leroy-Beaulieu, *L'État moderne et ses fonctions* (Paris: Guillaumin, 1900), x.

48. Ibid., 460.

49. Quoted in John Offer, introduction to *Herbert Spencer: Political Writings,* by Herbert Spencer, ed. John Offer (Cambridge: Cambridge University Press, 2012), vii. For Spen-

cer's life and career, see John Offer, *Herbert Spencer and Social Theory* (Basingstoke: Palgrave Macmillan, 2010).

50. Herbert Spencer, "Parliamentary Reform: the Dangers and the Safeguards," *Westminster Review* 73 (1860): 486–507.

51. Herbert Spencer, *Man versus the State: With Six Essays on Government, Society, and Freedom* (Indianapolis: Liberty Classics, 1981), 56.

52. Ibid., 26.

53. Edward Bristow, "The Liberty and Property Defence League and Individualism," *Historical Journal* 18, no. 4 (1975): 761–789.

54. Sandford Elwitt. "Social Reform and Social Order in Late Nineteenth-Century France: The *Musée Social* and Its Friends," *French Historical Studies* 11, no. 3 (1980): 445.

55. Max Weber, *Political Writings* (Cambridge: Cambridge University Press, 1994), 70–71, 159.

56. For the American response to the 1848 Revolutions, see Daniel Howe, *What Hath God Wrought: The Transformation of America, 1815–1848* (Oxford: Oxford University Press, 2007), 792–836.

57. Quoted in David Hackett Fischer, *Liberty and Freedom: A Visual History of America's Founding Ideas* (Oxford: Oxford University Press, 2005), 295.

58. Quoted in Richard C. Rohrs, "American Critics of the French Revolution of 1848," *Journal of the Early Republic* 14, no. 3 (1994): 374.

59. J. K. Bluntschli, "Lieber's Service to Political Science," in Lieber, *Miscellaneous Writings,* 8.

60. Frank Freidel, "Francis Lieber, Charles Sumner, and Slavery," *Journal of Southern History* 9, no. 1 (1943): 75–93.

61. Lieber, "Anglican and Gallican Liberty," 382–383.

62. Ibid., 386.

63. Ibid., 387–388.

64. Lieber, *On Civil Liberty,* 37–40.

65. Ibid., 237.

66. Howe, *What Hath God Wrought,* 408.

67. The next few paragraphs are based on Hugh Brogan, *The Penguin History of the United States of America* (London: Penguin, 2001), 280–345.

68. Quoted in Eric Foner, *Forever Free: The Story of Emancipation and Reconstruction* (New York: Vintage Books, 2006), 89–90.

69. Quoted in ibid., 148.

70. Quoted in ibid., 124.

71. Ibid., chap. 7.

72. Brogan, *History of the United States of America,* 418–446.

73. Ibid., 413–414.

74. Francis Parkman, "The Failure of Universal Suffrage," *North American Review* 126 (1878): 1–20. See also Eric Foner, *The Story of American Freedom* (New York: W. W. Norton, 1998), 119.

75. See John Sproat, *"The Best Men": Liberal Reformers in the Gilded Age* (New York: Oxford University Press, 1968); Nancy Cohen, *The Reconstruction of American*

Liberalism, 1865–1914 (Chapel Hill: University of North Carolina Press, 2002). For an account that stresses intellectual exchange between Gilded Age liberals and their European counterparts, see Robert Adcock, *Liberalism and the Emergence of American Political Science: A Transatlantic Tale* (Oxford: Oxford University Press, 2014).

76. For William Graham Sumner's life and career, see Richard Hofstadter, "W. G. Sumner, Social Darwinist," *New England Quarterly* 14, no. 3 (1941): 457–477.

77. William Graham Sumner, "Republican Government," in *The Challenge of Facts and Other Essays,* ed. Albert Keller (New Haven, CT: Yale University, 1918), 226–227.

78. William Graham Sumner, "Advancing Social and Political Organization in the United States," in *Challenge of Facts,* 335.

79. Ibid., 334.

80. William Graham Sumner, "Politics in America, 1776–1876," *North American Review* 122, no. 250 (1876): 51–53.

81. William Graham Sumner, "State Interference," in *War and Other Essays,* ed. Albert Keller (New Haven, CT: Yale University Press, 1919), 213–228.

82. Ibid.

83. William Graham Sumner, "The Forgotten Man," in *The Forgotten Man and Other Essays,* ed. Albert Keller (New Haven, CT: Yale University Press, 1918), 481.

84. William Graham Sumner, *What Social Classes Owe to Each Other* (New York: Harper and Brothers, 1911), 120.

85. Richard White, *The Republic for Which It Stands: The United States during Reconstruction and the Gilded Age, 1865–1896* (Oxford: Oxford University Press, 2017), 448.

86. Michael Les Benedict, "*Laissez-Faire* and Liberty: A Re-Evaluation of the Meaning and Origins Of *Laissez-Faire* Constitutionalism," *Law and History Review* 3, no. 2 (1985): 293–331, quote on 331.

87. Alexander Keyssar, *The Right to Vote: The Contested History of Democracy in the United States* (New York: Basic Books, 2000), 137.

88. See Adcock, *Liberalism,* 201.

89. Henry Sumner Maine, *Popular Government,* introduction by George W. Carey (Indianapolis: Liberty Fund, 1976), 66.

90. Ibid., 211.

91. Ibid., 242–243.

92. Quoted in Yasmin Sabina Khan, *Enlightening the World: The Creation of the Statue of Liberty* (Ithaca: Cornell University Press, 2010), 109.

93. June Parvis, "Emmeline Pankhurst (1858–1928) and Votes for Women," in *Votes for Women*, eds. Sandra Holton and June Purvis (London: Routledge, 2002), 109–134.

94. Emmeline Pankhurst, "Address at Hartford," 13 November 1913, reprinted in *Speeches and Trials of the Militant Suffragettes: The Women's Social and Political Union 1903–1918,* ed. Cheryl Jorgensen-Earp (Cranbury, NJ: Associated University Presses, 1999), 327.

95. Quoted in Karen Offen, *European Feminisms, 1700–1950: A Political History* (Stanford, CA: Stanford University Press, 2000), 154.

96. It should be noted that the idea that the late nineteenth century was characterized by a "long depression" is controversial, as economic historians point out that economic output continued to grow in most countries during this period. However, as Eric

Hobsbawm has pointed out, there can be no doubt that contemporaries experienced this period as one of prolonged slump and economic malaise, as prices and profits declined compared to earlier decades. See Hobsbawm, *The Age of Empire, 1875–1914* (New York: Vintage Books, 1989), 34–36.

97. For left-wing movements in Europe between 1880 and 1945, see Dick Geary, ed., *Labour and Socialist Movements in Europe before 1914* (Oxford, NY: Berg Publishers, 1989) and Dick Geary, *European Labour Politics from 1900 to the Depression* (London: Macmillan, 1991). For the European Left's contribution to democratization, see Geoff Eley, *Forging Democracy: The History of the Left in Europe, 1850–2000* (Oxford: Oxford University Press, 2002).

98. John A. Scott, *Republican Ideas and the Liberal Tradition in France, 1870–1914* (New York: Octagon Books, 1966), 119–125.

99. Ferdinand Buisson, *La politique radicale: étude sur les doctrines du parti radical et radical-socialiste* (Paris: V. Giard, 1908), 219–221.

100. Jacques Kergoat, "France," in *The Formation of Labour Movements 1870–1914: An International Perspective*, 2. vols., ed. Marcel van der Linden and Jürgen Rojahn (Leiden: Brill, 1990), 1: 163–190.

101. Jean Jaurès, *Libertés,* ed. Gilles Candar (Paris: Ligue des droits de l'homme / EDI, 1987); my translation.

102. Jean Jaurès, *A Socialist History of the French Revolution,* ed. Mitchell Abidor (London: Pluto Press, 2015), 249–251.

103. For the decline of liberalism as a political force in late-nineteenth-century France, see Alan Kahan, *Liberalism in Nineteenth-Century Europe: The Political Culture of Limited Suffrage* (Houndmills: Palgrave Macmillan, 2003), 172, 192.

104. Sidney and Beatrice Webb, *Industrial Democracy* (New York and Bombay: Longmans, 1897), vol. 2, 847. For the centrality of the concept of industrial democracy to the Webbs' political outlook, see Lisanne Radice, *Beatrice and Sidney Webb: Fabian Socialists* (London: MacMillan, 1984), 10.

105. John Hobson, *The Crisis of Liberalism: New Issues of Democracy* (London: King, 1909), 93, xii.

106. See Peter Clarke, *Liberals and Social Democrats* (Cambridge: Cambridge University Press 1978); Michael Freeden, *The New Liberalism: An Ideology of Social Reform* (Oxford: Clarendon Press, 1986).

107. L. T. Hobhouse, *Liberalism* (London: Williams & Norgate, 1919), 57.

108. Ibid., 214.

109. Ibid., 48, 54–56.

110. L. T. Hobhouse, *Democracy and Reaction* (London: T. F. Unwin, 1909), 222–223.

111. For an attempt to explain the survival of British liberalism in a comparative perspective, see Kahan, *Liberalism in Nineteenth-Century Europe,* 172–192.

112. Gregory Claeys, *Marx and Marxism* (London: Pelican, 2018), 173–187.

113. Karl Marx and Friedrich Engels, *The Marx-Engels Reader,* ed. Robert Tucker (New York: W. W. Norton, 1978), 484–485.

114. Ibid., 491.

115. Karl Kautsky, *The Class Struggle (Erfurt Program),* trans. William Bohn (Chicago: Charles H. Kerr, 1910), 122–123.

116. Marx and Engels, *The Marx-Engels Reader,* 556. For Marx's and Engels's views of the state, see Gareth Stedman Jones, "The Young Hegelians, Marx and Engels," in Jones and Claeys, *History of Nineteenth-Century Political Thought,* 579–585.

117. Claeys, *Marx and Marxism,* 232–243.

118. L. T. Hobhouse, *Democracy and Reaction* (London: T. F. Unwin, 1909), 235.

119. Eley, *Forging Democracy,* chaps. 1 and 2.

120. Mark Mazower, *Dark Continent: Europe's Twentieth Century* (London: Penguin Books, 1998), 8–11.

121. Gareth Stedman Jones, *Karl Marx: Greatness and Illusion* (London: Penguin, 2016) chap. 12, note 66.

122. V. I. Lenin, *Collected Works, Vol. 28 (1918–1919)* (Moscow: Progress Publishers, 1974) 455–477. For the role of the concept of proletarian dictatorship in Bolshevik doctrine, see Neil Harding, "The Russian Revolution: An Ideology in Power," in *The Cambridge History of Twentieth-Century Political Thought*, ed. Terence Ball and Gareth Stedman Jones (Cambridge: Cambridge University Press, 2008), 257–261.

123. See Massimo L. Salvadori, *Karl Kautsky and the Socialist Revolution, 1880–1938* (London: Verso, 1990), 251–293.

124. Communist International, *Manifesto and Governing Rules of the Communist International (Adopted by the Congress of the Communist International at Moscow, March 2–6, 1919, and Signed by Comrades C. Rakovsky, N. Lenin, M. Zinovjev, L. Trotzky, and Fritz Platten)* (Chicago: Chicago Labor Printing, 1919). For the division of Marxist socialism between a democratic and communist bloc, see Eley, *Forging Democracy,* chap. 9.

125. Ludwig von Mises, *Liberalism: The Classical Tradition,* ed. Bettina Bien Greaves (Indianapolis: Liberty Fund, 2005), 30.

126. Ibid., 30, viii.

127. Ibid., 119, 151.

128. Ibid., 120.

129. For a classic analysis of the decline of liberalism in the interwar period, notably in Britain, see George Dangerfield, *The Strange Death of Liberal England* (London: Constable, 1935). For an analysis of the more recent debate about the causes of this decline, see G. R. Searle, "Did the Liberals Still Have a Future in 1914?," *Historian* 35 (1992): 10–12.

130. Mazower, *Dark Continent,* 27.

131. Charles Postel, *The Populist Vision* (New York: Oxford University Press, 2007).

132. Jill Lepore, *These Truths: A History of the United States* (New York: W. W. Norton, 2018), 363.

133. For progressivism and new liberalism in the United States, see Douglas Charles Rossinow, *Visions of Progress: The Left-Liberal Tradition in America* (Philadelphia: University of Pennsylvania Press, 2008).

134. John A. Thompson, *Woodrow Wilson* (London: Longman, 2002), 43–64.

135. As one of the founding documents of American liberalism, Wilson's *The New Freedom* has been much discussed by historians. Two very different interpretations have been offered. Arthur Link describes the new freedom as an ambitious program to broaden popular control over government and emphasizes Wilson's desire to redistribute income and limit corporate power. Martin Sklar, by contrast, describes Wilson's pro-

gram as affirming corporate-industrial capitalism. For a good overview of this debate, see W. E. Brownlee, "The New Freedom and Its Evolution," in *A Companion to Woodrow Wilson*, ed. R. A. Kennedy (New York: Wiley and Sons, 2013), 106–132. This author agrees with Link's interpretation.

136. Woodrow Wilson, *The New Freedom: A Call for the Emancipation of the Generous Energies of a People* (New York: Doubleday, 1913), 55–78.

137. Ibid., 243–244.

138. Ibid., 15.

139. Ibid., 284.

140. Henry F. Pringle, *The Life and Times of William Howard Taft*, 2 vols. (New York: Farra & Rinehardt, 1939), 1: 34.

141. William Howard Taft, *Popular Government: Its Essence, Its Permanence and Its Perils* (New Haven, CT: Yale University Press, 1913), 34.

142. Ibid., 66.

143. Ibid., 15.

144. Ibid., 197–199.

145. Keyssar, *The Right to Vote*, 216.

146. Brogan, *History of the United States of America*, 503, 512–513.

147. Herbert Hoover, "Principles and Ideals of the United States Government," October 22, 1928, https://millercenter.org/the-presidency/presidential-speeches/october-22-1928 -principles-and-ideals-united-states-government.

148. Brogan, *History of the United States of America*, chap. 22.

149. Ibid., 542

150. Franklin D. Roosevelt, "Fireside Chat 6: On Government and Capitalism," September 30, 1934, https://millercenter.org/the-presidency/presidential-speeches /september-30-1934-fireside-chat-6-government-and-capitalism. For Roosevelt's liberalism, see Rosenblatt, *Lost History of Liberalism*, 260–261.

151. John Dewey, "The Future of Liberalism," *Journal of Philosophy* 32, no. 9 (1935): 227.

152. Franklin D. Roosevelt, "Speech at the Democratic National Convention," June 27, 1936, https://millercenter.org/the-presidency/presidential-speeches/june-27-1936 -democratic-national-convention.

153. Hackett Fischer, *Liberty and Freedom*, 488–494, quote on 491.

154. Franklin D. Roosevelt, "State of the Union Message to Congress," January 11, 1944, http://www.fdrlibrary.marist.edu/archives/address_text.html. See also Foner, *Story of American Freedom*, 235.

155. Quoted in Foner, *Story of American Freedom*, 235.

156. Labour Party, "Let Us Face the Future: A Declaration of Labour Policy for the Consideration of the Nation" (1945), http://www.politicsresources.net/area/uk/man/lab45 .htm.

157. Quoted in Sheri Berman, *The Primacy of Politics: Social Democracy and the Making of Europe's Twentieth Century* (Cambridge: Cambridge University Press, 2006), 177.

158. Quoted in Jan-Werner Müller, *Contesting Democracy: Political Ideas in Twentieth-Century Europe* (New Haven: Yale University Press, 2013), 144.

159. Odd Arne Westad, *The Global Cold War: Third World Interventions and the Making of Our Times* (Cambridge: Cambridge University Press, 2007).

160. Tony Judt, *Postwar: A History of Europe Since 1945* (New York: Penguin, 2005) 211, 207.

161. For a different account of Cold War liberalism, see Jan-Werner Müller, "Fear and Freedom: On 'Cold War Liberalism,'" *European Journal of Political Theory*, 7 (2008), 45–64.

162. Bruce Caldwell, introduction to *The Road to Serfdom: Texts and Documents. The Definitive Edition*, by F. A. Hayek, ed. Bruce Caldwell (Chicago: University of Chicago Press, 2007), 1–36.

163. Hayek, *Road to Serfdom*, 100–111, quote on 110.

164. Ibid., 82.

165. Ibid., 110–111.

166. Ibid.

167. Caldwell, introduction to *The Road to Serfdom*, 18–19; Theodore Rosenof, "Freedom, Planning, and Totalitarianism: The Reception of F. A. Hayek's Road to Serfdom," *Canadian Review of American Studies* 5, no. 2 (1974): 150–160.

168. For Berlin's life and work, see Michael Ignatieff, *Isaiah Berlin: A Life* (London: Vintage, 2000).

169. But compare Jan-Werner Müller, "The Contours of Cold War Liberalism (Berlin's in Particular)," in *Isaiah Berlin's Cold War Liberalism*, ed. Jan-Werner Müller (Singapore: Palgrave Macmillan, 2019), 37–56. Müller argues that Berlin's defense of the welfare state was principled and not pragmatic.

170. Isaiah Berlin, "Political Ideas in the Twentieth Century," *Foreign Affairs* 28, no. 3 (1950): 383.

171. Ibid., 377.

172. Ibid., 378.

173. Ibid., 383.

174. Ibid., 385.

175. For a different reading of Berlin's *Two Concepts*, arguing that Berlin was a defender of both negative and positive liberty, see Joshua L. Cherniss, *A Mind and Its Time: The Development of Isaiah Berlin's Political Thought* (Oxford: Oxford University Press, 2013), esp. chap 8.

176. Isaiah Berlin, *Political Ideas in the Romantic Age: Their Rise and Influence on Modern Thought* (Princeton, NJ: Princeton University Press, 2014), 90, 205.

177. Isaiah Berlin, *Two Concepts of Liberty* (Oxford: Clarendon Press, 1958), 48, 14.

178. Ibid., 12.

179. Isaiah Berlin, *Freedom and its Betrayal: Six Enemies of Human Liberty* (London: Chatto & Windus, 2002), 73, 67.

180. Berlin, *Two Concepts*, 8.

181. Ibid., 14.

182. Marshall Cohen, "Berlin and the Liberal Tradition," *Philosophical Quarterly* 10, no. 40 (1960): 216–217.

183. "The Fate of Liberty," *Times,* December 6, 1952.

184. Raymond Aron, *Essai sur les libertés* (Paris: Calmann-Lévy, 1965), 230; my translation.

185. Ibid., 149; my translation.

186. Ibid., 228; my translation.

187. For a similar argument with regard to Judith Shklar, see Samuel Moyn, "Before—and Beyond—the Liberalism of Fear," in *Between Utopianism and Realism: The Political Thought of Judith Shklar,* ed. S. Ashendem and A. Hess (Philadelphia: University of Philadelphia Press, 2019), 24–46.

188. Aron, *Essai sur les libertés,* 230.

189. J. Roland Pennock, *Liberal Democracy: Its Merits and Prospects* (New York: Rinehart and Company, 1950).

190. Glenn Negley, review of J. Roland Pennock's "Liberal Democracy: Its Merits and Prospects," *Political Science Quarterly* 67, no. 2 (1952): 289–290.

191. Hannah Arendt, "What Is Freedom?," in *Between Past and Future: Eight Exercises in Political Thought* (New York: Penguin Books, 1954), 149. See Kei Hiruta, "Hannah Arendt, Liberalism, and Freedom from Politics," in *Arendt on Freedom, Liberation, and Revolution: Philosophers in Depth,* ed. Kei Hiruta (Cham: Palgrave Macmillan, 2019), 17–45. Note that, according to Hiruta, Arendt was probably unfamiliar with Isaiah Berlin's *Two Concepts of Liberty.*

192. Arendt, "What Is Freedom?," 150, 157.

Epilogue: Freedom in the Twenty-First Century

1. Daniel Hannan, *The New Road to Serfdom: A Letter of Warning to America* (New York: HarperCollins, 2010).

2. Mark R. Levin, *Liberty and Tyranny: A Conservative Manifesto* (New York: Threshold Editions, 2009), 17–18.

3. Walter E. Williams, *Liberty versus the Tyranny of Socialism: Controversial Essays* (Stanford: Hoover Institution Press, 2008); Ron Paul, *Liberty Defined: 50 Essential Issues That Affect Our Freedom* (New York: Grand Central Publishing, 2012).

4. For a recent, sophisticated defense of this view, see Randy Barnett, *Our Republican Constitution: Securing the Liberty and Sovereignty of We the People* (New York: HarperCollins, 2016).

5. Fareed Zakaria, *The Future of Freedom: Illiberal Democracy at Home and Abroad* (New York: W. W. Norton, 2003), 20, 24–27.

6. Yascha Mounk, *The People vs. Democracy: Why Our Freedom Is in Danger and How to Save It* (Cambridge, MA: Harvard University Press, 2018), 14.

Acknowledgments

I started thinking about this book in 2009. At the time, I was living near the University of California, Berkeley. One day I ran into a group of conservative protestors holding signs that depicted Barack Obama with Adolf Hitler's characteristic mustache. That got me thinking: In what universe did it make sense to compare the first black president of the United States to Hitler? What kind of freedom was Obama supposed to be undermining? To answer these questions, I undertook what would become a journey through more than two thousand years of thinking and talking about freedom by figures dating back to Herodotus and ranging all the way to the present.

Perhaps this was a bit more than the original puzzle warranted. It certainly took me a lot longer than I had expected. (Never believe an academic when she says her second book will be a short one!) But overall, it was an enjoyable ride, all the more so because of the companionship and generosity of so many friends and colleagues on both sides of the Atlantic. Special thanks goes to Aaron Belkin, Lars Behrisch, Josine Blok, Luara Ferracioli, René Koekkoek, Ido de Haan, Martin van Hees, Lynn Hunt, Bruno Leipold, Samuel Moyn, Maarten Prak, Sophia Rosenfeld, Enzo Rossi, Eric Schliesser, Quentin Skinner, Daniel Steinmetz-Jenkins, Martha Schulman, Siep Stuurman, Wyger Velema, and Michael Zuckert for taking the time to read (parts of) the manuscript and to provide invaluable feedback.

I am also deeply indebted to Robin Mills, Adrian Blau, and Eric Boot for organizing workshops at King's College London and Leiden University where I was able to discuss the manuscript as a whole with an intimidating array of experts. To all participants in these workshops: thank you so much. Many thanks also to my dauntingly efficient research assistant Annelot Janse, who helped with footnotes and provided assistance in locating and obtaining art and illustrations. Last but not least, I would like to express gratitude to Kathleen McDermott and Simon Waxman, as well as to the anonymous reviewers for Harvard University Press, whose thoughtful comments and suggestions made this book far better than it would have been otherwise.

This book could not have been written without the support of the Netherlands Institute for Advanced Study, where I was able to work on my manuscript without interruption as a research fellow in 2015 and 2016. This proved to be the crucial push that turned this manuscript from an idea into a reality. At the institute, fellow historians Frances Andrews and Karen Hagemann encouraged me to think better and harder about what I wanted to say. I would also like to thank the Independent Social Research Foundation, whose generous grant provided me with enough research time to finalize this book in 2018 and 2019. Thanks also to the Alexander von Humboldt Foundation for awarding me a fellowship in 2015, even though personal circumstances kept me from accepting their generous offer.

Finally, I would like to thank my family and friends for their love, care, and wise council. A special shout-out to Rens Bod, who first suggested that I start with the ancients rather than in the eighteenth century (as originally planned); he is thus singlehandedly responsible for delaying the completion of this project for another two years. On the other hand, I have Dominique Reill to thank for the fact that this book did not balloon into a global history of freedom, which would have surely doomed the project altogether. Liza Mügge inspired me by continuing to ask about the place of women in the history of freedom. Without my parents, this book never could have been written, as they have always encouraged me to follow my dreams. Finally, and above all, I want to thank my wife Tanja and our daughter Nora for traveling with me on the long and arduous road to freedom (from this book). I love you both.

Illustration Credits

Index

Buisson, Ferdinand, 314, 315
Bulis (Spartan envoy), 15–17, 18, 27,
  110, 155
Burckhardt, Jacob, 133–134
bureaucracy, 298, 306
Burke, Edmund, 4, 223–224, 235, 242, 246,
  247, 263
Busenello, Giovanni, 149–150
Byzantine thinkers, 119–120

Caesar, Julius, 89–93, 100–102; assassination
  of, 92, 103, 130, 132–133; Dante's view
  of, 130; Plutarch on, 110; as tyrant,
  132–133, 167; views of in Renaissance,
  144
Caesar Augustus (Octavian), 94, 95–99,
  105, 107, 113, 115, 137
Calanus, 66, 67
Calvin, Jean, 153, 171. See also Reformation
Cambyses (Persian king), 28, 29–30, 110
capitalism: natural rights doctrine and,
  174. See also free-market economy;
  market societies
Carthage, 81
Cassius, Gaius, 92, 93, 95, 97, 130, 132–133,
  147, 148
Cassius Longinus Ravilla, Lucius, 75, 83
Cato: A Tragedy (Addison), 207
Cato of Utica (Cato the Younger), 91, 92,
  100, 102–103, 108, 155, 207
Cato the Elder, 76
Chaeronea, 61, 68, 101
Chambers, Ephraim, 179, 181
Charlemagne, 120, 121
Charles X (king of France), 257
Chateaubriand, François-René de, 235
checks and balances, 246, 264, 308
Christianity: conceptions of freedom in,
  116; Dante's description of hell, 129–132;
  defense of one-man rule, 114–118; defense
  of Roman Empire, 119; early attitudes
  toward political power, 113–119; individual
  and, 278; inner freedom in, 118–119;
  liberating function of, 116–117; Machiavelli
  on, 141; in Roman Empire, 106, 113–119;
  slavery in, 116–117. See also Church;
  Protestants; Reformation; religion
Church: independence from secular
  authority, 122–123. See also Christianity;
  Reformation

Cicero, Marcus Tullius, 9, 83–84, 85–87,
  93–94, 100; on Cato, 91; death of, 6;
  eulogy for Cato, 100; Petrarch's admiration for, 136; Philippics, 100–101;
  Plutarch on, 103–104
cities, Italian, 123–124, 125, 144. See also
  Florence; Rome; Siena; Venice
citizens, ordinary: views of political capabilities of, 235. See also independence,
  individual; poor; private life; working
  classes
citizens, ordinary Athenian, 44–47
citizens, ordinary Greek, 40, 62, 64
citizens, ordinary Roman, 71–72; conflict
  with elites, 81–86, 91; response to
  Caesar's death, 93; in Roman Empire,
  97–99; in Roman Republic, 78–81.
  See also plebeians; populares
citizenship, in Athens, 50
citizenship, Roman, 80
city-states: individual independence in,
  41; institutionalizing freedom within,
  7–8; medieval Italian, 123–125 (see also
  individual cities)
civil liberty, 176, 217–218; in dictionaries,
  248; in Great Britain, 236–237; modern
  liberty as, 251, 252–254 (see also modern
  liberty); vs. natural liberty, 232; in
  Netherlands, 245; vs. political liberty,
  232–233, 234, 236–237, 241, 251, 252,
  262; securing, 254. See also independence,
  individual; liberty, modern; rights,
  individual; security, personal
Civil Rights Act of 1866, 302
Civil War, American, 4
classics: influence on Atlantic Revolutions,
  214–215; loss of memory of, 121; revival
  of study of, 135 (see also humanism;
  Renaissance)
class interests: defense of, 4–5. See also
  citizens, ordinary; elites; poor; wealth;
  working classes
Cleisthenes, 21, 36, 43, 44
Cohen, Marshall, 337
coins, 83, 96, 120, 148, 181
Cold War, 5, 279, 330–340, 343. See also
  liberalism, Cold War
collective mediocrity, 290
collectivism, 4, 294–297. See also property
  rights
commercial societies. See market societies